# IT'S ONE FOR THE MONEY

Also by Clinton Heylin

*E Street Shuffle: The Glory Days of Bruce Springsteen and the E Street Band*
*All The Madmen: A Journey to the Dark Side of British Rock*
*So Long As Men Can Breathe: The Untold Story of Shakespeare's Sonnets*
*Still on the Road: The Songs of Bob Dylan vol. 2 (1974–2008)*
*Revolution In The Air: The Songs of Bob Dylan vol. 1 (1957–73)*
*The Act You've Known For All These Years: A Year In The Life of Sgt. Pepper and Friends*
*Babylon's Burning: From Punk to Grunge*
*From The Velvets To The Voidoids: The Birth of American Punk*
*All Yesterday's Parties: The Velvet Underground in Print 1966–71* [editor]
*Despite The System: Orson Welles versus The Hollywood Studios*
*Bootleg – The Rise & Fall of the Secret Recording Industry*
*Can You Feel The Silence? – Van Morrison: A New Biography*
*No More Sad Refrains: The Life & Times of Sandy Denny*
*Bob Dylan: Behind The Shades*
*Dylan's Daemon Lover: The Tangled Tale of a 450-Year-Old Pop Ballad*
*Dylan Day By Day: A Life In Stolen Moments*
*Never Mind The Bollocks, Here's The Sex Pistols*
*Bob Dylan: The Recording Sessions 1960–94*
*The Great White Wonders: A History of Rock Bootlegs*
*The Penguin Book of Rock & Roll Writing* [editor]
*Gypsy Love Songs & Sad Refrains: The Recordings of Sandy Denny & Richard Thompson*
*Rise/Fall: The Story of Public Image Limited*
*Joy Division: Form & Substance* [with Craig Wood]

# IT'S ONE FOR THE MONEY

## The Song Snatchers Who Carved Up
A Century of Pop
& Sparked a Musical Revolution

Clinton Heylin

Constable • London

CONSTABLE

First published in Great Britain in 2015 by Constable

1 3 5 7 9 8 6 4 2

A CIP catalogue record for this book
is available from the British Library.

ISBN: 978-1-47211-190-6 (hardback)
ISBN: 978-1-47211-966-7 (trade paperback)
ISBN: 978-1-47211-200-2 (ebook)

Typeset and design in Garamond by TW Typesetting, Plymouth, Devon
Printed and bound by CPI Group (UK) Ltd, Croydon, CR0 4YY

Constable
is an imprint of
Constable & Robinson Ltd
Carmelite House
50 Victoria Embankment
London EC4Y 0DZ

*To Steve Jump and Dave Dingle,*
*who would have loved this.*

# Contents

# Intro: All Song Is Theft

'About twenty years ago somebody discovered this beat,
[which] was such that husbands would rape their wives . . .
It would turn intellectuals into babbling idiots;
good girls get bad when they hear this beat, and bad girls
get worse.'

Bruce Springsteen's introduction to the first live performance<br>of 'She's The One'.

It is early October 1974, and the Jersey Devil himself is back in New York, at the plush Avery Fisher Hall, débuting the third song from his forthcoming fab waxing, the barely begun *Born To Run*. As the E Street Band begin to play a familiar riff, the Boss man drops into one of his raps, this one providing a little historical context. The song they seem on the verge of launching into sounds like something from that Chess master, Bo Diddley. It could be one of many, because once Bo hit upon his formula, he rode it from sunrise to sunset. But to the audience that night, it was simply the 'Bo Diddley riff'.

The riff in question – at least as far as most attendees were aware – had indeed been unveiled 'about twenty years ago'; back on 2 March 1955, to be precise, at Chess studios in Chicago. It happened the moment Bo and his band of crack Chess players, featuring the likes of Lester Davenport on mouth harp and Leroy Kirkland on tom-toms and bass drum, began to repeat the most basic of riffs. Not so much simple as elemental.

Leonard Chess was there that day, presiding over another cache of colourful characters whose records for the label bought him not only the shirt on his back but Muddy Waters' first Cadillac (which he duly charged to Waters' account). In keeping with a tradition dating back to the first time he heard Waters, when he'd supposedly exclaimed, 'What's he singing? I can't understand what he's singing . . .', Chess didn't think 'Bo Diddley' was a stone-cold hit. He put 'I'm A Man' on the A-side of Diddly's first Checker single (and misspelt Bo's name into the bargain, consigning him – à la Shakspere – to an extra 'e'). 'Bo Diddley' was hidden away on the flip side.

It mattered not. In those days, the *Billboard* charts were based as much on radioplay as singles sales. And so Checker 814 spawned not one, but two, number ones on the weekly's R&B chart.* The difference in initial impact, if it could be quantified, was down to eleven weeks on said chart for 'I'm A Man' and eighteen for 'Bo Diddley' (both sides were listed on two of the three R&B listings published in *Billboard* at the same time – Jukebox and Sales – but only 'Bo Diddley' was listed on the Airplay chart). Both were to become R&B standards.

In fact 'I'm A Man' was the first McDaniel composition to be purloined and by Chess labelmate Waters. His 'Mannish Boy' was a thinly veiled rewrite with added bragging (even *Billboard* noticed, describing Muddy's effort as 'an exciting Deep South parody on Bo Diddley's "I'm A Man"'). But it was 'Bo Diddley' which seeped into the very marrow of modern music. And though it never crossed over from the R&B charts to the Pop charts, its first important convert was a white bo' from Lubbock, Texas, name of Buddy Holly.

Holly recorded a straight cover of the original on his first demo session for Norman Petty, at his Clovis studio in January 1956, though that version would not be released until 1963 (when it still managed to make number four in the UK). Petty already had his eye on Holly's publishing, and he wasn't about to put out an already-copyrighted Chess cut on a Buddy Holly and The Crickets single. Instead, Holly was encouraged to put the riff to something he could call his own; only for Petty to make the same mistake as Chess, hiding the results away as B-side to

---

* It was on Checker because Chess wanted a crossover hit, and he considered the Checker label more r 'n' r than r 'n' b.

The Crickets' 'Oh Boy'. The song in question was 'Not Fade Away'; and though it would not launch Holly's career, it would set the world alight soon enough, turning The Rolling Stones from also-rans into genuine contenders when issued as a single in February 1964.

Only at this point does it appear that Bo himself became aware of the brazen larceny of the late Mr Holly, presumably because in the late fifties he paid as little attention to the *Billboard* pop chart as it paid to him. He observed, 'I thought The Rolling Stones had ripped me off when I heard "Not Fade Away," because the song was just like one of mine. I didn't find out until sometime later that it was a Buddy Holly song . . . I wish I'd heard his version while he was alive. I'd have told that dude something.'

The 'Bo Diddley riff', though, had hardly reached the end of its journey with Holly's backhanded B-side *or* the Stones' third-hand act of appropriation. Having already become part of the R&B lexicon, it spawned the crossover hit Chess had been looking for in 1959, just not for one of his labels. Johnny Otis – who had already claimed a hand in 'Hound Dog', until Leiber-Stoller made a legal matter of its authorship – created a fad of his own with 'Willie and The Hand Jive'. This time Bo's riff made it all the way to the Top Ten on the Pop charts.

With the Stones' solid-state success, self-consciously smelted on the south side of Chicago, the sound of Bo passed directly into pop's mainstream. There, in 1965, another production team concocted a composite pop song by putting the 'Bo Diddley riff with new bubblegum-punk words' (to quote punk songsmith Richard Hell). Bob Feldman, Jerry Goldstein and Richard Gottehrer were three ambitious young New York producer-writers who, by pretending to be Australian (and as such presumably exotic) members of a non-existent pop band called The Strangeloves, took 'I Want Candy' to number eleven on the Hot Hundred.

Barely two years later, Pete Townshend temporarily found himself clean out of ideas for hits after the surefire 'I Can See For Miles' stuttered to a halt at the nether end of the UK Top Ten. He hastily demoed what he later called 'a Voodoo-Dub-Freak-Out of a Nothing song'. The result, 'Magic Bus', using that Bo riff again, was 'destined to become [our] most requested live song', and restored The 'Oo to chart favour on both sides of the pond, giving the quartet both a four-minute single and a fourteen-minute encore in one swell foop.*

If The 'Oo were among the first to stretch that 'Bo Diddley' riff to breaking point in concert, they were certainly not the last. Back in 1974 Bruce's six-minute 'She's The One' confined its history lesson to a brief spoken intro. By 1978, the whole song – which many nights ran to twelve minutes plus – was a crash-course in appropriation. The '78 E Street Band would riff away on 'Mona' (another Diddley song the Stones had covered, and credited, though he still received diddley squat) before seguing into Buddy boy's 'Not Fade Away' and sometimes even Van Morrison's 'Gloria', the latter's debt to 'Bo Diddley' now displayed in all its revelation. Only then were audiences deemed ready for 'She's The One'.

By the time Springsteen was connecting dots for his fans, Diddley was screaming blue murder at Leonard Chess and all the other so-called rock & rollers who dun stole from Bo. 'Cept it turns out they didn't. Bo no more originated the riff to which he gave his name than the King, or I. As cult rockabilly artist Sleepy LaBeef, who had a minor hit of sorts with Diddley's 'Ride On Josephine', told music historian Spencer Leigh: '"Bo Diddley" was simply "Hambone" with the old fiddle ending of "shave-and-a-haircut-two-bits." You keep repeating that fast and you have the Bo Diddley beat. It was being performed long before Bo Diddley was born . . . A few of us . . . have cut that beat. Most people would call it a Bo Diddley beat, but they [just] don't know its origin.'

Nor was The Crickets' Jerry Allison in any doubt about its roots. Of 'Not Fade Away', he told the same indefatigable researcher, 'The rhythm came from "Hambone," and we'd heard that long before "Bo Diddley."'

Diddley was not even the first R&B artist to put it to use. Back in February 1952, when Mr McDaniel was still trying to get his foot in the front door, specialist R&B label Okeh had released a song called

---

* That they knew the original is not in dispute. They had covered 'I'm A Man' on their first UK LP.

'Hambone', credited to Red Saunders and His Orchestra 'with Dolores Hawkins and the Hambone Kids'. As far as Saunders was concerned, 'Hambone' was his take on a traditional children's chant, popularly known as 'Mockingbird' because one of the verses went thus: 'Papa's gonna buy me a mockingbird, and if that mockingbird don't sing, Papa gonna buy me a diamond ring/And if that diamond ring don't shine, Papa gonna take it to a five and dime.'

Diddley was to preserve elements of the original in his famous non sequitur, 'Bo Diddley buy baby a diamond ring, if that diamond ring don't shine, he gonna take it to a private eye.' But whereas Saunders got his own trio, the self-styled Hambone Kids, to emulate the West African chant-rhythm by slapping and singing 'the hambone', Diddley plugged in and made that playground chant *jump*.

Where Bo himself first encountered the hambone is not documented. It is possible he came across it while having his shoes shined (or more likely, shining shoes himself). White folk would certainly first have heard the well-known 'shave and a haircut, two bits' beat when it was popularized in the pre-war era by black shoeshine boys. As such, its adoption by the rock n' roll fraternity was only a matter of time – and opportunity. After which, contrary to any claim from Arc Music on behalf of Mr Diddley, it was fair game.

Others who shared that fabled Chess studio with Bo have taken a more phlegmatic view about those who beg, borrow or steal songs. Chuck Berry, asked to reveal the source of the genre-defining 'Johnny B. Goode', retorted, 'That riff comes from ideas that influenced me. Somebody else influenced him. It all comes from somebody else. I've been stealing all these years, man.' Berry could well have been thinking of a specific 'cop' – say, Louis Jordan's 'Ain't It Just Like A Woman' where Carl Hogan's distinctive guitar intro sounds a lot like Mr Goode's. But his point is well made.

It is equally well made by another, obscurer originator of classic rock riffs. In his accomplished monograph on a dozen classic Who singles of the sixties, The Only Ones' John Perry (of 'Another Girl Another Planet' fame) devised Perry's First Rule of Songstealing: '"Ripping off" is a matter of context. Everyone steals; it's not what you nick, but the way that you nick it. As a rule, *interesting people steal more interestingly*, because they can't help putting something of themselves into what they steal . . . Someone sets out to copy an idea, but can't quite get it right. In the process, the original idea mutates into something new and unexpected.'

Although less recognized pop artists may have been more coy about their lifts, cops or plain steals, it seems one can hardly contain these folk once the millions start to roll in, so keen are they to affirm the scale of former appropriations. It was Paul McCartney, no less, who told *Guitar Player* in 1990, 'What do they say? A good artist borrows, a great artist steals – or something like that. That makes the Beatles great artists, because we stole *a lot* of stuff.'

One of McCartney's early inspirations was New York songwriter-for-hire Gerry Goffin. He was equally brazen, suggesting in a latterday interview that he and songwriting partner Carole King, when holed up in the Brill Building turning out hit after hit, sometimes applied their patented glass-against-wall method of songwriting: 'Barry [Mann], Cynthia [Weil], Carole and I used to plagiarize each other's songs. Because we had cubicles directly next to each other. Carole could hear what Barry was playing, and I could hear what Cynthia was writing. And we'd end up finishing each other's songs. Some of the ideas sorta drifted through.'

It seems Goffin took Bob Dylan's mantra – 'Open up your eyes and ears and you're influenced' – rather literally. Dylan himself, having penned a couple of songs with Goffin in the early nineties, was later inspired to come clean himself. In a 2004 interview he openly admitted: 'I'll take a song I know and simply start playing it in my head. That's the way I meditate . . . I'll be playing Bob Nolan's "Tumbling Tumbleweeds," for instance, in my head constantly . . . People will think they are talking to me and I'm talking back, but I'm not . . . At a certain point, some of the words will change and I'll start writing a song.'

Not a bad way to make a living – and he ain't complainin' none. And neither is Elton John, whose gross publishing revenue may even exceed Dylan's. He once described to *Rolling Stone* how he came to write 'Crocodile Rock', a classic 1972 hit: '[It] is just a combination of so many songs, really. "Little Darling," "Oh Carol"; some Beach Boys influences . . . are in there as well, I suppose. Eddie Cochran. I mean, it's just a combination of people.' Another case of '*interesting people steal[ing] more interestingly*'.

As for Springsteen, he talked openly about his own songwriting (and influences) in his keynote address at that MusicBiz orgy of self-congratulation, South By Southwest, in March 2012. Here he spoke about influences general and specific, obvious and unexpected, the most telling of which was his heartfelt debt to The Animals, Eric Burdon's bunch of belligerent Geordies who began life belting out r&b as black as the coal their forefathers dug up: 'The Animals were a revelation . . . "We Gotta Get Out Of This Place" had that great bass riff, that was just marking time. That's every song I've ever written. Yeah. That's all of them. I'm not kidding, either. That's "Born to Run," "Born in the USA," everything I've done for the past 40 years.'

The Animals, as Bruce knew full well, stand as one of the great might-abeens of the British beat scene. Like Bo, they had gussied up a song as ancient as the hills, or in their case the oldest profession, generating a number one both sides of the Atlantic; only to find the publishing on 'House of the Rising Sun' had gone south, along with the one Animal who considered himself more equal than the others.

Unlike Bo, The Animals did not allow such a hard lesson in economics to eat away at them. They simply produced a string of classic singles – 'It's My Life', 'We Gotta Get Out of This Place' and 'Don't Let Me Be Misunderstood' among them – that redefined Britpop and inspired at least one teenage beachcomber hanging out under the boardwalk in Asbury Park, New Jersey. It was a lesson they were not alone in learning too late. As McCartney told his biographer Barry Miles, 'John [Lennon] and I didn't know you could own songs. We thought they just existed in the air. We could not see how it was possible to own them.'

\* \* \*

It turns out that even the breakthrough songs – like 'Bo Diddley' – have lifted their imprint from the past. Because *nothing* in Pop is original; everything comes from somewhere and (usually) someone identifiable. And often the only thing separating the rich from the poor is how well one of them has managed to disguise it. Carole King once admitted she would 'play someone else's material that I really like, and that sometimes unblocks a channel. The danger in that is that you're gonna write that person's song for your next song.' It's a danger all songwriters succumb to, sooner or later.

Only since the twentieth century has this become a problem. Because something that for hundreds of years had been communal, by the early 1900s had become a form of property which could, like any commodity, be bought and sold. Everything changed not when Edison ensured a song could be recorded and mechanically reproduced; but when the quality of what came out was such that one could say the recorded performance was not only unique but, in terms delineated by the 1909 US Copyright Act, original. This is where the trouble started, and where we enter the frame. Seems like a hundred years ago . . .

# PART ONE

# Stealin' Back To My Good Ol' Used To Be

# CHAPTER 1

# 1914-38: Stepfather of the Blues

*Featuring*: 'St Louis Blues'

'If you go for what has a chance of surviving, then you have to go for songs. You can go for artists, but to what degree has Bessie Smith survived today, by her recordings? . . . A lot more people know "St Louis Blues" than know Bessie Smith . . . A song is capable of having several life-spans.'

Paul Simon, *Rolling Stone*, 1972

At least Bo Diddley always had 'Bo Diddley'. As its singer-songwriter, he was both the song's main cheerleader and, in theory at least, its biggest beneficiary. But a songwriter always needs someone to sing his or her songs. So it is not surprising that Paul Simon explicitly associates 'St Louis Blues' with Bessie Smith's 1925 recording. Smith cut the song eleven long years after its author, W.C. Handy, penned what he called – the same year Smith sealed it as a standard – 'a composite, made up of racial sayings in dialect'.

William Christopher Handy had already waited twice as long as Smith before committing lines he heard sung by a heartbroken drunk in St Louis to the song that would make his name and secure his place in the American popular canon. For it was the summer of 1914 when the forty-one-year-old ex-bandleader and horn player became more than a bit player in the transmission – and transmutation – of 'the blues'.

Back before he became Memphis midnight revellers' favourite bandleader, in the late 1900s, Handy had had very little exposure to the undersoil of Afro-American song. He was a pro – a fan of ragtime and minstrelsy, paid to play what the people wanted. And he did it for pay, nightly. But he had always fancied himself something more than an arranger. He saw himself shaping songs out of his imagination, with (more than) a little help from his black musical heritage. And, starting in 1909, with 'Mr Crump', an election song based heavily on a favourite blues commonplace, he began crafting – and more importantly, publishing – a steady stream of blues tunes that to the 'educated' classes sounded like the real thing.

Fortunately for Handy, if not for popular song, the same summer he wrote his 'St Louis Blues', nine New York music publishers sealed the future of the medium by forming a song publishers' union of sorts – the American Society of Composers, Authors and Publishers (ASCAP). (By then, Handy fancied himself as all three.) Taking as their cue a provision in the 1909 US Copyright Act that allowed the performance of a copyrighted song to be licensed 'publicly for profit', ASCAP set about demanding payment for all public performances of the published songs of their constituent members.*

Not surprisingly, a fair few establishments 'took to adapting old melodies for the new trot and rag dances' rather than pay the fledgling song union, and *Variety*'s pages were soon full of advertisements for 'tax free' music; but the future course of pop music was now set. The public domain would increasingly become the purview of published denizens, and that, at the time, meant membership of ASCAP; for which one needed to be able to transcribe music, fixing it for print (and, therefore, copyright).†

For Handy, who had entered the publishing business expecting to rely on sheet-music sales, any potential revenue from performances of his songs was but gravy. However, in the case of one composition, his cup soon runneth over. By the time Bessie gave Handy a leg up, 'St Louis Blues' was well on its way to over 1,600 documented versions on record

---

* The valuable performance right was actually first recognized in US law in 1889, with the right of mechanical reproduction added in 1909, though it was intended to relate only to piano rolls.

† As noted in *This Business of Music*, 'Under the 1909 Copyright Act the sale of recordings was not considered a "publication" of a composition; and would not be until 1976'!

and innumerable public performances that would make Handy a legend in his lifetime.*

This was because this solitary song sounded the bugle on a revolution. As David Jansen and Gene Jones wrote, in their compelling 1998 survey of early black songwriters, *Spreadin' Rhythm Around*:

> In the era of 'We'll Have a Jubilee In My Old Kentucky Home,' 'How's Every Little Thing in Dixie?' and 'Mammy's Little Coal Black Rose,' Handy's song was more than a breath of fresh air. It was a new wind blowing. If the . . . lyrics [seemed] innovative, its music was revolutionary. Its harmonies literally put new notes into the pop music scale, and its structure showed writers a new way to build popular songs.

If it took the full decade between Handy stitching it together and Smith tearing it apart for 'St Louis Blues' to make its mark in the notoriously competitive field of American song publishing, over the next half-century it would become the most valuable copyright this side of Irving Berlin. And its impact on popular song itself would be hard to overestimate. Chart historian Joel Whitburn considers it the second most covered song (after 'Silent Night') of the pre-rock & roll era.

Such a song should have made Handy a rich man – and would have, if he had handled his other copyrights as astutely. Unfortunately, Handy soon began to believe his own press, ironic given he generated most of it himself. (As early as June 1919 the all-black daily *The Chicago Defender* wrote that Handy was 'well known the world over as the "Daddy of the Blues"', a claim which can only have come from the man himself.)

Handy soon convinced himself 'St Louis Blues' was something other than what it actually was – a fluke. 'St Louis Blues' may have been as radical as songs come, but its author was by temperament a reactionary and, in general, a poor judge of what worked and why. Hence his chequered career

---

* Tom Lord's definitive jazz discography details nearly 1,500 versions of 'St Louis Blues'; the Library of Congress lists 1,605 renditions across every musical discipline.

as a song publisher and non-existent career as a recording artist. (On his one and only session for Columbia in 1917, he passed over his patented blues hybrids, even 'St Louis Blues', for the likes of 'Fuzzy Wuzzy Rag', 'The Old Town Pump', the waltz-like 'Moonlight Blues' and 'Snakey Blues', all recently copyrighted by his newly formed publishing company.)

So how did Handy chance upon a song that 'literally put new notes into the pop music scale, and . . . showed writers a new way to build popular songs'? The answer is, by taking building blocks from Afro-American tradition and judiciously applying the glue of a tutored pop sensibility. Even he admitted of 'St Louis Blues', in his 1941 autobiography, that 'the twelve-bar, three-line form of the first and last strains, with its three-chord basic harmonic structure . . . was already used by Negro roustabouts, honky-tonk piano players, wanderers and others of their underprivileged but undaunted class'. His own contribution – or so he claimed – 'was to introduce this, the "blues" form, to the general public, as the medium for my own feelings and my own musical ideas'.

In Handy's mythic account of his musical epiphany, it was 1903 when, in a train station in Tutwiler, Mississippi, he first heard the blues. The music was played by a black guitarist with a knife.* Yet it was 1909 before he penned his first blues hybrid, 'Mr Crump', at the age of thirty-six. Even after nearly two decades as a cornettist, bandleader and/or music teacher, he still required a couple of dry runs to learn (by being fleeced) the ropes of song publishing and discover what elements of the 'twelve-bar, three-line form' a popular audience would buy. Only then would he strike St Louis gold.

Handy insisted he was always looking for a way to render 'the blues' commercial. And the way he achieved this was to create, in his own words, 'three distinct musical strains . . . as a means of avoiding the monotony that always resulted in the three-line folk blues'. To Handy's mind, this

---

\* Some blues scholars fondly imagine this was Charley Patton, but it seems unlikely that the great Mississippi bluesman, who would not be recorded by Paramount until he was in his forties, was sitting there in Tutwiler in 1903 when no more than sixteen years old.

made him a composer and a creative force, someone who used the blues as 'a medium for my own feelings'. Actually, *his* blues were patchwork quilts compiled from commonplace couplets and appropriated melodies.

Some scholars, after a recent spate of revisionism regarding Handy's place in popular song, have grown less inclined to champion his innovations. David Evans' seminal *Big Road Blues* (1982) contrasted 'the folk blues aesthetic [which] emphasized truth in the lyrics and musical and structural freedom' with 'the aesthetic of the blues songwriters [like Handy, who] emphasized storytelling, lyrical originality and novelty within fixed musical structures' – and found the latter wanting. Francis Davis, in his wide-ranging *History of the Blues* (1995), felt compelled to observe, 'Nothing about "St Louis Blues" was original, except for Handy's elan in tossing together these seemingly disparate elements.' While T-Bone Walker, a bluesman through and through, dismissed the song with these loaded words: 'It's a pretty tune, and it has kind of a bluesy tone, but it's not the blues. You can't *dress up* the blues.'

Handy thought he could 'dress up the blues'. In fact, he deemed it a veritable necessity that he stitch 'seemingly disparate elements' together, something he'd done with 'Mr Crump', the very first blues he wrote. When he rewrote this – as 'Memphis Blues' – in 1912, he took two twelve-bar (i.e. traditional blues) strains and inserted a single one of sixteen bars. Even the latter strain was folk-based, taken from the traditional melody known as 'Mama Don't 'Low'.*

It apparently did not occur to Handy that the song's ready acceptance in his adopted city of Memphis might be less down to his melodic 'innovations', and more because everyone liked 'Mama Don't 'Low' (or what he had done with it). When he tried to take 'Memphis Blues' further afield, publishing it as an original instrumental, it had less impact. Having put his own money into a print run of a thousand song-sheets, Handy was obliged to sell the publishing outright to a white midwestern publisher called Theron C. Bennett for a token $50.

---

* The authentic original would still serve an arch-bluesman like Tampa Red on two recordings dating from 1929.

Bennett smartly realized that what the song really needed was a new set of words, not necessarily from the blues idiom. He set professional lyricist George A. Norton to it. The words Norton devised cleverly name-checked its author in a slightly condescending way: 'I will never forget the tune that Handy called the Memphis Blues/Oh them blues . . . That melancholy strain, that ever-haunting refrain/Is like a Darkies' sorrow song.'

Norton's words and Bennett's contacts made a hit of Handy's first composite. 'Memphis Blues', thanks largely to Bennett, made Handy's name, ensuring subsequent efforts would be accorded a degree of interest. This obliged Handy to concoct a story about how he had been conned out of the song by Bennett – whom he accused of surreptitiously printing his own sheets alongside Handy's, and marketing them in direct competition. In fact, his next blues composite, 'Jogo Blues', issued the following year by the newly formed Pace & Handy Publishing, sank without a trace, probably because of 'the eccentricity of a structure consisting only of twelve- and eight-bar strains, which lack[ed] the glue of melodic coherence'.

Fortunately for Handy, his earlier effort, 'Memphis Blues', soon became the standard accompaniment to a new dance sensation, the Fox Trot, courtesy of dance team Vernon and Irene Castle, and he was again a name to be reckoned with. At the end of 1914 it was ranked the twenty-eighth best-selling song of the year. Meanwhile, chastened by the failure of 'Jogo Blues', Handy reverted to the same structure as 'Memphis Blues' for his breakthrough blues. Yet his reuse of the central strain of 'Jogo Blues' as the third, resolving strain of 'St Louis Blues' confirmed a limited musical palate.

The faith he had in the earlier melody would prove well founded, even if, like most of 'St Louis Blues', it was not actually his. New Orleans piano-player Jelly Roll Morton, a French Quarter legend, would subsequently suggest in print that the whole of 'Jogo Blues' had been written by Guy Williams, a guitarist who had worked in Handy's band in 1911, but because 'Williams had no copyright as yet', Pace & Handy simply copyrighted it in the latter's name. Whether or not this is so, the tune's main motif had been lifted from an already copyrighted work by Antonio Maggio, a New Orleans ragtime player, who had published it as early as 1908 as the first strain of a ragtime song called 'I Got The Blues'. (Maggio insisted Handy had heard his work on a visit to N'Orleans.) Handy made light of the similarities, yet he never explicitly denied the debt.

'Jogo Blues' had always been an uncharacteristic piece for Handy, but with 'St Louis Blues' he reverted to the triple-ply approach of 'Memphis Blues', sandwiching a tango between two twelve-bar slices of the blues. This time, though, he applied his 'own' set of words, traditional couplets that already constituted a familiar template for 'the blues'. Handy later claimed this was the very first time a published song had used the AAB format of traditional folk blues.

The real debutant was Leroy White's 'Nigger Blues', published the previous year. But it was Handy's lyric which introduced into popular parlance the plaintive complaint called the blues. His had been studiously acquired over the past two decades, beginning with the opening line of the final verse, 'My man's got a heart like a rock cast into the sea'; these were words he had heard in St Louis back in 1893, sung by a drunken woman stumbling through the streets late one night. Another element that helped place the song was a caustic couplet of disaffection from the common pool of Afro-American rhyming gripes: 'St Louis woman, wid her diamon' rings/Pulls dat man roun' by her apron strings'.

Throughout the compositional process, and it *is* a beautifully crafted song, Handy only ever saw the music of his own people – the deep dark blues of a much-oppressed minority – as a way of enabling his personal elevation to the rank of commercial composer.

Commercially speaking, his key innovation was making the middle strain of 'St Louis Blues' a tango, in deference to the success the Castles were enjoying with their latest dance craze. As David Evans puts it, in *Big Road Blues*: 'Even though these compositions . . . of Handy did often contain some lines or stanzas drawn from the traditional folk blues, . . . for [Handy] the folk blues' value was their potential as material to be reworked . . . As W.C. Handy said of folk blues singers, "Their music wanted polishing, but it contained the essence," an essence he rarely transferred to his own blues.'

Although Handy convinced himself he was the first to make such a radical departure, the idea was centuries old. In fact, it had been adopted by Scotland's national poet, 'Rabbie' Burns, who did exactly the same with large chunks of Scottish folksong as Handy had now with America's, arranging traditional tunes and adapting traditional lyrics.

Burns published the results in six highly influential volumes, *The Scots Musical Museum*, between 1787 and 1803.* And it was here that the likes of 'Auld Lang Syne', 'My Love Is Like A Red, Red Rose', 'Lady Mary Ann' and 'My Heart's In The Highlands' first appeared, all songs recrafted (or bastardized, depending on your point of view) by Burns from the rich core of Scottish tradition. In the process Burns cleaned up some of the choicer turns of phrase, and in general made the songs fit for the parlours of the very people he professed to despise. One can't help but lament, with the irascible folklorist Gershon Legman, that whether or not Burns 'ornamented and improved every folksong he ever revised, ... from the simple viewpoint of the reliable transmission of folk-collected texts ... one is driven almost to the heresy, sometimes, of wishing that Burns had just simply left his folksong texts as he found them.'

And Handy was no Burns. With hindsight, his act of musical sophistication seems rather presumptuous. After all, as Fiddlin' John Carson, A.P. Carter and Blind Lemon Jefferson would demonstrate in the next decade, Americans were bound to catch up with their common musical heritage soon enough. As it is, because they thought 'the blues' was supposed to be played with a full ensemble and a mutable number of strains, the success of 'St Louis Blues' convinced Handy – and the popular urban audience who embraced this new fad – that he was the 'Daddy of The Blues'. It took an unnamed blues pianist, quoted in the *Chicago Tribune* the following year, to point out, in an article with the intriguing title, 'Blues is Jazz is Blues', 'The blues are never written into music, but are

---

* Edinburgh engraver James Johnson, who had begun the project without Burns, completed it after Burns' death using notes the poet left behind.

interpolated by the piano player or other players. They aren't new. They are just reborn into popularity. They started in the south half a century ago and are the interpolations of darkies originally.'

Handy seized his long-awaited opportunity with alacrity, relocating first to Chicago and then to New York and branding the Pace & Handy Publishing Company as 'The Home of the Blues' – having published exactly two of his constructs. The move proved premature. Before the Original Dixieland Jass Band's 1919 recording of 'St Louis Blues', this was *not* the Handy song one heard in Southern saloons and theaters. 'Memphis Blues' still held dominion, followed by 'The Yellow Dog Rag' and 'Joe Turner Blues', two wartime songs which continued mining authentic blues motifs – or, as Handy himself asserted, 'followed my frequent custom of using a snatch of folk melody in one out of two or three strains of an otherwise original song'.

In fact, his songs were already becoming less and less inventive with each recalibration. As Peter Muir has recently noted, '[Handy's] "Joe Turner" is much closer to an unmediated traditional twelve-bar blues than anything Handy had produced earlier. Indeed, it is arguably the closest he ever came to the style of pure folk blues.'

The best known, if not the oldest, song in the canon of traditional blues, 'Joe Turner' had already been published, albeit in the wholly academic *Journal of American Folklore*, by Howard Odum, along with 114 other negro secular songs. And as Odum also discovered, and duly noted, Handy was hardly alone in claiming authorship of songs which were 'anonymous for the best of reasons':

The singers are often conscious that they are singing folk-songs, and they attempt to pose as the authors . . . Many negroes maintain that they are the original authors of the songs they sing, and they are able to give apparent good evidence to substantiate the statement. Even if one were inclined to accept such a testimony, it would be a difficult matter to select the author from a number who thus claim to have composed the song. This is well illustrated by the young negro who wished to call out his name before each song which he was singing into the gramophone. 'Song composed by Will Smith of Chattanooga, Tennessee,' he would cry out, then begin his song; for, he maintained, these songs would be sung all over the world, and he deserved the credit for them.

The itinerant black entertainers known as songsters even made their own joke of the practice exemplified by the two Wills, Handy and Smith. A coda to the ubiquitous 'Boll Weevil Blues' offers this observation: 'If anybody axes you who writ this song/Tell 'em it was a dark-skinned nigger/Wid a pair of blue-duckins on.'

Though Odum had the foresight to record his informants, only to subsequently lose those priceless recorded originals, he ended up simply publishing the lyrics, many of them commonplaces, none of them authored. Already, any claim to authorship of the blues, most less than a quarter of a century old, was being lost in oral tradition. Thus fifteen years later, when collector Dorothy Scarborough tried to track down the person behind 'Boll Weevil Blues', she was informed by the principal of the negro school in Greenville, Mississippi, '"The Boll Weevil" was composed by a man in Merivale, I believe. It is like many other ballads written by men in this state. The tune is made, the writer sings it and sells his song. His hearers catch the sound – and on it goes.'

Fortunately for Handy, few others had yet displayed the requisite foresight to copyright any of the folk melodies or sayings he considered mere building blocks for his own patented form of the blues. But he was not the first. It turns out that the first sheet music to describe itself as a blues was a 1909 piano rag by the New Orleans pianist Robert Hoffman; and not only did Hoffman's 'Alabama Blues' predate 'Memphis Blues' by three years, it also made extensive use of two traditional blues melodies, being itself a thinly veiled reworking of the well-known 'Alabama Bound'. The gesture went largely unnoticed.

For now, Handy had the field of published blues pretty much to himself, and he was determined to publish every vestige of folk blues he could dredge up before other black songwriters caught on. In 1915 – after his first attempt at using blues imagery in a standard 32-bar pop song, 'Shoeboots Serenade', proved a resounding flop – he copyrighted 'Hesitating Blues', his take on the steadfastly traditional 'Hesitation Blues'. Only one problem: white Kentucky songwriting team Billy Smythe and Scott Middleton had copyrighted the song under its 'correct' title five weeks earlier. And Handy knew it.*

He, of all publishers, did not need to be told that existing US copyright law recognized no such form of fair usage. Had 'Hesitating Blues' been a hit of similar proportions to 'St Louis Blues', Smythe and Middleton would have been well within their rights to sue the 'father of the blues'. Instead, they did a service to Song by emulating the traditional blues, musically and lyrically, even as folklorist Newman White was collecting three contradistinct versions of the same traditional song in Auburn, Alabama.

Actually, by the 1920s these pesky folklorists were becoming a real nuisance to a small band of black songwriters who had holed up in New York's Gaiety Building – rechristened by some wag 'Uncle Tom's Cabin' – copyrighting elements of their racial heritage. Following Handy's lead, Perry Bradford and Clarence Williams had proven just as keen to copyright anything from the common store of negro song – but only after recrafting it with all the skill and subtlety of the worst broadside balladeer.

But if the likes of Robert Winslow Gordon, who had a regular

---

* The stock phrases, 'I woke up this morning with the blues all 'round my bed' and 'I'll have to leave this town just to wear you off my mind', both appear in 'Shoeboots Serenade'. In 1926, in his own skewered anthology of 'The Blues', Handy got the unquestioning Abbe Niles to state, in his introduction for Handy's unadopted 'Hesitating Blues': 'At about the same time . . . a "Hesitation Blues" or "Must I Hesitate?" was published by Smythe and Middleton of Louisville, which used this same melody in a slightly different arrangement . . . Neither song was stolen from the other, but the basis of this version here given was played and sung to Handy by a wandering musician who said he had it from a hymn (yet unidentified) and suggested its use.' A convenient explanation that predictably placed Handy's acquisition of 'his' blues several years before this *a priori* copyright claimant.

column in the popular *Adventure* weekly, or society novelist-folklorist Dorothy Scarborough, stumbled across a folksong, they had an annoying habit of publishing it, tune and all, *without copyright*, thus fixing it for all time in the eyes of US law as *traditional*. And therefore uncopyrightable.

Fortunately for those in 'Uncle Tom's Cabin', these earnest white folklorists were having a real hard time transcribing the results of their excavations. As one correspondent wrote to Scarborough, 'I cannot begin to tell you of the difficulties [my music transcriber] met with in trying to translate the songs "from African to American music," as she expresses the process. There are slurs and drops and "turns" and heaven knows what of notes not to be interpreted by any known musical sign.'

Handy thus had an edge because he had a genuine gift for arranging and transcribing the blues. It was one he could have used for the common good had he not convinced himself – and the newly formed ASCAP – that what he was doing qualified as composing, not song snatching.

Meanwhile, his partner at Pace & Handy, Harry Pace, had begun to realize popular song's future lay in recordings, not printed song-sheets. As such, in 1921, he sold his share in the publishing business to Handy and set up the Black Swan Phonograph Company (originally the Pace Phonograph Company), giving it the catchy – if misleading – slogan, 'The Only Genuine Colored Record, Others Are Only Passing For Colored'.

Unfortunately for Pace, his judgement as to what constituted 'Genuine Colored', or indeed authentic blues, was even more askew than that of his erstwhile publishing partner. That same year he passed on Bessie Smith after she auditioned for the label, signing Ethel Waters instead. It was to prove a costly error. Black Swan ultimately sank without trace. Meanwhile, Mamie Smith and her 1920 phonographic phenomenon, 'Crazy Blues', had proved there was a substantial market for ersatz blues sung by black vaudeville/theatre singers, and a host of female blues singers now felt obliged – at their A&R men's behest – to cover commercial blues. Much of it gave a namecheck to W.C. Handy. The man himself could sit back and watch the money roll in.

Instead, Handy was inspired to again set about raising his pen, though this time he was (re)writing songs which had definitely already been collected and published. This didn't stop him from copyrighting the likes of 'Careless Love', 'John Henry' and 'Make Me A Pallet On The Floor' – as 'Loveless Love', 'John Henry Blues' and 'Atlanta Blues' respectively – between 1921 and 1923. But none of the pseudo-traditional trio took hold, or superseded now-familiar originals, as 'St Louis Blues' once had.

Around this time, Handy seemed inclined to admit his own role in the commercial exploitation of the blues form. He told Dorothy Scarborough, then hot on the trail of negro folksongs for her 1925 collection of the same name: 'Each one of my blues is based on some old Negro song of the south, some folk-song that I heard from my mammy when I was a child . . . some old song that is a part of the memories of my childhood and of my race. I can tell you the exact song I used as a basis for any one of my blues . . . They are essentially of our race, and our people have been singing like that for many years. But they have been [only] publicly developed and exploited in the last few years.'

And when Howard Odum and Newman White followed Scarborough into print with collections of negro secular folksongs, Handy responded with his own *Blues: An Anthology*, though – not wishing to appear immodest – he left its introduction and notes to lawyer and part-time journalist Abbe Niles, a confirmed Handy acolyte. Meanwhile, Odum's *Negro Workaday Songs* was complaining that, 'It is no longer possible to speak with certainty of the folk blues, so entangled are the relations between them and the formal compositions.' If Handy bore much of the blame, Niles' laudatory introduction to Handy's own best-selling anthology dispensed only plaudits his way:

It was [W.C.] Handy who first appreciated the universal appeal of the Negro blues, and who introduced into American 'popular music' the qualities of these folk-songs . . . Handy wrote the first and several of the most famous of the published blues, thereby starting a revolution, a fundamental change in the character of the

*15*

popular music of this land comparable only to that brought about by the introduction of ragtime. The blues, after that introduction, became embedded in our music so rapidly that, for a number of years, their folk source and their history tended to be overlooked.

Needless to say, Handy's own anthology of 'the blues' was nothing of the sort, standing in stark contrast to the authentic excavations of Odum, Scarborough and White. Already, though, the tide in men's affairs was turning and Handy was being left behind in the wash. The year 'his' anthology appeared, Paramount released the first Blind Lemon Jefferson 78 ('Booster Blues'), thus signing the death warrant on ersatz blues – though it would take till the end of the decade for the sentence to be carried out.

By then Handy was a wealthy man, who could afford to spend his time boosting his credentials in public and collecting his copyrights in private. In the mid-thirties, a young bassist named Red Callendar approached Handy for a copyist job, and was apparently informed: 'Son, I've got to tell you that this office is just a front to get me out of the house. I've been living off "The St Louis Blues" for the past twenty years.'

Such a comment rather suggests Handy was worried he might be called out on earlier claims of primacy, especially those made on his behalf by Abbe Niles. Such fears were duly realized in 1938 – around the time he made recordings of ten songs he had 'used as a basis for . . . my blues' at the behest of the Library of Congress. That summer a destitute, aggrieved, royally ripped-off Jelly Roll Morton came out of the woodwork to challenge Handy's claim to fatherhood of the blues in a lengthy letter reprinted in both the Baltimore-based *African-American* and *Down Beat* magazine, the premier jazz journal of the era.

In *Down Beat* Morton's article was headlined 'I Created Jazz in 1902, Not W.C. Handy', and when he wasn't asserting his own claim to be the 'originator of jazz and swing', Morton spat metaphorical blood at Handy's unmitigated gall:

In . . . 1908, I was brought to Memphis by a small theatre owner, Fred Barasso, as a feature attraction and to be with his number one company for his circuit which consisted of four houses, namely Memphis, Tenn., Greenville, Vicksburg and Jackson, Mississippi. That was the birth of the Negro theatrical circuit in the USA. It was that year I met Handy in Memphis. I learned that he had just arrived from his hometown, Henderson, Ky. He was introduced to me as Prof. Handy. Who ever heard of anyone wearing the name of Professor, advocate *Ragtime, Jazz, Stomps, Blues*, etc.? Of course Handy could not play either [sic] of these types . . . I know Mr. Handy's ability, and it is the type of Folk Songs, Hymns, Anthems, etc. . . . Mr. Handy cannot prove anything is music that he has created. He has possibly taken advantage of some unprotected material that sometimes floats around . . . [because of] a greed for false reputation . . . Please do not misunderstand me. I do not claim any of the creation of the blues, although I have written many of them even before Mr. Handy had any blues published. I had heard them when I was knee-high to a duck.

With *The African-American* carrying an even blunter headline – 'Handy Not Father of Blues, Says Jelly Roll' – Handy had little choice but to respond; and respond he did, with a long, rambling letter to *Down Beat* entitled 'I Would Not Play Jazz If I Could . . .' In it, the old Handy came out to play. He bragged of his personal contribution to black music – 'because of my exceptional ability to write down the things peculiar to [the Negro], I *created* [my italics] a new style of music which we now know as the "Blues" '– while repeatedly boasting of all the copyrights he had assigned to himself, knowing full well Morton had done nothing of the sort:

I feel perfectly sure of my position in the musical world and of my ability as a pioneer, creative musician and composer . . . [having] traveled with Maharas' Minstrels . . . of Chicago in 1896, in which

I arranged and played unusual, unpublished Negro music . . . This minstrel show traveled throughout the United States, Canada, Cuba, and Mexico. I had the opportunity to hear what Negroes were playing in every city and hamlet all over the south, and . . . created a new style of music which we now know as the 'Blues' . . . [I also] had vision enough to copyright and publish all the music I wrote so I don't have to go around saying I made up this piece and that piece in such and such a year like Jelly Roll and then say somebody swiped it. Nobody has swiped anything from me. And, if he is as good as he says he is, he should have copyrighted and published his music.

In fact, Morton was not the first to suggest Handy was a relative late-comer to the form he was still claiming to have created. Back in 1934, in his memoir of the early Memphis music scene, *Beale Street: Where the Blues Began*, George Lee had written about how, 'long before Handy's day, Charlie Bynum organized the Bynum and Jim Turner Band. Bynum was the first [band]leader on Beale Street to play the blues, but, not real-izing their potential commercial value, he never thought of trying to set them to [sheet] music.'

One by one, blues scholars began querying Handy's claims to pri-macy. As far back as 1901, Chris Smith, a capable songsmith specialising initially in ragtime, had published a song called 'I've Got De Blues', though attached to a most unblueslike tune. And in 1912, Handy had been beaten to the copyright on a blues he claimed as a signature piece for his Memphis-based band. 'The Last Shot Got Him' was instead assigned to Smith, who by then had been plying his trade for more than a decade. And the same year, Smith reused his 1901 title for a commercial blues co-written with Tim Brymn – 'I've Got the Blues But I'm Too Blamed Mean To Cry'. Along with Franklin Seals's 'Baby Seals' Blues' and Hart Wand's 'Dallas Blues', Smith demonstrably published his own brand of the blues pre-Handy. So much for Handy creating 'a new style of music which we now know as the "Blues"'.

Handy still had one more trick up his sleeve. He was going to write his life story and 'set the record straight' – which meant singularly ignoring the contributions of Jelly Roll Morton, Chris Smith and Guy Williams. Instead, he painted a series of fanciful vignettes in which he encountered the blues in a variety of out of the way places that no one could challenge because at the turn of the century no one was jotting down notes. After toying with the idea of calling the book *Fight It Out*, presumably a reference to Morton, he adopted a suggestion of James Weldon Johnson. Published in 1941, just as Morton was gasping his last breath, it was called, without the slightest hint of irony, *Father Of The Blues*.

A near-blind Handy would live long enough to see a statue erected in a park named after him in his adopted hometown of Memphis; to hear an entire album of his best-known songs recorded in his honour by the great Louis Armstrong; and to witness the completion of a Hollywood biopic based on his 1941 memoir, the part of Handy being assigned to Nat King Cole, of all people. For the film's release in 1958, at the height of rock & roll, the studio press department even managed to out-hype Handy, producing a poster which proclaimed the film to be 'based upon the life and music of W.C. Handy – Daddy of Rhythm and Blues'. It seemed there was no end to the achievements of someone who fathered a musical form the older Morton had learnt when 'knee-high to a duck'.

Yet Paul Simon got it wrong. 'St Louis Blues' has not outlived Bessie Smith's famous torch-song. In the CD era, Smith's work has been remastered by Sony Legacy and discovered by a new generation for whom Handy is merely a name on a statue (or two). And now in the YouTube age, anyone with a computer can sit and watch the early movie short Smith made of her most famous song back in 1929, four years after her original Columbia recording. Even when obliged to simultaneously act out a cliched storyline, Bessie sings the blues. Not the Handy blues, but the *blues*, returning the song to its emotional roots with a performance that makes it (and her) live again. (As her own A&R man once put it, 'I . . . never heard anything like the torture and torment she put into the music of her people. It was the blues, and she meant it.')

However, Handy's descendants still get the last laugh. Fifty-five years after his death, and a hundred after he stitched the song together, 'St Louis Blues' remains in copyright in most countries. Bessie Smith's definitive recording, though, fell out of copyright more than a decade ago, returned to the public domain from which most of its elements came.

# CHAPTER 2

# 1920–37: He Done Me Wrong

*Featuring*: 'Dink's Song'; 'Crazy Blues'; 'Down Hearted Blues'; 'Backwater Blues'; 'See See Rider'; 'That Black Snake Moan'; 'Keep A Knockin''

> The women's songs were chiefly the sweetest of them all . . . [but] were rarely sung by the males. The women might sing some of the men's pieces, but the men seldom sang those of the women. They appreciated their sweetness but they felt the songs did not belong to them . . . Most of the men sang at the inns, and their pieces were consequently . . . publicly known, while the women's songs . . . might not often have been heard out of doors.
>
> Alfred Williams, *Folk Songs of The Upper Thames* (1923)

In the summer of 1993, Sony's hottest new singer-songwriter was plying his trade in New York at a dinky downtown bar called Sin-e (pronounced like Sinead), learning his craft before curious crowds in increasingly cramped confines, while the air-con rattled and hummed. Jeff Buckley, as the son of the late Tim, had pedigree. But what he didn't have was his father's rich musical roots. And so in the previous two years, since he stunned the audience at a St Ann's tribute to Tim with his ghostly rendering of his father, he had been given a crash course in popular song courtesy of friends like guitarist Gary Lucas (with whom he briefly shared a stage in Gods and Monsters) and WFMU DJ Nicholas Hill. One of the pair even turned him on to a Dylan bootleg recording of a song known simply as 'Dink's Song'. The gut-wrenching refrain, 'Fare thee well, my honey, fare thee well', suited Buckley's wailing tenor perfectly, and the song soon became a nightly tour de force on these heady East Side evenings.

Tragically, Buckley died in 1997 in a drowning accident in Wolf River

Harbor, near the Memphis park they named after W. C. Handy, without fulfilling his abundant promise. It would be 2003 before a recording of *his* 'Dink's Song' (actually from Sin-e) would see the light of day. Two years later, Sony went as far as issuing, on the seventh of Dylan's official *Bootleg Series*, the December 1961 Bob Dylan home recording Buckley had learnt it from. Both credited the song as 'Trad. arr.', though, like 'Bo Diddley', its ostensible author's name was there in the title.

Indeed, the circumstances of its 'capture' in 1907 were known to Dylan, who had undoubtedly read folklorist John Lomax's memoir, *Adventures of a Ballad Hunter* (though the young tyke claimed to have learnt the song from Dink herself):

> I found Dink washing her man's clothes outside their tent on the bank of the Brazos River in Texas. Many other similar tents stood around. The black men and women they sheltered belonged to a levee-building outfit from the Mississippi River Delta, the women having been shipped from Memphis along with the mules and the iron scrapers, while the men, all skilful levee-builders, came from Vicksburg. A white foreman volunteered: 'Without women of their own, these levee Negroes would have been all over the bottoms every night hunting for women. That would mean trouble, serious trouble. Negroes can't work when sliced up with razors.' . . . But Dink, reputedly the best singer in the camp, would give me no songs. 'Today ain't my singin' day,' she would reply to my urging. Finally, a bottle of gin, bought at a nearby plantation commissary, loosed her muse. The bottle of liquor soon disappeared. She sang, as she scrubbed her man's dirty clothes, the pathetic story of a woman deserted by her lover when she needs him most – a very old story. Dink ended the refrain with a subdued cry of despair and longing – the sobbing of a woman deserted by her man.

Like Handy before him, Professor Lomax had stumbled on a secret side of Southern life, the sorrow of the negro woman set to song. Dink was by no means unique, even given the long and winding passage of her song from crude wax recording to the pages of Lomax's *American Ballads and Songs* (1934) and thence, via the folk revival, to Ramblin' Jack Elliott, Bob Gibson, Dylan, and ultimately Buckley. Lest we forget, Handy carried for twenty years the haunting refrain of the St Louis woman who (first) sang, 'My man's got a heart like a rock cast into the sea.'

Even before Handy's own epiphany, Johann Tonsor had written 'his' defining 1892 article on 'Negro Music', in which 'he' observed, 'It is quite a common thing for the negro women to improvise words and music while they are at work, a sort of Wagnerian "melos," or endless melody, as it were. I have often heard them drone softly thus all through the live-long, bright summer day.' Tonsor's estate would go on to claim a half-share of the most valuable song copyright in Christendom. Because Tonsor was really Mildred J. Hill, author of the melody to the school song belatedly copyrighted in 1932 as 'Happy Birthday To You'.

Back in the day Hill/Tonsor was simply a music teacher with a special interest in Negro spirituals (and given that her most famous song was published the year after her article on 'Negro music', perhaps she based the western world's favourite melody on some jaunty spiritual). If so, Hill was one of the first song snatchers to publish her own work – as 'Good Morning To All' – in the 1893 blockbuster, *Song Stories for Kindergarten*, and one of the few female songsmiths not taken to the cleaners by the patriarchal hegemony of publishing, destined to remain the exclusive purview of men well into the 1950s.

Unlike Dink, Hill was lucky enough to be born white and middle class. Like Katharine Purvis, who in the same year 'Good Morning To All' first appeared in print, wrote an execrable poem based on the structure of 'Auld Lang Syne' called 'America The Beautiful', as well as the two Adas – Blenkhorn ('Keep On The Sunny Side of Life') and Habershon ('Will The Circle Be Unbroken') – Hill found in such song 'writing' a sideline from a life spent expecting one's reward on the other side.

For women singers, especially if black, opportunities to break into the professional world of song at the turn of the century were somewhere between slim and non-existent. When they did manage to burst their metaphorical bonds, it merely prompted headlines like the one in a 1910 issue of *The African-American*, 'Mothers Taking Innocent Daughters to Houses of Ill Fame to Play Piano'. Even a great singer like Dink was stuck washing clothes in the river, not able to cross over.

In the 1890s and early 1900s blacks who travelled about singing to fellow blacks in makeshift shacks for a living were called songsters, and were invariably male. Howard Odum described the life this creed led in his 1911 survey of negro folksong: 'Songsters gather to render music for special occasions, such as church and private "socials," dances and other forms of social gathering . . . The wandering songster takes great pride in . . . singing with skill some of his favourite songs . . . As he wanders from negro community to community, he finds lodging and solace. So the negroes at home take up the [songster's] songs, and sing them to their companions.'

Few whites ever enjoyed the privilege of witnessing such occasions. Odum, who *was* permitted that honour, explicated what 'black' music the average white Southerner was allowed to hear: 'In the smaller towns, such negroes not infrequently organize a small "orchestra," and learn to play and sing the [popular] new songs. They often render acceptable music, and are engaged by the whites for serenades or for occasions of minor importance. They do not, however, sing the negro folk-songs.' Which explains why, for more than a quarter of a century, white popular audiences remained oblivious to a strong undercurrent of Afro-American song which ran contrary to the popular fare of 'coon songs', parlour ballads and such.

This only began to change after the turn of the century, as medicine shows, first, and then a nascent black vaudeville circuit began to introduce black singers – and specifically black *female* singers – to a lowbrow version of their own fare. The first of these to make a large splash was billed as 'Ma' Rainey. The larger-than-life lass once remarked, 'White folks hear the blues come out, but they don't know how it got there,' but she did not encounter the blues herself until 1902, when she was officially sixteen, but like as not twenty.* Like John Lomax, Gertrude Rainey first heard it from a downhearted female, this one from a small Missouri town, 'who came to the tent one morning and began to sing about the "man" who had left her. The song was so strange and poignant' she asked the girl to teach it to her. She then began to incorporate it into her act, though the title of the song is now lost.

Marrying a fellow minstrel-show performer, Will 'Pa' Rainey, in 1904, the woman who in the twenties would be branded 'Mother of the Blues' perennially toured the south with the famous Rabbit Foot Minstrels. Yet songs they performed, like 'Kansas City Blues' and 'Jelly Roll Blues', were closer to ragtime than anything Odum's informants sang. Between 1914 and 1916, Rainey was touring with Tolliver's Circus and Musical Extravaganza, aka 'The World's Largest Colored Show', packing them in as she belted her way through 'Walkin' The Dog', 'A Good Man Is Hard To Find', two of Handy's off-shoots – 'Memphis Blues' and 'Yellow Dog Blues' – and a song she seems to have heard along the way, 'See See Rider'. For a brief period in 1912, she even toured with a young, untutored Bessie Smith, who, for now at least, remained in awe of her musical idol.

By this time 'the blues' – thanks in no small part to Handy's misappropriation of the brand-name – had become, in the words of Alain Locke's important 1936 study of negro song, 'a generic name for all sorts of elaborate hybrid Negroid music'. Even Handy's first blues was essentially a 'very bluesy rag' which happened to use a twelve-measure strain. In fact, it bore a strong resemblance to one penned by another white female music teacher, Geraldine Dobyns, and published – in Memphis – in 1908. Dobyns' 'Bull Dog Rag' sounds an awful lot like the A and C strains of Handy's 'Mr Crump', supposedly composed the following year. And as the line between folk blues and commercial blues grew increasingly blurred, those women blues singers obliged to play to the crowd were party to a widespread deception. Designed to appeal to both sides of the

---

* According to the 1900 census, Gertrude was born in 1882 not 1886, as she always claimed.

racial divide, they concocted a new kinda hybrid from their own musical heritage. But what a sassy sisterhood it was, ready and willing to be captured on the new-fangled shellac records.

There was only one major problem. In the acoustical era, women's voices – being higher in pitch – were a lot more difficult to record than men's. Before the invention of electric microphones in the mid-twenties, a female singer was required to 'put her head as far as it will go into the [recording] horn when she's on her very low notes, and when she soars to the heights she must draw her head quickly back and sing straight to the ceiling' – or so read the guidelines provided by a Columbia Records executive in 1898. This evidently took some practice. In fact, one account of the first session in February 1920 by the original woman blues recording artist, Mamie Smith, suggested that, twenty-two years later, they still hadn't quite figured out how to record the real thing:

> When Mamie arrived, [Fred] Hager looked hard at her. She wasn't exactly the 'little girl' Perry [Bradford] had talked about; but she seemed to know her way around. They went into the studio at once, where Charley Hibbard had the equipment ready for a test recording. Just as they were starting, [Ralph] Peer walked in. After spotting Mamie at the recording horn, he gave Hager a quick look but didn't say anything. Hager gave the go ahead . . . [and] Mamie began. A short piano introduction, and a full shouting voice began to pour forth. After a few bars, Hager cut it off and said, 'Now, let's play that much back.' As they heard the first line, everybody winced, and Peer went and sat down at the door. That was it, as far as he was concerned. Hibbard was listening intently, and as the cow-like sounds issued from the speaker he nodded his head. 'I think I can fix that to sound like it should.' 'I hope so,' said Hager. 'They'd run us off the market with that cutting.'

At this historic Okeh session were three figures who between them were to revolutionize the record industry – singer Smith, the songwriter-publisher

Perry Bradford, and Ralph Peer, the assistant to Okeh's director of production, Fred Hager. The last of these would go on to make the most seismic contribution, but for now, Smith took centre stage, while it was Bradford who stood in the wings pulling strings. Having grown tired of scraping a living from touring, with Jeannette Taylor, as a comedy double-act, Bradford had become a songwriter-publisher. And it was he who had been hustling Hager to allow 'his' Mamie, whom he had been managing since 1917, to record two of his own commercial blues, the likes of which he had been publishing since 1916.

The songs recorded that Valentine's day – 'That Thing Called Love' and 'You Can't Keep A Good Man Down' – were typical Bradford takes on 'the blues', being 'closer in spirit to the marital sitcoms of vaudeville than to the sorrowful folk stories of the [traditional] blues singers'. Still feeling his way into the world of song publishing, he had sold the former to W.C. Handy, thus ensuring Handy would reap the benefits of Bradford's unswerving self-belief and also owe Bradford a favour.*

Like Handy, Bradford had songs bearing a more traditional hue in his portfolio, including half a dozen with blues in the title: 'Lonesome Blues' (1916 and 1918), 'Harlem Blues' (1917), 'Broken Hearted Blues', 'Nervous Blues' (both 1918) and 'Don't Care Blues' (1919). Of these, 'Don't Care Blues' leant heavily on the ubiquitous 'Make Me A Pallet On The Floor' while 'Lonesome Blues' was a halfway house between those two traditional standards, 'Hesitation Blues' and 'I'll See You When Yo' Troubles All Like Mine' (both also appropriated by Handy). But Bradford wasn't about to chance his arm with either of these after hustling so hard to get Mamie a shot at single success.

Okeh soon discovered Mamie's single was selling rather well; and in August they scheduled a second session for the gal. This time Bradford got to peddle what he thought of as a real blues song.

It wasn't. 'Crazy Blues' was one of his ham-fisted pseudo-blues, being largely plagiarized from his own earlier compositions. Of the song's

---

* Handy may well have returned it when he gave Bradford the reference he needed to take an office down the hall in the Gaiety Building after Mamie Smith's breakthrough.

four sections, the first derived from 'Harlem Blues', the second from his (unpublished) 'Nervous Blues' and the fourth from 'Broken Hearted Blues' – while the latter's chorus melody was identical to the middle section of 'Crazy Blues', a song with which it also shared two lines of lyrics.*

Yet 'Crazy Blues' sounded different enough to send shockwaves through the fledgling record industry. This time, sales were not only surprisingly – in fact, spectacularly – good, but were coming from what seemed like the most unlikely places. 'Crazy Blues' was a genuine phenomenon, a moment when the world of song temporarily tilted off its axis. Barely a month after its release, Okeh were ushering Mamie back in the studio, expecting Bradford to come up with another hit, such was the unprecedented demand. The song he gave them, 'Fare Thee Honey Blues', once more drew on elements of 'Make Me A Pallet On The Floor', and also made use of 'Fare Thee, Baby, Fare Thee Well', two chips off the folk-blues block.

Such were the limits of his imagination, the latter would be pillaged by Bradford a second time, in 1923, for his 'Fare Thee Blues'. By then, women blues singers had become a full-blown phenomenon, even as Bradford lost his own management rights to the increasingly unmanageable Mamie. His fly-by-the-pants approach to publishing was to have a more unwelcome by-product. When Lucille Hegamin had a hit with a song Bradford thought he had bought outright from Lem Fowler in October 1922, he received a writ. It turned out the flighty Fowler had already sold the song in question, 'He May Be Your Man, But He Comes To See Me Sometimes', to the Ted Browne Music Company. Bradford perjured himself in an affidavit responding to Browne's suit, and ended up serving a four-month jail sentence for his pains.

Bradford was finding out there were just as many sharks in the world of songwriting as in the ocean. Unencumbered by any great creative gift, he at least knew which way to swim. When Mary Stafford recorded 'Crazy Blues' for Columbia in January 1921 without the prestigious company

---

* Unfortunately for Bradford, he had previously sold the last of these outright to another publisher, Frederick Bowers.

making any royalty agreement with its composer, Bradford went to the Columbia offices to sort the matter out. An executive blithely informed him they shouldn't have to pay any royalties because Columbia could make a song which was fast approaching a million sales 'a popular hit'. Columbia even had the gall to send Bradford a contract with a clause that specifically waived all royalties. Bradford's retort was a peach: 'Please be advised that the only thing Perry Bradford waves is the American flag.'

Columbia, not for the first or last time in its semi-illustrious history, was hopelessly out of touch. Actually, all the established record companies proved slow to grasp the change signalled by 'Crazy Blues', and showed themselves hopelessly ill-equipped to gauge the needs of this new audience. In February 1921, the *Chicago Defender* reported that 'one of the greatest of all "blues" singers . . . Miss Bessie Smith, . . . is at present making records, with the aid of six jazz musicians, for the Emerson Record Company.' No such record ever appeared, presumably because Emerson – like Black Swan – shied away from anybody who *really* sang the blues. This didn't stop the labels from now signing a bewildering bevy of black girl singers. As *The Metronome* presciently reported the following January, 'Now every phonograph company has a colored girl recording. Blues are here to stay.'

However, the blues these girls were cutting – usually two at a time – in single-afternoon sessions were not exactly authentic. Rather, as D.D. Harrison observed in her study of women blues singers, *Black Pearls* (1988):

A new blues tradition [had] evolved as the women incorporated existing practices – the break in the second half of each four bars of the first two lines of the standard twelve-bar blues; talking in breaks; [the] improvising [of] new verses for endless repetitions – into their own innovative styles . . . They [also] altered non-blues songs such as 'He Used To Be Your Man But He's My Man Now', 'Give Me That Old Slow Drag', and 'Daddy Your Mama Is

29

Lonesome For You', to fit the blues format and to evoke the blues feeling . . . Although most of the songs blues women sang were either composed or arranged by professional songwriters such as Clarence Williams, Chris Smith, Perry Bradford and W.C. Handy, many [soon] wrote their own blues, too.

Of the *few* who actually sang and 'wrote their own blues', Alberta Hunter was perhaps the first to make a splash – and the first to be treated like she was fresh off the banana boat. The black blues queen had run away to Chicago when she was twelve, preferring to wash dishes in a whorehouse until the opportunity to sing professionally arose. She finally wowed Chicago's Dreamland cabaret in 1918, her rendition of 'A Good Man Is Hard To Find' making her the talk of the town (and as a Pace & Handy copyright, lining Handy's pockets). As a result, the popular white actress-singer Sophie Tucker sent her maid to ask Hunter to come to her dressing room and teach her the song. Hunter later recalled: 'The white shows used to come in from New York and everybody was down there to see us work, . . . Al Jolson, Sophie Tucker, everybody . . . She wanted that song, and that's how they were, always trying to get something out of us, always trying to pick up on our little tricks.'

Though Hunter held out, Tucker was sure she would get her way. Though their concern was not wholly based on skin colour, in 1918 the very idea of recording Hunter, or Smith or Rainey, would never have occurred to New York-based record labels. Signed to Black Swan Records in 1921, Hunter found herself within a year on the Paramount label, run by Maurice Supper – a former mechanical engineer put in charge of the record division by its parent furniture company because he was a good draughtsman.

Having let Black Swan have its way with personnel and song-choice on her debut sessions in May 1921, by the time of her first Paramount session in July 1922 Hunter was ready to unleash her timeless 'Down Hearted Blues'. The song would become her best earner, and the one she would be remembered for, though she found herself obliged to share any windfall with Lovie Austin, pit pianist at Chicago's Monogram Theater, for knowing – or so Hunter claimed throughout the remainder of her long life – how to 'fix' the tune for copyright purposes:

**Alberta Hunter:** 'Downhearted Blues' was composed at the Monogram Theater in Chicago . . . One day I was talking to Lovie [and she] heard me hum that thing and she said, 'Oh, that's a good song. That's a good song. We put that down.' Now, Lovie put the music down that I hummed to her. They had it on the [sheet] music that Lovie Austin wrote the music to 'Downhearted Blues'. Lovie Austin did *not* write the music – *I* am the composer of 'Downhearted Blues' – words and music. Lovie Austin put the notes down on a piece of paper in order for it to go to the copyright department. Because I knew nothing about having to have a song copywritten [sic] . . . Now, I will give her credit for this one thing . . . She was kind enough and honest enough to put my name as the writer of the words . . . She could've been nasty enough to have stolen the whole thing from me. A song called 'Down South Blues', I wrote the whole thing to that, and Ethel Waters and Fletcher Henderson . . . put their names [to it].

One suspects Hunter may be doing Austin a disservice. What Hunter described as 'put[ting] notes down on a piece of paper' was most likely arranging the song; this was considered Austin's forte, one which put her in great demand and resulted in her working not just with Hunter, but also Ma Rainey, Ethel Waters and Ida Cox.

Austin also did Hunter another favour. She placed the song with publisher Jack Mills, who was at least a great white shark, thus ensuring that Paramount's Maurice Supper did not get his hands on the publishing for a nominal few dollars tagged onto the session fee begrudgingly doled out by his label.

Such a practice was very much the norm in the 'race records' business in 1922 – and, for that matter, 1942. This industry model, such as it was, meant that, 'whether written by the artist or by the black talent scout-producer, race songs were assigned to a publishing company owned by the latter, to which royalties were paid. Talent was paid by the piece, from the $25 to $50 per side that prevailed for many years to the $200 a song Columbia paid Bessie Smith . . . Although unfair to those performers whose recordings were popular, the system served to cover the cost of failures and  eventually became "what everybody did."' As a result, publishing was often lost in perpetuity, a place where real money could eventually be made.

Certainly 'Down Hearted Blues' would never have had the long life it did if Supper had controlled the publishing. For starters, Frank Walker, head of Columbia's 'race division', would never have allowed the song to be recorded at the debut session of the still 'unknown and practically broke' Bessie Smith in February 1923. It's lucky he did, because the second the Empress of the Blues started singing Hunter's blues he knew he had a star in the making: 'There was one line in the ["Down Hearted] Blues" that did it. It was the first time that it was used and it made that record a hit. It was, "Got the world in a jug, got the stopper in my hand."'

Though Smith was clearly a natural, Walker was hardly diffident about taking the credit for tutoring someone who had been pounding the boards for the past decade. As the label manager, W.G. Monroe, informed the papers when Bessie's first blues broke all previous records, 'Her first few recordings were terrible, for her voice was absolutely uncultured. However . . . Mr Walker, realizing that she possessed latent talent, put her through a course of training. She finally came through in splendid style.' What Monroe – and Walker – meant was that they had turned Bessie's 'uncultured' raw blues voice into something refined enough to ensure no Columbia record exec. choked on his New York strip-steak upon hearing her.

Less fortuitously for Smith, her backing musicians at that first session included the chancer Clarence Williams plonking away at the piano. Before ascending the stairs of the Gaiety Building, Williams had scuffled in the foothills of song publishing longer than most. Having hung out with the likes of Jelly Roll Morton and Tony Jackson upon arriving in New Orleans in 1906, he sought out a niche where his limited musicianship was not a major handicap. By 1915, he had set up a publishing company with a popular local violinist, Armand J. Piron. By 1919, he had opened another office in Chicago, then the second home of song publishing, where the same year an amateur songwriter, Lucy Fletcher, brought in a song lyric, 'Sugar Blues'. Williams added a tune of sorts, putting his name alongside hers. In time 'Sugar Blues' would prove to be his most valuable copyright, helping to fund a move to New York in 1921.

From here he bought out Piron, though not before publishing 'I Wish I Could Shimmy Like My Sister Kate'. This was a song Piron initially claimed full copyright on, but of which he later admitted – after Louis Armstrong laid claim to it, too – 'That tune is older than all of us. People always put different words to it, some of them . . . too dirty to say in polite company.' And the move east evidently worked out because, later in 1921, when Handy found himself suffering one of his periodic downturns and had to borrow $25,000 to stay afloat, Williams offered to be one of his creditors.

Williams was present at Bessie Smith's first session because, like Perry Bradford, he wanted his piece of the pie. This is why he ensured Bessie's electrifying take of 'Down Hearted Blues' was backed by his own 'Gulf Coast Blues'. In fact, Williams might have been allowed to collect publishing on both of Bessie's sides if Alberta Hunter had not personally written to Walker with a copy of the sheet music to 'Down Hearted Blues', suggesting he let a Columbia act record it.*

Whether two Clarence Williams songs *and* two of his piano accompaniments on a single 78 would have driven away potential punters, we will never know. As it is, Williams knew that one side of a record sold exactly the same number of copies – and received exactly the same royalty – as the other. He also knew that sheet music sales of this new style of popular song by February 1923 were trailing some way behind record

---

* Walker was hoping to prise Hunter away from Paramount, until he realized he had found what he really wanted in Bessie Smith.

sales. Indeed, the word 'publishing', when it came to popular songs, was beginning to take on a new meaning – the acquisition of copyrights for licensing purposes. Here was the future.

What Williams didn't know was that Bessie's new boyfriend, Jack Gee, had begun taking a keen interest in her business affairs. Gee was unimpressed to find that Williams was not only grabbing a slice of the publishing (a concept neither he nor Bessie really grasped), but was also pocketing half of Bessie's 'selection fee' from Columbia, which already stood at a generous $125 a cut. It turned out – a trick Williams probably learnt from his fellow Gaiety leaseholder, Perry Bradford – that Bessie's recording contract had been drawn up not directly with Bessie herself but between Clarence Williams and Columbia.

Unluckily for Williams, the ever-persuasive Bradford was in jail when Jack and Bessie came to call, seeking to straighten things out using a language Williams might understand. If the ever-alert Williams promptly crawled beneath his desk to avoid a kicking from Jack, Bessie needed no such help in this department, being more than capable of holding her own in a bar-room brawl. When she jumped him and began pounding at him with her clenched fists, Williams decided the management game was not for him and released Bessie from any further contractual obligations. He perhaps already suspected the Empress of the Blues might prove something of a handful – even for the more muscular Gee.

Yet barely had Bessie extracted herself from one serpentine bosom than she sank her teeth into another, and this one held her recording career in the palm of his hand. Back at Columbia Frank Walker was quick to learn about the little spat – probably from Williams himself. Having offered the requisite sympathy, he promptly signed Smith directly to Columbia, making himself her manager in all recording matters while promising her a minimum of $1,500 a year (still at $125 a side) with an option to renew at $150 a side. He also carefully omitted the standard artist's royalty clause, offering instead to copyright any of her own songs with his Frank Music Company, thus allowing himself to collect royalties from all Smith compositions he recorded. And it was he who decided what she recorded.

Williams, meanwhile, wisely made his peace with Bessie, still offering his perfunctory piano playing at her sessions while feeding her the kinda songs she needed to fulfil her expansive new Columbia contract. Clarence already knew that any lost selection fee was mere chicken feed compared with the potential rewards that came with publishing a hit, if it had his name on it.

It often did. As Jansen and Jones sarcastically observe, 'Clarence Williams' name is on many good songs, usually sharing credit with a better songwriter, [making] every Williams hit come with an implied question mark. Did Spencer Williams, Fats Waller, James P. Johnson, Chris Smith, or Willie the Lion Smith consistently run into problems in composition that could be solved only by the input of Clarence Williams? Probably not.' An older, wiser Williams had an explanation for this: 'That's the way the music business worked in those days. If you couldn't get a piece of the copyright, it didn't pay to publish it. Songwriters understood that putting the publisher's name on it, along with his own, was part of the original deal.' And those that didn't understand, didn't last long.

Through 1932 Williams kept Bessie Smith supplied with a steady stream of his copyrights – the best of which was 'Tain't Nobody's Bizness If I Do', a song ostensibly written by Porter Grainger and Everett Robbins but heavily based on the traditional 'Tain't Nobody's Business But My Own'. In September he even lent a hand (and took a co-credit) on the first 'original' song Smith recorded for Columbia, 'Jailhouse Blues'. By then, Smith had found a better pianist, but Williams continued to supply songs for Smith right up to her final Columbia session in November 1931, on which he was her sole accompanist.

Smith herself was too busy whooping it up and trading blows with Gee to really get a handle on the way publishing worked. She seemed content just to be allowed – every now and then – to record a song of her own in a style she found more comfortable than the cluttered, jazzy efforts preferred by Walker and/or the powers-that-be. Thus it was that in April 1924 she recorded her second original, 'Sorrowful Blues'; and for the one and only time, she was allowed to accompany herself with just guitar and violin, not piano and/or jazz band. Here for three magical minutes is Bessie the pure blues singer. Even the lyrics are clearly in a traditional style; two of the verses are the same as ones sung by Ida Cox on 'Chicago Monkey Man Blues', suggesting a common pool of inspiration.

If Cox took credit for almost all of her own blues. Smith was only rarely allowed to dip into her own pool of material, and it would be another nine months before she recorded her third original, 'Reckless Blues' (with Louis Armstrong on cornet). At this juncture she seems to have realized where the real power lay, and from now on she made it a point to generally record at least one original at a scheduled session. Yet it would take her until February 1927 to reach the high watermark of her self-composed blues, 'Backwater Blues', written after she got caught in a flood on her way from Cincinnati. In the words of her sister Maud, Bessie 'had to step off the train into little rowboats that took us to where we were staying . . . Bessie looked around and said, "No, no, I can't stay here tonight." But there was a lot of other people there, and they were trying to get her to stay . . . She got the title [and the idea] from those people down South.'

'Backwater Blues' was recorded at the same session as another song Bessie claimed for her own, 'Preachin' The Blues', and both receive the same piano accompaniment. But it would be two and a half years before she was allowed to record another pair of originals with just P. Johnson at the piano. By the time those recordings were issued, the Wall Street Crash had landed with a wallop that shook the world, and the market for blues queens was receding fast.

Despite taking Bessie's publishing for his own, Walker remained a trusted trustee of the Smith audio library through the Roaring Twenties. Even after the Crash, he stood by her, continuing to pay her that substantial selection fee (which now stood at $200) for each track cut, though demand had not so much sloped off as died off. Only after her November 1931 session did Walker bow to the inevitable. By 1932 there was barely a blues queen – or race label – left standing.

Other labels had already jettisoned even bestselling artists of yes-teryear when austerity came a-knockin'. Paramount, predictably, were among the first to bail on their blues queens, dispensing with Ma Rainey and Ida Cox before the first economic aftershock had even been felt. By this point, neither singer could count on their long-time protector and general cheerleader, Clarence's namesake, Mayo J. Williams, to run inter-ference with the man upstairs sniffing furniture polish.

Such had been his precarious hold on his position at Paramount – talent scout, producer and music publisher rolled into one, each of these duties unsalaried – that Mayo Williams's only way of making a living was to take a half-share of the publishing on any track released under his audiophonic auspices. Because as Jansen and Jones suggest, 'His money mostly came from the shady sidelines of publishing companies that didn't publish and from songs that he didn't write . . . He was usually on com-mission, betting that the royalties he received on his companies' products . . . would add up to a living.'

As it happens, Williams made a very good living, because he was very good at all his unpaid jobs. However, he came up short when selecting Paramount as the place he should ply his skills. Set up as an afterthought by manufacturers of (equally shoddy) phonograph players in 1918, the label paid small advances, used cheap materials, recorded in the most corner-cutting way possible, and generally produced a product that screamed, *Cheap is how this feels*. Paramount had been running on empty for five years when this keen young negro presented himself at their Port Washington, Madison, headquarters in the spring of 1923, claiming to be a journalist. Maurice Supper was happy to give the man a job, just as long as he didn't want paying. In fact, he had in mind the job Supper had himself been hired to do: run the race records division.

For finding, arranging and recording new talent, Williams would receive a position at Chicago Music, a publishing division Supper had set up after losing out on 'Down Hearted Blues'. Chicago Music did not actually publish any music. What it did was collect the two-cents-per-record publishing royalty on every record sold; and out of those two cents, Williams would get one. This crucially meant that Williams was only interested in signing singers who either wrote their own songs or, more likely, applied a Handyesque twist to a traditional, and therefore public domain, blues.

As such, his first signing was the underrated Ida Cox, who had made her name at the Monogram Theater in Chicago. Pianist Lovie Austin tipped off Williams, and in June 1923, the three of them assembled at Paramount's sorry excuse for a studio to record three Cox 'originals': 'Any Woman's Blues', 'Bama Bound Blues' and 'Lovin' Is The Thing I'm Wild About'.

Ida seems to have been steeped in blues lore, with many a Cox couplet turning up on more 'authentic' Delta blues after her recording career had ground to a temporary halt in the year of the Crash.* She was to prove a steady seller – but nothing like Williams's next signing, the great Ma Rainey. It was Rainey who put Paramount on the map, Chicago Music on an even keel, and Williams (temporarily) on easy street. Surprisingly, it had taken Rainey until June 1923 to be snapped up. Even then it was only Williams who took a chance, tying her to a label whose legendary parsimony spread through the company like dry rot.

Paramount needed Rainey, because at the end of 1924 Alberta Hunter flew the coop, having failed to find the label any more appreciative of their good fortune than Black Swan Records. (The latter company went under shortly after they started using Paramount's pressing plant, ensuring that even a pro like Hunter sounded like someone recorded at the bottom of a slurry pit.)

At least Paramount let their artists record what they wanted – which in Rainey's case was usually her take on a hard life. And rather than be dissuaded by her larger than life persona, her age (she was already forty-one

---

* Her 'How Long Daddy How Long' would influence and inspire at least three country blues classics, Leroy Carr's 'How Long, How Long Blues', the Mississippi Sheiks' 'Sitting On Top of The World' and Robert Johnson's 'Come On In My Kitchen'. And on 'Ramblin' Blues', she directly anticipated Son House with an archetypal opening couplet: 'Early this morning the blues came walkin' in my room [x2]/I said, blues, please tell me what are you doing here so soon.'

in 1923) and her non-beauty-queen looks, Mayo Williams smartly marketed her as the Mother of The Blues. It was a title to which she certainly had a greater claim than the one adopted by W.C. Handy, after plying her professional wares since the turn of the century.

Rainey was also remarkably prolific, recording ninety-four sides for Paramount in her six-year stint. Almost all of them bore her name, though she invariably incorporated lines found floating in the folk-blues pool. She was, after all, a country gal, as were most of her audience, hence the songs about bo' weevils and moonshine at her very first Paramount session and reports of her performing live with country jug bands when touring away from the big cities.

It was also Rainey who first fixed the couplet, 'Lord, I stand here wonderin'/Will a matchbox hold my clothes?', on 1924's 'Lost Wandering Blues'; while her 'See See Rider' would become a perennial for any number of emulators white, black, male, female, long before Elvis opened his seventies shows with it.* Nor did Rainey need any help notating a song, though she used Lovie Austin at many of her studio sessions, presumably because she needed someone adept enough to get things down in one or two takes: this was Paramount, after all, and time was money. In many ways, Rainey was a smart cookie. But she still ended up having to surrender her publishing to the label that recorded her, and specifically the man who signed her.

Not only did Rainey sell records but she stockpiled enough songs to set up her own publishing house of the blues. As long as Mayo Williams's place at Paramount was dependent on Maurice Supper, however, he needed her songs to make ends meet. Despite her impressive output, in 1925 his little publishing empire was placed in jeopardy after Supper left the label to set up his own mail-order record business. Supper's replacement as Sales Manager and Recording Director was Arthur C. Laibly; and Laibly not

---

* Her 'Jealous Hearted Blues' even sounded traditional enough for A.P. Carter to recast it as 'Jealous Hearted Me', making it one of the first recorded blues to cross the race/hillbilly divide.

only considered Williams's position at Paramount anomalous, he fancied himself as something of a talent scout.

Fate initially smiled on Laibly. In late 1925, an important regional record salesman wrote to him from Dallas, Texas, telling him about a local gospel singer called Blind Lemon Jefferson. When the two resultant gospel sides didn't do much, Laibly summoned Jefferson to Chicago in March 1926 to record four sides under his personal supervision. This time Jefferson stuck to the blues.

The first Blind Lemon 78, 'Long Lonesome Blues', broke all records and Laibly wanted more, promptly recording a further dozen Jefferson songs before year's end. All were credited to Jefferson; Laibly however assigned the publishing to himself, including 'That Black Snake Moan', the song that turned Jefferson from Paramount's premier artist into their very own cash machine. 'That Black Snake Moan' was to shift the very sands of popular song, reversing the 'Crazy Blues' fad and returning black popular music to its country roots. That it had already been recorded and 'published' by one of the blues queens, Okeh's Victoria Spivey, fazed neither Laibly nor Jefferson – even when the blind bluesman's old friend came looking for him, demanding her cut.

**Victoria Spivey:** Way back before my 'Black Snake Blues' was recorded I met Lemon one night in Galveston, Texas, where I was working as a blues singer and pianist. And he helped me out by sitting in and singing his blues giving me an opportunity to take a break and mingle with my friends. His blues were so full of soul and made a big hit with the people. Lemon and myself continued meeting at house parties where we would give one another much needed intermissions . . . We were buddies and everything went along swell until I heard his recording of 'Black Snake MOAN' on Paramount which came out some months after my original 'Black Snake BLUES' on Okeh. It was so much like my 'Black Snake Blues', [even] including the moan. I was really angry for a while knowing that Lemon and myself were like brother and sister in our jobs. I could not understand how it happened. He had heard me sing the 'Black Snake' at different house parties way before I recorded it. John Erby and myself met Lemon in St. Louis and we straightened the matter out . . . 'Black Snake MOAN' not only made Blind Lemon Jefferson, but pulled him out of the sticks. It was so good for him that Paramount had him make more versions of it for future records.

This was the diplomatic account Spivey gave in a 1966 *Record Research* article, after Jefferson had been in the ground twenty-five years. However, at the time the singers' labels went to war over the song. Spivey herself responded to Jefferson's brazen thievery by cutting a 'New Black Snake Blues' with guitarist Lonnie Johnson. As of March 1927, Jefferson himself had been temporarily enticed to join Spivey at Okeh, where he cut the song again (along with his other showstopper, 'Matchbox Blues'), thus providing blues fans with their one and only opportunity to hear Jefferson minus the ubiquitous Paramount crackles and pops. Paramount enticed him back with threats, promises, or both; then convinced him to cut his own sequel, 'Black Snake Dream Blues' (credited to pianist George Perkins, perhaps to make Spivey think twice about hunting down her old friend a second time).

But for Mayo Williams and his roster of blues queens, Jefferson's success signalled the end. Laibly was convinced he had the Midas touch, and remained convinced even after he brought Paramount to the brink of bankruptcy – which he had by the time Jefferson went missing during a snowstorm, in 1930. Jefferson's success certainly had wider implications, but they were ones Laibly proved too ill informed to exploit. Even before the Great Depression struck like a thief in the night, the blues queens' era was drawing to a close.

Having cut the prescient Williams loose, Laibly could only guess what came next. Williams finally quit Paramount in 1928, moving to Vocalion where he continued to discover – and claim a part-share of the publishing on – a second wave of notable blues artists. He even signed the last of the great blues queens, Memphis Minnie, in June 1929.* By now, Williams had learnt that the only guaranteed way to ensure the publishing stream kept flowing was to put his name in the mix, and preferably on the label. At some point he began doing what the artists he had recorded for Paramount and Vocalion had always done, copyrighting to *himself* the occasional folk standard.

Most notable of these was 'Corrine, Corrina'. Blind Lemon Jefferson had included a verse of the song in 'Corrina Blues' (his 1926 version of Ma Rainey's 'See See Rider'), and both Clayton McMichen and James Wiggins had recorded it in 1929–30 in 'traditional' guise. Yet by 1932 it had been copyrighted to Williams *and* Bo Chatman, occasional member of the Mississippi Sheiks, a band of black bluesmen who set their wacky take on the blues to the sound of fiddles and even the odd hillbilly-like instrumental busk. Chatman had recorded three different versions between 1928 and 1932, just in time for Red Nichols and His Five Pennies to take it into the pop mainstream and Cab Calloway to take it further downstream; by which time Williams had jumped on board.

Nor did Williams allow the hunt for publishing opportunities to distract him from recognizing talent. Tampa Red and Georgia Tom (a.k.a. the great gospel songwriter, Thomas A. Dorsey) were signed to Vocalion in 1928, and when Williams transferred his affiliation to Decca in 1934, they almost immediately had a minor hit with Kokomo Arnold's 'Milk Cow Blues', a song which holds the unique privilege of having been covered by Robert Johnson, Elvis Presley, Bob Dylan and (albeit as a tuneless jam at Abbey Road during the interminable *Let It Be* sessions) The Beatles.

Mayo also got to sit back and watch a couple of old guard creditstealers – one of them his namesake, Clarence – get into an argument about who stole what, first. In the months before the world went to war, Clarence Williams and Perry Bradford started their very own playground spat. It

---

* Like Ida Cox, Minnie put her own inimitable mark on the songs she recorded, though this did not stop the likes of Chuck Berry ('I Wanna Be Your Driver') and Led Zeppelin ('When The Levee Breaks') from later removing it, putting theirs on instead.

was all over an old Bradford copyright, 'Keep A Knockin'', which had become a hit for the new king of the dance floor, Louis Jordan. It turned out Bradford had carelessly neglected to copyright the song until *after* the Jordan recording was made, and since it sounded a lot like a song Williams had claimed as his own back in 1933, 'My Bucket's Got A Hole In It', Williams set out to claim this, too.

The fact that a prototypical 'Keep A Knockin'' had been among the negro folksongs collected by Howard Odum in the 1900s, and everyone knew 'My Bucket's Got A Hole In It' was an old New Orleans folk tune, mattered not. What mattered to this pair, tutored in the school of Handy, was who filed first. In the end Bradford prevailed, retaining the rights to 'Keep A Knockin''; and Williams reinforced his copyright on 'My Bucket's Got A Hole In It', which in the end would prove equally valuable.

By 1939, both Bradford and Williams were convinced that just about every worthwhile copyright from folksong's store had already been scooped up. In fact, there was still quite a hoard of unsung classics, one of which was 'Dink's Song'. Because John Lomax had returned to banking, he had not got around to fixing it in print until 1934; and when he did publish it in *American Ballads and Songs* he copyrighted only the compilation, not the song itself.

As a result, 'Dink's Song' stayed firmly in the public domain, from whence it passed into the folk revival and out into the wider world of pop culture. At its reappearance, 105 years after Lomax collected it, as the theme tune to the Coen Brothers' *Inside Llewyn Davis*, it received another sex-change from Marcus Mumford and Oscar Isaac. At least it had escaped the strip mining of tradition during the twenties and thirties, much of it done at the behest of the man who coined the terms 'race' and 'hillbilly' in popular music. In the process, he would accumulate wealth the likes of Perry Bradford and Clarence and Mayo J. Williams could only dream about. That man was Ralph Peer.

---

* This was an oversight his son would belatedly (and unsuccessfully) try to remedy.

CHAPTER 3

# 1917-27: The Only True Valid Death You Can Feel Today

*Featuring*: 'The Wreck Of The Ol' 97'; 'The Prisoner's Song'; 'Casey Jones';
'Frankie And Johnny'; 'Good Ol' Mountain Dew'

'Quite by accident I unearthed and developed the business of recording Negro artists to make records for sale to the colored population. Two years later, I had the good fortune to stumble across the fact that throughout our Southern states there existed a separate and distinct repertory of popular music, not connected in any way with the productions of New York and Chicago songwriters. I supervised recordings of material taken from this folkloric goldmine using local artists. This led to the development and expansion of the travelling recording studio, and brought up the necessity for a name which would distinguish this special repertory from the New York brand of popular music. After trying several names unsuccessfully, the word hillbilly took the popular fancy and has since become universal.'

Ralph Peer, *The Meridian (Miss.) Star*, 26 May 1953

In later life Ralph Peer liked to recall one particular assignment, when transferred to Columbia's Chicago office in 1915 as a hungry 23-year-old anxious to learn the ropes of the recording industry. He was charged with looking after W.C. Handy when the older man changed trains in Chicago on his way from Memphis to New York to record for the label. Handy, though he devoted several pages of his autobiography to the trip in question, makes no mention of Peer. Yet it would be the well-bred white boy from Independence, Missouri, who would do the greater service to the blues, and indeed to popular music in general. Starting with the revolutionary Mamie Smith 'Crazy Blues' session, which he attended in a subsidiary role as his boss at Okeh, Fred Hager, coaxed the requisite performance out of the anxious Mamie, he would prove to be something of a lightning rod for almost every change in the air through the tumultuous twenties.

It seems to have been Peer who first realized the significance of Smith's statements of intent; and he who coined the label 'race records' under which this new, exciting musical genre could be marketed. Ever the company man, he had been intrigued enough by initial sales to investigate their source, and he thus set out to

. . . do a little exploratory work to find out just who was buying Mamie's records with such enthusiasm. He looked over the orders from outlying districts and saw that an unusual number came from out-of-the-way places – from retailers not normally noted for large orders. Amongst these was a furniture store in Richmond, Virginia. He decided to investigate and headed for Richmond. He had hardly shaken hands when the dealer started enthusiastically, 'This is a wonderful Okeh idea, Mr Peer – great. Business is terrific. The coloured folk are buying records and record players like crazy. They don't really have that kind of money to spend. It's these records of Mamie Smith's.' . . . From then on Okeh was in the race record business [Kirkeby].

As far as companies were concerned, the new genre was not the blues, which already carried worrisome connotations. Okeh, fighting for market share with bigger, better-funded rivals, was prepared to set up a whole division to push the new genre. Peer had found his niche. And gradually he began to convince the powers-that-be there was another kinda artist they should also be recording.

The cogs at Okeh turned slowly, though, as did the technological changes necessary for Peer's plan to be realized. Initially, it seemed easier to pay a singer's New York fare than to ship an entire recording studio by rail. But what if there were dozens of these singers, each with only a couple of songs the label could use? The idea that Okeh should go to the very font of vernacular American song, rather than wait for its practitioners to hop a freight train east, was a radical one, which it took the success of the race division to justify. Finally, in the spring of 1923, Hager gave Peer the green light to go scout potential recording artists in a part of the country he knew well – the south.

And so in June, Peer undertook the first-ever field trip by a record producer (as opposed to a folklorist) looking to make recordings of folk performers 'in situ'. The first city to which Peer shipped Okeh's still-cumbersome 'portable' recording equipment was Atlanta, Georgia – at least partly at the behest of a regional Okeh distributor by the name of Polk Brockman, who ran a furniture store there, doing talent scouting in his spare time. He directed the label to a vacant warehouse on Nassau Street where Charles Hibbard, a one-time associate of Thomas Edison, and his team of engineers set up the equipment Okeh had sent ahead. Initial results did not reinforce Peer's belief that there was an untapped well of talent waiting to gush forth from the south, but his instincts were to prove spot-on.

According to Brockman, a primary goal all along was to record a local fiddle-player known as Fiddlin' John Carson. Given that the first pressing of the resultant Carson 78 was between five hundred and a thousand copies, pressed at Brockman's behest wholly for the local market without even being assigned an official Okeh release, this seems unlikely. Peer's own account rather suggests Brockman had talked up how much talent there was to be found in Atlanta. He already feared it might prove a wasted trip – which would not reflect well on him after angling for such an opportunity, probably scuppering any future sorties – when Carson seized his opportunity.

**Ralph Peer:** We went down there to get Negro stuff. This [local] fellow began scouting around [Atlanta] but to my amazement he didn't know of any Negro talent . . . So to take up that [allocated] time, my distributor brought in Fiddlin' John Carson. He said, 'Fiddlin' John had been on the radio station and he's got quite a following. He's really not a good singer, but let's see what he's got.' So the beginning of the hillbilly [thing] was just this effort to take up some time.

Adding credence to Peer's account is the fact that on the day he recorded Carson's tracks (probably 14 June), he also cut two blues songs, both by women singers, 'The Pawn Shop Blues' by Lucille Bogan from Alabama, and 'Grievous Blues', by Fannie Mae Goosby. Both would be invited to New York to record further tunes later in the year, as would Carson. Peer also ended up recording a white dance band, a few novelty acts, and a group of gospel singers from the local college. Hardly your average folkloric expedition!

Already, Peer was setting a pattern for his (and fellow A&R men's) field trips, one which drew precious little distinction between black and white rural performers. Wherever and whenever Peer lay his hat and his record company's equipment, Jim Crow was barred. At no point did Peer discriminate along lines of colour. He would record the likes of Frank Stokes, Tommy Johnson and Blind Willie McTell – three of the Delta's finest bluesmen – on these travels, often at the same sessions he recorded the likes of Ernest Stoneham, Jimmie Rodgers or Alfred G. Karnes.

However, he was too much of a record man to think he could *market* Lucille Bogan and Fiddlin' John Carson to the same constituency. When Carson's debut 78 – 'The Old Hen Cackled' b/w 'Little Log Cabin In The Lane' – started selling like hot molasses, Peer needed to find another label with which to market this unearthly sound. For now 'Old Time Ballads' would have to do. But by 1925, he was calling it hillbilly music.* Recording Carson also reminded Peer just how hard it was to capture the authentic feel of old time music on the equipment he was obliged to use:

---

* Any pejorative connotations later applied to 'race' and 'hillbilly' only came with hindsight. Neither term brought the slightest sales resistance at the time.

**Ralph Peer:** [Carson] was a very difficult recording proposition because it was before the invention of the so-called electrical recording system. We had to use large horns and it was really troublesome getting both the fiddle played by Carson and his voice all into the mouth of one horn. When the wax recording got back to New York and had been processed, I listened to [both] items, and believe me they were terrible.

Thankfully for Peer, and the future of recorded sound, a solution was not far off. The electric microphone – invented and refined by Western Electric – would not only usher in the era of the 'talkies', but would make field trips like the one Peer had embarked on in June 1923 a lot easier, even if the change left Victor's Nipper howling at the moon. Indeed, it is hard to argue with music historian Donald Clarke's assessment that 'the invention of electric recording in 1925 . . . changed everything: singers . . . did not have to be shouters, like the singers of the coon-song era, but could use the microphone to sing apparently to each individual . . . listening at home . . . The access of African-Americans, hillbillies and other minorities to the recording studio [also meant] that never again [could] the music of "the common people" be ignored.'

Within eighteen months of Carson's first New York session, Peer would have electric microphones on hand to capture not just the fiddle-player, but all the country folk he fancied, the 'common people' having bought Carson in their thousands, and ultimately tens of thousands. Peer had once again ensured himself and his bosses end-of-year bonuses, while unlocking another rich vein of American song for other diggers to strip-mine.

But in June 1923 it was Polk Brockman – a man who wouldn't have known a Child ballad from a parlour ballad – who claimed the publishing on both sides of the first Carson 78. Though it devolved to Peer to protect Okeh's interests, and his own, he went along with Brockman on this occasion. With 'Little Log Cabin In The Lane', by William Shakespeare Hays, he knew full well he was chancing his arm; it 'was too well known to everybody, [being] an old minstrel song', he explained:

**Ralph Peer**: But after that, when[ever] I worked with Fiddlin' John, I wouldn't let him record . . . anything that already had wide distribution [orally]. [Thankfully,] he had a repertoire of about three hundred songs that you've never heard of before, things he'd acquired in his circus days, from other performers . . . [And] they were now all duly copyrighted and put over as new songs.

Carson, who had been writing his own folksy compositions for a decade or more, even printing and selling them on the streets, was smart enough to soon broker a deal direct with Peer. And, successful as Carson's initial release proved to be, it was still far enough off the radar to pass New York's cabal of credit-stealers by. The song-snatchers only really took notice after Peer returned to the city and remembered a rough demo he had made back in March, when an annoyingly persistent harmonica player had presented himself at his New York office and insisted Peer record him. Having reviewed that ragged recording, largely made to humour the man, Peer realized that while it had all the deficiencies of Carson's cuts it also contained that same Southern spirit. Henry Whitter was duly summoned back to Okeh, this time going from demo to disc. His first release paired 'Lonesome Road Blues' – a song Dorothy Scarborough had recently collected for her negro folksong collection – with 'The Wreck Of The Ol' 97', one of the popular ballads describing a fatal crash on Virginia's Southern Railway the night of 27 September 1903.

Despite the proximity of the incident that directly inspired it, 'The Wreck Of The Ol' 97' had already taken on a life of its own, with at least two distinct narrative ballads becoming intermingled in oral tradition. Just to confuse matters further, both had taken as their template an earlier disaster ballad, 'The Ship That Never Returned', ostensibly written in 1865 by Henry Clay Work, while there had been 'train wreck' parodies of Work's work since at least 1888. Nevertheless, Whitter allowed himself to be paid $200 by Fred Hager for what was supposedly clear title to 'The Wreck Of The Southern Ol' 97', as it was called on its release at the turn of the year.

The song clearly struck a chord with the public and was soon covered by another Southern singer, Ernest Thompson. But it was a 'pop version' on Victor Records by a popular tenor, Vernon Dalhart, which truly put the cat among the canaries. It was paired with another quasi-traditional tune, 'The Prisoner's Song', supposedly at the behest of Victor A&R man Nathaniel Shilkret, who told Dalhart he feared a 'cover' of a recent hit might need something different to entice punters to part with a buck. What really motivated Dalhart was a share of the song publishing. 'The Wreck Of The Ol' 97' was already spoken for. 'The Prisoner's Song', on the other hand, was something his guileless cousin, Guy Massey, had brought him, agreeing to sign it over to Dalhart for a measly five per cent of the publishing.

Released in October 1924, Dalhart's 78 purportedly sold an eye-watering seven million copies in the US alone, and spent thirty-two weeks in the 'charts'.* Predictably, these spectacular sales prompted an all-American flurry of legal threats, claims and counter-claims, initially centring on the authorship of 'The Prisoner's Song', thus proving two well-known maxims: if you have a hit, expect a writ; and, success has many failures, but failure is an orphan.

Shilkret later claimed that Dalhart had brought him the song, and that he thought it needed some work and rearranged it, rewriting part of it into the bargain. Meanwhile, Guy Massey, having already surrendered 95 per cent the publishing to his country cousin, owed half of his share to his brother, Robert, an arrangement he confirmed in a letter dated 20 October 1924, before the size of his debt became apparent. This seemingly generous gesture was really Guy's way of acknowledging the song's true provider, as Robert's widow later revealed: 'Guy always stayed with us

---

* Chart information and sales information comes from *Billboard* historian Joel Whitburn's *Pop Memories*, but is impossible to verify. In fact, Whitburn places this Dalhart 78 fourth in the best-selling singles of the pre-rock 'n' roll era.

when he came to Dallas, and I was with them while my husband sang it and Guy wrote it down. He said he wanted to take it to New York. Well, he did and he copyrighted it in his own name . . . Guy tried to put it on record, but he failed, then their cousin, Vernon Dalhart, recorded it, and it just went like wildfire. In his will, Guy willed it back to my husband, but he never did admit that he didn't write it.'

As to where Robert found it, his widow grew distinctly vague. Apparently, 'Up until the time we were married, Robert travelled around over the country, and he picked up part of it somewhere, and put [more] words to it.' It turned out that Robert had spent time in jail and probably learnt the song, sung by many a fellow in a correctional facility, while incarcerated.

Unfortunately for each of these latterday claimants, Frank C. Brown in North Carolina, Robert Winslow Gordon in Washington, Mellinger E. Henry in 'the Southern Highlands' and Roy W. MacKenzie in Nova Scotia had already captured versions of the very same song from authentic oral tradition. Not only that but a composite text from these assorted variants would account for every verse, chorus *and* the tune of Dalhart's rendition.

Nor were the song's traditional origins a trade secret for very long. When Carl Sandburg published his influential *American Songbag* in 1927, his introduction to the source tune read:

'The Prisoner's Song,' a 1925–26 'hit', got its melody from 'The Ship That Never Returned,' and its verses from another old timer, 'Moonlight.' That is, two songs Broadway launched and forgot, lived on and changed, mellowed and sweetened among the mountaineers. Years later the tune of one forgotten 'hit' joined to the verses of another, sweeping the country as a Broadway triumph. Such, in short, is the history of 'The Prisoner's Song.'

Through it all, Dalhart clung to his copyright – one which helped make him a wealthy man. He was able to watch from the sidelines as Victor, who had already been forced to settle a suit with Okeh resulting from claiming the publishing on 'The Wreck Of The Ol' 97', fought a ten-year court battle to prove that the song in question was not the work of a certain David Graves George. George only came forward in March 1927, writing to the *Richmond News Leader* to assert, 'I with others composed the poetry of 97.' (When the letter was produced in court, the phrase 'with others' had been crudely erased and replaced with the word 'alone'.) And because no one could *disprove* George's wafer-thin claim, made twenty-five years after the accident he supposedly witnessed, this protracted suit – which went as high as the Supreme Court and took until 1936 to finally be resolved, after interchangeable judgments, in Victor's favour – would change the face of publishing and the attitude of record labels to traditional songs.

In fact, Robert Winslow Gordon, who was at the time employed as the folksong archivist at the Library of Congress, had already collected versions of 'The Wreck Of The Ol' 97' from two credible claimants to (at least) one ballad on the subject, though even they couldn't agree about who originated what. Charles Weston Noell was seventeen years old at the time of the Ol' 97 accident, and told Gordon he had written 'the song' about the wreck. However, the very same evening, when Gordon drove to Concord, North Carolina, his interviewee, Frederick Jackson Lewey, insisted *he* had composed the ballad, and had taught it to Noell. Gordon later testified in the Victor/George case that he believed Lewey had been the first to write a song about the crash.

To his credit, Gordon had seen all of this coming. As he duly observed in a series of articles in the *New York Times*, 'Both the author element and the folk element are to be found in all folk-songs of civilized people today.' And that raised a potential legal minefield.

With a degree of prescience, Gordon had written to Victor Records in the summer of 1925, informing the label that they 'were treading on very dangerous ground in certain instances where copyright was, to say the least, extremely questionable'. Accompanying this information with an offer to become their 'folksong consultant' – Gordon was forever short of funds for his own songhunting – he went further, pointing out, undoubtedly a reference to Vernon Dalhart, 'that in a number of cases the firm was paying royalty to unscrupulous pretenders who had no [vestige] of right[s] in the texts they sold'.

The issue of whether 'the author element' conferred a copyright on a particular variant was one the labels themselves – knowing almost nothing about the *nature* of the 'race' and 'hillbilly' songs they claimed publishing on – were not disposed to address. Even before Victor became embroiled in their legal spat, the copyrighting of traditional songs had become a minefield for the talent scouts and A&R men, who were inclined to simply assign songs acquired from rural songsters on 'field trips' to themselves.

Whereas blues singers were of necessity obliged to piece together disparate elements for their brand of folk blues – at this juncture little more than a lexicon – hillbilly singers mined a far more codified tradition, one that had already been thoroughly trawled by subscribers to the *Journal of American Folklore*. Richard A. Peterson encapsulates the state of affairs at the midpoint of the twenties, as talent scouts and record producers kept an eye on the prize:

> Within the folk tradition out of which commercial country music was emerging, there was no such thing as 'song publishing.' Songs were not written and read by trained musicians; they were just sung and heard, and gifted performers would commit many hundreds of songs to memory . . . Musicians [thus] developed a repertoire of 'their own songs', as they usually thought of them, but the songs were not so much their 'compositions' as . . . assemblages of melody, sound styling, rhythm, and words constructed from fragments of songs in the generally available stock of song elements, edited, rearranged, and supplemented to fit their own styles.

In such a free-for-all, the repertoires of the good and the great overlapped a great deal. And so, while Ernest Stoneham happily included

'The Sinking of The Titanic', 'The Wreck Of The Ol' 97', 'John Henry', 'Frankie and Johnny' and 'Don't Let Your Deal Go Down' in his, George Reneau claimed 'The Sinking of The Titanic', 'Casey Jones', 'The Wreck Of The Ol' 97', and 'Turkey In The Straw' for himself. Gid Tanner also asserted his right to a piece of 'Casey Jones', 'The Wreck Of The Ol' 97', and 'Turkey In The Straw', as well as 'John Henry' and 'Frankie and Johnny'; whereas Fiddlin' John Carson staked a claim to 'Casey Jones', 'Turkey In The Straw', 'John Henry', 'Hesitation Blues' and 'Don't Let Your Deal Go Down'. Then Charlie Poole wanted the last two, along with 'Frankie and Johnny'.

Nor should it be surprising to find these pioneers of country music regularly traipsing across each other's turf, all the while deferring to each other's right to lay something down tilled from the same ground. They were equally unconcerned by Richard 'Rabbit' Brown putting a black man's stamp on 'The Sinking of The Titanic'; or Mississippi John Hurt making 'Frankie and Johnny' his own; or Henry Thomas getting real friendly with 'John Henry'. It was all fair game.

What the wider world of publishing had yet to realize was just how entwined the black and white strands of tradition had become since the Civil War. Although the commercial blues composers had been first out of the traps with their 'popular' arrangements of songster material, the white folk on the other side of the picket fence were just as familiar with 'John Henry', 'Stack O'Lee', 'Frankie and Albert', 'Ain't Nobody's Business', 'Make Me A Pallet On The Floor', 'Salty Dog', 'Easy Rider', 'Poor Boy', 'Corrine Corrina', 'Careless Love' or 'Turkey In The Straw'. And they weren't about to share any of 'their' publishing with W.C. Handy or Clarence Williams; would not even have grasped what the larcenous pair were claiming they originated.

But if none of the above acts were claiming 'authorship' of ongoing revenue streams like 'Casey Jones' and 'Frankie and Johnny', there were those who had already transferred them to songsheet on behalf of every would-be broadside balladeer. At some point B.H. (Before Handy), a small band of professional songwriters 'fixed' songs in common currency not for the record divisions of New York, but for the vaudeville circuit and/or early twentieth-century parlour pianists. For them, sheet music superseded the broadside in fact, if not in spirit. And these folk retained a sense of what the lower classes liked – disaster ballads, for one.*

Among this all-American brand of balladry, the most lucrative song would be written by two vaudevillians, T. Lawrence Seibert (words) and Eddie Newton (music), and published in 1909. It concerned another train wreck which occurred just months before the 'Ol' 97' crash. This time the song served to celebrate the exploits of Cayce Jones, whose gung-ho attempts to make up time with a passenger train leaving Memphis ninety-five minutes late, bound for Canton, Mississippi, led to a collision with the caboose of a southbound freight and to a single fatality – Mr Jones himself.

The song evidently struck a chord with people who knew nothing of the historical circumstances of Cayce's crash – like the individual who labelled the Seibert-Newton songsheet 'The Only Comedy Railroad Song'. A year after Billy Murray and The American Quartet took their 1910 recording of the Seibert-Newton version to number one for eleven weeks, Peter Mulligan of the *Railroad Man's Magazine* contacted the writers, querying the source of their song. They confessed it was their own adaptation 'from an old negro song . . . Nobody knows how many verses it had, and as near as we can trace it back it started about an old engineer named John Luther Jones . . . We have searched back, and so far as we can learn, an old darkey by the name of Wallace Saunders, working in a roundhouse, started the first of the Casey Jones song[s].'

This was hardly the whole truth. As Norm Cohen has shown in his meticulous history of railroad songs, *Long Steel Rail* (1981), lyricist Seibert self-consciously drew on '*two* independent thriving traditions about Casey Jones . . . having borrowed from both . . . Stanzas 3, 4 and 6 [being] taken mainly from the blues ballad tradition . . . [while] their first

---

* The sinking of the *Titanic* in 1912 provided a particular bonanza, combining as it did sanctimony and self-sacrifice in roughly equal measures.

two quatrains . . . [had been] taken directly from the 1908 version,' a reference to a lyric previously published in the March 1908 issue of *Railroad Man's Magazine*. The latter, which begins with the commonplace, 'Come all you rounders . . .', runs to ten verses and was very much in what Cohen correctly calls the Anglo-American 'vulgar ballad' tradition. Seibert's prompt response to Mulligan's query from the same magazine suggests he was probably a regular reader three years earlier, having incorporated the 1908 opening for his own purposes.

Seibert was guilty of no greater a subterfuge than W.C. Handy when he crafted his blues out of the few strands of tradition he had gathered up. And for now, he was free and clear to continue the practice, though when the likes of Fiddlin' John Carson, Riley Puckett and Furry Lewis got around to recording 'their' 'Casey Jones' in the 1920s they reserved the right to sing (and copyright) it their way.*

Another song, published a couple of years before 'Casey Jones', has had an even more productive life in popular culture, having spawned several PhD theses, a coupla books and a film, while also being recorded by everybody from Elvis to Dylan, Jimmie Rodgers to Johnny Cash – all of whom claimed tradition as their ultimate source. It took as its ostensible narrative a shooting in October 1899 which resulted in another rounder lying dead: the adulterous Allen Britt, killed at the hands of his jilted lover, a wildcat named Frankie Baker.

Fittingly, neither of its common forms, 'Frankie and Albert' and 'Frankie and Johnny', had the decency to get the murdered man's name right. Yet claims to the authorship of some such song came early. According to a St Louis reporter, Ira Cooper, writing at the time of Britt's murder, 'On the night following the shooting, Bill Dooley, a negro pianist and songwriter, composed a sorrowful dirge which was played thereafter in many Negro saloons and resorts.' Factually accurate, but failing to tally

---

* In Furry Lewis's case this was far enough removed for him to claim it as his own, though his compelling 1928 version, split across two sides of a 78 to accommodate all thirteen verses, came up 1,996,000 sales short of Seibert's broadside ballad, give or take.

with either of the variants copyrighted in the decade after the shooting, the title of the song Dooley allegedly authored was 'Frankie Killed Allen'.

The first sheet music publication of a 'Frankie' song came in 1904, under the title 'He Done Me Wrong'. It carried the subtitle 'Death of Bill Bailey' (presumably because the copyright claimant, Hughie Cannon, had previously written a popular hit called 'Won't You Come Home, Bill Bailey', and knew nothing of the circumstances surrounding the song he now appropriated). This is the 'Frankie and Albert' derivative, though Cannon, like Seibert, was guilty of rendering anodyne an already vital tradition. Four years later another variant was published. Credited to Frank and Bert Leighton, 'Bill, You Done Me Wrong' was closer to the 'Frankie and Johnny' version, and it was this version which retained a stronger hold in rural tradition, perhaps because it was adapted from a murder-ballad earlier than any Bill Dooley could have written.*

Dooley's is hardly the only name to have been put forward as the original 'author' of the 'Frankie' ballad. Nick Tosches, in his wide-ranging *Country* (1977), asserts unequivocally, 'The song was written by Mammy Lou, a singer at Babe Conner's cabaret in St. Louis.' And his theory does have the considerable advantage of suggesting a female authoress. (Does 'He was a man and he done her wrong' *really* sound like the kinda line a black man would have written in 1899?!) Nor is it reliant on testimony from a 1942 court case by a 'researcher of Negro folklore', Nathan B. Young, who made the ludicrous claim that 'Tin Pan Alley' songwriters in the 1890s would 'come here to St Louis negro clubs, listen to the improvised songs, then go back East and write their own versions'.

Frankie Baker herself had been acquitted of murder back in the day,

---

* Those who assume 'Dooley's ballad' and these subsequent derivatives must have a common origin should bear in mind that Tradition usually has a mind of its own. To cite just one instance, a contemporary diarist writing about the infamous murder of the second Earl of Moray – pronounced Murray – by the Earl of Huntly in 1592, referred to a number of 'common rhymes and songs' being made up on the spot about the incident. Of the two that survived in tradition – the first of them, to the present day – one was finally written down in 1724, the other not until 1810. And there is no way of knowing if either represents one of the 'rhymes and songs' James Melvill reported in 1592.

the judge ruling it was self-defence, and later brought a suit for defamation against Republic Pictures for their portrayal of the incident in a 1936 movie, based on the now-endemic popular ballad. Intriguingly, Republic based their defence on establishing that the song existed prior to 1899, and therefore the movie could not have been based on the 'Frankie Baker' incident. They won their case – and not because, as Cecil Brown asserts in his ill-informed 2005 essay, the jury was white – so evidently the court accepted the defence's argument.

In fact, the evidence is pretty substantive on this matter. Because between the initial publications of two distinct 'Frankie' songs as sheet music, a far more significant version of a rather similar murder-ballad was published in the *Journal of American Folklore* by our old friend Howard Odum. His version was not called 'Frankie and Johnny' (though he refers to 'Frankie' as an alternate title in the notes), but 'Lilly', and it was collected in Newton County, Georgia, not St Louis, Missouri, around 1907.

Here again, the song smacks of a woman's pen. But it does not simply repeat the repetitive hook, 'He was her man and he done her wrong'. Instead, the anonymous balladeer varies 'her' burdens across some twenty-one verses, beginning with, 'Her man certainly got to treat her right' and ending with, 'Well, it's all dat you got's daid an' gone'. In 'Lilly', the victim is called Paul and the shooting occurs on Bell Street – which is in Atlanta, not St Louis – but it is self-evidently the same template, beginning, 'Lilly was a good girl – ev'body knows' and ending with, 'Well, it's fohty-dollar hearse an' rubber-tire hack/Carry po' Paul to cemetary, but fail to bring him back.' The whole song not only feels like a prototype for *both* forms of 'Frankie', but suggests a more inventive poet than Bill Dooley, Mammy Lou, Hughie Cannon and the Leighton Brothers put together.

In all likelihood, this is the ballad that Leonard Feather, in his *Biographical Encyclopedia of Jazz* (2007), claimed was sung at the 1863 Siege of Vicksburg and the self-same one Carl Sandburg, in his *American Songbag*, suggested was widespread before 1888, i.e. before it could start intermingling with tangential 'Frankie' offshoots.

After all, in the 1900s neither 'Frankie and Johnny' nor any other negro murder-ballad (and 'Stack O' Lee' was at least as popular) needed some dandy from the big city to spread the word. The idea that one person could set in stone, or *own*, a song like 'The Wreck Of The Ol' 97', 'Casey Jones' or 'Frankie and Johnny' would have struck any traditional singer as plumb crazy. For such folk, oral tradition would continue to exercise its recreative magic for another quarter-century or more. It would take the combined clout of the electrical microphone, voracious A&R men and talent scouts of the record labels, and a lack of basic protection from America's backward copyright laws to short-circuit this endlessly (re)creative process; and even then, it would still take half a century for the new way to wholly subsume the old. It would come at a cost.

Initially, the ubiquitous nature of such songs – in both black and white tradition – did not faze the A&R men who swept up the last leaves of tradition in the pre-Crash years. This was a period when the hillbilly and race divisions were run by a small number of white men all sharing a belief in the American Dream, with an ear for its more arcane songs. They were content to take the publishing on the performances they captured, knowing full well that Gid Tanner's 'Casey Jones' no more resembled Mississippi John Hurt's than did his 'Frankie and Johnny'.

At the same time, there was a real sense of competition between men like Frank Walker at Columbia, Ralph Peer at Okeh and Art Satherly at Paramount as they strip-mined the song reservoirs of the south. What happened next, though predictable enough, seems to have taken them all by surprise: '[Initially] there [had] seemed to be an inexhaustible supply of songs . . . [but] as the search for songs that were different and uncopyrighted became common practice, this aboriginal mother lode of commercially interesting available songs was essentially mined-out in a few short years. [Peterson]'

Each of these key figures adopted their own approach to the problem of how to mine 'this aboriginal mother lode', and still stay true to the music. The English-born Art Satherly seemed to take a genuine delight in new discoveries. He would travel large distances if he heard about a hillbilly singer 'who has a very original ballad'. What really interested him was the approach of the singer, not the strength of the material, which often walked a tightrope between turgid moralizing and saccharine sentimentality. His own description of the music he sought out says it all: 'Simplicity of language, an emotional depth in the music, sincerity in the rendition, and an indigenous genuineness of dialect and twang . . . But, above all, sincerity – even if it's awkward, unpolished sincerity.'

Frank Walker, too, hankered after 'awkward, unpolished sincerity', yet he set a higher bar on the musicality of those acts he brought to Columbia. He knew his music. Indeed, when fiddle player Clayton McMichen, the most ambitious member of the Atlanta-based Skillet Lickers, famously told Walker he wanted to record popular rather than traditional music, Walker pointed out there were considerably better bands in New York playing that kinda music, and he had lugged the recording equipment all the way to Atlanta to record hillbilly songs, not bad pop music.

The Skillet Lickers, fronted by Gid Tanner, proved one of Walker's most productive finds. Another was Charlie Poole and The North Carolina Ramblers, whose 1925 recording of 'Don't Let Your Deal Go Down' was both the first and best of the many renditions released in the pre-Depression era. Walker's return on the $75 he paid Poole for the publishing was a hundred thousand sales – at two cents a time. Indeed, if the history of rural recordings had been written before August 1927, Walker would undoubtedly have merited a larger entry than Ralph Peer.

Yet even Walker generally took only what he could copyright from a given singer; only when they achieved sales like the Skillet Lickers and the North Carolina Ramblers did he bother to track them down again. He usually adopted a method which took the best and left the rest: 'Their repertoire would [usually] consist of eight or ten things that they did well and that was all they knew. So, when you picked out the three or four that were best in a man's so-called repertoire you were through with that man as an artist . . . It was a culling job, taking the best that they had.'

The labels' retinue of local talent-scouts, like Polk Brockman and the legendary H.C. Speir, were prepped to adopt a similar approach. When in 1927 the great Tommy Johnson, who was probably the best-known blues singer in Jackson, Mississippi, approached Speir, then part of a talent-scout network operated by and for Ralph Peer, he only had two copyrightable originals. Speir told him it was not enough – he needed four. Johnson heeded the lesson and came back with two more.

By then, Ralph Peer had jumped the Okeh ship and after a game of brink-manship, washed up at Victor in charge of their 'hillbilly' and 'race' divisions. His contract seemed on the face of it disturbingly like the one which made Mayo J. Williams consider his position at Paramount, one that paid no salary but raked in the cents on publishing. Peer had seen the wider picture, though, and the Victor directors had not. He was sure he had something they wanted and only he could provide: his peerless sense of what hillbilly music sold.

An awareness that he was missing out financially may well have dawned the day he read (or even penned) an article in a December 1925 issue of *Talking Music World*.* Headlined 'What the Popularity of Hill-Billy Songs Means to Retail Profit Possibilities', it cited three songs Peer had produced for Okeh in the past year:

'The Death of Floyd Collins', 'Wreck of the Shenandoah', 'At My Mother's Grave' [sic], and other such songs . . . may mark the initial move in the passing of jazz . . . The fact that the public or a fair portion of it has decided on a funer[e]al dirge type of offering should not be taken as an atavistic tendency. It is rather a desire for something different. This desire can be taken advantage of by both the popular music publisher and record maker, [with] songs of good ballad order, love songs and other numbers particularly lending themselves to solo voices with a minimum of arrangement.

---

* It is perfectly possible Peer authored the article anonymously. In which case, it was his last open letter to his rivals in A&R.

Peer himself now wanted to be 'both the popular music publisher and record maker'. So, at the end of 1925, he quit Okeh, tired of making money for others and for his troubles collecting a weekly pay cheque. In fact, he ended up taking home $16,000 that year including his annual bonus, a figure most other companies would have been hard-pressed to match. But to his credit, he did not flinch when Victor Records offered him $5,000 a year to do the same job. He just politely declined, biding his time; and by the start of 1927, Victor accepted it was between a rock and a shareholders meeting.

The biggest record company in the world needed someone who knew the hillbilly market, and Peer knew it inside out. It was at this point that Peer made his 'no win, no fee' proposal – he would work for Victor for a dollar a year on one condition: he would retain the copyright on all the music he recorded. As he later bragged, 'I had considered the matter very carefully and [realized] that essentially this was [a] business of recording new copyrights, and [I made it clear] that I would be willing to go to work for [Victor] for nothing with the understanding that there would be no objection if I controlled these copyrights.'

In order for this to work, Peer would need a Gid Tanner and/or a Charlie Poole, with a repertoire of traditional-sounding songs that would last far beyond a single cull. He also needed the artists tied to him, not the label he ostensibly represented.

Peer had seen what happened when someone like Polk Brockman had tried to demand loyalty after fleecing songsters of their copyrights for a fixed payment. Brockman always had his eyes on the short-term prize, collecting publishing on a hit song. 'The Death of Floyd Collins' was a written-to-order contemporary disaster ballad commissioned from the Reverend Andrew Jenkins the second Collins got buried in a Kentucky mine in April 1925. Brockman convinced Fiddlin' John Carson to record it for the hillbilly audience and Vernon Dalhart for the citybillies, and was duly rewarded with his one and only million-seller. But Brockman saw only the quick buck, not the future of song-publishing.

Looking to build a publishing empire, Peer took the longer view. So when he hitched his wagon to the Victor train, he made sure he 'signed most of his artists to three separate contracts: a recording contract with Victor that generally paid them $50 a side up front, as well as a modest royalty on each record sold; a song publishing contract with Peer's newly formed Southern Music publishing company; and a personal management contract with Peer himself'. Thankfully, any legal impediment to such a clear conflict of interest lay some way off.

Peer was still taking something of a gamble. He was now as reliant as Mayo Williams on finding singers with songs that were either theirs, or could be *made theirs*. To live inside the law or starve. And though in later years he would give the impression he always thought he could find the former, it was really the latter he set out to unearth when he arrived in Bristol, Tennessee, the first week of August, 1927.

Bristol was serendipitously positioned on the border of Tennessee and Virginia, at the foot of the Appalachians, a mountain range which had yielded such an abundant musical crop that English folk collector Maud Karpeles needed two volumes to publish the 274 traditional songs she and Cecil Sharp found on their 1917–18 expeditions. Its geographic significance was not lost on Peer, who informed the Bristol newspaper on his arrival: 'In no section of the South have the pre-war melodies and old mountaineer songs been better preserved than in the mountains of east Tennessee and Southwest Virginia, experts declare, and it was primarily for this reason that the Victor Company chose Bristol as its operating base.' This would be a trip with a very specific remit.

Most of what Peer recorded in Bristol on that historic jaunt was either in the gospel field (thirty-one songs recorded) or 'traditional' (thirty-five songs). In fact the first act given more than the statutory four-song session that week was one he had booked in advance, in case auditions proved a bust. Ernest Stoneham was someone Peer had already recorded for Okeh and wanted back on board, with good reason. Stoneham didn't do the same old traditional songs everybody did. Rather, as Peer said, 'He'd made something new of the Titanic poem – and could find newer songs with modern-sounding lyrics, such as "Sinful to Flirt" and "Don't

Let Your Deal Go Down." And Pop could always pick up a new song in a hurry.' Stoneham recorded ten songs in all at Bristol with his Dixie Mountaineers, six of them religious.

Peer later insisted he was ruthless about the acts he recorded in Bristol: 'I didn't want any old material or standard songs . . . I never recorded an established selection, I always insisted on getting artists who could write their own music.' But he simply could not afford to be so dogmatic at this stage – and he wasn't. The four songs of B.F. Shelton, the greatest traditional singer he recorded at Bristol (and perhaps the greatest of them all, if only we had more on which to judge him), were all firmly drawn from tradition and had already been collected and recorded several times, in the case of 'Pretty Polly' and 'Darling Cora' – and several dozen times in the case of 'Cold Penitentiary Blues'. Peer would just have to take his half-cut on the arrangements he copyrighted to his publishing company. But by the time he returned to Bristol the following year, Peer was no longer interested in recording any more Sheltons. By then he had turned Jimmie Rodgers, the odd one out in hillbilly combo The Teneva Ramblers, into 'The Blue Yodeller'.

Initially, though, his great Bristol discovery seemed to be the Carter Family, who sang both gospel and traditional songs. The Carters – a folk trio formed by A.P. Carter, wife Sara and sister-in-law Maybelle to sing mountain songs for fellow mountain folk – had come into town from their Appalachian homesteads after reading in the local *News Bulletin* the previous week about how 'the Victor Co. will have a recording machine in Bristol for ten days'.

Carter, his wife and her sister were exactly what Peer had hoped to find. And he knew it for what it was: 'As soon as I heard Sara's voice – that was it. You see, I had done this so many times that I was trained to watch for the one point . . . As soon as I heard her voice, why, I began to build around it and all the first recordings were [done] on that basis.'

Jimmie Rodgers, Peer's most lucrative discovery that week, was unexpected, being no repository of 'pre-war melodies and old mountaineer songs'. Like Tommy Johnson, Rodgers had made his first approach to H.C. Speir. After Speir told him straight, 'Jimmie, you're not ready to record right now . . . Go back to Meridian and when [you've] worked up four or six more songs, bring them back and see me again,' Rodgers had sought an alternative route to Peer's palace. As the great traditional singer Bascom Lamar Lunsford confirmed in a 1971 interview, he wrote Rodgers a letter of introduction to Peer; and Lunsford was a name Peer took note of. Sought out by folklorists and talent-scouts alike, Lunsford had recorded for Peer's Okeh in 1924. He was known to have a great ear, and would happily steer A&R men and folklorists to singers he rated.*

As Rogers wrote to his wife, Carrie, shortly after Speir's rejection, 'Folks everywhere are getting kind of tired of all this Black Bottom-Charleston-jazz music, junk.' Finding a band he thought he could mould, then calling themselves The Teneva Ramblers, he rechristened them The Jimmie Rodgers Entertainers. He was still doing mostly theatrical standards and pop tunes of the day, with only the odd 'old plantation melody' or 'river ballad' thrown in, and he still didn't have enough songs he could call his own. Nonetheless, the next thing Speir heard, Rodgers had jettisoned the Entertainers (or they had jettisoned him) and was recording for Victor.

In fact, having turned up to record with Peer in tandem with the Entertainers, his 'sometime backing band', Rodgers found himself surplus

---

* Lunsford's generosity didn't stop there. The author of the country standard, 'Good Ol' Mountain Dew', he sat and watched Scott Wiseman steal this traditional-sounding song, copyright it to himself and then offer Lunsford a cut of his own song. As Wiseman conveniently explained: 'The original "Mountain Dew" was made up by Bascom Lunsford . . . After I returned from Chicago, I remembered the melody and composed a new set of verses for it. Lulu Belle and I cut a Vocalion record of it in 1939 in Chicago. Roy Acuff and other Nashville singers learned it from our record and started singing it . . . Mr Lunsford came to Chicago after our version of the song became well-known . . . He, John Lair and I sat in a Chicago hotel one evening discussing old songs. Mr Lunsford said, "I believe I know how to pay my bus fare back to Asheville. I'll just sell Scotty my interest in 'Mountain Dew' for $25." I wrote a brief agreement on hotel stationery and closed the deal. After we retired, he came to visit us. I called the publisher and BMI and gave them instructions to pay him 50 per cent of all royalties on the song during his lifetime.'

to requirements – perhaps because he made it plain he thought the others were 'just' his backing band. Peer expressed amazement that Rodgers and the Teneva Ramblers had ever been a partnership, believing that the Ramblers' records 'would have been no good if Jimmie had sung with this group, because he was singing Negro blues and they were doing old time fiddle music'. When the other Ramblers decided to audition without Rodgers, Peer gave them three bites of the cherry. Of the three songs the Ramblers recorded, one would go on to earn a great deal of money, though not for Peer. 'The Longest Train I Ever Saw' would be the first commercial recording of a traditional variant later made famous by – and copyrighted to – Leadbelly as 'Black Girl (In The Pines)'. Rodgers himself would get just two bites, neither destined to set the world on fire:

> **Ralph Peer**: We ran into a snag almost immediately because, in order to earn a living in Asheville, [Jimmie Rodgers] was singing mostly songs originated by the New York publishers, the current hits. Actually, he had only one song of his own – 'Soldier's Sweetheart' – written several years before. When I told Jimmie what I needed to put him over as a recording artist . . . [he said] if I would give him a week he could have a dozen songs ready . . . I let him record his own song, and as a coupling his unique version of 'Rock All Our Babies To Sleep'.

Peer was making an exception, perhaps in deference to Lunsford's judgement, despite having his own way of sorting the wheat from the uncopyrightable chaff. When a group came to audition above the furniture store he had rented for the week, he would let them do a song of their own choice first, to get a sense of where their strengths lay. Usually the song they chose was well known, often something heard on the radio, at which point he would ask them if they had any songs of their own. 'If they did another popular song,' Peer recalled, 'I never bothered with them.'

Peer later insisted he heard something unique in Rodgers' way of putting a song across that very first time: 'In spite of the lack of a repertoire,

I considered Rodgers to be one of my best bets. Accordingly, I asked him to sign a management contract, [and then] explained to him the necessity to find new material.'

But if he really thought Rodgers had such potential, Peer took his own sweet time releasing the only two Rodgers cuts he'd recorded. Whereas with the Carter Family he had already hedged his bets, recording six tunes. Soon after he put them into the world, each title copyrighted to 'A.P. Carter' and published by Southern Music, all three Carter 78s were selling tens of thousands, and Peer could relax. He was now in the publishing game, and from now on he would produce only those artists who could take something traditional and render it anew. He did not know it yet, but he had just signed two 'singer-songwriters' who in the next decade would revolutionize American popular song, and he was about to be handsomely rewarded for his foresight and his faith.

# CHAPTER 4

# 1927–39: Après Le Déluge

*Featuring*: 'Wildwood Flower'; 'Will You Miss Me When I'm Gone'; 'I'm Thinking Tonight of My Blue Eyes'; 'Will The Circle Be Unbroken'; 'Blue Yodel #1'; 'In The Jailhouse Now'; 'Waiting For A Train'; 'This T.B. Is Killing Me'

> Most [acts] . . . expected to record for nothing. When on top of this fifty dollars I gave them royalties on their selections, they thought it was manna from heaven . . . I could just as easily [have] bought [the songs] for $25 each, or taken them for nothing, as far as that goes. But fortunately, I wasn't quite that greedy, and therefore I built up the business.
>
> Ralph Peer

Jimmie Rodgers and A.P. Carter, Ralph Peer's favourite miners of rural music, met just once, for a staged photoshoot and recording session at his behest. Though each shared the poverty and instinctive feel for music that was most Southerners' lot in life, they were cut from very different cloth. But, between them and their relentless outputs, they would transform Victor Records, Peer's publishing company and the whole hillbilly genre.

What their releases didn't do was make either artist rich. Even at the height of their commercial success, pre-Depression – when 78s by both were selling six figures – the sums coming their way were enough to keep them going, for A.P. to buy a new farm or Rodgers a new car. But there would be no mansion on the hill for either.

In a sense, though, this was never Peer's intent. Rather, as Richard Peterson points out, 'In giving performers a financial stake in writing and finding new songs, he gained their personal loyalties and ensured the steady flow of new songs. Thus Peer, more [than] other record producers, transformed tradition into a renewable resource.'

It was an inspired strategy. One, it provided the most telling of incentives to produce – money. Two, it did not require any capital outlay on Peer's part. All the costs of acquiring the artists with the songs and advancing money against potential sales were met by Victor Records. His own publishing company 'was simply a named entity for holding copyrights' – plus all the money he was soon making.

The loyalty he inspired from 'his' artists was crucial to Peer's plan. Without his ability to hold each at arm's length, both the label and those artists might have come to realize, after he had discovered them and established their commerciality, that they did not actually need him. Eventually both *did* realize Peer was something of a third leg, but at different times: in the label's case, when the publishing money started rolling in and they weren't getting any; in the Carters' case, when sales began to tail off as the Depression started to bite and publishing alone wasn't enough to maintain their relatively affluent new lifestyle. (Jimmie Rodgers had the (mis) fortune to die before the money ran out, which at the rate he was spending it would have been some time soon.) Hence Maybelle Carter's famous verbal barb, 'Mr Peer made us famous and we made him rich.'

It was no exaggeration. In the first quarter after the relationship with Victor was formalized, the royalty payment to Southern Publishing – the company Peer was putting most of his copyrights in – came to a quarter of a million dollars. In 1927! By 1928, more than a third of all non-classical music recorded by Victor was under Peer's control; 22.9 per cent being hillbilly and 21.7 per cent race.

The volume of sales in these rural styles took everyone at Victor but Peer by surprise. After an explosion in the availability of phonograph players early in the 1920s had led to the industry's greatest year in 1921 ($106.5 million – a figure not topped until 1947), sales had dipped. But by 1927, they were back around the $70 million mark, and continued growing steadily until the Wall Street Crash. (After that, sales did not so much dip as plummet. By 1933, they were a tenth of what they had been, and still falling.)

Though Peer tried to hide the scale of his publishing income in the pre-Crash years by forming a number of companies to collect on the songs, by late 1928 – preferring to honour a deal made in good faith by breaching it, a tradition which has made American corporations the envy of the world – Victor wanted to renegotiate the terms of their agreement. But by then, Peer had made himself invaluable; and with those personal management contracts in place, he could have walked out on the label, taking Rodgers and the Carters with him. So Victor needed to proceed cautiously. They dangled him a carrot – an empty promise to give him the publishing on any publisher-free popular works recorded by their popular and classical divisions – and in return Peer unwisely agreed to turn over the operation of Southern Music to the record company, while retaining sole control of existing copyrights.

In the Carters' case, these already included the most precious jewels in their country crown. No matter how much incentive Peer gave A.P. to excavate further gems, the best earners from the Carters' cache of classics remained those from their core repertoire – songs their daddies and mammies taught them, either literally or metaphorically. Even before Jimmie Rodgers tried to convince Peer he could craft 'new' songs according to Peer's 'spec.', A.P. Carter knew *his* family's appeal was directly related to their 'old timey' feel. The songs their audience demanded had to have at least one foot in the clay of traditional song. As long as A.P. stuck to his brief – 'pre-war melodies and old mountaineer songs', the obscurer the better – copyrighting them required the audio equivalent of smoke and mirrors.

The Carters' first session for Peer after the storming success of their Bristol recordings was scheduled for May 1928. This time they were summoned to Camden, New Jersey; field trips were generally for finding talent, not milking it. The twelve songs they recorded across the two May days would define the Carters' repertoire unto the grave: 'Meet Me By The Moonlight Alone', 'Little Darling, Pal of Mine', 'Keep On The Sunny Side', 'John Hardy', 'Will You Miss Me When I'm Gone', 'River of Jordan', 'Anchored In Love', 'Wildwood Flower' and 'Forsaken Love'.

If these songs were all that the Carters ever produced, they would still warrant legendary status in country music. They also served to demonstrate that A.P. Carter – and Ralph Peer – sometimes sailed awfully close to the wind when copyrighting compositions which had been around as long as those wildwood flowers.

'Wildwood Flower' itself was an inspired choice. It was obscure, out of copyright and a song they had already made their own. And it came from the hearth. As Maybelle recalls, 'The first time I heard the song, I was just a kid. My mother sang it and her mother sang it. It has been handed down for years and years. It's the most popular song we ever recorded.'

It was also a song whose meaning had been rather lost in translation from vaudeville to oral tradition to shellac. (The Carters' recording contains the mystifying lines, 'I'll twine with my mingles and waving black hair', and, 'The pale and the leader, and eyes look like blue'.) 'Wildwood Flower' was actually a vaudeville number by that maudlin dame Maud Irving, circa 1860. By the 1910s it had passed into tradition, being collected by folklorists in North Carolina and southwest Virginia. No matter. Neither version conferred a copyright, and A.P. Carter duly claimed 'dibs' on behalf of the Carter clan – and Southern Music.

Peer, the most informed A&R man of the era, generally knew when something was too familiar to bear scrutiny, but took a chance with 'Meet Me By The Moonlight Alone'. One of the Carters' most powerful performances, its tune and chorus were unmistakably those of 'The Prisoner's Song', over which there had already been much controversy. However, the Carters' version (which A.P. and Sara had been singing for years) had been grafted on to 'The Prisoner's Song' long *before* Robert Massey wrote it down. And Peer probably knew Vernon Dalhart was unlikely to rock the boat given his own dubious title to the song.

He wasn't quite so lucky with 'Will You Miss Me When I'm Gone', another staple of the family repertoire and a gospel favourite they had known for years. It turned out it was still in copyright – though only just, having first appeared in an old hymnal around 1900. As Maybelle duly noted, '*They* had to pay for it.'*

And the Carters were even more careless with their version of 'Anchored In Love', which they not only took from a popular 1911 songbook, *Crowning Praises*, but sang almost exactly as it appeared there, something Peer only learnt after the recording was released. On the other gospel standard recorded in Camden that May, 'River of Jordan', they could hardly claim primacy either. It had been recorded by the Fisk University Male Quartet the previous year. But the song itself – which also went by the titles, 'Streets of Glory' and 'Some of These Days' – was ubiquitous enough to have escaped an individual copyright.

Peer soon realized he could not be quite so trusting about the material A.P. was coming up with, and pushed him to be more creative with the songs, to individualize them and render them *his*. His motive may have been money, but Carter's method was one adopted by every would-be songster from Guthrie to Dylan. Having been told to research his songs better, Carter began his transition into the first professional song catcher who really knew his way around the Southern mountains.

A.P.'s greatest find wouldn't be a song but a one-man repository of song. From October 1928 many of the more gospel or blues-inflected songs in the Carters' repertoire would come from a black guitarist, Lesley Riddle, Carter's very own song-catcher-on-call throughout much of the family's tenure at Victor.

A.P. had encountered Riddle in Kingsport Town, while searching for a usable version of the resolutely traditional 'Motherless Children Sees A Hard Time'. The person he initially sought out was called John Henry Lyons. By chance, Riddle was at Lyons' house when he came to call, and Carter quickly realized he had happened upon a mine of useful melodies. He immediately began to badger Riddle for more, as the latter recalled to folklorist Mike Seeger some decades later:

---

* Under the 1790 US Copyright Act – which was only superseded in 1909 – the author's copyright lasted just fourteen years, renewable for another fourteen, if s/he was still alive and sought its renewal.

**Lesley Riddle:** I played him a couple of pieces. He wanted me to go home with him right then and there. I went over to Maces Spring with him. Stayed over there about a week . . . I continued for about three or four years, going over to his house and going where he wanted to go. I went out with A.P. about fifteen times to collect songs. He'd just go in [someone's house] and tell them, 'I was told by someone that you got a song, kind of an old song. Mind letting me hear it?' . . . He'd go ninety miles if he heard someone say that someone had an old song that hadn't been recorded or didn't have a copyright . . . I was his tape recorder. He'd take me with him and he'd get someone to sing him the whole song. Then I would get it, then I'd learn [sic] it to Sara and Maybelle . . . They never sang for me. I'd have to do all the picking and singing when I was over there . . . I'd be settin' over there sometimes, you know, and pick up the guitar and play something – four or five months from then, I'd be coming down the street and I'd be hearing it. The Carter Family would be singing it.

Riddle, though, was no recondite repository of that great speckled chimera, 'pure' tradition. He probably got his version of 'Motherless Children' from a record, and a magnificent one at that, Blind Willie Johnson's 1927 recording for Columbia. Thankfully, Peer was less concerned about recordings in the other popular genre he had given its nomenclature. The Carters recorded their version of the gospel standard the following year.

Riddle was similarly coy about the source of a song recorded by the Carters as 'The Cannon Ball'. This shared the same tune as Charlie Poole's 'White House Blues'. Riddle later admitted he had learned it from a Blind Lemon Jefferson recording. Its blues characteristics even A.P. couldn't hide. Verses like, 'Yonder comes a train/Comin' down the track/Carry me away/But ain't a-gonna carry me back' would ultimately find their way back into black tradition via Junior Parker's 'Mystery Train', and journey back to white pop via Elvis.

Carter quickly discovered his new-found friend was also replete with sacred songs he'd heard in church. Southern Baptist church. Or perhaps from records; Riddle wasn't saying. The Carters' most fiery gospel performance, and one of their best-known gospel tunes (partly because it was appropriated by one of their imitators, Woody Guthrie), was also acquired from Riddle. Again, the song, 'When The World's On Fire', had already been recorded and released by Blind Willie Davis, as 'Rock of Ages'. Maybelle even played in the same bottleneck style as Davis, presumably because she'd been taught to play this way by Riddle.

The Carters happily learnt all Riddle would show them, even a song like 'Lonesome For You', which Riddle later claimed he had worked up himself. On the Carter recording, though, it was (as always) attributed to the ever prolific 'A.P. Carter', and Riddle voiced no dissent at the time. It was all grist to Peer's publishing mill. And though he probably asked more questions about a song's provenance than A.P. ever did, he took a rather patriarchal view of proceedings, crediting even songs which self-evidently originated with Sara and/or Maybelle to the gruff father-figure, assuming that any financial windfall would be duly passed around. When Sara suggested 'I'm Thinking Tonight Of My Blue Eyes', an old song she'd known all her life, it was A.P.'s name that appeared on the song credit. When Maybelle and Sara found some lyrics in a pamphlet set to the platitudinous notion, 'you are my flower', Maybelle 'changed some of the words and fixed a tune to it'. It still became an A.P. Carter composition, and a country standard.

And A.P. continued insisting on the final say. He had the trust of Peer, who knew by now he would do (just) enough to ensure each song qualified for a new copyright. In fact, after those initial issues of appropriation at that first Camden session, the Carters remained remarkably free of copyright controversies – unlike the other mainstay of the Southern Music empire, Jimmie Rodgers.

Even their best-known song, 'I'm Thinking Tonight Of My Blue Eyes' – recorded at a second series of Camden sessions in February 1929 – remained free of counter-claims, even though the melody and sentiments had already served the Stoneham Family (as 'The Broken Hearted Lover') and Welby Toomey ('The Thrills I Can't Forget'). Recorded at the same sessions as that other perennial, 'Little Moses' – which had appeared in a 1905 folksong collection but was otherwise free and clear – 'Blue Eyes' proved the commercial clincher as far as the Carters' country fans were concerned.

Peer, though, did not abandon his scouting field trips, or give up searching for new talent just because, two days apart, he had found the Carters and Rodgers. In fact, a year on from those revolutionary discoveries, he returned to the self-same furniture store to re-record some of the previous year's 'other' finds. Alfred G. Karnes and Ernest Phipps, both of whom had recorded songs of salvation the previous August, continued to come up with new ways of spreading the good news. The ever-dependable Ernest Stoneham had also brought his extended family of singers and ragbag of songs, some for sweethearts, others intended to save souls.

Indeed, that 1928 trip covering two months was to prove Peer's most productive; and not just because Bristol yielded its bounteous booty a second time. Sessions in Memphis through September allowed him to capture not just Furry Lewis, Ishman Bracey and Charlie McCoy, but also Cannon's Jug Stompers and Will Shade's Memphis Jug Band at the peak of their collective powers, while in Atlanta he not only arranged to catch up with Jimmie Rodgers and Henry Whitter again, but also the peripatetic Blind Willie McTell and the Carolina Tar Heels. Only Nashville – still an outpost of Memphis to most musicians – failed to yield much in the way of copyrightable repertoires.

But if A.P. was too busy accumulating songs to bring the Carters' wares to Bristol that fall, he already knew Peer had enough material from May to tide him over till the new year. By the end of 1928, A.P. had become a man on a mission, just as his name began carrying some weight locally. His daughter Janette recalls: '[My father] was known in the Valley and in the area, and people would tell him if they heard somebody had a song, and he'd go see them. Or sometimes he'd just be driving by and stop and go up to a little house up in the hills to see if they had a song . . . He'd just tell 'em who he was, and that he was looking for songs.'

Carter seemed to take a particular delight in rewriting nineteenth-century parlour songs, some of which even he found too hokey for words. The nineteenth-century lyricist, William Shakespeare Hays, proved especially useful. A self-styled Kentucky newspaperman/broadside poet – as the fanciful middle name suggests – Hays liked his 'pale moons, withered flowers, ageing mothers and dying children'. Among his many atrocities was the perennially popular 'Jimmy Brown, The Paper Boy', which Carter rescued from itself with a few choice rewrites, trimming the sails of the high-flown poetaster and turning Hays's half-baked homilies into home truths.

By the mid-1930s, however, A.P.'s song production was in a slow, steady decline. Having all but exhausted his own imagination, drilled through Riddle's full repertoire and trawled all the ol' songbooks he could find, he resorted to plundering old recordings of Ma Rainey ('Jealous Hearted Me') and Blind Lemon Jefferson ('Sad and Lonesome Day', the Carters' clever recasting of 'See That My Grave Is Kept Clean'), probably at the behest of Riddle.

They still sold. But now Maybelle began to pick up the slack, imposing her taste on latter Carter recordings. Thus, 'There's No One Like Mother To Me', recorded for Decca in June 1936, was (almost verbatim) a poem Maybelle cut out of a magazine, set to her own tune. As was 'You Are My Flower'. She also suggested 'Little Black Train' and 'Sweet Heaven In My View', two hymns she used to sing at the local Holiness revivals.

A.P. also proved his continuing worth by rewriting the words of a song by that prolific English hymn-writer from the turn of the century, Ada R. Habershon. Habershon's song was published in 1907, as 'Will The Circle Be Unbroken?', with music by Charles H. Gabriel. But Carter discarded the original Gabriel melody and rewrote Habershon's words. The melody he ended up using was his own adaptation of the gospel number, 'Sunshine In The Shadows', which the Carters had already recorded back in 1931. It mattered not; the Carters' 'Can The Circle Be Unbroken?' proved to be their best seller of 1935. It was also the standout track from their first set of recordings for ARC, the family having abandoned their Victor home at the end of 1934.

The defection reignited an internecine struggle between Peer and Victor's Eli Oberstein to retain the recording services of The Carter Family. In March 1935, Oberstein wrote to A.P. Carter baldly stating that Peer could not be trusted but he (and Victor) could: '[Peer] is naturally trying to keep things for himself and get all he can . . . I offered to get together with Mr Peer but as usual he wants everything and would like to give you people little or nothing . . . The point he is angry about is that we want to give you copyright royalties and he wants those for himself with a very small portion to you.'

It was Oberstein's last roll of the dice in a game of brinkmanship that began after Peer had unwisely brought him from the Okeh bookkeeping department in order to have someone on staff protecting his manifold interests. It was a rare miscalculation. Instead, as Peer put it, Oberstein 'wanted to take [the copyright business] from me – he saw how I was operating and he wanted to take this over'.

But Victor itself had been taken over in 1929 by the Radio Corporation of America. And in the end, Oberstein alienated RCA's head mogul, David Sarnoff, who was – literally – more concerned about the big picture: the recent acquisition of Victor and RKO Pictures potentially exposed the company to anti-trust laws. In 1932, Sarnoff ordered the return of Southern Music to Peer for essentially what he'd paid in 1928, adjusted for the economic downturn. Peer even got back the copyrights Southern had acquired in the interim. As he enjoyed pointing out, 'Oberstein . . . really didn't get much out of the deal, because I had all these people signed to me in my original arrangements with Victor, so it all sort of kicked back on him.'

Oberstein was still smarting in March 1935, but A.P. Carter never even considered his proposal. He and Peer had a good thing going. The move to ARC by the Carter Family had other consequences, too. Since Peer owned both the copyrights and their management contract, he had always been keen to ensure his performers did not record their songs for other record companies. This was an extremely common practice for many artists, whether under an assumed name – as Blind Willie McTell did, repeatedly – or simply as oneself. (Vernon Dalhart recorded his 'Prisoner's Song' no less than seventeen times between 1924 and 1934.)

It was a control Peer now willingly relinquished. The Carters re-recorded most of their greatest hits for ARC in a marathon set of sessions that spawned some forty songs across five days in May 1935. Victor no longer had an exclusive on Carter Family recordings, and at this rate might soon have very little Carter fare unique to their catalogue.

At least Victor still owned the entire Jimmie Rodgers catalogue – even if Peer had regained full control of the publishing in the corporate clash of 1932. Sadly, Jimmie was no more. His oft-prophesized death from that ol' TB at New York's Taft Hotel in May 1933 had robbed them of their most reliable seller, indeed the most commercial pre-war country star of them all. What they perhaps did not realize, because Peer had kept Rodgers under his personal tutelage, was that at the time of his death the man who'd come to be known as the 'Singing Brakeman' was rapidly running out of songs. It was one of the best-kept secrets in song publishing that Rodgers had always been heavily reliant on the input of compositional confidants.

Back in August 1927, Rodgers had made a promise to Peer (and his wife), on leaving Bristol, that he would return – and if 'they want these old-fashioned things . . . love songs and plantation melodies and the old river ballads, well, I'm [gonna be] ready with 'em'. Yet just ten months later, with two days of sessions scheduled to produce follow-ups to a pair of spectacular smashes, 'Blue Yodel #1' and 'In The Jailhouse Now', he was phoning sister-in-law Elsie McWilliams, saying, 'Sis, I've got an opportunity, but I haven't got the time to write the songs. I've got to have some original ballads, so you've got to write 'em.'

Such was the backdrop to the creation of 'Jimmie Rodgers, the Singing Brakeman', a hard-workin', hard-lovin' man of the people. It relied on his audience believing *he* was the person he sang about in his songs. The truth is, although 89 of the 108 songs he recorded credit 'Jimmie Rodgers' as author or co-author, he wrote very little of the material Peer copyrighted on his behalf.

Peer happily gave Jimmie the credit for turning that material into a self-contained body of work, stating in 1953: 'Although much of [Rodgers's] material came from traditional sources, he imposed upon it his own innate concepts and left it indelibly stamped with the elements of his peculiar brand of back-country genius – the driving unorthodox guitar runs, his freight-train whistles and [those] lyrical yodels.'

Actually, though, precious little of Rodgers' material 'came from traditional sources', and those songs which did were usually rendered unrecognizable, such was the mess of blues, folk and vaudeville running through his tubercular bones. Norm Cohen's introduction to the first serious Jimmie Rodgers discography divided his 108 'distinct musical selections' into five categories:

(1) nineteenth-century sentimental ballads and songs;
(2) novelty songs probably from minstrelsy or vaudeville;
(3) blues pieces (blue yodels);
(4) traditional folksongs or songs derived from folksongs;
(5) contemporary hillbilly songs written by Rodgers, alone or with co-authors, or written by other songwriters of the late Twenties (generally expressly for Rodgers).

And in that all-important fourth category, Cohen highlighted four songs, 'Waiting For A Train', 'Frankie and Johnny', 'Those Gamblers Blues' (Rodgers' take on the already contentious 'St James Infirmary') and 'Hobo's Meditation'; of which only Rodgers's 'Waiting For A Train' could be considered a definitive representation.

Of course, the lexicon for his many blue yodels was traditional, too; but the format was his alone. And it was these which made him country's first star. 'Blue Yodel #1' was Rodgers' icebreaker when he turned up unannounced at Peer's New York office in November 1927 – barely three months after the Bristol sessions, and just seven weeks after Victor had finally shipped his first 78: 'The Soldier's Sweetheart' b/w 'Sleep Baby Sleep'.

He had evidently spent very little time working on 'old-fashioned things . . . love songs and plantation melodies and the old river ballads', and a lot more listening to records by 'the competition' and looking for a niche. His widow, Carrie, later wrote in her memoir of how 'he [had] brought phonograph records by the ton . . . Working tirelessly toward the betterment of his own brand of music-making, he would play those records over and over.' He wasn't looking for material. He was critiquing others' approach. On one occasion he told Carrie, 'That fella's got a good voice . . . You can make out what he's singin', too. Only thing is, no . . . tellin' if he's feelin' bad about it – or good.'

Jimmie was castigating the 'classic impersonality' of traditional singers like Bascom Lunsford, who had proven more popular than him on radio precisely because he sang the 'correct' folk way. What Rodgers came up with in those precious few months was a cross between the 'worried blues' of white bluesman Frank Hutchison – released by Okeh the previous year – and the 'lovesick blues' of Emmet Miller, recorded a year earlier.

It is therefore not surprising that the one 'original' song he did work on tirelessly in those months was a white man's take on blues common-places. 'Blue Yodel #1', if one forgets he sings it like a brakeman whose brakes just failed, was 'just' a composite of stray lines (mostly) from negro tradition, familiar to the race market, if not at this juncture to most pho-nograph-owning hillbillies. As John Greenway wrote of the song, 'The first stanza is the only one not ubiquitous in Negro bad-man/bad-woman songs that were old long before Jimmie Rodgers began singing publicly.'*

---

* Greenway cites two lyrical lifts, both collected in 1915. One, 'Kentucky water drinks like sherry wine' was from Georgia, the other, 'Gonna get me a pistol with a shiny barrel/Gonna kill the first fellow [sic]/Fooling with my long-haired girl', from Alabama. He could just as easily have cited the famous lines in which a little water boy addresses a captain, which had already appeared on record by both the blues singer Tom Dickson and the popular partnership, Lonnie Johnson and Texas Alexander. As for 'T For Texas', it had already been collected by Mellinger Henry.

But Peer knew the minute he heard that first blue yodel the song had the indelible stamp of originality, in particular 'the driving unorthodox guitar runs [and] his . . . lyrical yodels'. Though he was nonplussed by Rodgers' appearance at his office that November day, and was not entirely sure the sales of 'The Soldier's Sweetheart' warranted a second chance, he grabbed at 'Blue Yodel' with all his might.

Again, though, Rodgers had arrived short of material. Of the four songs they recorded in a single Camden afternoon, only two could be claimed as Rodgers' own work – and only one was. Peer's previously voiced concern that Rodgers simply did not have enough songs to call his own still seemed like a potentially insurmountable stumbling block. For now, 'Blue Yodel #1' would more than do. Barely had Victor released the song in February 1928 than it started racking up sales from all corners of the south (total sales would eventually top half a million).

The problem – forever and always – was how to follow up such blazing success. When Rodgers was hastily summoned back to Camden, the eight songs he and Peer recorded across two days in February 1928 included two further riffs on 'Blue Yodel', two co-authored with Ellsworth T. Cozzens (of 'The Three Southerners', a harmonic construct intended to provide more musical interplay than Rodgers' solo work), and one given him by sister-in-law Elsie McWilliams, 'A Sailor's Plea'.

In fact, this session might have been a Bristol-like bust if Rodgers hadn't produced, on the second afternoon, another song he insisted was traditional. 'In The Jailhouse Now' was to become almost as much a country standard as 'Blue Yodel #1' and Peer again beamed his benefi-cence down on Rodgers. Sensing he had another huge hit on his hands, he went ahead and released the song. He might not have done so if Rodgers had revealed he had learnt it – as he probably did – from a Blind Blake Paramount 78 released barely two months earlier.*

When both 'In The Jailhouse Now' and its follow-up, 'Blues Yodel #2' replicated the almost unprecedented success of 'Blues Yodel #1', Peer

---

* Nor was Blake the first to take this familiar folk tune for a spin. Whistler's Jug Band had cut it as 'Jailhouse Blues' in 1924.

suggested Rodgers return to Camden in June, when they could record something more solidly commercial than the half-dozen left overs from the November and February sessions. But the well was already beginning to run dry. Hence Rodgers's frantic call to his sister-in-law, who travelled with him to Camden, teaching him the nine songs she had penned along the way.

McWilliams' contribution was largely lyrical. She already knew that when it came to 'the music part, he would change it anyway'. And for now, she received full credit for her contribution on all but 'My Little Old Home Down In New Orleans', even though she had told Rodgers 'not to put my name on anything'. As yet, neither Peer nor Rodgers fully appreciated how invested in Rodgers' whole persona his listeners were, and how keen they were to believe these experiences were his own.

Peer was never entirely convinced McWilliams' songs were what this audience *really* wanted, and he held back from releasing anything from the June session until the November and February recordings had been fully plundered. These included another 'Blue Yodel', #3, and a song Rodgers had recorded the previous November, 'Mother Was A Lady', released in August 1928. Rodgers convinced Peer he had, in the words of one biographer, '"fixed it up" from traditional and therefore copyrightable sources'. He had done nothing of the sort – it was a marginal rewrite of an old show tune by Edward B. Marks called 'Whisper Your Mother's Name', a fact well known enough to draw comment from Abbe Niles in his *Bookman* column at the time.

Peer didn't cave in when challenged by Marks. He insisted that Rodgers had come up with his own tune (as he usually did, largely because his transpositional skills were such he could rarely copy what he heard verbatim, he *had* to adapt). In a 1931 letter to Rodgers, Peer patiently explained the settlement he'd reached: '[They are] giving you credit for the music and giving Marks credit for the words . . . [because] you used the lyric practically word for word . . . This is going to cost you from $250 to $300 . . . but that is better than losing the entire amount.'

Rodgers got off lightly. As it happens, the song had failed to set the world alight in quite the same way as its predecessors. Meanwhile, Peer had been given a timely reminder to be more sceptical about Rodgers' claims of authorship or provenance. He later suggested he still had to cut Jimmie short on a number of occasions: 'Jimmie would bring in some famous old minstrel song and just do it word-for-word, and . . . I'd stop that immediately. I'd say, "You didn't compose that."'

However, he did not apply the brakes to a song Rodgers produced at his next session in October 1928. Peer was in Atlanta on his longest-ever field trip. The label was demanding more shellac and Peer had assembled a five-piece 'orchestra' of local talent – comprising cornet, clarinet, guitar, steel guitar and bass – hoping to add an extra dimension to Rodgers's sound. Rodgers had brought just four tunes with him, one of which was another minor Rodgers-McWilliams co-composition ('I'm Lonely And Blue'), while a fourth 'Blue Yodel' (subtitled 'California Blues') hardly suggested someone about to break new ground. They needed something else. So Rodgers came up with 'Waiting For A Train'.

This time Peer knew Rodgers was playing him something that had its roots somewhere and with someone else. As he duly recalled: 'Somebody sent him a garbled version, and Jimmie said, "Well, I know that song." So he picked up his guitar and he starts to do this thing . . . [but] Jimmie couldn't fit the chords he knew to those words, and, anyway, he didn't like the words the way they were – so he changed those. We ended up with what has never been challenged as a completely new song.'

Elsie McWilliams, again on hand, suggested both she and her sister, Jimmie's wife, helped rewrite the words at the session, which certainly represent *someone*'s departure from its ostensible source, the folksong 'Ten Thousand Miles From Home'.* The original was part of the lexicon; it had already been recorded by George Reneau, Riley Puckett, Vernon Dalhart, Dock Boggs and Ernest Stoneham. Rodgers had little choice but to make it his own, though he clearly used as his template a version close to the one quoted in a letter to the *Railroad Man's Magazine* in July 1909:

---

* One of many: 'Danville Girl', which Guthrie would later rework, would be another, as would Bill Tuttle's 'The Romain Musician', Clayton McMichen's 'Free Wheeling Hobo' and Cliff Carlisle's 'Box Car Blues', all of which postdate Rodgers's recasting.

> While standing on the platform, waiting for a train,
> Cold and hungry, I lay down, out in the cold and rain,
> Thinking o'er those good old times I ne'er shall see again,
> Ten thousand miles away from home, I've bummed a railroad
>     train.

Whatever its roots beforehand, though, 'Waiting For A Train' was tradition made anew. Rodgers had penned himself another standard, selling 365,000 copies on 78. From here on, though, he was obliged to expand his cabal of co-composers as the demand for product grew, and his health declined. Twice more, he felt the need to resort to traditional staples – 'Frankie and Johnny' and 'Those Gambler's Blues' (a.k.a. 'St James Infirmary') – while displaying little familiarity with either song. (He only recorded 'Frankie and Johnny' after Elsie McWilliams taught him the lyrics, while his version of 'Those Gambler's Blues' sounds like his attempt at another 'Waiting For A Train' which came up short. Perhaps he needed to live with it some more.)

In each case, the best contemporary version was by a blues singer, though the latter's prototype dated back to at least 1790 (and as far away as Dublin town). What was slightly surprising was that Peer took a risk on releasing 'St James Infirmary/Those Gambler's Blues'. Only a month before Rodgers's July 1930 recording, a New York Appellate Court had ruled that, although 'Gambler's Blues' was 'an old gutter song of the Southern slums' [sic], the copyright resided with Irving Mills and Mills Music.

Mills was another savvy Brill Building brigand who happily bought songs outright, only to fiercely protect *his* copyrights as if they were his own flesh and blood. His greatest coup had come in July 1929 when he purchased nineteen songs outright from Fats Waller, including that perennial classic 'Ain't Misbehavin', for a desultory $500. He also laid claim to 'Minnie The Moocher', 'Lovesick Blues' and the lyrics to Duke Ellington's 'Mood Indigo', which had actually been written by Mitchell Parish, the lyricist of 'Stardust'.

The New York court not only gave Mills ownership of the copyright, but others were thereby enjoined from using either 'St James Infirmary' or 'Gambler's Blues' as a title or adopting any similar tune. But perhaps the very idea of Mills laying claim to a folk standard like 'St James' so offended Peer that he was prepared to defy the courts. Whatever his reasoning, Mills wisely refrained from testing the legal waters a second time, and Peer smartly claimed an arrangement credit on Rodgers's behalf.

Even as her name appeared less frequently among the song-credits, which more and more reflected the marketing of Rodgers as *auteur* of his Singing Brakeman persona. Mrs McWilliams continued to provide a steady supply of songs her brother-in-law could bend to his whipperwill. Despite such input, though, by 1930 Rodgers had to resort to buying songs from correspondents, who would send them along hoping he would record them. According to Peer, there was no shortage of such generous souls out there: 'People would send Jimmie songs, usually just lyrics, and if he liked them he had instructions from me, he would buy these lyrics and pay them $25, $50, something like that, and have them sign a full bill of sale. Buy them outright.'

Peer paid royalties to Rodgers to keep him producing and personally beholden. He did not feel any such sense of obligation toward these correspondents, as the penitentiary-bound Ray Hall – one of Rodgers' more regular ports of call in later years – soon discovered. Rodgers first recorded a Hall song in June 1930, but 'Moonlight And Skies' went unreleased until October 1931, by which point he had already received a co-credit and a flat payment of $50 for his contribution to Rodgers's version of 'T.B. Blues'.

Hall evidently considered the latter to be 'substantially Jimmie's work – he had merely supplied a batch of maverick stanzas from which Rodgers could pick and choose'. However, 'Moonlight And Skies' was another matter entirely. In fact, he had already gone so far as to have the song copyrighted, no easy matter given he was banged up in the Texas State Penitentiary and the Copyright Office was in Washington. When sent the usual 'bill of sale' by Peer, Hall returned it, saying he wanted a royalty contract.

By this time the song was scheduled for release, leaving Rodgers little choice but to go down to the prison and straighten matters out. He evidently succeeded, because Hall continued to feed Rodgers songs right up to his last sessions in May 1933. But he never got that royalty contract – or if he did, it was never honoured. When Peer registered the song at the US Copyright Office (two years after Hall's original registration) the credits read simply, 'Words and Melody of Jimmie Rodgers'. Evidently, Mills' methods weren't entirely off-limits, even for Peer.

Waldo O'Neal, who was *not* doing life without parole, was another long-distance correspondent who became difficult. After sending Rodgers lyrics as pitch-perfect as 'Hobo Bill's Last Ride' and 'Pistol Packing Mama', he said he would prefer a royalty agreement with Southern Music. Rodgers advised against it: 'I don't know if you are wise or not regarding this royalty business, but it is a good racket and very hard to get into.' Peer wasn't about to welcome him into the fold. O'Neal was offered the usual flat fee and told to 'like it or lump it', and elected to like it.

Even when Rodgers used songwriters who already had ties to the Peer publishing empire – like Kelly Harrell ('Away Out On The Mountain') or Andrew Jenkins ('A Drunkard's Child') – he expected his half share of the publishing, credit or not. Such continued to be the case even after he began tailoring material to the persona, not the man. In this sense, entrusting his songwriting to those, like Hall and O'Neal, who invested something of themselves in *that* Jimmie Rodgers was a smart move, even if it leaves a great big question mark hanging over the man. As his (and Peer's) biographer, Barry Mazur, has noted, 'The image of Jimmie Rodgers as a solitary, confessional singer-songwriter is complicated by the undeniable fact that he wrote only a minority of his songs outright, alone. In fact, he wrote neither of the two songs that seem most intensely autobiographical, "T.B. Blues" and "Jimmie The Kid."'

'T.B. Blues' may just be the point at which Rodgers crossed some indefinable line. His actual *performance* of 'T.B. Blues' inhabits the present

like few other early hillbilly recordings, a contradiction he left still unre-
solved when death came a-creepin'. Yet what seems on the face of it like
a brave confessional blues about his own chronic condition took as its
central motif a couplet appropriated by W.C. Handy some years before:
'Well, the graveyard must be an awful place/Lay a man on his back and
throw dirt on his face.' Nor was Rodgers the first to address the T.B. blues
in song. Victoria Spivey recorded her 'Dirty T.B. Blues' in October 1929,
barely three weeks before Bessie Tucker recorded her 'T.B. Moan'. And
although Leadbelly would not record his own 'T.B. Blues' ('T.B. Woman
Blues') until 1935, it was evidently a song he had learnt some years earlier.
Even if Rodgers didn't know any of the above, which seems unlikely, he
almost certainly knew Willie Jackson's 1928 recording when he asked Ray
Hall in 1929 for '*your* [my italics] version of T.B. Blues'. If the condition
they 'called consumption' was bound to kill Rodgers, it still did not drive
him to plunder his own imagination.

The end was assuredly nigh when he finally tackled the subject head-
on, with the apparently self-composed 'Whippin' That Old T.B.', recorded
in August 1932. It was always (intended to be) two parts bravado to one
part 'blue yodel'. But most of Rodgers's latter material continued to be
written by others seeking to articulate his, and his audience's, perceived
concerns. So it was O'Neal who largely penned 'My Time Ain't Long',
ahead of five days' session work in Dallas in February 1932. And it was
Bill Halley whose name appeared on the heartfelt and homesick 'Miss
The Mississippi And You', even as the royalties rolled Peer's and (Carrie)
Rodgers' way. Shortly before his penultimate set of Victor sessions, in
August 1932, Rodgers wrote to Clayton McMichen – whom Peer had now
enlisted to beef up his studio sound – and informed him, 'Mr Peer says he
wonts me to do at least 10 numbers so if you have any thing of your own
be sure to bring it along because Im pretty sure I can get several of your
songs Recorded.' By then a number of regular sources had been wrung
dry, and he needed songs.

Rodgers' death, at the sickeningly young age of thirty-five, merely confirmed his status as a true original in every way but one, the art of original

composition. His heroic last sessions, undertaken between bouts of spitting blood, even included one last blue yodel (released posthumously as 'Jimmie Rodgers' Last Blue Yodel', though this was not its working title). Meanwhile, Peer was hoping to stop traipsing round the south searching for sung gems as the Depression bit into the sales of his cherished hillbilly and race records like no other. He would be a respectable music publisher by the time country came up with its next true original, fifteen years down the line.

# CHAPTER 5

# 1926–50: My Time Ain't Long

*Featuring*: 'Matchbox Blues'; 'Goodnight Irene'; 'Midnight Special';
'Cottonfields'; 'Rock Island Line'; 'This Land Is Your Land'

> When [Blind Lemon Jefferson] sings, 'That's all right, mama; that's
> alright for you' on 'That Black Snake Moan', it isn't just that we
> suddenly know where both Arthur 'Big Boy' Crudup and Elvis
> Presley came from . . . With just a little imagination, you can hear
> a world opening up in Jefferson's records, a social order shifting,
> hitherto suppressed voices making themselves heard, the oldest
> black traditions feeding into something new, a mass culture in
> which blacks would play a dominant rather than a submissive part.
>
> Francis Davis, *A History of The Blues* (1995)

Jimmie Rodgers not only brought the blues to a wider, whiter audience, he
also enjoyed a genuine cross-cultural appeal. When Furry Lewis recorded
'Dying Hobo', his own take on the 'Waiting For A Train' template, he
threw in a yodel; while the Mississippi Sheiks, Blind Willie McTell and
Robert Johnson all felt obliged to learn the Singing Brakeman's songs in
case they got a request, like as not from someone with the same colour
skin. Unfortunately, not one of these black artists ever recorded a
Rodgers original. We have to rely on hearsay to connect such dots – an
indirect consequence of A.P. Carter and Jimmie Rodgers' transformation
into country's first 'singer-songwriters'; one of Peer's profounder legacies, pushing others to emulate his reinvention of Carter and Rodgers as
singer-songwriters.

The fusion of folk-based styles that had blown such a breath of fresh
air through the mid-to-late twenties record industry, and was to inform

the whole of Harry Smith's quixotic *Anthology of American Folk Music*, became something the labels – and particularly A&R men – frowned on. When the A&R men of the thirties discovered black talent, they not only demanded as a matter of course copyrightable songs but insisted they be in the style of Blind Lemon Jefferson and Charley Patton.

From this time forth, black singers were obliged to tailor their songs to people they never knew, playing phonographs hundreds of miles away (lawd, lawd). It signalled the death of the songster, a common figure in the south through the first quarter of the century. Howard Odum again provides our most apposite description of this dying breed, who, 'with a prized "box," perhaps his only property . . . wander[ed] from town to town . . . working only when compelled to do so, gathering new songs, and singing old ones . . . [as they] mingle[d] every kind of song into one . . . Thus "coon songs," "rag times," "knife songs," "devil songs," "corn songs," "work songs" – all alike [would] become love songs or dancing "breakdowns."'

These distinct categories of negro secular folk music were known to one and all at the turn of the century ('corn songs' and 'devil songs' got a mention in print as far back as 1867, in a collection of religious slave songs). But of the few songsters who survived into the 'field-trip' era only Henry Thomas, who was in his fifties when he cut twenty-three sides for Vocalion between 1927 and 1929, seems to have studiously refused to cater to the new fad, recording his unique combination of reels, gospel songs, minstrel pieces and ragtime numbers. Even his handful of blues were, in Nick Tosches's words, 'of a style that predates the standard verse structure of the blues. It is a blues that has not yet been tamed.'*

Possibly knowing already that he was not long for this world, Thomas disappeared for good after a session in October 1929. The success of one

---

* Eventually those two dozen precious cuts would be selectively plundered by Dylan, The Lovin' Spoonful (his 'Fishing Blues' having provided a glimpse of their jugband roots), Canned Heat (who reworked his 'Bull Doze Blues' as 'Goin' Up The Country' in 1968) and the Grateful Dead; but appreciation of Thomas's dying art came too late for him – and his breed.

particular songster, Blind Lemon Jefferson, had already done for the rest of his union. Before dying of a heart attack in a mid-West snowstorm in December 1929, Jefferson had recorded just shy of a hundred masters for Paramount (and two precious masters for Okeh, the only Jefferson cuts which don't sound like they were recorded down a mine). And by recording all the blues he knew for a label which had no more imagination than a boll weevil, Jefferson defined the kind of records which would sell to black buyers before (almost) anyone had market-tested the various other song-styles once enjoyed of an evening.

After his first session, when he recorded two gospel songs under the fabulous pseudonym Deacon L.J. Bates, Jefferson stuck dogmatically to the blues, though only his 1926–7 recordings really hint at the diversity of styles with which he had grown up. When Paramount advertised their premier seller's wares in a 1926 trade ad as 'real, old-fashioned blues, by a real, old-fashioned singer', they were not only contrasting Jefferson with the jazz/rag fusion that had passed for commercial blues music in the previous decade, they were suggesting Paramount's blacks played the *blues*. Period.

The problem Jefferson almost immediately encountered – after 'Booster Blues' and 'Got The Blues' broke down musical barriers no one knew existed – was similar to the one Jimmie Rodgers was to face two years later, with the equally revolutionary 'Blue Yodel #1'. A repertoire honed over years was now plundered in a matter of months by a label who thought the blues was a bottomless well. In fact, as blues scholar David Evans observed after forensically dissecting Jefferson's recorded repertoire, '[Like] most folk blues artists who recorded regularly, [Jefferson] soon ran out of traditional material that was "original and different" and had to compose blues that were thematic, or else use the compositions of other songwriters, which were also thematic,' i.e. one that adhered to a single theme, rather than jumping from commonplace to commonplace.

Others pressed to record after they had exhausted their core repertoire had already attempted such a transition. Indeed, the first time Jefferson had need of a 'thematic' blues, he simply plundered a song his friend, Victoria Spivey, had already made her own, 'Black Snake Blues'.

The startling success of this 78 may even have convinced him to emulate the old blues queen, though not until he'd used up all the blues tunes he knew. Like his contemporary Jimmie Rodgers, Jefferson's transition into a 'thematic' singer-songwriter proved a drawn-out process. But, as Evans' meticulous analysis makes clear, by 1928 he had successfully reinvented himself as a blues auteur of the first water:

> In 1926 [Jefferson] relied almost wholly on traditional verses and never fully developed a single theme in a blues. He continued in this vein for most of his 1927 recordings, but in that year he also recorded three original thematic blues by another composer . . . [But] the year 1928 marked an almost complete reversal of his original style. Perhaps after recording thirty-three mostly traditional blues, he had [simply] run out of traditional verses and had been forced to produce original material . . . [because] in his last two years Jefferson did not record a single non-thematic blues . . . He recorded only one blues during this period with mostly traditional verses, 'Prison Cell Blues'.

After the genre-defining success of 'Black Snake Moan', Blind Lemon found the commercial rewards which accrued from imposing thematic integrity on his recordings to be mixed, at best. Just like Rodgers – and blues contemporaries like Barbecue Bob and Sleepy John Estes – he achieved his best sales with his earlier records, 'which tended to be more traditional in content'. Certainly the songs for which he is largely remembered these days – 'Corinna Blues', 'That Black Snake Moan', 'Broke And Hungry', 'Match Box Blues', 'Easy Rider Blues' and 'See That My Grave Is Kept Clean' – come exclusively from those 1926–7 sessions, suggesting his audience may have been less bowled over by his departure from his folk-blues roots.

For Jefferson personally, bound as he was to the wheels of commerce, it mattered little whether the newer songs outsold the older as long as they *sold*. He was a Paramount artist, and Paramount artists got paid a flat fee, by the song. The publishing, such as it was, went into Mr Laibly's pocket. He just needed something (else) to sing, and found when he put his mind to it, he could construct a thematic blues out of commonplaces as well as any bluesman; at least until Robert Johnson claimed his crown.

For proof there had once been a different Blind Lemon, a singer who embraced all the traditional styles of the songster, we are largely beholden to the testimony of an old travelling companion and fellow songster, Huddie Ledbetter. Ledbetter, better known as Leadbelly, had the (mis)fortune not to be discovered at the time of the Delta blues craze in the late 1920s/early 1930s, because he was either doing time for nearly killing a man – for what would have been a second time – or trying (unsuccessfully) to stay away from hotbeds of temptation.

When he and Blind Lemon became travelling companions, some time around 1912, there was no commercial blues platform and Jefferson played what biographer Charles Wolfe called 'a variety of music, folk as well as the current favourites, sinful as well as religious, ragtime and dance tunes as well as ballads'. Blind Lemon's example quickly rubbed off on Leadbelly as they worked together in Texas, specifically the notorious Deep Elum district of Dallas-Fort Worth, through 1914.

At that time, Ledbetter, though older by five years, was the apprentice, and Jefferson – born in 1893, sixty miles south of Dallas – the tutor. Among the songs Blind Lemon seems to have shown and shared with Leadbelly were 'Careless Love', 'The Sinking of The Titanic', 'Three Nights Drunk' (and perhaps that other Child ballad, 'Gallows Pole'), 'The Darktown Strutters Ball', his own version of 'C.C. Rider' and a long narrative blues Leadbelly later recorded on Jefferson's behalf, called simply 'Blind Lemon Blues'.

By the time Leadbelly was placed in front of a recording machine by former English professor John Lomax in July 1933 his old friend had been dead for three years, and the blues boom he had presided over had all but died on its feet. Paramount itself stopped making records in 1932, and would be out of business by the time Leadbelly made his first *studio* recordings, on 21 January 1935.* Leadbelly had emerged from a second spell in prison in August 1934 to a changed musical landscape; and though he hoped he could still make a living as a songster, he quickly realized he would have to reinvent himself – not as a blues singer like Blind Lemon, but 'as a folk artist who contributes to the tradition'. That was the way his 'discoverer', John Lomax, described the singer in his introduction to *Negro Folk Songs as Sung by Lead Belly* (1936).

Leadbelly would not have understood the distinction between a folk-singer and 'a folk artist who contributes to the tradition'. But then he was not burdened down by the kinda weight two hundred years' worth of academic idealization of 'the folk process' produced. He was just happy to oblige when a father and son team came to Louisiana State Prison in the summer of 1933, carrying an unwieldy and unreliable disc-recording machine, hoping to document American oral tradition barely ten years after Carson's recording debut, and seven years after Blind Lemon's. It seemed to the pair that all things traditional were in danger of being lost to the world because of the insidious spread of phonographs and (now) radiograms.

John and Alan Lomax were the team dispatched by the Library of Congress to record the 'real' America with their blessing, a few blank discs and extremely limited funds. As Lomax Jnr later noted, 'We were looking for the genuine oral tradition – not a type of song.' Results in the first six weeks of travelling were patchy, but when they pulled up at the gates of the infamous Angola penitentiary, the Lomaxes remained optimistic they would find at least one (idealized) noble savage on the other side, ready and willing to raise his voice in Song. (To put such racial condescension in context, Aldous Huxley's *Brave New World* had been the literary phenomenon of 1932.)

Though the Lomaxes weren't entirely sure what 'type of song' – or man – they were looking for, they were pretty sure they'd found him when Leadbelly unleashed 'The Western Cowboy', 'Honey, Take A Whiff On Me', 'Angola Blues', 'Frankie And Albert', 'You Can't Lose Me Cholly'

---

* Three of the songs Leadbelly recorded that day were interpretations of Blind Lemon hits, 'Corrina Blues', 'Matchbox Blues' and 'Black Snake Moan'.

and 'Ella Speed'. In their excitement, it does not seem to have occurred to either Lomax that 'a supposedly authorless and uncopyrighted song learned by ear for generations might be in reality a song once featured in a vaudeville revue, or written and recorded by some long-forgotten professional entertainer' [Wolfe/Lornell].

Such was precisely the case with the last song recorded that day, listed simply as 'Irene'. Neither Lomax knew the song in question because it had gained little traction in oral tradition, though another Library of Congress field unit captured a singer in Little Rock, Arkansas, dropping its memorable chorus into another misogynistic blues, 'The Girls Won't Do To Trust', as a floating verse before Leadbelly's version had even been published.

When the pair enquired from the singer as to the origins of 'Irene', he was predictably vague, saying he had learnt the refrain and 'a couple of verses' from his uncle Terrell. The Lomaxes recorded another Ledbetter uncle, whose version was virtually verbatim. The uncle in question explained he had learnt it exactly that way from Terrell 'twenty years ago'.

Where Terrell got it is less clear, but a nineteenth-century minstrel song called 'Irene, Goodnight' shared a chorus and maybe the underlying idea of the song with Ledbetter, albeit gilded with the overwrought diction of the Victorian songhall. The song in question was penned by a prolific black songsmith, Gussie Lord Davis, who probably adapted an old folk tune, as his near-contemporary Stephen Foster had been wont to do in a far less heavy-handed way.

Whatever Leadbelly – and/or his uncle Terrell – did to the song, to their mind it was neither creation nor recreation. It was what a songster did. In the last few months of his life, Ledbetter provided Fred Ramsey of *Playback* magazine with an explanation of how such songs came about: 'He stated that he took a melody from any given song, combined it with words of another or of his own free rhyming, and then had the piece he was ready to sing. Some he felt he should change a great deal; others he left pretty much as he found them.' Whether 'Goodnight Irene' – destined to become one of the biggest-selling records in pop history – was the former or the latter, Leadbelly would take to his grave.

\* \* \*

What neither Leadbelly nor the Lomaxes could know, that afternoon in Angola, was whether this remarkable repository of songs, popular and folk, negro and Anglo-American, had a commercial future; and if so, as what? Perhaps the next blues revival was just around the corner. In which case, what better connection to Blind Lemon's lineage was there than his old friend Huddie? Which was presumably why in January 1935, Art Satherly – now in charge of ARC's race division – decided to test the commercial waters with the recently released murderer, recording the bluesier parts of his repertoire the Lomaxes had to date expressed little interest in.

Making his blues credentials explicit, Leadbelly even recorded a reminiscence of Jefferson called simply 'My Friend Blind Lemon'. Recordings of 'T.B. Woman Blues', 'Red River Blues', 'New Black Snake Moan' and 'C.C. Rider' showed Leadbelly to be a recreator the likes of whom popular song had little truck with since Peer rewrote the rules. Whether he was producing versions that *could* be copyrighted in this brave new world was unclear. The Lomaxes were wrestling with this very issue even as Satherly made recordings suggesting 'real, old-fashioned blues, by a real, old-fashioned singer'.

The Lomaxes had already published three of the variants Leadbelly had given them that hot and humid day in prison, 'Take A Whiff On Me', 'Frankie and Albert' and 'Ella Speed'. All were in a collection that professed to represent this 'genuine oral tradition' they had convinced themselves could be found behind bars erected by society. *American Ballads and Songs* (1934), though, broke the golden rule of all post-Child folk collectors – thou shalt not create composite texts out of multiple variants.* That is *not* unsullied tradition. The pair also took a rather laissez-faire approach to citing sources – as if they wanted to muddy

---

* Harvard professor Francis J. Child single-handedly broke previous anthologists' habit of producing 'composite' versions of folk ballads, and insisted on a respect for authentic oral tradition, however fragmentary or contradictory the results might be. When he died in 1896, his five-volume *English and Scottish Popular Ballads* had become the benchmark all future folk collections aspired to.

the waters of tradition (something they needed to do when producing composite texts from both published and unpublished sources without clearing copyright on the former).

Leadbelly's eclectic repertoire may not yet have made the Lomaxes rethink their own preconceptions about the nature of America's *Volkslieder*, but it was only a matter of time. Satherly was certainly in little doubt that Leadbelly had learnt a fair number of the blues he had just recorded for ARC from early commercial blues records – some of which Satherly himself had been responsible for. Indeed, as Leadbelly's biographers state, 'Blues songs that he absorbed from recorded sources ultimately became an important part of his repertoire . . . "Backwater Blues" (Bessie Smith), "It's Tight Like That" (Tampa Red), "Midnight Special" (Sam Collins) and "Outskirts of Town" (Big Bill) all appeared on race records long before Leadbelly recorded them.'

Of these, 'Midnight Special', a song about the Southern Pacific train which passed the Sugarland prison about midnight, would prove the most popular – and problematic. The song had already appeared in Sandburg's *American Songbag*, a year after the first commercial recording, by Dave Cutrell; while the first version by a bluesman was Mississippi's Sam Collins's 'Midnight Special Blues', recorded in September 1927 for the Starr Piano Company. Yet it would be Leadbelly's own template that would inspire versions by everyone from Paul McCartney (via Lonnie Donegan and The Quarrymen) to Creedence Clearwater Revival, Bob Dylan (as sideman to Harry Belafonte) to Van Morrison (twice, once with Donegan). In every single case the song was credited as traditional – which it was. All, however, indubitably derived from Leadbelly, who included at least one unique verse referring to four contemporary Houston law officers: 'Bason an' Brock will arrest you/Paton an' Boone will take you down'.

Whereas Ralph Peer had shown few qualms about copyrighting the work of those who adapted tradition, the Lomaxes perforce sat on the fence separating folklore from popular songwriting. This would be a problem throughout Leadbelly's musical career, especially for the Lomaxes. On the one hand they were determined to present him as an authentic repository of a lost tradition and on the other, to copyright his work to *themselves*. Meanwhile Leadbelly was paid a third of the publishing on songs where the Lomaxes' own contribution consisted of turning a tape recorder on.

The elder Lomax had form when it came to appropriating others' work, and when called to account by touchy folklorists, denying any wrongdoing. Though it would take until 1975 for someone to publish the full, sordid story of Lomax's first collection, *Cowboy Songs* (1910), there had been mutterings for years before the well respected D.K. Wilgus blew the gaff:

[Around 1890] Nathan Howard (Jack) Thorp, a young easterner turned cowboy, became interested in the songs sung on the range ... He discovered on his collecting trip[s] that 'none of the cowboys who could sing ever remembered a complete song.' he collected verses here and there until he had something like a complete song ... Finally, in 1908 he ... printed 2,000 copies of a red paperbound pamphlet of fifty pages, 23 songs – the first edition of *Songs of the Cowboys* ... [But] Thorp was more than a collector and editor; he was a singer and composer; and five of the pieces in *Songs of the Cowboy* are his own. On this fact turns the quarrel with [John] Lomax. 'Little Joe The Wrangler' appeared in the [original] 1910 edition of *Cowboy Songs*, and the other four . . . in the edition of 1916 . . . The Lomax papers contain no texts of the four songs added in 1916. In fact, there is but a list of the songs 'Thorp claims to have written' and the following, in a letter to J.W. Jones [from] 1923: 'Thorp's book . . . is largely cribbed from mine, with a lot of so-called songs to which he signs himself as author.'

This was the man to whom Leadbelly tied his fortunes on his release from prison. Not that the singer had many other options. When John Lomax got the *March of Time* newsreel company to do an item on his great discovery, shown in just about every US cinema through 1935, he even made a painfully uncomfortable Leadbelly utter the immortal words, 'I'll drive you all over the United States and I'll sing all songs for you. You be my big boss and I'll be your man. Thank you, sir, thank you, sir.'

So, when Lomax signed a book deal with Macmillan for a collection of Leadbelly songs – the advance and copyright of which would reside with him, doled out to the book's author as he saw fit – he knew he needed to find a way of presenting the contents as neither folk songs nor pop songs. His preferred solution was a fudge at best: 'We present this set of songs . . . not as folk songs entirely, but as a cross-section of Afri-American songs that have influenced and have been influenced by popular music; and we present this singer, not as a folk singer handing on a tradition faithfully, but as a folk artist who contributes to the tradition.'

Not surprisingly, the publisher was nervous about which, of the sixty-plus Leadbelly songs the Lomaxes recorded, he had 'change[d] a great deal' and which 'he [had] left pretty much as he found them'. Though John allayed their fears, he knew full well *Negro Folk Songs As Sung By Lead Belly* (1936) was an amalgam of both. While 'Irene', 'Roberta' and 'Blind Lemon' were Leadbelly's 'finders-keepers' takes on tradition, 'Midnight Special', 'Ella Speed', 'De Titanic' and 'Bring Me A Little Water Silvy' were all directly acquired from other traditional singers.

After the Lomaxes brought in a recognized musicologist, Columbia professor George Herzog, to transcribe and arrange Leadbelly's songs, Herzog expressed concern that most of the melodies were already familiar to him. In the end, he insisted on qualifying his own contribution, prefacing the transcriptions with a note: 'More than half of these melodies and texts have been published in other collections, in some other version. Others are of white parentage, some are white tunes pure and simple.'

Unperturbed by Herzog's concerns, the Lomaxes pressed ahead, but at the last minute they were forced to drop 'You Don't Know My Mind' from the collection because Lomax Snr discovered the song had been published and copyrighted by Clarence Williams in 1924. Given Williams' own history of credit stealing, this does not mean Leadbelly's version was not itself traditional. But a copyright was a copyright.

John's high-handed approach to Leadbelly and his work served to frustrate and ultimately alienate the singer, who was soon angling to extricate himself from the Lomaxes and get *his* songs back. It proved easier said than done. (At one point, he was advised he might not even be able to perform the songs contained in the Macmillan collection without the permission of John Lomax.) When Leadbelly consulted a lawyer, Lomax agreed to pay him off, but retained control of the material published to date, retiring to Texas to write his self-justifying memoir, *Adventures Of A Ballad Hunter.*

By freeing himself of the folklorists, Leadbelly (and, more importantly, his estate) would retain a share of three valuable copyrights: 'Cottonfields' (which his publisher initially forgot to copyright, before being reminded by The Highwaymen's 1962 version), and 'In The Pines' and 'Rock Island Line' (two traditional songs the same publisher proceeded to claim). In the last instance, Leadbelly had John Lomax to thank for learning the rudiments of a song he went on to make his own. Lomax collected it from two black chain gangs in Arkansas on his 1934 tour of the state's prisons. The newly freed Leadbelly, employed as Lomax's chauffeur for the trip, when required would strap on his guitar and provide a shining example for the more taciturn convicts of what Lomax wanted. Unlike Lomax, Leadbelly didn't need no recorder to memorize a song for later use. 'Rock Island Line' was soon a staple of his repertoire.

Lomax's patronizing attitude to his discovery was not the only trigger which convinced Leadbelly to cash up and leave the Lomaxes' employ. He also had a problem with their ultra-narrow view of the kinda songs he should sing in public. As the ARC recordings demonstrate, he had more strings to his bow than the 'folky' songs they demanded. (He was hardly alone in finding John, in particular, to have a rather fixed view of American folksong.) John Lomax had made a rod for Huddie's back the minute he introduced him at his first New York public performance with the words, 'Northern people hear negroes playing and singing beautiful spirituals, which are too refined and are unlike true southern spirituals. Or else they hear men and women on the stage and radio, burlesquing their own songs. Lead Belly doesn't burlesque.'

He might not 'burlesque', but Leadbelly still liked playing songs he had heard 'on the stage and radio'. Lomax Snr would later complain, 'For his programs Lead Belly always wished to include "That Silver Haired Daddy of Mine" or jazz tunes such as "I'm In Love With You, Baby" . . . He could never understand why we did not care for them.' Lomax could never comprehend that the big black man was a songster, pure and simple; all he seemed to care about was selling Leadbelly's 'authenticity' to the east coast media. And he evidently succeeded, because when Leadbelly *did* play Gene Autry's 'That Silver-Haired Daddy of Mine', it prompted the *Brooklyn Daily Eagle* to bemoan, 'Already the pure nigger in him shows signs of becoming corrupted.'

As befits a songster, Leadbelly loved all kinds of music, black, white and blue. He especially loved those early country exemplars, Jimmie Rodgers and the Carter Family. And in this particular passion, he would find a fellow acolyte one night in March 1940, when booked to perform at a benefit show organized by the actor, Will Greer. Also on the bill that night was another self-styled songster newly come to New York. And this time, it was the ex-convict who was sitting there thinking these tunes sure sounded familiar – and not entirely 'folky'.

We do not know whether on this occasion Woody Guthrie sang – actually, debuted – a song he had penned just ten days earlier, in response to Irving Berlin's jingoistic 'God Bless America'. Woody's altogether more caustic view of the great country he had experienced on his many travels, then known as 'God Blessed America', did not inspire any more faith in Guthrie than the 'last refuge of the scoundrel' patriotism to which Berlin's song pandered. He may even have felt he was taking too great a risk singing lines like, 'Was a big high wall there that tried to stop me/A sign was painted, said Private Property', at a time when the country stood on the brink of war. He put the song away, and when he located it again at the end of the war he decided the opening line, 'This land is your land, this land is my land', might convey a more universal appeal were it to become the title.

But before the song could begin its stately passage towards universality, Guthrie needed a tune. And as was his wont, he chose one of those old-time hillbilly records he grew up with, the Carter Family's 'When The World's On Fire', whose melody the Carters themselves had appropriated from their good friend, Lesley Riddle. Though the tune also bears a resemblance to an earlier A.P. Carter 'original' – 'Little Darling, Pal of Mine' – Guthrie knew his Carter songs, and it was Riddle's tune he decided suited his lyrics. In fact, he stole Riddle's note for note.*

Guthrie himself was no respecter of property laws, especially intellectual property. He usually assumed – correctly or not – that any tune utilized by the Carters or their kin was de facto traditional. Usually, he was right. His famous epic ballad, 'Tom Joad', took 'John Hardy' as its melodic model, specifically the arrangement used by the Carters on their first Camden recording; while 'The Reuben James' purloined the Carters' 'Wildwood Flower'. Even his first noteworthy composition, 'Philadelphia Lawyer', was based on a traditional folk ballad recorded by Gid Tanner, Kelly Harrell and Vernon Dalhart in the 1920s, 'The Jealous Lover'.

Such sources reflect Guthrie's early ambition to be a country singer, hopefully a popular one. For, as country historian Bill C. Malone noted, 'Guthrie never used the word "folk" or "folksinger" to refer to himself before he made his move to New York. The Woody Guthrie of the pre-1938 period was a hillbilly singer who sang for hillbilly audiences. His guitar accompaniment was a modification of that of Maybelle Carter, and the lyrics of his songs . . . were set to older melodies of [both] commercial and non-commercial origin.' Indeed, throughout the forties and fifties Guthrie wore his influences on his sleeve – even as he began to see with

---

* As Joe Klein, Guthrie's first biographer, has written, 'Sometimes he'd change the notes of an old tune here and there to make the melody fit his words better, thereby creating a new one – but the music was usually an afterthought [because] he wrote his songs at the typewriter.'

his own eyes the maltreatment of America's underclass, inspiring written retorts like the one directed at Russian émigré Irving Berlin.

While remaining in his forerunners' melodic thrall, once radicalized by his experiences Guthrie began to parody the attitudes of those he had once hoped to emulate. In 1937, he wrote his first out-and-out parody of a Jimmie Rodgers song, 'Dust Pneumonia Blues', to the melody 'Blue Yodel #8 (T For Texas)'. Guthrie even had the temerity to lampoon his idol by interjecting, 'Now there ought to be some yodelin' in this song, but I can't yodel for the rattlin' in my lungs.'

He even seemed to blame Rodgers for painting a rose-tinted picture of California in his 'California Blues', as if Hollywood's picture palaces had not done the job thoroughly enough some years before. And perhaps his final act of apostasy from those former idols, the Carters and Jimmie Rodgers, was his written introduction to a protest ballad Sarah Ogan Gunning set to the tune of 'I'm Thinking Tonight of My Blue Eyes', and published in *Hard Hitting Songs for Hard Hitting People* (1967): 'Didn't Jimmie Rodgers sing a song like that, too? I think so. But his sounds blank and empty and all vacant compared to this one that Sarah Ogan sings from the graves of her loved ones that sacrificed their lives at the feet of the rich coal operators.' Needless to say, they're still singing and playing the Carters' exquisitely overwrought original; Gunning's bleating ballad never made it off the page, let alone into the proletariat's hearts.

There remained for Guthrie one last act of appropriation, one that would fuel not just a single song but an entire category of folksong he could make his own: the talking blues. Again, his actual source for the style was a twenties country singer from North Carolina, named Chris Bouchillon, whose original 1926 'Talking Blues' was a homage to the half-spoken, half-sung blues he had heard songsters perform when knee high to a sharecropper. As Columbia's contemporary press leaflet was at pains to point out, 'When Chris Bouchillon says anything he does it in such a dry, humorous sort of way that you can't help but laugh.'

For a man like Guthrie, who in the words of biographer Joe Klein 'wrote his songs at the typewriter', the talking blues was an answer to his prayers. Now every verse had a punchline, and every song a punch. With this kinda song, 'he didn't have to sing at all, just talk rhythmically while backing himself with a simple, bouncy three-chord progression on the guitar'. Guthrie wrote half a dozen of 'em, all musically identical. His disciple Dylan duly wrote half a dozen more.

Back in the spring of 1940, one suspects, Guthrie and Leadbelly spent many an evening listening to and learning from the Carters and Rodgers, after Leadbelly graciously offered the Okie a couch to crash on. If Guthrie eventually recorded his own version of 'Muleskinner Blues' without even a namecheck for the blue yodeller, Leadbelly captured latterday versions of Rodgers' 'Daddy and Home' and 'My Rough and Rowdy Ways'. He was free at last to perform a cross-section of all the styles an old-fashioned songster had in his locker.

By now, neither Leadbelly nor Guthrie had any expectation they would ever enjoy the kind of success their country cousins had enjoyed in their lifetimes. They didn't even expect to hear one of their songs on a regular radio station, let alone get paid for the songs that they'd crafted, partly or wholly, from the common store. For now, their kinda music existed only between the commercial cracks.

Such a state of affairs was destined to remain just as long as members of the American Society of Composers, Authors and Publishers retained an almost total monopoly on union gigs and airplay. Folksingers, as far as ASCAP's largely white membership was concerned, were little better than inbred hillbillies and nig'rahs. But that was all about to change – and with that change would come a folk boom which would rattle those walls, make Guthrie and Leadbelly household names, and the publisher of 'Goodnight Irene' and 'This Land Is Your Land' – Howie Richmond – rich. The emergence of BMI (Broadcast Music Inc.) as storm clouds of war gathered would finally allow songs like 'Cottonfields', 'This Land Is Your Land' and 'We Shall Be Free' a share of America's seemingly end-less bounty.

# CHAPTER 6

# 1940–54: Are You Sure Hank Done It This Way?

*Featuring*: 'The Wabash Cannonball'; 'Great Speckled Bird'; 'The Precious Jewel'; 'I Saw The Light'; 'Move It On Over'; 'Lovesick Blues'; 'My Bucket's Got A Hole In It'; 'Cold, Cold Heart'; 'Jambalaya'; 'That's Alright Mama'

> The formation of BMI had results reaching far beyond competition in the field [of song publishing] . . . Authors of black and hillbilly music . . . could now receive advances and royalties from BMI that they had never had from ASCAP. Furthermore . . . by 1950 there were 1,517 independent [radio] stations compared with 627 network affiliates; half of the independents served single-station local markets, and courted them with more country music and rhythm and blues than the networks did. The outcome of all this was that . . . BMI unwittingly fed and watered the seedbed from which rock & roll would grow.
>
> Donald Clarke, *The Rise and Fall of Popular Music* (1995)

BMI's emergence was only possible because by 1940 ASCAP had become too big for its boots. Having grown from 182 members at the end of 1914 to several thousand by the outbreak of hostilities in Europe, ASCAP put the interests of the publishers ahead of even the songwriters it professed to represent, while a third of its revenues in the early 1930s went on 'operating expenses'. Not content with 3 per cent of advertising income from commercial radio stations, it bumped it up to 5 per cent in 1935, leading several major broadcasters to start looking for sources of non-ASCAP music. The seeds had been sown for a rival collection agency, and BMI was formed in 1939 by a conglomerate of broadcasters led by Sydney Kaye, a CBS lawyer.

Since 1914 ASCAP's own apartheid system had successfully ensured only its members could receive revenue from radioplay – by far the most important arbiter of popular music – or play union halls like Carnegie. It excluded on grounds of musical genre as much as colour, its underlying raison d'être being that only people who could read music could make music, or at least get paid for making music. If power corrupts, monopolies corrupt absolutely, and by 1940 ASCAP was spoiling for a fight with US broadcasters, demanding a 50 per cent bump in the ceiling on fees it received for radioplay. The broadcasters said, Nein.

ASCAP had been the playground bully too long to back down, and at midnight on 31 December 1940, it instituted a blanket ban on its members' music across American airwaves. But ASCAP's was a monopoly in name only. There was plenty of music, located on the outskirts of town, ASCAP and its members did not own. It just didn't happen to be the usual muzak people were used to hearing on their radiograms. Folk music, hillbilly music, world music, none of these had been previously offered shelter 'neath ASCAP's umbrella. All would benefit from the blanket ban.

The prime beneficiary would be music made by and for hillbillies – meaning both kinds: country *and* western (swing). This was because, thanks to Ralph Peer, this kind of music had been registered with its own publishing houses, ASCAP affiliates who could nonetheless see the advantages of competition and were amenable to change. The acquisition of Edward B. Marks' countrified catalogue by BMI in July 1940 signalled a sea change in popular song. Soon enough, BMI were enticing Peer's Southern Music and the Chicago-based M.M. Cole to also jump the ASCAP ship.

Peer, in particular, proved an important coup. He had stayed ahead of the game by extending his tentacles into world music, specifically Latin music; and when ASCAP belatedly realized it needed to sign up the best of South American music, it found Peer had got there first. 'Perfidia', a 1941 hit for Glenn Miller, was the first of many such hits for Peer, who also sewed up the Cuban market. All these songs went to BMI. But, with hindsight, the newcomer's greatest acquisition came in 1942, at the height of the dispute, when songwriter Fred Rose assigned his new partnership to BMI.

Rose was a most unlikely convert to the joys of country. Elected to ASCAP in 1938 when still based in Chicago, he had written a number of hit songs for Sophie Tucker, of which 'Red Hot Mama' was the most notable. Moving to the west coast, he had written more than a dozen songs for Hollywood's favourite singing cowboy, Gene Autry, having found he had a natural gift for songs with a melancholic twang. Nonetheless, his next career choice was unexpected. He moved to Nashville, Tennessee – hardly a hub of song publishing *or* music making in 1940 – and became staff pianist for Station WSM, home to 'the Opry'.* And while at WSM, Rose met and heard the affable Roy Acuff, a popular country singer who had already sussed out that publishing was the key to prosperity – even for a non-ASCAP songwriter like himself.

Acuff had learnt the ropes the hard way, by making records for ARC in 1936, where William R. Calaway was an A&R man. As Nick Tosches notes in his irreverent history of *Country*, 'Calaway had a bad reputation for stealing the copyrights of his singers. During an eight-year period, he deposited approximately 100 songs with the Copyright Office in Washington, D.C. The last copyright he attempted to register was "The Wabash Cannon Ball" in 1938.' That was Acuff's song.

When Calaway first approached him two years earlier, after hearing him sing a religious piece on his noon radio programme at WROL in Knoxville, Tennessee, Acuff knew enough to be wary. The song in question was 'Great Speckle Bird' – its title taken from the ninth verse of the twelfth chapter of Jeremiah, 'Mine heritage is unto me as a speckled bird, the birds round about are against her' – and Acuff would enjoy the biggest country hit since the Carters when Calaway released it as his ARC debut.

---

* When Hank Williams was asked in a 1952 interview how come Rose ended up in Hicksville, he replied, 'Fred Rose came to Nashville to laugh, and he heard Roy Acuff and said, "By God, he means it."'

In fact, 'Great Speckled Bird' owed more than a nominal debt to the first family of country. Its tune, magically transformed into a Roy Acuff melody, was a marginal rearrangement of 'I'm Thinking Tonight of My Blue Eyes'.

Acuff had originally heard 'Great Speckle Bird' played at the radio station by the Black Shirts, but it had a different melody. He asked the group's leader, Charlie Swain, to write down a set of the lyrics for him – Swain charged him two quarters for it – before transposing them to Carterland; for which service he assigned himself half the publishing. Now he just needed to find out who wrote the words. But that proved more problematic than he might initially have imagined.

The researches of the Ozark folklorist Vance Randolph uncovered a general attribution of the lyrics to Guy Smith, and his research perhaps calls into question whether even the Carter tune was actually Acuff's idea.* Acuff himself would later claim Smith's original text did not contain enough verses, and that he and his father had to produce four more to help less scripturally versed listeners understand what seeing this great speckle bird *meant* – just the sort of problem one encountered when claiming to have authored a song that already had a string of recorded claimants closer to the source. It nonetheless allowed Acuff to cut himself an extra slice of the publishing pie.

Similarly contentious were the origins of 'Wabash Cannonball', recorded the day after 'Great Speckle Bird'. Again, Acuff seemed to have done very little to a song the Carter Family had recorded back in 1929, even as he claimed another cut of the publishing. The fact that the Carters'

---

* Collecting the song from oral tradition less than half a decade after Acuff reaped rewards from its first commercial recording, Randolph observed: 'This piece is very popular with the "Holy Rollers" and brush-arbor evangelists. Some backwoods singers claim that it is at least forty years old, others say that it was written about 1934 by a radio entertainer of Springfield, Mo., known as "Uncle George," whose real name is Guy Smith. One text was printed anonymously in the *Aurora* (Mo.) *Advertiser* Mar. 26 1936. Another version was copyrighted in 1937 by the M.M. Cole Pub Co., of Chicago, with the words credited to Rev. Guy Smith and the music to Roy Acuff, a radio singer of Nashville, Tenn. . . . It is often sung to a tune very similar to that of "I Am Thinking Tonight of my Blue Eyes."'

recording had not itself been issued until November 1932 has led country historians to assume 'Peer didn't pick this as one of the big hits from the [original] session'. It seems more likely Peer knew it was in copyright until June 1932. It had been copyrighted by William Kindt in June 1904, though no author was listed on either the published sheet music or its copyright entry, perhaps because Kindt had made merely cosmetic changes to a lyric written back in 1882 by J.A. Roff and titled 'Great Rock Island Route'. Kindt cut two verses, put the trimmed words to a traditional tune ('The Jealous Lover') and claimed it as his own – a quarter of a decade before the Carters thought they'd dreamed up this very ruse.

Having grown increasingly distrustful of Calaway after 'Great Speckle Bird', Acuff switched his allegiance to Art Satherly at Columbia. When his 1936 recording of 'Wabash Cannonball' was released by Columbia in 1938, it quickly generated sales of over a million. Peer promptly copyrighted the Carters' version, though with words closer to Acuff's (which included a 'new' verse about coming 'down from Birmingham one cold December day'). Acuff responded by copyrighting the song himself in April 1940; the words were credited (erroneously) to Kindt, with 'revised lyrics and arrangement' by Acuff. Presumably this was a retort to Peer, who could hardly argue Kindt didn't have the prior claim.

The same month, Acuff recorded another new song, 'The Precious Jewel', whose melody borrowed from tradition ('The Hills Of Roane County') but whose publishing went directly to Acuff. It sold almost as many as 'Great Speckled Bird' and 'Wabash Cannonball'. The man clearly had an instinct both for what country fans wanted to hear and what the Copyright Office might allow.

So when Acuff and Rose – names now synonymous with Nashville, country music and publishing – met at the WSM radio station some time in 1940, it was a meeting of like minds. Their decision to affiliate their fledgling publishing company with BMI, the same collection agency as Peer's Southern Music, would ultimately seal the deal on the agency's long-standing association with country music. Meanwhile, Acuff-Rose's expanding roster through the forties, Acuff's continued presence on the

*Grand Ole Opry* and in the *Billboard* charts, and Fred Rose's seemingly effortless transition into a country songwriter made Nashville first, and the offices of Acuff-Rose second, magnets for all would-be country songwriters.

Such was the case when a 23-year-old colt called Hank Williams presented himself to Fred Rose, reportedly during a table-tennis game at WSM, after he had just failed an(other) audition for the *Grand Ole Opry* in September 1946. There have been a number of accounts of that fabled first meeting between Fred and Hank. One of the less likely has Rose asking the fledgling songsmith to prove he hasn't just purchased the songs he has brought with him – a practice still current in the frontier town – by writing a song about a woman who leaves someone she truly loves to marry a rich man on the spot. Hank supposedly returned with 'A Mansion On The Hill', a song he would not assign to Acuff-Rose for another fourteen months.

At least one aspect of this anecdote does sound like our young singer-songwriter. 'A Mansion On The Hill' was another of Hank's poached melodies, this one from Bob Wills' 1928 recording of 'I Wonder If You Feel The Way I Do'. Because at this stage, although he already fancied himself a songwriter, Hank had taken at least one leaf from Acuff's songbook – picking up tunes from common ground.

One song he certainly played Rose in the first few months of their association was 'Pan American'. His first railroad song, its tune was clearly 'Wabash Cannonball'. And like Woody Guthrie before him, Williams first published his songs in a collection of ten lyrics without tunes. *Original Songs Of Hank Williams* [sic] included 'A Tramp On The Street', which he claimed as 'author unknown'. However, even slowing down a song that dated back to at least 1877, and had been copyrighted as recently as 1939, until it was essentially a blues, did not confer copyright.

Yet it was probably this purloined song that really brought him to the attention of Fred Rose, who heard Molly O'Day singing the song Hank's way on the radio when he was down in Gatlinburg, Tennessee, with Art

Satherly. An intrigued Rose asked Molly's husband, Lynn Davis, whose it was. He steered Rose in Hank's direction, and when Satherly duly signed Molly O'Day, Rose pushed the still-unknown Williams to provide her with more songs like 'A Tramp On The Street' (though he quickly surrendered any claim to *that* copyright).

Hank promptly produced 'When God Comes and Gathers His Jewels' and half a dozen similar pastiches from country's self-plagiarizing tradition. At the same time he started demoing songs for Acuff–Rose, 'Pan American' among them, not sure if he had a future as singer or a songwriter. It turned out to be both. With surprising ease, Rose secured him a short-term deal with Sterling Records, for whom he duly recorded 'Pan American', his own take of 'When God Comes and Gathers His Jewels' and his first minor hit, 'Honky Tonkin'. This proved enough to pique interest from a major label, and by April 1957, he was an MGM artist.

For now, though, Hank remained stuck halfway between song snatcher and songwriter. At the first MGM session, he cut two of his most memorable, and ultimately valuable, songs – 'I Saw The Light' and 'Move It On Over' – kickstarting his career in the process. But he was taking a chance on both songs. The former is probably still his best-known gospel song, but at the time few would have missed its melodic and lyrical debt to the great gospel composer Albert E. Brumley (of 'I'll Fly Away' fame), specifically his evergreen 'He Set Me Free'.

The debt owed by 'Move It On Over' was more generic, yet equally unmistakable. As Williams's biographer, Colin Escott, notes, 'The melody was as old as the blues itself; a variant ha[ving] done business as [Jimmy Witherspoon's] "Your Red Wagon."' What Hank did with it, though, was entirely original – even revolutionary – because this was a song which hollered, when I shift gear you better get outta the way. When Jim Dawson and Steve Propes asked their book-long question, *What Was The First Rock & roll Record?*, they appositely placed 'Move It On Over' halfway between 'Good Rockin' Tonight' (the 1948 Wynonie Harris original) and 'Blue Suede Shoes'.

Suddenly Williams was a genuine hit songwriter, albeit one who initially struggled to live up to the billing. On his next session, he had to rely on his own publisher to write him some songs (Rose came up with two: the self-satisfied 'I'm Satisfied With You', and 'Fly Trouble', a surprisingly tame follow-up to 'Move It On Over'). All Hank had was a song which began as an unholy alliance of the traditional 'Lakes of Pontchartrain' and 'The Prisoner's Song'. Even then, he needed the helping hand of Ramona Vincent to finish 'On The Banks of The Old Pontchartrain'. Neither side struck the requisite chord with country fans.

The next set of sessions – in November 1947 – thus became make or break. This time Rose offered his version of what country/pop fusion might sound like ('Rootie Tootie'), while helping Hank develop his own songwriting skills. Williams was a naturally gifted lyricist, but not the most disciplined of wordsmiths. When a song did not come immediately, he was as likely to move on to another as finish it.* He also had a tendency to write too many verses. Rose encouraged him to write bridges instead, trim the weaker verses and drop the archaisms which were a hangover from the broadside ballads he mistook for authentic tradition.

Rose served as a methodical editor for Hank's lyrics. How much he contributed creatively to the songs we will never know – most of the time he was content to take his (handsome) cut as the songs' publisher and leave sole credit to Hank – but on a handful of occasions he did take a co-credit, presumably because he felt his own contribution to be substantive. And among these was 'A Mansion On The Hill'. One of eight songs Williams recorded at those November sessions, it was the first real hint he could be more than just a rockin' song catcher.

On its belated release – the last of four A-sides released by the label, who had stockpiled singles ahead of an impending musicians' strike destined to suspend all studio activity in 1948 – 'Mansion' gave Hank yet another country hit, affirmed a distinctive lyrical gift and laid the ground for his impending passage into mass acceptance. That was to come with his next single and first post-strike recording, 'Lovesick Blues'.

---

* Hence the 2011 CD of various artists, Dylan and Lucinda Williams included, offered the chance to finish songs from *The Lost Notebooks of Hank Williams*.

If one were to believe Nick Tosches, in its 1925 guise this had already been revolutionary, sung by the yodelling vaudevillian, Emmet Miller. In Hank's hands, it was simply a coming together of all the disparate styles he'd been trying on for size till he was ready to emerge as country's first fully fledged superstar.

Yet neither Miller nor Williams recorded 'Lovesick Blues' first. That honour goes to a popular contralto named Elsie Clark, who cut it in March 1922. Whether Williams had heard either Miller or Clark is a matter of heated debate, but there is no doubting his direct source – Rex Griffin's September 1939 Decca recording. Though Griffin modelled his version on (one of) Miller's, it was to Griffin's solo guitar arrangement Williams tipped his wide-brimmed hat, supposedly with the artist's blessing. In fact, Williams told Rose he had bought the song outright from Griffin, though later comments about the song's provenance suggest he knew it wasn't Griffin's: 'I'd been singing ['Lovesick Blues'] for years. It was an old minstrel tune. I liked it and my audiences liked it.'

The audiences at the *Louisiana Hayride*, country's second most popular weekly radio show, certainly liked it. And so did record buyers north and south. A quarter of a century after Elsie Clark's 'pop' version sank without trace, the song's success would make Hank Williams a household name. It would also bring a shitstorm of recriminations and accusations down on him – as perhaps Rose, if not Williams, should have known. After all, the *Shreveport Times*, reporting the song's imminent release on 9 January 1949, was already suggesting that 'the authorship of ['Lovesick Blues'] is much disputed and under investigation'. The essential problem was that Hank knew he had nicked the song. He just didn't know that the person he had knowingly nicked it from had nicked it, perhaps unknowingly, from one of the most litigious publishers of all, the infamous Irving Mills, still sitting on 'Stardust' and 'Ain't Misbehavin''.

Unfortunately for Fred and Hank's bank balances, the minute this song broke out of *Billboard*'s country charts and into the 'real' charts – the Hot Hundred – Williams was a bona fide pop star, and as such worthy of Mills' interest. And lyricist Cliff Friend's interest, too. Because

'Lovesick Blues' was as much his as it was Mills', or so Friend suggested. Indeed, when it was set for inclusion in the Country Music Foundation's collection of country's greatest lyrics, *Sing Your Heart Out, Country Boy*, Friend claimed it was his, and his alone:

> **Cliff Friend**: I was a flier-pilot in the First World War at Wright Field, Dayton, Ohio. I was impressed by the lovesick boys who left their young wives and sweethearts for the service, [feeling] blue. I had been writing songs since I was twelve. So I wrote 'Lovesick Blues'. After the war I went to New York City. Cliff Edwards [as Ukelele Ike] recorded [it] . . . but the song, ahead of its time, was a flop. I took the song back from Jack Mills. Twenty years went by and . . . a stranger in Alabama who met Hank Williams, sold him 'Lovesick Blues' as his song for $100. Fred Rose published it, but I had the copyright. When Williams's record hit the market, I flew to Nashville and took all the money, since I was also the publisher. Meanwhile, [crooner] Frank Ifield in England had sold 4 million, and altogether, the song has sold 10 million.

In fact, Friend had already sold all rights in the song to the ever-methodical Mills for $500; and it was Mills – the ostensible lyricist for 'Lovesick Blues', and a host of other songs he had no hand in but collected on – who stood to exact his pound of flesh from a concerned Acuff-Rose. After an agreement was brokered by Frank Walker, who was now at MGM, Mills and Rose agreed to split the publishing on Hank's recording, in recognition of the 'promotional' work that Acuff-Rose had done on the song's behalf. Mills retained a 100 per cent interest in all other rights pertaining to the song he had chisselled out of a former Friend. And Rose learnt an important lesson – never trust the artist, trust the Copyright Office.

Hank was less inclined to learn *his* lesson. Barely had the furore died down than he was back in the studio recording 'Mind Your Own Business', a song about gossipmongers – a favourite subject of his – that he had bought in embryonic form from a Montgomery musician, Smokey Metcalfe. And when it was decided that nothing recorded that day would do as the follow-up to 'Lovesick Blues' – even though the session included two of Hank's most enduring originals, 'You're Gonna Change (Or I'm Gonna Leave)' and 'Honky Tonk Blues' – he returned nineteen days later with another song he had acquired, from well-known Knoxville guitarist and song-hustler Claude Boone.

Almost as notorious as Boone was James Arthur Pritchett, a local alcoholic, who when he needed a drink – which was most of the time – would stand outside the WNOX studio in Knoxville with a little box of songs, priced between ten and twenty-five dollars. 'Wedding Bells' was one of Pritchett's pricier picks, but Boone bought it and sold it on to Acuff–Rose for a share of the publishing and a namecheck. According to Colin Escott, his immediate return on his $25 investment was at least $40,000. The song peaked at number two in the country charts, though it did not emulate the effortless transition to the pop charts 'Lovesick Blues' achieved.

For that, Williams would need to find a voice of his own. Instead, he decided to record a song he definitely knew had been copyrighted in 1933 by another notorious New York-based credit stealer, Clarence Williams. Actually, Hank's version of 'My Bucket's Got A Hole In It' was nothing like his namesake's – itself purloined from a version recorded six years *before* Clarence copyrighted it, by Tom Gates for Gennet Records. Hank's had far more in common with Washboard Sam's 1938 retake, at least in spirit; and Washboard Sam had already refused to share the copyright on *his* version with Clarence.

Rose, though, wasn't inclined to risk it all again. Giving song credit to the elder Williams, who had already sold his copyrights to Decca, a label who could afford lawyers, he simply ensured the other side of the 78 gave Hank's side of the story. In fact, although both sides generated steady airplay, it was 'I'm So Lonesome I Could Cry' which suggested Hank was well on his way to becoming the finest singer-songwriter of the pre-Rock era.

From here on, there would be no stopping the reborn Nashville songwriter. In 1950–1, he would rack up five number ones on the *Billboard* 'country and western' charts (so named in 1949), every one of them a Hank Williams 'original' and an Acuff-Rose copyright: 'Long Gone Lonesome Blues', 'Why Don't You Love Me', 'Moanin' The Blues', 'Cold, Cold Heart' and 'Hey Good Lookin'.

Not that publishing disputes became a thing of the past. 'Cold, Cold Heart' instigated a case which would outlive not only Williams, but also Fred Rose. The melody (and its sentiment) was one Williams had knowingly adapted from Texas Tyler's recording of 'You'll Still Be In My Heart', a song originally written by Ted West, then rewritten by Buddy Starcher, who had ceded it to his business associate, Clark Van Ness, in July 1943.

Van Ness, who knew how to play the game, waited until 'Cold, Cold Heart' hit the top of the country charts before he issued proceedings, by which time Acuff-Rose had already paid Hank his initial share of the royalties. This time, though, Acuff-Rose did not consider the song's debt an open and shut case and contested the claim; and though Dixie Music ultimately won the judgment, they were awarded just $2,500 in damages and double that sum in court costs.

Hank's song had already earned four or five times that amount; and it would go on to ring yet more cash registers when Johnny Cash, Ray Charles and Jerry Lee Lewis got through with it. But even this stone-cold country classic did not restore Williams to the pop charts. That would take until July 1952 and a song that showed there was almost no genre of folk music Hank could not summon to his command.

'Jambalaya (On The Bayou)' owed its genesis to a fellow singer-songwriter, 'Moon' Mullican, who was enjoying his own heyday at King Records; 'I'll Sail My Ship Alone', 'Mona Lisa' and 'Cherokee Boogie' had all stormed the country charts in the past eighteen months. Unfortunately for Moon, he was signed to a long-term contract with Syd Nathan's King Music in Cincinnati, and his publishing arm, Lois Music. Nathan was one of that group of ambitious, independent entrepreneurs in the fifties who knew all about the means of production yet proved positively mean about paying for what their artists produced. As a result, he lost as many as he kept.*

Mullican already knew if he assigned his portion of 'Jambalaya' to Nathan, as he was contractually obliged to do, he would never see a jumping bean. So he and Hank cooked up a deal whereby Williams instructed Rose to surreptitiously pay Mullican 25 per cent of the publishing. Which he did – until Hank died, six months later, and Rose less than two years after that. Fred's son Wesley assumed the helm, and the payments to Mullican dried up. As King Records chronicler Jon Hartley Fox drily observes, 'It probably cost Mullican at least a million dollars in lost income.'

But Mullican wasn't to know what the future held; and what he did receive was probably still out of all proportion to what he brought to the tune. 'Jambalaya' was essentially a clever rearrangement of the Cajun stalwart 'Gran' Texas', for which Chuck Guillory might have received his own slice of the songwriting given that his 1946 recording was almost certainly Hank (and Moon)'s main melodic template.†

Some of Williams' songwriting sheen had begun to rub off on his one-time mentor, because in 1952 – Williams's last year on this earth – Rose presented him with songs as good as 'Setting The Woods On Fire' and 'Take These Chains From My Heart', as well as lending enough of a hand to take co-credits on 'Kaw-Liga' and the seemingly prophetic 'I'll Never Get Out Of This World Alive'. Hank simply raised the bar again, writing 'Your Cheatin' Heart' and 'You Win Again' solo. Sadly, though, this was the end of the line for Hank. Whatever musical direction he was heading in, he reserved for the heavenly choir.

---

* Jethro Burns, of country duo Homer & Jethro, later revealed how *he* got out of their King contract. Nathan had claimed the copyright on a song of theirs ['I Feel That Old Age Creeping On'] after the fact: 'Well, then, Syd took the song, changed one word in it . . . and had Wynonie Harris record it. Of course, it was a big hit . . . Syd took half of the song. It was out and out thievery. He just took the song. I had him over a barrel and he knew it. I said, '. . . Give me Homer & Jethro's contract.'

† It would take Mullican most of the fifties to extricate himself from King, and when he finally did, he had just enough time to record one last hit. This was Riley Puckett's unabashed 'Ragged But Right', to which Mullican attached his own name.

Though Hank had anticipated the musical blend of country and R&B to come, he had ultimately shied away from making his own leap into pure rockabilly. Perhaps if he had recorded two hundred miles east, in Memphis, Tennessee, he would have set the charts on fire with just such a fusion ahead of that pre-ordained meeting with his Maker. But he was someone who never really liked being produced. He brought in the songs and everyone fell in behind him. Hank recorded everything like he was in a hurry. And it seems he was.

On the other hand, a callow would-be crooner from Tupelo, who kept hassling producer Sam Phillips at Sun Records in Memphis to let him make a 'country' record, needed all the help he could get. He didn't write songs, he didn't have a band, he didn't know his strengths and weaknesses musically, and he could display pretty atrocious taste when it came to picking which songs he thought he should record.

Yet in the eighteen months that separate Hank Williams' death in the backseat of a limo from the most famous session in popular song, Elvis Aaron Presley kept playing a particular 1946 record by Arthur 'Big Boy' Crudup to death as he told himself, 'If I ever get to the place where I could feel all that Arthur felt, I'd be a music man like nobody ever saw.' By July 1954, he had also set his sights on turning Bill Monroe's 'Blue Moon Of Kentucky' into an unholy brew of blues and bluegrass. What he did breathed new life into two forties songs from opposite sides of the musical divide; and in the process he made them – and popular music itself – whole.

As to whether he did any of this consciously, the jury is still out. The one person who can genuinely say she 'discovered' Elvis was Marion Keisker, the Sun secretary who screened every would-be singer who wanted to sing for Sam. And she has no doubt it was 99 per cent intuitive: '[Sometimes] Elvis would do something absolutely extraordinary and . . . something would go wrong before the tape was completed. Sam would say, "Well, let's go back, and you hold on to what you did there. I want that." And Elvis would say, "What did I do? What did I do?" Because it was all so instinctive that he simply didn't know.'

In many ways, Elvis was the last of the songsters. For him, a song was there to be played around with. Authorship and publishing was for the birds – he just had a sound in his head he needed to expel if he was gonna keep from going mad. All he really needed at this (turning) point was a producer like Phillips who knew how to catch white lightning, and rather than bottling it, transfer it to tape. Phillips had already done it with Howlin' Wolf, B.B. King, Ike Turner and Rufus Thomas. All *he* needed now was a white boy who sounded just like them.

Legend has it that Presley broke into Crudup's 'That's Alright Mama' as part of an impromptu jam during a break at his first Sun studio session in the first week of July 1954. But he had evidently put some thought into the song, and what it meant. Because whereas Crudup sang interchangeable commonplaces like, 'Babe, now if you don't want me, why not tell me so/You won't be bothered with me 'round your house no more', Elvis injected a sense of momentum all his own, coming up with the swaggering couplet: 'I'm leavin' town now, baby, I'm leaving town for sure/Well, then you won't be bothered with me hangin' round your door.'

In the blink of an 'I', as Greil Marcus noted, 'Elvis reduces the blues-man's original to a footnote. He takes over the music, changing words and tightening verses to suit himself . . . He turns Crudup's lament for a lost love into a satisfied declaration of independence . . . It's the blues, but free of all worry, all sin.'

In this sense, Elvis deserved a share of the publishing – as did Blind Lemon Jefferson for 'That Black Snake Moan', another song that coopted Crudup's central couplet. But the publishing of 'That's Alright Mama' was owned by the last of the great pre-war song snatchers, Lester Melrose. Like Mayo J. Williams, from whom he learnt the ropes, Melrose was strictly old school when it came to signing would-be singer-songwriters; he 'signed the acts [he would record] directly to himself, then farmed them out to the record companies. He made the rules and he set the prices, and the blues musicians could either like it or lump it.'

Unfortunately for Crudup et al., by the early forties Melrose was the only show in town, at least if that town was Chicago. He had the likes of Tampa Red, Memphis Minnie, Lonnie Johnson and Memphis Slim at his beck and call, all collecting scraps working as sidemen on one another's records. He even got a first pop at recording Muddy Waters, four years before Leonard Chess made his play. But Lester was too set in his ways to recognize the next generation's sound when it came banging at his door.* Crudup was convinced he had lost out on untold millions, complaining to anyone who would listen, 'I was making everybody rich and I was poor.'

In fact, 'That's Alright Mama' stayed a strictly Southern phenomenon, Sun having the kinda independent distribution – and cashflow restraints – that made the very idea of a pop hit as likely as Man landing on the moon. It changed the world f'sure, but 'That's Alright Mama' (and Sun's four follow-ups in the ensuing eighteen months) didn't even make Sam Phillips or Elvis Presley rich.†

For that to happen sunny Sam was gonna have to find someone who actually wrote the songs they sang. And Elvis was gonna have to find a manager who could make anyone who wrote the songs he wanted to sing sign over half their publishing to 'him'. By the end of 1955 the future King of Rock & Roll had found the right uncle, Tom Parker, a colonel in the army of hustlers and hucksters who made a living from that most modern of medicine shows – pop music. When Phillips cashed the $40,000 cheque he had received from RCA for surrendering his pop prodigy to this carney of commerce, he was convinced he had already captured his next cash cow on tape. And this one had songs he could record *and* publish.

---

* Perhaps he sensed as much, because by the time Presley became a Hill & Range artist himself, in January 1956, Melrose had retired to Florida and sold his publishing to that larger concern.
† The Beatles and Dylan both recorded the song – in the latter's case in 1962, 1963, 1969 and 1975 – but neither released a version until recent archival trawls.

# PART TWO

# FREE-FOR-ALL

# CHAPTER 7

# 1953–6: A Piece Of The Pie

*Featuring*: 'Blue Suede Shoes'; 'Folsom Prison Blues'; 'Heartbreak Hotel'; 'I Got A Woman'; 'Tutti Frutti'; 'Maybellene'; 'Promised Land'; 'Matchbox'

> Elvis Presley, one of the most sought-after warblers this year, signed two big-time contracts as a recording artist, writer and publisher. RCA beat out the diskery competition and signed the 19-year-old to a three years-plus-options contract. Besides which, Hill & Range inked him to a long-time exclusive writing pact.
> 'Double Deal Hurls Presley Into Stardom', *Billboard*, 3 December 1955

When Sam Phillips had asked the Pop genie for a white man who could sing like a black, he should perhaps have added the caveat – and write songs. Even as the phenomenon he quickly became, the Sun Presley was always living on borrowed time creatively, and Phillips was always living on borrowed time financially. Phillips, though, was no fool. Once Elvis had proved 'That's Alright Mama' was no fluke, he pushed him to make at least one side of each single a cut he could collect the publishing on, beginning with 'Baby Let's Play House'; which was backed by Stan Kesler's 'I'm Right You're Left She's Gone', a song Kesler says he 'based on the Campbell's soup advert . . . written as a western swing type thing'. Not in Elvis's hands, it wasn't.

Next up was 'Mystery Train'. This was a song on which Phillips had taken a co-credit back in 1953, when he had recorded Junior Parker's version – though for what is not entirely clear. (If anyone should have been sharing the credit with Parker it was A.P. Carter – or Lesley Riddle – whose 'Worried Man Blues' provided the underlay Parker had carpeted over.) Bad blood between Parker and Phillips, perhaps over said credit, spilt over into a court case when Parker allowed himself to be poached by Don Robey's Duke label. So the decision to induce Presley to record 'Mystery Train' as his fifth Sun A-side was both payback to Parker (who never saw a dime from the Presley remake) and payday for Phillips.

And once Phillips decided to make 'Trying To Get For You' Elvis's sixth shot at the prize, he looked around for a B-side he could assign to his Hi-Lo Publishing. Presley obliged by attempting to record 'When It Rains, It Really Pours', but (as of yet) he couldn't relate to its sentiments and successive takes only took the song further away from him. He was spared a further stab at it when 'Colonel' Tom intervened, telling Phillips he would get him $40,000 for a release from his Sun contract. He proved as good as his word.

This was a real stroke of luck on Phillips' part. He had serious cashflow issues at this point – and the unprecedented demand for Presley product only made the situation worse. Every time the advance orders for the next Presley single shot up, he needed to find the cash to press it, because it would be months before the revenue river began to flow the other way. Forty thousand bucks gave him the cushion he needed. Meanwhile, Sun's two other great white hopes had given him songs he could collect both the 'mechanicals' and publishing on, each a stonewall classic.

It turned out the 'next' Elvis had been at Sun Records all along, though Sam had been keeping him on a short leash. All that changed when Carl Perkins entered Sun's studio for a third time in December 1955 to record his follow-up to 'Let The Jukebox Keep Playing' (a Hank Williams pastiche that kept its revolutionary wares – the high octane original 'Gone Gone Gone' that was its B-side – well hidden).

As Perkins remembered it, 'We had been playing country music because Sam did not want two [white] artists doing coloured music like Elvis, but at this session he said to go right ahead and rock.' And rock they did, sensing that the label's future was now riding on the high hope that Perkins had a coupla songs which could crack the same code as the departing Presley. Or as he later put it to *Musician*'s Bill Flanagan, 'I played country songs and put in speeded-up black blues licks.' The songs he had brought along that day were 'Blue Suede Shoes' and 'Honey Don't'. With a pairing this explosive, rock & roll had truly arrived.

By the time Presley entered an RCA studio on the afternoon of 10 January 1956 – five weeks after *Billboard* proclaimed him an RCA artist – Phillips had already released into the world Johnny Cash's 'Folsom Prison Blues' (a song he'd been holding back since July, presumably because of cash flow) and Perkins's 'Blue Suede Shoes'. The feedback on both the Cash and the Perkins – issued on 15 December 1955 and 1 January 1956 respectively – was most encouraging. If the Cash 78 looked like it might top the country charts, Perkins' double-shot of rock & roll redemption looked like shattering the glass ceiling *Billboard* placed on most indie-label releases.

When Elvis called on Phillips at the Memphis studio, a couple of days after that first RCA session, he found his former producer surprisingly sanguine about his departure. Phillips' decision to put all his weight behind Sun's two singer-songwriters, and let Presley go, seemed about to pay dividends. Meanwhile, Presley's new producer/A&R man at RCA, Steve Sholes, was privately voicing his concerns to guitarist Chet Atkins that 'he'd bought the wrong one'.

In fact, 'Blue Suede Shoes' would have made a perfect RCA debut for Presley – if he hadn't already given his word to Phillips and Perkins that he wouldn't compete with Sun's big chart play. He had seen the effect the song had on audiences when touring Arkansas and Mississippi with Perkins and Cash the previous December, as his career lay in label-less limbo for a few frustrating weeks. It was at an earlier Sun show that Cash had had the original idea for the song; which he took to Perkins, feeling it was more likely he could do something with it. Perkins's response was, 'I don't know nothin' about them shoes, John.' So Cash began relating an experience he'd had in the Air Force with a bootblack called C.V. White:

> We wore our fatigues when we worked on our job in the Air Force,
> but when we got a three-day pass everybody would dress up in Air

Force blues and black shoes . . . C.V. White was a friend of mine. And before he'd go on his pass to go to town, he'd always come by and get me to inspect him, because he wanted to look the best he could look for those women in Munich. I'd look him up and down and say, 'You sharp, C.V. You got your shoes shined up really good.' And he said, 'Those are not Air Force black. Those are *blue suede* shoes tonight. And . . . don't step on my blue suede shoes.'

Perkins, not a prolific songwriter at the best of times, was struggling to find a way into the song when he remembered a jump-blues called 'Rock Around The Clock', which began thus: 'One for the money, two for the show, three make ready, four let's go . . .' (The song in question by Mercury saxophonist Hal Singer was itself a knock-off of Lucky Millinder's 1942 78, 'Let It Roll'.) Cut three years before Bill Haley appropriated the title – and much of Wynonie Harris and Jimmy Rushing's 1945 record, 'Around The Clock' – it was, to Perkins' mind, fair game.*

Singer evidently agreed, although that didn't stop a song publisher from that renowned hub of publishing, Pasadena, Texas, claiming Perkins had plagiarized '*the title*, theme and tune' from a song he had 'cleared through BMI on August 22, 1955'. Phillips' response was somewhat confused, but presumably sufficient, as he never heard from Pasadena again. He asserted the song was 'a joint work of two of our artists, Johnny Cash and Carl Perkins, and was virtually composed, over a period of several months, in our studios'. Yet he had just released the record attributed solely to Perkins. If the man in black had done more than suggest the title, he was entitled to quite a chunk of cash.

On the other hand, he knew he might at some point have to give back all the royalties accrued on his own 'Folsom Prison Blues', heavily based as it was on 'Crescent City Blues', a self-composed song Gordon Jenkins had included on his 1953 album, *Seven Dreams*. Cash had heard it from fellow recruit Chuck Riley while serving in Germany. In fact, he asked

---

* With lines like, 'Well, we looked at the clock and the clock struck five, everything in the joint was jumpin', jumpin' like it was alive', Haley's debt is clear.

to borrow the record from Riley to write down the lyrics, which he was determined to relocate to Folsom Prison after seeing a documentary film about the godforsaken place. In the process, he barely modified the Jenkins narrative, which starts, 'I hear the train a-comin'/It's rollin' down the bend/And I ain't been kissed, lord/Since I don't know when,' and ends with the couplet, 'Far from Crescent City is where I'd like to stay/And I'd let that lonesome whistle blow my blues away.' So, same song.

In Jenkins's case, though, he was stuck in Crescent City 'just watching life mosey by'; whereas Cash's narrator was in Folsom Prison, doing life without parole because he famously 'shot a man in Reno just to watch him die'. It was the one line that was all Cash, and it struck a chord. When he played the song to Sam Phillips, Cash admitted his debt to Jenkins. But Phillips shrugged it off and happily assigned the song to his publishing company, Hi-Lo. In fact, according to Marshall Grant, Cash's bassist, 'John was a little nervous about ['Folsom Prison Blues'] because he had taken so much of the song from Jenkins, so he told Sam about the two songs. But Sam didn't seem to care at all. Everyone was taking stuff from old songs, he said. He didn't even ask to hear the Jenkins song.'

Cash's sole credit wouldn't have cut much mustard with any judge, which makes it astonishing it took the length of a life sentence for Jenkins to notice the two songs shared almost identical lyrics and do something about it. (It would be 1975 before Jenkins threatened to sue. He received a one-off payment of $75,000 but failed to insist on a co-credit meaning the million-dollar song remains credited to Cash alone.)

Fortunately for Cash, 'Folsom Prison Blues' was initially only a smash in the country charts.* 'Blue Suede Shoes', on the other hand, was making short work of the Hot Hundred's lower reaches. Though it had entered the pop charts eighteen places behind Presley's RCA debut, 'Heartbreak Hotel', the following week it was at twenty-three, while 'Heartbreak Hotel' lay at twenty-eight.

---

* Where it reached number four, ten places higher than its predecessor, 'Cry Cry Cry', but three places shy of its successor, 'I Walk The Line'

RCA were already sweating over what to release as a follow-up to 'Heartbreak Hotel', which they feared might yet stall short of the all-important Top Ten. When Presley returned to CBS-TV's *Stage Show* on 17 March for his fifth appearance, after a four-week break, he finally delivered a version of 'Heartbreak Hotel' that set teenage pulses racing. But even better was his performance of 'Blue Suede Shoes'. He had now performed the song twice on the show, having recorded it at his first New York RCA session (30 January) with enough ferocity for Perkins to fear the worst. Presley stayed true to his word, though, nixing any suggestion it be issued as his second RCA single.

RCA's point-man Sholes got around the problem by releasing it at the end of March as the lead track of Elvis's first EP (called simply, and rather unimaginatively, *Elvis Presley*). On the same day, RCA released Presley's debut album with the same title and cover, and the same lead track. Perkins, by then, was lying with his feet up in hospital as 'Blue Suede Shoes' mounted four consecutive unsuccessful sorties against 'Heartbreak Hotel', safe in its top berth. A car crash on his way to New York to appear on the Ed Sullivan and Perry Como shows finally put paid to Perkins' dash for glory (the latter, broadcast in direct opposition to CBS's *Stage Show*, usually had significantly superior viewing figures). Presley stopped by to see his friend at the hospital in Dover, Maryland, on his way to his sixth and final *Stage Show* appearance, where he finally nailed 'Heartbreak Hotel'. This time he substituted 'Money Honey' for 'Blue Suede Shoes'. His triumph over his former Sun labelmate was assured.

It had been a close run thing. And Presley had needed to fight RCA and his new publisher, Hill & Range, tooth and nail to make sure 'Heartbreak Hotel' was his first RCA single, and 'Blue Suede Shoes' was not his second. He was as yet unaware that it was Hill & Range, not RCA, who had paid the lion's share of the Sun transfer-fee.

Presley had been angling to record 'Heartbreak Hotel' ever since its (co-)author, Mae Axton, had played him the song at the Country Disc

Jockey Convention in Nashville the previous November. According to Axton, 'The moment I played it for Elvis, he was hooked. He went back and played it ten times.' Steve Sholes and Colonel Parker were unimpressed, and they became apoplectic when Axton, who had done some of Hank Snow's advance press work on the Colonel's behalf and knew how he worked, refused to sign the song over to Hill & Range, though she willingly gave Presley a third of the publishing for displaying faith in the song in the first place. (She had already promised the other third to her 'real' co-author, Buddy Killen, and his Tree Publishing.)

'Heartbreak Hotel' had been one of two songs Presley recorded at his first RCA session on the afternoon of 10 January 1956. The other was 'I Got A Woman', a Ray Charles song Presley had been keen to release (preferably as a single) for months. And it would have been a smart move. Though Charles's version had topped the R&B charts in the winter of 1955, it never crossed over to the pop charts. It was also a song Presley had been singing live for the past nine months, and it had not failed him yet – which is probably why he chose it for his national TV debut on Tommy Dorsey's *Stage Show* on 28 January 1956. But Parker knew there was precious little chance of getting the publisher of this particular song to 'split' the publishing. It was Ahmet Ertegun at Atlantic, an adversary even Parker took seriously.

Whether Charles himself was entitled to (all) the publishing on this classic slice of soul was another matter entirely. When record producer 'Bumps' Blackwell heard Charles's single, upon its December 1954 release, he was shocked as much by Brother Ray's audacity as his audible achievement: 'I couldn't get over it. He'd taken a gospel song that Alex Bradford had recorded for Specialty and made it into an R&B number.' Nor was Blackwell referring to some obscure pre-war gospel 78, but rather a 1954 single by Professor Alex Bradford, 'My Jesus Is All The World To Me'.

Charles wasn't about to stop now as he set to plundering the gospel mine. Within six months he had transformed 'This Little Light of Mine' into 'This Girl of Mine', and by the time Elvis had given up on the idea of

'I Got A Woman' as an RCA single, he had made 'You Better Leave That Liar Alone' into 'Leave My Woman Alone', and 'Hallelujah I Love Him So' into 'Hallelujah I Love Her So'. In each case, Jesus (and/or the Devil) received the requisite sex change. Not surprisingly, Charles caught some flak for turning such sacral standards into songs of sin: 'I caught hell for turning around old church songs into pop songs like "This Girl of Mine." [But] to tell the truth, I didn't give a shit. Music is music. The church was part of me. Church music was part of me. I was being honest, and besides, the records were selling.'*

Presley would have to wait eight more years to release a Ray Charles classic as an A-side, by which time he needed all the help he could get. And that song, recorded at the *Viva Las Vegas* sessions and backed by the title track, had its own country heart. Whether Presley realized it or not, Charles had taken Hank Snow's 'I'm Movin' On', a song Presley grew up with, and inverted the riff till, in the words of Atlantic producer Jerry Wexler, it 'became the underpinnings of "What'd I Say," the song that propelled him to the top of the charts'. (Charles later demonstrated the trick by recording 'I'm Movin' On' itself.)

If Hill & Range would never have countenanced 'I Got A Woman' as a follow-up single to 'Heartbreak Hotel', neither was Elvis about to record the kinda songs his A&R man insisted on offering him. In the weeks leading up to that first RCA session he had been spinning the ten demo discs Sholes had sent him before Christmas, asking him to listen to them and tell him which ones he liked. The answer was, none of 'em, and a list of some of the titles would tell anyone with five Sun singles and two ears why: 'I Need A Good Girl Bad', 'Shiver and Shake', 'Old Devil Blues', 'Automatic Baby' and 'Wam Bam Hot Ziggety Zam'.

Elvis was having none of it. Instead he recorded 'I Got A Woman',

---

* Charles could have mounted a more spirited defence, pointing out that he was merely reversing the historical atrocity perpetrated by Scottish poet James Wedderburn in 1549, when he first published his *Buike of Godlie and Spiritual Sangs, changed out of Profane Sangs for avoyding of Sinne and Harlotrie*. Culled from traditional songs the world needed him to *preserve*, he instead transformed the material into sanctimonious dreck.

'Heartbreak Hotel' and 'Money Honey' as potential A-sides on the 10th; and then, in a gesture intended to satiate Sholes, cut two ballads Hill & Range *did* own ('I'm Counting On You' and 'I Was The One') as possible B-sides on the 11th.

Presley continued playing the field with his song choices after he landed in New York at the end of the month, performing 'I Got A Woman' and 'Shake, Rattle and Roll' (into which he interjected part of another Big Joe Turner song, 'Flip, Flop and Fly') on his national TV debut. The following week, he performed his old Sun single, 'Baby Let's Play House' and the Little Richard hit, 'Tutti Frutti' (which he reprised on *Stage Show* a fortnight later). What was he playing at?

It got worse. When Elvis entered RCA's New York studios for three days of sessions in the week between his first two TV appearances, he insisted on cutting both the Turner and the Little Richard songs, as well as Lloyd Price's 'Lawdy Miss Clawdy'. Sholes, in his frustration, penned a letter to the Colonel trying to get Presley to adopt a more conciliatory position: 'On Friday we didn't have any new material that suited Elvis so we recorded "Lawdy Miss Clawdy" and "Shake, Rattle and Roll." Neither one of the two will be suitable for single release.' He meant not without a half-share of the publishing.

Like 'I Got A Woman', 'Lawdy Miss Clawdy' had been a number one single in *Billboard*'s R&B charts for Lloyd Price back in 1952, but had not replicated that success in the Pop charts. As such, it could easily have made up a double A-side with the Charles cut, making for a twin-set of R&B at its finest. But that would have meant cutting a deal with Art Rupe at Specialty, a thief among princes.

Ditto 'Tutti Frutti', which Little Richard had sold outright to Rupe for $50, only to find he had called in Joe Lubin, who had written for Vera Lynn, Doris Day and Anne Shelton and once had a big hit with 'Shoemaker's Serenade'. As Lubin told Spencer Leigh, 'The publishers of "Tutti Frutti" . . . called me in to clean up the song so that Pat Boone, who was a million-selling artist, would record it.' The changes were relatively minor ("She knows how to love me, yes indeed" became "She's a real gone cookie, yes sirree").* Anyway, Richard Penniman had already done a perfectly good job disguising the true meaning of the song, which in its original guise was an unambiguous paean to anal sex: 'Tutti frutti, good booty, if it don't fit don't force it, you can grease it, make it easy.'

For this reason alone, Penniman had never really thought about recording it – 'it was just something I did'. Rupe allayed his concerns, and then gave 'his' cleaned-up version to Boone. Though by the time Boone released it, Little Richard's raw wail had already risen to seventeen in the pop charts, and even the pale-faced Boone struggled to climb five places higher. Presley, as the bridge between black and Boone, made a better fist of it, but the song was only three months old. And it was already becoming clear to the labels that sales resistance to black R&B singers among white teenagers was not what it used to be.

Part of the acclaim for this crucial change should go to popular DJ, Alan 'Moondog' Freed, a one-man publicity machine who not only claimed to have coined the term 'rock & roll', but was taking credit for certain R&B hits becoming pop successes. His WABC show, from New York, was seen as an important indicator of each 'next big thing'. And he had started taking advantage of those who bought into this perception by putting his name to songs by bands he brought to labels, specifically Chess Records. Even now he is listed as a co-composer on no less than forty-four songs in the BMI database, including 'Down In The Valley', 'Sincerely', 'Nadine' and 'Sweet Sixteen'.†

'Nadine' (not the Chuck Berry song, which came later) had been cut by The Coronets, who were trying unsuccessfully to get a record deal when band member Sam Griggs sought out Freed at the WJW studios in Cleveland, where he worked in 1953. Having been told by the station

---

* Lubin was only credited on the English single, while in recent reissues producer 'Bumps' Blackwell's name has now been added to the litany of contributors.

† The BMI database is an online resource available to all, though for a one-stop shop of American song publishing the Harry Fox Agency website combines both BMI and ASCAP compositions.

manager Freed would not see him, Griggs was about to give up when Freed's wife, Jackie, heard them talking and agreed to get him 'a quick minute' with Alan. Freed took the demo of 'Nadine' from Griggs and several weeks later, The Coronets found themselves being offered a contract with Chess, where they duly re-recorded 'Nadine'. But when the single was released in September 1953, the writing credits read simply, 'Alan Freed'.

Freed also arranged the signing of another harmony group, The Moonglows, to Chess, and was in turn listed as co-author (with Harvey Fuqua) of their debut single, 'Sincerely'. When the McGuire Sisters, a white pop-oriented trio, enjoyed a million-selling number-one hit with the song early in 1955, having copied it note for note from The Moonglows, Freed realized he had a good thing going.

Less than three months later he found his name on another Chess single, though his sole contribution seems to have been playing it on regular rotation and telling Leonard Chess 'it was his biggest record ever'. Freed was right. Which is perhaps why it was a slightly unfortunate choice on Chess's part for settling some outstanding debts with a dubious song-credit – or two. The song in question, 'Maybellene', rose to number five on the pop charts. But its actual author, a certain Chuck Berry, soon found he was receiving only a third of the publishing (and even that had to go through the Chess mill of creative accounting):

**Chuck Berry**: My first royalty statement made me aware that some person named Russ Fratto, and the Alan Freed I had phoned, were also part composers of the song. When I later mentioned to Leonard Chess the strange names added to the writing credits, he claimed that the song would get more attention with the big names involved. With me being unknown, this made sense to me, especially since he failed to mention that there was a split in the royalties as well.

Russ Fratto, a Chicago record distributor and the Chess brothers' landlord, was an even less credible co-author than Freed. But at least he had the decency to give up credit and his share of the royalties sometime in the sixties. However, as Berry ruefully revealed to *Rolling Stone* in 1972, Freed not only 'grabbed a third of the writing of "Maybellene" in lieu of my rookiness', he was still waiting for the Freed estate to return what was rightfully his.

Well, almost his. Because 'Maybellene' was actually a well-known country song disguised as R&B. As a country song it was known from the Adirondacks to the Appalachians – 'cept here it was called 'Ida Red'. And it was as traditional as they come. Recorded by Bob Wills and The Texas Playboys in 1938 and 1950 (when it reached number ten in the country charts crossing Berry's radar), it had previously enjoyed a degree of fame at the hands of Riley Puckett, Clayton McMichen, Gid Tanner, the Shelton Brothers et al. Berry would later deny they were the same song, telling Bill Flanagan, 'I planned to call it "Ida Red" but there was already an "Ida Red." Different song, different words, different melody. The other "Ida Red" had no messages whatsoever.'

Everyone else concerned knew the two began life as the same song, with a common melody and a touch of western swing. But when Leonard Chess heard it, he was inspired to make one of his little suggestions. In the words of Johnnie Johnson, Berry's pianist, 'It was [as] a western tune that Chuck wrote [it] and we had been playing [it] . . . [However, when] Leonard Chess heard it, he liked the song, but not the name.' Chess's essential objection was that it sounded too rural and Chess was an urban label with an urban sound. Drawing on his background as a cosmetician, Berry looked to the Maybelline beauty line for inspiration, changing the spelling to ensure no contravention of the Maybelline trademark.

The song still had that western feel. And since what Chess himself knew about song arranging wouldn't have filled a postcard, he deferred to his sometime session bandleader, Willie Dixon, to offer *his* three cents' worth: 'The first time I heard [Chuck Berry] he had more of a country & western style. At that time he had his song "Maybellene" sounding just like "Ida Red." I told him he should do something about it; it wasn't having the effect on people it should because it was too close to "Ida Red." I made a couple of suggestions and we found a way to record it.'

It is tempting to discount Dixon's version of events. As someone known for taking his share of credit (and royalties) on old-time blues songs rearranged for the Chess sound, and being something of an all-round hustler, can we really attach credence to his claim he told the poet laureate of rock & roll how to arrange his debut single? Actually, he probably did – though, for once, he did not get a credit on the song.

As it stands, the start of 'Maybellene' breaks all the rules of R&B songwriting. Instead of launching into the first verse, 'Maybellene' opens with its chorus and, tellingly, that chorus is a straight AAB twelve-bar blues: 'Maybellene, why can't you be true [x2]/You done started back doin' the things you used to do.' It is a daring inversion, setting the listener up to expect a straight blues. And it's precisely what Dixon had been doing with songs like 'I Just Wanna Make Love To You'. It taught Berry a vital lesson. From here on, there would be no stopping him:

> **Chuck Berry:** When I wrote 'Maybellene' I had no idea about how the business worked. Then, when that record was a hit, Leonard Chess said, 'Now write some more.' . . . They'd say, 'We need four more tracks,' and I'd just knock off some blues. You can write blues songs in no time. 'Baby please don't go, baby please don't go, I love you so, baby please don't go.' What's to that?

Berry's love of old-time country music, as profound as Leadbelly's and as deep as Ray Charles's, did not go away just because he reinvented himself as a (rhythm and) bluesman. Growing into his role as the leading songwriter of rock & roll, he simply learnt how to disguise the fact he'd 'been stealing all these years, man'. Very few noticed that 'Thirty Days', cut the same day as 'Maybellene', and riding its shirt-tails into the R&B charts, took its tune from 'When The Saints Go Marching In'. It just sounded like another of Berry's blues.* And the lyrical approach adopted on his 1964 classic, 'Promised Land', sounded so original – a black boy

---

* This did not stop Ronnie Hawkins calling it 'Forty Days' and claiming a song-credit for himself, when he recorded it for Roulette.

from Norfolk, Virginia travels all the way to California as if he were a Jew heading for the promised land; except when he reaches it, he doesn't write a gospel, he calls the operator collect and sings, 'Tell the folks back home, this is the promised land calling, and the po' boy is on the line' – that the song's distinct debt to 'Wabash Cannonball', one of Berry's favourite list songs, passed most listeners by.

A favourite of both Dylan and Springsteen, 'Promised Land' would be revisited by Elvis in 1973. By then he was struggling to command any critical attention for his current work, so mired in the past were his current performances, and so out of touch had his manager become about how to acquire material in an era when songwriters personally managed their publishing. By the time Presley's version was released, as the title track and lead single to a 1975 album, he no longer commanded centre stage in pop culture, and it charted no higher than fourteen.

When Presley had really needed songs cut from the same precarious precipice as his Sun sides – at the end of 1956, as the first adrenalin rush of success began to subside – he was already being steered away from his country roots and towards the middle of the road. And all because Hill & Range demanded a piece of the pie. At least one person Presley encountered that year was prepared to spell out the price he would pay. Bill Haley, who found himself on a package tour with the man who had made *his* kinda rock & roll redundant, told him straight, 'Elvis, you're leaning too much on ballads and what have you. You've got a natural rhythm feeling, so do your rhythm tunes.'

Elvis, in his mid-fifties pomp, clearly longed to record some of Chuck Berry's 'rhythm tunes'. He had sung 'Maybellene' at the *Louisiana Hayride* when it first charted in the summer of 1955, and seized a similar opportunity when he found himself lured into a loose jam at the end of a Carl Perkins session in December 1956. Though the so-called 'Million Dollar Quartet' focused largely on gospel standards, he found time to belt out both sides of Berry's most recent single: 'Too Much Monkey Business' (a song he was to return to in 1968) and 'Brown Eyed Handsome Man'.

Both hit the R&B charts, neither crossed the pop divide – leaving it open for Presley to do some steering of his own. If only.

In fact, it would be 1963 before he was allowed to record one of Berry's Chess pieces, presumably because Arc Music, the publishing company set up by Leonard Chess with Gene and Harry Goodman, brothers to big-band leader Benny Goodman, simply refused to surrender any of the publishing. The song in question, 'Memphis Tennessee' – which had only ever been a Berry B-side back in 1959 – again went unreleased. And when Elvis returned to it the following year he unwisely played his spruced-up version to Johnny Rivers. An inspired Rivers took the song into the studio himself and to number two in the charts, making an Elvis single out of the question.

Thankfully for fans of Elvis's early RCA oeuvre – which might have come out even more compromised – by the second half of 1956 the smarter indie-label bosses specializing in R&B realized a rapprochement with Presley and Parker was a way to cross the great divide. Also Sholes realized they were still short of material Presley was prepared to play in the studio, and had just a three-day window at the beginning of September to record the bulk of that difficult second album. Art Rupe at Venice Music (Speciality's publishing arm) worked out a deal whereby three of 'his' songs – 'Long Tall Sally', 'Ready Teddy' and 'Rip It Up' – would appear on the disc.

A meeting between Presley and Sholes on 1 July 1956, the day before Presley entered RCA's New York studio for another 'make or break' session, had finally led to an understanding of sorts between the artist and 'the money'. Between rehearsals for Elvis's debut on the Steve Allen Show (the famous occasion he sang 'Hound Dog' to a bemused basset hound), 'Sholes sat down with the young artist and tried to clear up some of their past problems and come to an agreement about material.'

Sholes presumably reiterated (or perhaps revealed to Presley for the first time) the terms of RCA's arrangement with Hill & Range. The publishers had provided a substantial part of the purchase price for Elvis's Sun contract, with the clear understanding that he would receive half of the two-cent statutory mechanical fee and half of the two-cent broadcast fee on all new Hill & Range compositions he recorded. These would be registered through his own publishing company, Elvis Presley Music. If the singer also claimed a (wholly unjustified) song-credit on any released cut – a tradition which went all the way back to Al Jolson – he would increase his cut by a further two cents a side. All he needed to do was play ball.

For now, though, the priority remained making Presley the undisputed Pop King. And that required songs which suited his way of projecting 'em – from the pelvis out. As a result, in advance of the 2 July session, a great deal of negotiation had been undertaken to ensure that one, the songs were to Elvis's liking and two, the publishing had been tied up.

'Any Way You Want Me' was a ballad (co-)written by Aaron Schroeder – who had been responsible for 'I Was The One', B-side to 'Heartbreak Hotel'. And like that earlier hit, Elvis loved it and saw how he could make it his own. He was less enamoured with the other four demos Sholes offered him. Again the titles say it all: 'Anyplace Is Paradise', 'I Ain't Studying You, Baby', 'Naughty Mama' and 'Too Much'. But, if one can believe Anne Fulchino's sleeve-notes to *Elvis' Golden Records* (1958), Sholes also presented one more demo to Presley at the session itself:

> While sipping coffee, Steve Sholes pulled out a demonstration record of 'Don't Be Cruel' and told Elvis it was a new song written by Otis Blackwell, whom Elvis had long admired as a rhythm and blues artist. It took just a few bars to convince Presley that it was a perfect song for him, and he decided to cut it right away. Presley learned the song within minutes – he has an inherent musical sense – and in short order a great master was put on tape.

In fact, the song required twenty-eight takes. But it was certainly written by Blackwell, a fair to middling R&B singer hustling his way into the songwriting game. Blackwell happily agreed to a co-credit and a 50 per cent cut in his share of the publishing just to get on board the Presley Express.

Jerry Leiber and Mike Stoller were not inclined to be so obliging when it came to 'Hound Dog'. Presley had performed the song twice on national TV in the past month and the resultant uproar, and paroxysms of moral panic, were greater than anything America had seen this side of Orson Welles's 1938 *War Of The Worlds* radio broadcast.* A failure to capitalize on such infamy by not releasing 'Hound Dog' as the next Elvis A-side would have been unthinkable. Thankfully, Leiber and Stoller, businessmen first and songwriters second, were not the final arbiters of who covered their song or what they themselves received. Though the pair had retained credit on their song, 'Hound Dog' was published at the time by Don Robey, another indie label boss who would not have been out of place in *The Sopranos*.

With the copyrights sewn up, RCA could finally release their third Presley single, 'Hound Dog' b/w 'Don't Be Cruel', on 13 July, just eleven days after both tracks were recorded. (The second RCA 78 had included another Arthur Crudup cover, 'My Baby Left Me', as flipside but failed to replicate the success of 'Heartbreak Hotel' – which it was never likely to.) The double A-side broke every record going, with both sides topping the charts, 'Hound Dog' for five weeks and 'Don't Be Cruel' for six. At the same time they topped both the Country and the R&B charts – a first for everyone, Elvis included.

The following month, RCA issued the entire contents of Elvis's eponymous debut album as singles, marking the debut of his version of 'Blue Suede Shoes' on the singles charts. Despite all the album and EP sales it had already enjoyed, it still made the Top Twenty. At the same time, a fully recovered Carl Perkins received his first royalty cheques from Sam Phillips, one in the form of mechanical royalties from Sun itself, the other

---

* Writing about these performances at a twenty-year remove, Greil Marcus, as per, sought to capture their revolutionary nature, suggesting 'Elvis's early TV performances caused so much trouble [because] Elvis, clearly perceiving the limits of what America had learned to accept as [its] shared culture, purposefully set out to shatter them.'

publishing royalties from Hi-Lo. The former was just over $12,000, the latter little more than $14,000 – a chunk of money to be sure, but hardly the stuff of Midas's dreams.

Something wasn't right. Not only had the Sun single got to number two on the pop charts under its own steam, the song had been covered by Elvis, who had sold more records than the rest of RCA put together in the last six months (fact). As related in Perkins' authorized biography, he decided to show the cheques to his wife:

> Valda [agreed] something was amiss. While attempting to decipher the accounting statement, she told Carl, 'There's no way this can be right.' Carl admitted that other artists had told him he would probably make $100,000 from his first royalty payment, given how mammoth a record 'Blue Suede Shoes' had been out of the box . . . [But] as they looked at the accounting together, one item caught their attention: Sam had deducted the price of the Cadillac from Carl's artistic earnings. So much for the grand gesture honoring Sun's first million-selling record . . . 'The accounting that Sam Phillips gave Carl was not to where you could really even count it up yourself,' Valda recounts. 'It was just so vague. Even without it, there was no way that amount of money could be right.' . . . Urging Carl to question Sam, Valda emphasized to Carl, 'Look, it's your money.' . . . He could not make himself believe Sam would cheat him.

Perkins found out the hard way that, yes, Southern Sam 'would cheat him'.

However, even if Phillips' accounting was to prove as creative as his production techniques, Carl was too busy trying to get his own career out of first gear after that calamitous car-crash to make an issue of any shortfall. Of more concern to him at this juncture was the failure of his last two singles, 'Boppin' The Blues' and 'Dixie Fried' b/w 'I'm Sorry, I'm Not Sorry', to replicate even a tenth of the sales for 'Blue Suede Shoes'. Could it be Perkins was destined to be a one-hit wonder? Or was Phillips simply not issuing the right records?

The latter certainly seemed to be the case with 'Boppin' The Blues', recorded just a fortnight before Perkins' crash. Recorded the same day but not even accorded B-side status was 'Everybody's Trying To Be My Baby', a song Perkins had adapted from an earlier one of the same title recorded by Rex Griffin, of 'Lovesick Blues' fame, back in 1936.

Questioned by his acquiescent biographer, Perkins admitted to hearing a 1938 recording by 'a group out of Dallas headed by Roy Newman . . . that combined elements of western swing and Dixieland. Lyrically the songs share some similarities in their first verses but . . . Carl has no recollection of ever hearing Newman's recording . . . and his best guess is that somewhere along the honky-tonk trail someone must have been playing the song when he was around.' It was the same song – Griffin's – which Newman (and Johnny Barfield) later covered. Perkins now changed it around and took the copyright.

Phillips had missed a trick, and four long-haired louts from Liverpool knew it. The song was a winner, as they proved when they covered it for their fourth album, *Beatles For Sale*, along with the B-side of 'Blue Suede Shoes', 'Honey Don't'. Even after the accrued worldwide sales of a Beatles LP, Perkins was no better off. Phillips was still cheating him.

Phillips's instincts failed Perkins again when he stuck 'Dixie Fried', Carl's first post-accident recording, on the B-side of the next Perkins single. A song about fighting in a dance hall, one couplet – 'Rave on, Trouble, I'm with you, Rave on, Cat, she cried/It's almost dawn and the cops have gone, So let's all get Dixie Fried' – would inspire a boy from Lubbock to rave it up too.

Perhaps, in his desperation to replicate that first chart fix, Perkins was trying too hard. On 4 December 1956, he decided to go back to his roots. The single he recorded that day was his most commercially compelling since 'Blue Suede Shoes', and again its tipping point came from a song he grew up with, Blind Lemon Jefferson's 'Matchbox Blues'. Not that he was about to admit as much. Again, his chosen biographer lamely suggested the songwriter 'had never heard Jefferson's song at the time . . . and apart from the first verse supplied by [his father] Buck, the two brook no

*141*

comparison . . . Carl remembered hearing Buck singing that same lyric around the house on occasion, but had never heard the complete song.'

Perkins had never heard of Hal Singer or Rex Griffin either, yet ended up appropriating their work. At every turn he had an explanation, just never the obvious one. But at least in the case of Jefferson, Perkins was on safe ground. That Paramount copyright was more worn than the suede shoes he left out in the rain. And his version of 'Matchbox Blues' was as raw and vital as the two songs he cut twelve months earlier, when there was still a crown for the king of rockabilly to claim.

As Perkins finished up the session, the undisputed King of Pop turned up, not to taunt his old friend but to swap some songs. One would like to think Presley was impressed by Perkins' new single, even as he remembered how it used to sound. They didn't, however, duet on it when the fabled Million Dollar Quartet jam session started – or if they did, Phillips had yet to realize history was being made and it was time to roll some tape.

'Matchbox' was released on 27 January 1957 but again Phillips sabotaged Perkins's chart chances by making it the B-side of 'Your True Love', which peaked at a disappointing sixty-seven on the Pop charts. Elvis's latest single, 'Too Much' b/w 'Playing For Keeps' released three weeks earlier, was already closing in on number one, where it would stay for three weeks. Both songs had been written to order, and copyrighted and published by the Hill & Range subsidiary, Elvis Presley Music.

They were also bloody awful. There would be more great music to come from Elvis, but it would be twelve years before he again stamped his foot and told his publisher and label he was gonna record what *he* wanted. By then, the once-hippest man on the planet had spent nigh on a decade making music for people who liked slippers and a pipe of an evening.

## CHAPTER 8

# 1956–62: Ain't Nothing You Can Do

*Featuring*: 'Hound Dog'; 'Pledging My Love'; 'Why Do Fools Fall In Love?';
'Susie Q'; 'That'll Be The Day'; 'Not Fade Away'; 'Oh Boy'; 'Peggy Sue'; 'Love
Me Tender'; 'It's Now Or Never'; 'Can't Help Falling In Love'

> There are many who enjoy glory plus financial gain's abundance,
> even in the millions, who should be digging ditches or sweeping
> the streets. Lack of proper protection causes this. I could dig up
> many tunes that were published, and benefits reaped accredited
> to one who never wrote the first note, no arranger got paid for his
> work, and the cash went to the one who was the actual thief.
>
> Jelly Roll Morton, *Down Beat*, 1938

By the standards of the day – which would run the last days of the
Roman Empire close in the moral bankruptcy stakes – Elvis Presley's
publisher was generous to a fault in offering to share the publishing on
one of the King's hits. Generally, as in Jelly Roll Morton's day, all 'the
cash went to the one who was the actual thief'. Indeed, such had almost
been the case with the song which had turned Elvis from one-hit wonder
to full-blown phenomenon, 'Hound Dog'. No wonder Jerry Leiber and
Mike Stoller, a couple of Jewish songwriters from the east who first met
at LA's City College in 1950, were wary of the first offer Hill & Range
made.

College had not been wasted on these smart cookies. After writing R&B hits for Jimmy Witherspoon, Little Willie Littlefield and Big
Mama Thornton in the early 1950s, encountering along the way numerous label bosses in shark-skin suits, they had formed their own label,

Spark Records, with mentor Lester Sill, in 1953. Signing doo-wop combo The Robins (an early version of The Coasters), they had given them the likes of 'Smokey Joe's Café' and 'Riot In Cell Block No. 9'. Bought out by Atlantic Records, Leiber and Stoller insisted on a clause which would allow them to produce for other labels – retaining a degree of autonomy when others were busy binding themselves in chains of legalese.

So when Hill & Range expressed an interest in their song, they could do as they saw fit. At least the publishers weren't suggesting putting Elvis's name to 'Hound Dog' – as would be the case with two Otis Blackwell cuts at the 'second album' sessions, 'Don't Be Cruel' and 'Paralyzed'. The pair had already had quite enough of other names appearing alongside theirs on the song, which had topped the R&B charts for seven weeks when sung by Big Mama Thornton back in 1953.

In fact, the success of Elvis's version merely stirred up the same vipers' nest all over again – with even Presley's publishing company finding itself embroiled in its first legal spat. In October 1956, the success of Presley's version prompted Valjo Music, a publishing company owned by bandleader and singer Johnny Otis, to sue Leiber and Stoller (and Elvis Presley Music). Otis wanted to be 'restored' as co-writer of 'Hound Dog' and recoup 'lost' royalties. Given that he had already lost one such case because, in the great tradition of Perry Bradford, he didn't realize forging documents was actually illegal, Otis was the one looking to get stung. But he was nothing if not tenacious when it came to unscrupulous self-aggrandizement.

Leiber and Stoller had been first introduced to Otis back in July 1952, by Federal Records boss Ralph Bass. Even then, Otis needed songs for artists he represented like Little Esther, Little Willie Littlefield and Big Mama Thornton, preferably from naive young songwriters. Leiber and Stoller were rookies, but they could still read. In particular, they read and understood the agreement they and Otis signed, which gave Otis a one-third interest in any songs Leiber-Stoller assigned to Otis's company, Valjo Music Publishing. However, that agreement did not give Otis the right to assign any of their songs to another company

– especially one owned by the notorious Don Robey – or add his own name to the mix.

When it came to 'Hound Dog', Mike Stoller recalled, '[Otis] had asked us for a third of our end of the song which we agreed to on a certain basis, but the basis was not complied with. We were *all* to co-publish the song . . . We formed a firm to publish the song[s] and then unilaterally he signed [that] song to Don Robey's firm.' When the song was initially copyrighted on 9 September 1952, it had been credited to Don Deadric Robey and Willie Mae Thornton, with Lion Publishing Co. identified as the registered publisher. By the time Leiber-Stoller produced that original signed agreement, before Thornton had taken 'Hound Dog' to the top of the R&B charts, Robey fully lived up to *his* reputation for double-dealing. Otis and Robey were kindly providing the pair with a crash-course in chicanery second to none:

> **Mike Stoller**: The exhilaration of creating something [as] good [as 'Hound Dog'] was one thing, but the reality of the cold-blooded music business was something else. Later, we learned that Johnny Otis [had] put his name on the song as a composer and indicated to Don Robey, the label owner, that he, Johnny, had power of attorney to sign for us as well . . . When we saw what he was doing, we got an attorney and a new contract from Robey . . . We were given an advance check for $1200. The song hit the R&B charts, but the check bounced.

Welcome to the Music Biz, boys! Once again, success turned a song from Orphan Annie into heir to a fortune, with a host of potential suitors. But what suitors! Otis had struck his own deal with Robey, intended to cut himself in on the song-credits, without reading the agreement previously executed with the real songwriters and had been caught out. Knowing he would need the approval of all parties if push came to shove, Robey now asked for all three signatures on the writer/publisher contract. Otis simply took matters into his own pen-toting hand. As later court-papers confirm:

Otis signed not only his name but also signed – or perhaps [more accurately] forged – the names of Stoller and Leiber to it. The president or proprietor of Lion Music Publishing Company noted the similarity of the handwriting of the signatures and made contact with Leiber and Stoller who advised him that Otis had no authority to sign their names to the agreement and that Otis was not a co-author of the song, although he was entitled to receive one-third of the royalties. Lion then arranged for a contract with Leiber and Stoller alone for the publishing rights.

Otis was not alone in wanting a share of the glory. Mama Thornton herself would later claim, 'I started to sing the words and put in some of my own, all that talkin' and hollerin' – that's my own.' *She* had a point. Her performance made Ma Rainey seem like a shrinking violet. In fact, such was the drama of her delivery that Presley made no attempt to emulate it. Rather, as Jerry Leiber notes, 'Elvis knew Big Mama's version, but that wasn't the one that got him to do it. He had heard it sung by a lounge act at the Sands Hotel in Vegas – Freddie Bell and the Bellboys. Apparently he liked the rhumba feel to the rhythm, and told his boys to work up an arrangement. So Elvis was really covering a cover.'

Otis continued to cry wolf, insisting the original verses 'had lyrics about knives and scars, all negative stereotypes. I took out a line and put in one of my own that went, "You ain't lookin' for a woman/You just lookin' for a home." . . . It was a legal swindle and I got beat out of it.' Being hoist by his own petard had left him scarred but unrepentant.

Leiber and Stoller, knowing the kind of man Otis was, and anticipating a potential problem when the Elvis version went global, had presciently got Otis to sign a release on 26 August 1956, in which he renounced all claims to the song in exchange for $750. In court, Otis would claim he had only done so because he had discovered the defendants were legal minors (i.e. under twenty-one) at the time of the original 1952 contract. But on 4 December 1957, Valjo's claim was roundly dismissed in the New York Federal Court in a damning judgment which stated that Otis himself was 'unworthy of belief' (courtspeak for pathological liar), and besides forging Leiber and Stoller's signatures on a declaration to Lion Music, had signed that release for $750 just two months before bringing the case.

All that was left for Otis was his own appropriation of the 'Bo Diddley riff' on behalf of Willie and his hand jive, and several decades of going on the radio to explain how he 'had a working arrangement where Leiber and Stoller would bring in the songs and I would edit them, make a contribution or occasionally rewrite them'. By then, Leiber and Stoller had definitively proven they needed no such help, and it was bye bye Johnny. Their experiences also taught them to steer a wide berth around Don Robey. If Elvis, or his publishing company, wanted any more Leiber-Stoller songs, they were going to have to deal direct.

Robey, like most of his fellow Dons, tended to focus on short-term gain rather than wait to see the whole picture. He had adopted the self-same stance with the late great Johnny Ace, who didn't stick around long enough to discover the downside to Robey's way of doing business. Instead, on Christmas Eve 1954, backstage in Houston with Big Mama Thornton and a young lass he was keen to impress by playing Russian Roulette, Johnny put the barrel of a .22 pistol to his head with a single bullet in its chamber and blew his brains out. As Big Mama later described it, 'The hair on his nappy head just stood straight up.'

Three weeks earlier, Robey had released the follow-up to Ace's minor hit 'Never Let Me Go' (exquisitely covered by Dylan and Baez in 1975). 'Pledging My Love' was a song he had been sitting on since the previous January, when Ace recorded it for his Duke label with the Johnny Otis Orchestra. Perhaps he was hoping the two songwriters responsible would forget they had written it: when the record appeared, it was credited to Ferdinand Washington and Don Robey. The former had indeed had a hand in it; Washington, a disabled DJ from Shreveport, home of the *Louisiana Hayride* radio show, had also written two other songs Ace recorded that day, 'Still I Love You So' and 'Anymore'. But he was no tunesmith – or lawyer. As his widow, Betty, revealed, 'He wrote "Pledging My Love" as a poem. Joe Scott, Robey's studio arranger, put [the] music to it. He wrote the music to all of Fat's [i.e. Ferdinand's] things. Don Robey never wrote a note . . . [but Fat] didn't know about copyrights. He lost all of his rights because the contract, down at the bottom, said "sold to."'

The reports of Ace's death proved good news for Robey's bank manager. The song sat for ten weeks at the top of the R&B charts, and this revenue stream was all Robey's. And although it pulled up at seventeen on the Pop charts, it would enjoy a second life when another fifties torch-balladeer released it as his last single in June 1977, only to see it stall at thirty-one. Again the Reaper lent a helping hand. When Elvis was found dead, not from a gunshot wound but 'with a whole lot of nothing running through his veins' (as Springsteen put it), 'Way Down' b/w 'Pledging My Love' reversed its chart descent and Presley's penultimate studio recording (made just before the equally prophetic 'He'll Have To Go') allowed Lion Publishing to roar again. Robey himself, though, had succumbed to a heart attack two years earlier – the first substantive proof he actually had one.

Robey would certainly have agreed with his business rival, Morris Levy at Roulette Records, that the most appealing aspect of music publishing was not just it 'accumulates into nice money', but 'it never talks back to you'. Both these label bosses disliked it when artists answered back, and disliked it even more when they sent in the accountants. The record business had always attracted its fair share of shysters, and the R&B boom of the early fifties had brought them all buzzing like flies on sherbert. Sam Phillips at Sun, Leonard Chess at Chess, Syd Nathan at King, Don Robey at Duke, were all members of a club with few scruples and fewer rules. But even these boys deferred to Morris Levy when it came to chiselling every last dime out of an act, spraying his largesse in ever decreasing circles until it all came back to him.

By the time Elvis ripped up the rock & roll rulebook, Levy was already learning to keep schtum (and make sure others did likewise) about cash payments intended to buy those all-important chart positions. The year-end 1955 issue of *Billboard* may have reported how 'the industry has its share of [disc] jockeys who indulge in doubtful extra-curricular activities – those with secret slices of publishing companies, hush-hush management contracts with recording artists, &c.', but even they weren't stupid enough to name a name like Levy.

Levy was as mobbed-up as most juke joints and jukeboxes across the land. But it was only after he bought the famous jazz club, Birdland, in the late forties that he had decided to enter the world of publishing. According to the Levy legend, it all began when he realized one had to pay BMI or ASCAP every time a song was publicly performed. So he hired George Shearing to write a theme song for the club, 'Lullaby of Birdland', and then persuaded him to sign over the copyright on the song to him. Persuasion, even then, was Levy's middle name; and when rock & roll came to stay, he was soon signing up more teenage bands than he could shake a stick, or baseball bat, at.

His most successful sortie into song publishing came in January 1956. He was nowhere near the studio when 'Why Do Fools Fall In Love?' was recorded by Frankie Lymon and The Teenagers, or the street-corner when it was first performed by doo-wop duo The Premiers. But by the time Gee Records – a label once wholly owned by George Goldner – released the Frankie Lymon version, Levy had acquired 50 per cent of the label through Joe Kolsky, a silent partner. Goldner had endeavoured to clear some gambling debts, and Levy, like all would-be mobsters, generally attached himself to 'degenerate' gamblers. It was a weakness put there by Jehovah for one of his Godless tribe of moneylenders to exploit.

The song was initially credited to Frankie Lymon, Herman Santiago and George Goldner, making it three songwriters in one – a fairly normal ratio for fifties rock & roll song-credits. If Goldner produced the record and Lymon gave it that unique, eunuchoid vocal, it was Santiago who actually (co-)wrote it, with his fellow Teenager, Jimmy Merchant (which was finally established in a 1992 court case – after the song had sold more than three million copies). During Levy's twenty-six years in charge, first Santiago's name dropped off the song and then, shortly after he bought Gee Records outright from its gambler-boss, Levy's name replaced

Goldner's. When Santiago protested to Levy personally, he was told in no uncertain terms, 'Don't come down here anymore or I'll have to hurt you.' Levy still didn't like it when those royalty cheques talked back.

Even after Levy formed his own label, Roulette, his business practices came directly from the Cosa Nostra handbook. Guitarist Robbie Robertson learnt all he needed to know about copyrights eight years before The Band's debut (when he applied all those lessons himself), by writing a couple of songs for frontman Ronnie Hawkins, then on Roulette. Robertson found 'there was my name under the song and a couple of people's names that I'd never heard of before'. And when Ritchie Cordell submitted 'It's Only Love' for Levy's big sixties act, Tommy James and The Shondells, Levy apparently returned the demo bent in half. The message came through loud and clear. If Cordell wanted the song released, Levy's name had better be on it.

Yet all the muscle that the bellicose Levy threatened to employ was rarely necessary. In most cases, it was easier to sign acts who would willingly, knowingly settle for a part share of something as opposed to 100 per cent of nothing. Leonard Chess, for one, liked to use this argument when settling some of his own debts with a share of someone else's publishing on songs the label was essentially bribing DJs to play. He remained undaunted even after *Billboard*'s December 1955 story suggested payola may yet become another word for something left to lose.

Chess was never one to discriminate. He would happily fleece any musician – red, white or blue. Thus, in spring 1957 – when he agreed to release an independent single recorded at Shreveport's top radio station, KWKH – on the Checker label, its ostensible author, Dale Hawkins, found out he had to share 'Susie Q', for it was she, with Shreveport store-owner Stan Lewis (presumably for soliciting Chess in the first place), and Eleanor Broadwater. That it should be Broadwater, and not her husband, Nashville DJ Gene Nobles, who got a credit suggests even Chess now thought it prudent to disguise such an obvious example of payola.

The real tunesmith, though, behind 'Susie Q' was not named on that label, though he was most assuredly on the Dale Hawkins recording – and a whole legion of rock's greatest moments over the next fifty years. Guitarist James Burton, another Louisiana boy brought up on Southern song values, was just seventeen when he played Hawkins an instrumental he had written, based around a 1954 Clovers record, 'I've Got My Eyes On You'. That tell-tale riff, though – one of the most distinctive series of notes in the whole of rock & roll – was all Burton's. The idea for the song's lyrics Hawkins took from an old Cotton Club Revue song called 'Doin' the Suzie Q'.

After the song rose to twenty-seven on the Pop charts, Hawkins was doing the Suzie Q all over the country. Chess, though, had insisted he leave his band behind in Shreveport; which Burton took as his cue to quit. This would be the last Leonard would ever see of the best white guitarist ever to grace a Chess record.*

Dale Hawkins was one of the many wannabe rock & rollers south of the Mason-Dixon line prepared to sell 'their' song rights for a shot at the prize. Indeed, when 'Susie Q' was finally released in May 1957, it was shipped into the shops by the same freight services that carried a new Decca single by a band from Lubbock, Texas: The Crickets. Catchily christened 'That'll Be The Day', the song was really the work of local singer-songwriter Buddy Holley. He just couldn't say so, for now.

Second only to Chuck Berry in the pantheon of rock & roll song-writers, but already in his twenties when the Crickets record appeared, Buddy was in a hurry to make Holly a household name (whereas Diddly acquired an extra 'e', Holley dropped his). In fact, he made his intentions plain when he presented himself to the record's producer, Norman Petty, at the latter's studio in Clovis, New Mexico, with the immortal opening line, 'If you can get Buddy Knox a hit, you can get me one.'

Holly was referring to a Knox 45 Petty had let slip through his hands

---

* Dale's cousin, Ronnie, treated his guitarists somewhat better, and thus continued to enjoy the services of Robbie Robertson and Roy Buchanan, the former until 1964, the latter until he noticed how intently Robertson watched his solos.

earlier that year. Even though Petty had produced 'Party Doll', it had ended up on Roulette, where success was assured, even if royalties were not. (It actually made number one on the *Cashbox* chart for a week.) Petty wasn't about to make that mistake again; or the one he made a year earlier, when he failed to sign the singer of another nonsense song recorded at Clovis – 'Ooby Dooby' – leaving Roy Orbison to re-record it a few weeks later at Sam Phillips' Sun shack.

As Knox later observed, 'Norm had a magic ear, he could spot things that you didn't know were there, but he [also] realized he had missed something by allowing us to get signed up in New York. he made sure he hung onto Holly.' That meeting of desperate minds in February 1957 came after Holly had already demoed versions of 'Bo Diddley' and 'Brown Eyed Handsome Man' at his own expense under Petty's greedy gaze. But neither of those songs came with copyright. The pair they recorded the evening of 24–25 February did – and between them, they would generate enough rancour to outlive both men.

Once again, the battleground would be song-credits. Petty would claim on a number of occasions in the quarter of a century he had on his Buddy, 'If I made a major change, my name went on a song; if I didn't . . . I didn't put my name on the song.' We have only one person's word on this – Petty's. All other parties involved say the exact opposite. In fact, Cricket Niki Sullivan told Holly's first biographers, 'I cannot remember *any* [my italics] songs that Norman definitely had a hand in.'

Even the song they recorded in two takes at two in the morning on 25 February 1957 ended up credited to Jerry Allison, Buddy Holly and Norman Petty. However, this was a song Holly and The Crickets had already recorded, seven months earlier, during a year-long try-out for Decca Records that resulted in just one flop single.

When that version of 'That'll Be The Day' was eventually released, it was identical in every way to the one Petty produced save for a beefed-up rhythm track and judicious use of Petty's echo chamber. Hardly enough to warrant a third share of a million-seller even if, as Petty regularly claimed, *his* production was key. (It is another claim the song's real co-author Jerry

Allison disputes: 'Norman did very little by way of production. I would say that Buddy and I really produced it . . . Norman put out the microphones and ran the board – he was [really] the engineer.')

The song itself had been written by Allison and Holly after the pair, in Allison's words, 'went to see [John Ford's] *The Searchers* . . . For a couple of days afterwards, we were mocking the way that John Wayne said, "That'll Be The Day." Then we wrote the song. The first time we recorded it was in Nashville for Decca Records. It was the summer of '56 and I had just gotten out of school. The producer [Owen Bradley] said, "That's the worst song I've ever heard in my life."'

At least Petty had the wit to realize it was nothing of the sort. In exchange for a large slice of the resultant pie – and every pie after that – he agreed to find Holly a record deal. Chastened by the loss of Orbison and Knox, he had hit on a way of doing business that was almost a return to the pre-Peer days. Rather than charging an act for session time – and Allison disputes even this, insisting 'we had paid for the session' at which 'That'll Be The Day' was recorded – Petty would offer 'an alternative deal involving as many free recording sessions as it took, followed by his best efforts to place the masters for release, in return for the music publishing on the song, which he in turn would split 50-50 with his co-publishers, Peer-Southern Music in New York.' In other words, the author/s would be lucky if they saw 25 per cent of their own song. How ironic that not only was Ralph Peer Petty's publisher, but as a result of this association Holly would later meet, date and marry Peer's receptionist, Maria Elena Santiago, who would drive a wedge between the pair and a stake into their one-sided partnership the minute she realized her new-found husband was being royally shafted.

In later life, Petty claimed his business methods were 'a romantic dreamer's way to handle business . . . We felt that the time we invested in creating copyrights merited spending all the time in the world doing it.' (What a telling phrase that is – not creating music, but 'creating *copyrights*'.) But Petty had simply devised a new way of exploiting other 'romantic dreamers'.

In keeping with standard practice in the fifties, if any song took more than a day to record, they were doing something wrong. In the case of The Crickets' first single it took just five hours, starting at 9 p.m. on 24 February, after a ninety-mile drive from Lubbock. Which means Holly ended up paying the highest session fee of all time on 'That'll Be The Day', a song which has earned seven figures in its own right, in exchange for a single night in a makeshift studio in New Mexico, large parts of which Petty had built with his own bare hands (and parts of whose echo chamber Holly himself apparently helped to build).

The minute Petty arranged Holly's record deal with Brunswick Records – a subsidiary of the label who'd rejected the singer some months earlier, unaware they already had 'dibs' on the song Petty was peddling – he assumed control of the purse strings. Any three-way cut on the publishing was merely for show. From the start, every member of The Crickets was required to give Petty power of attorney, while all income from publishing, touring and recording was fed through the same Petty funnel. If they (and the local Baptist church) were lucky, some of it might come their way. According to Cricket Joe B. Mauldin, they weren't: 'I don't think I ever received any money directly from the music publishers until after we split with Petty, after Buddy's death. All the money, even the BMI cheques, went to Petty.'

The choice of song Holly recorded that February night played right into Petty's hands. It contravened a prior agreement not to record any song from their 1956 Decca sessions for the next five years, even if – as in the case of 'That'll Be The Day' – the track remained unreleased. Petty, apprised of the problem, got around it by releasing the record as by 'The Crickets'.

There was still the issue of the publishing, which Holly had in theory already assigned to Cedarwood Music, co-owned by Webb Pierce, another Nashville singer who wanted it both ways. Fortunately, Holly had left Petty some negotiating room by 'forgetting' to sign the publishing contract previously sent him by Cedarwood. It is highly unlikely Petty revealed to Holly the nature of his settlement with Cedarwood

Music, but the result was Petty now owned the publishing, and was in a position to ensure nobody else received the kind of money they were expecting. Where it went, even Petty couldn't explain. When Holly had an audit done on one of Petty's bank accounts the week before he died, he was shocked to find less than $5,000 in it. Even after the famous 'church tax' Petty supposedly applied to the first Holly/Crickets recording, no one knew where all this money had gone.*

Petty was as careless about credit as he was about cash – *if* it happened to involve any contribution made by a Cricket, yet was remarkably consistent about adding his own name to the label, warranted or not. As Jerry Allison says, 'Until the records came out, we didn't know who would get the credits on the songs.' It was only when Brunswick released their third Holly single (after 'Peggy Sue' almost replicated his debut single's performance) that Jerry Allison found his name excluded from the B-side, 'Not Fade Away' – despite being responsible for 'that verse about my love being bigger than a Cadillac'. Instead, Petty made himself co-author of another song written around the old 'Hambone' riff. The song in question would prove one of Petty's most consistent earners.

Nor was it only members of the Crickets who could be mystifyingly absent from a song credit. Holly himself was missing from the credits when 'Peggy Sue' was first released (though, surprise, surprise, Petty wasn't). Petty even had the stones to claim, when challenged, that he wrote the lyrics. If he did, he never wrote anything like it again. Allison attributes just one line to the producer's input – 'Peggy Sue, Peggy Sue, pretty pretty pretty pretty Peggy Sue'. A natural born poet, indeed.

Other songwriters who fell prey to Petty were given no choice but to sign away a third of their songs if they wanted cast-iron success, in the

---

* According to Holly biographer Ellis Amburn, 'Petty strong-armed them [all] into donating a whopping 40 per cent of the royalties on their first record to the Baptist church. They all joined hands and prayed before signing the contract.' Later on, when Holly complained to Petty he couldn't even pay his church dues, Petty supposedly replied, 'Well, I'm tithing with y'all's money here at our church and it goes to the same place.' But as Buddy's brother, Larry, put it, 'He got all the money in, [and] did what he wanted with it.' The church got a new pipe organ.

shape of a Buddy Holly and The Crickets single. Sonny West, a rockabilly singer in his own right, had demoed 'Oh Boy' (co-written with Bill
Tilghman) at Clovis. When Holly heard it, he wanted it for himself. As
such West was summoned by Petty to sign some paperwork *if* he wanted
a Holly hit to his name: 'Norman Petty gave me no choice [about the
credits]. It was either that, or not get it [put] out. After I heard the way
that Buddy's version sounded, there was no way that I could turn it down.
Norman had the power and he did that to so many other guys. He took a
half or a third of almost every song there, plus the publishing.'*

But by the end of 1958 Holly was married to Maria. And, thanks to her
(or her aunt's) intimate knowledge of the Peer publishing set-up, he had
seen the light and cancelled Petty's power of attorney. As Jerry Allison
suggests, 'He was fed up with Norman Petty . . . Norman kept telling
us, "When the money comes in, we'll divide it up."' But the money never
came in. Petty retaliated by freezing the newlyweds' bank accounts, and
getting a court order stopping Coral Records and Southern Music from
dispensing funds directly to 'his' artist. Even after Holly's death, Petty
refused to surrender the unreleased masters he'd retained, insisting he
and only he would oversee their release.

In 1962, the estate reluctantly agreed to let him prepare some of these
masters for release. The results – full of crude, ill-conceived overdubs by
inappropriate backing singers and his personal pickup band, The Fireballs
– provided another instance of Petty's skill at 'creating copyrights'.
Thankfully, the British bands who had grown up with The Crickets'
recordings took that original template and ran with it, leaving Petty
embroiled with Maria in ever more acrimonious legal disputes. Holly's
widow claimed that even 'Buddy's original contract was suspect, and his
one with Brunswick as well. Norman Petty . . . had signed the contracts
and he had no reason to sign for Buddy Holly. Buddy couldn't remember

---

* West eventually stood up to Petty, after recording his own solo single, 'The Hula Hoop
  Song': 'I told him that I would not give him writer's credit on the song as he had nothing to do with it. He already had the contract typed out and he ripped it up and threw it
  down on the table . . . That's the last time I recorded there.'

signing anything. Even in litigation, they wouldn't let me see the [actual] contract.'

At least she had youth on her side. In 1984, Petty was finally required to explain to his God where those church funds had gone. Claiming to the end that it was the 'Holly-Petty partnership' that had made Buddy the great white hope of rock & roll after Presley spectacularly dropped the ball in 1957–8, he conveniently forgot Holly had already moved on when he took that last fateful flight and, with selections like 'Wishing', 'Love Has Made A Fool of You' and 'Learning The Game', was writing some of the best songs of his short life.

At the time, it probably seemed to Holly (and to Elvis's label) that the Presley phenomenon was in imminent danger of blowing itself out. Throughout 1958, RCA had been steadily issuing the few songs Elvis had cut before his army induction to keep the revenue stream flowing. But by the winter of 1959, they were running short of ideas – and compliant songwriters. Meanwhile, at a time when Otis Blackwell's offerings were becoming increasingly formulaic, and other rock & roll songwriters were saving their songs for themselves, Colonel Parker seemed determined to sabotage Elvis's working relationship with Leiber and Stoller.

Since the start of 1957, Leiber-Stoller had proven to be the most consistently inventive songwriters Presley could call on whenever he needed a new song. Having his name put to songs penned by others was something which had caused Elvis himself acute embarrassment (as he told one journalist straight, 'I've never written a song in my life'), and Leiber and Stoller had finally come on board after Hill & Range had put a new deal in place which meant Elvis no longer had his name attached to others' songs.

Instead, the songwriter/s would be asked to sign a document surrendering one-third of their royalties. This third was to be 'reserved out', to be 'paid to Elvis Presley personally'. It meant the real writers only got a third, instead of half the initial publishing, the remaining third going to the publisher. However, they retained the performance royalties paid by

ASCAP or BMI directly to the songwriter (or his publisher). Elvis took his 33 per cent royalty only on songs first recorded by him, and then only in their original incarnation.

This new arrangement suited Leiber-Stoller just fine. Their two-man song factory was soon pumping out songs for every Elvis occasion – a film soundtrack, a new single, even a Christmas album. But as they were soon to discover, anyone with a business head who got too friendly with the singer need fear the wrath of the Colonel. Elvis's manager would rather jeopardize his own artist's future than allow anyone else to shape Presley's universe. When Mike Stoller, prior to the first September 1957 session, played their latest song directly to Elvis, Parker instructed Hill & Range's Freddy Bienstock to set them straight. The song was 'Don't', and once again Leiber-Stoller demonstrated their commercial instincts were second to none. But rather than calling to express his gratitude for another surefire winner, Bienstock phoned Jerry Leiber to chew him out:

> **Jerry Leiber**: I get a call from Freddy Bienstock, 'What is your partner doing giving a song to Elvis Presley?' . . . He sounds enraged . . . 'Freddy, what's the problem, man? Did Elvis hate the song?' 'No, the problem is that he likes it.' 'That's a problem?' I ask. 'It is when we don't have a contract. Nothing's written down. You just don't hand a song to Elvis without a contract. In fact, you don't hand a song to Elvis at all. You hand a song to me or to Jean Aberbach. Then we get the business straight first.' 'Well, when Mike and I wrote the song, we presumed the business would be the same as all business with Elvis: the Colonel is going to demand that Elvis and the Aberbachs own the publishing rights, right?' 'Right . . . [but] it's a question of procedure. The Colonel hates it when anyone goes behind his back.'

Strike one. At the following day's session, the prolific pair played Presley another of their new songs, 'Santa Claus Is Back In Town'. Leiber immediately sensed that 'the Colonel thinks it's too bluesy and too black.

But before he can say anything, the King speaks out: "Now that's what I call a goddamn great Christmas song!"' The song stayed. And Parker fumed. Strike two.

Three months passed and Elvis needed songs for the soundtrack to his last pre-army film, *King Creole*. Again, it was Leiber and Stoller who came up with a right royal title track *and* the belligerent 'Trouble', reminding MGM (and Parker) that a real acting job, based on a proper book (Harold Robbins' *A Stone For Danny Fisher*), need not jeopardize Presley's pop crown.

By decade's end, however, Leiber-Stoller no longer needed Hill & Range like Hill & Range needed them. They had The Coasters, and very soon acquired their own record label, Red Bird. And at the end of 1959, Parker finally overplayed his hand, as he was wont to do, not realizing that without quality songs, and therefore compliant songwriters, Elvis was just a set of strong lungs and a nice haircut (the sexy sideburns he'd already surrendered to the GI bill). What happened next would have repercussions that would reverberate throughout Elvis's long, slow commercial decline. As Ernst Jorgensen relates in his epic Elvis sessionography, *A Life In Music*:

Paramount ha[d] asked that Jerry Leiber and Mike Stoller help out at the [*G.I. Blues*] recording sessions . . . but their request came just as tension was building again between the two writers and the Presley organization. Earlier, Jerry Leiber, without saying anything to the Colonel directly, . . . pitched the idea of Elvis starring in a film version of *A Walk On The Wild Side* . . . To Tom Parker this kind of unilateral meddling in Elvis's business affairs was tantamount to treason, and Leiber was warned in no uncertain terms that if he ever tried to intervene again it would be the end of their association with Presley. For Leiber and Stoller, that was the end of the line. They were already discouraged, even disgusted, with Parker's lack of artistic ambition and vision . . . What rankled them even further was the Colonel's insistence that Hill & Range get publishing rights to even the Leiber and Stoller songs that were *cut* from a soundtrack album . . . With the exception of 'She's Not You' [which they wrote with Doc Pomus in 1962], they never again wrote a new song for Elvis Presley.

Otis Blackwell, Presley's other tame A-grade songwriter, would soon buckle under the pressure of expectation – though not before he contributed 'Return To Sender', Elvis's last great single before Beatlemania crashed on his country's shores. Doc Pomus also managed to keep up a steady supply for the first three years of the sixties. But by the time The Beatles signed to Vee-Jay [sic] the only moments when Elvis seemed able to shake like he did before was when he remembered some old number by Ray Charles ('What'd I Say') or Chuck Berry ('Memphis Tennessee', 'Too Much Monkey Business'). Good songwriters always had other options – as Leiber and Stoller had proven.

The rot did not stop there. Jorgensen himself notes how the 'successful commercial and creative songwriters like Doc Pomus and Mort Shuman . . . Don Robertson, and Otis Blackwell eventually lost interest in writing for Elvis [because] not only were they required to give up a third of their normal songwriting royalties, but often as not they found their efforts rejected as movie title after movie title was discarded.'

Parker's particular method of song gathering – counting every red cent while the Presley punters revolted – was yielding less and less. Even Presley's personal songhunter duly admitted to a lack of quality control:

**Freddy Bienstock**: Elvis had contracts to make three motion pictures a year, and to be honest, there was never enough time to score them properly. I was given the script and we always managed to find a title song. The scripts never indicated where the songs should be, and I had to mark up where songs were possible. I would then distribute twelve scripts to twelve different teams, and tell them to work on songs for certain situations. I would get four or five songs for each situation and I would take them to Elvis who would select them. Both the mass production and the fact of being tied down to titles like *Kissin' Cousins*, *Wild In The Country* and *Harum Scarum* made everything very difficult. It was difficult to get hit songs, and the quality suffered.

Initially, Parker's (or Bienstock's) solution to this potential drought was surprisingly creative. Writing fresh lyrics to out-of-copyright songs was nothing new; it was just that – as the Carters and Rodgers had discovered – one had to tread carefully.* So the Colonel cast his mind back to a time when Elvis could do no wrong – the fall of 1956, and a song Hill & Range had claimed the publishing on after commissioning Ken Darby, a conveyor-belt film writer, to write new lyrics to the civil war ballad, 'Aura Lee'. Darby came up with 'Love Me Tender', a song which matched 'Hound Dog' for commercial impact – even if Elvis never sang those lachrymose lyrics straight again.

At an all-night session designed to get an album's worth of songs in the shops as the hype about Presley's release from the army hit hyperdrive, someone suggested reworking the old parlour ballad, 'Are You Lonesome Tonight?', last given the treatment by the Carters back in 1929.

Presley was also convinced to test his operatic range on 'O Sole Mio', an Italian folksong adapted by Tony Martin for his 1949 hit, 'There's No Tomorrow'. When Freddy Bienstock tried to secure the usual Elvis Presley Music cut-in on Martin's song, which Presley had always liked, he was rebuffed. So he simply commissioned his own set of English lyrics from Aaron Schroeder, who came up with 'It's Now Or Never'.

The following year, it was France's turn, as Elvis mined the nineteenth-century standard 'Plaisir D'Amour' for 'Can't Help Falling In Love'. The new version, written by George Weiss, supposedly in tandem with production team Luigi Creatore and Hugo Peretti, was perhaps the one redeeming feature from the otherwise awful *Blue Hawaii* film

---

* When, for example, Les Paul wrote 'Johnny (Is The Boy For Me)' in 1953, to the tune of a Romanian composer, Richard Stein, it turned out the 1937 composition ('Sanie Cu Zurg') was still in copyright.

soundtrack. And 'Can't Help Falling In Love' was to prove Weiss's calling card when later in 1961 he was asked to adapt another 'traditional' song from across the Atlantic.

It would be eight years before Elvis again scaled the chart heights reached by 'Can't Help Falling In Love', a number two single in October 1961. In that time, the Colonel's chosen course, which demanded composers give up half the publishing for the honour of an Elvis cover, had rarely deviated. But by the late sixties no serious songwriter sought out such an honour, and Presley was running out of songs he could stomach, let alone sing. The path to redemption opened up just once, during a heady month at Chips Moman's Memphis-based American Studios in January/ February 1969, when Elvis told all concerned he wanted the best songs, and the publishing could go hang.

No sooner had Elvis recorded his best album in a decade, though, than that ol' devil called publishing reared its head again. And this time the dispute centred on a song that everyone present knew could single-handedly revive Elvis's singles career. 'Suspicious Minds', a song Moman had suggested to Elvis, was given the kinda treatment that rekindled memories of the last time he recorded in Memphis.

But Moman – co-author of that perennial, 'Dark End Of The Street' – owned the publishing on the Mark James song. When Freddy Bienstock, still at Hill & Range, hustling on Elvis's behalf, became insistent about splitting the publishing, Chips suggested he take the $25,000 RCA had paid to rent Moman's studio and stick it up his ass.

If Bienstock thought he was negotiating from a position of strength he was wrong, so wrong. Even Elvis now knew. Marty Lacker, one of Elvis's so-called Memphis Mafia, remembers how at the end of the first set of American sessions in January 1969, 'We listened to [some] Hill & Range demos up in his office . . . [and] Elvis said, "I ain't got any more good songs." . . . I [finally] said something to *Elvis Presley* – "They don't need you anymore." He said, 'What?' I said, 'They don't want to give up the publishing anymore. There are lots of artists who write songs that sell a million records, but every time they come to us we have to send them to Hill & Range.'

Given that Hill & Range's Lamar Fike was in the room at the time, and was sure to report what Lacker said to Parker and Bienstock, his outburst took some nerve; but his old friend needed to hear the news: rock & roll was dead, and Steve Sholes was no longer at his side. Elvis's new RCA record rep., Harry Jenkins, knew just how much Elvis needed another number one, and came down on Moman's side. 'Suspicious Minds' duly became Elvis's seventeenth and last number one US single. Again Presley had proved that when he did put his foot down, he could still cut it. But as soon as he stopped stamping, it was a case of normal service resumed; the Colonel made damn sure he never worked with Moman again.

And still, a decade in the commercial wilderness failed to serve as the requisite reminder that without the right songs he was nothing but a jump-suit with a jumped-up manager. Presley's career returned to a rut, and once again, he voiced his dissatisfaction at the songs his publisher was bringing him. Parker's solution – 'to give Elvis more control over the songs he'd record, and also to keep more of the publishing money in their own organization' – required setting up for his artist a new publishing company, Whitehaven Music. And so began the hunt for a species everyone else suspected was extinct: the next great standard written by someone so desperate to have Presley put his stamp on it that they would surrender half the publishing in perpetuity.

Finally, in 1974, after a series of sessions at Stax studios in 1973 had produced very little chart material (the most promising cut – Presley's belated cover of Berry's 'Promised Land' – was held over), Whitehaven thought they had found the right song. 'I Will Always Love You', recently recorded by its authoress, Dolly Parton, and a number one country hit, had nonetheless stayed away from the Hot Hundred. Parker (and Parton) knew Presley, with that power-ballad voice of his, could take it there. If only the lady would give up half the publishing.

But Parton was cut from the same block of hard wood as Chips

Moman. Moreover she already had enough on her plate fending off the financial (and other) advances of her erstwhile partner-in-song, Porter Wagoner, for whom the song had in fact been written, as a plea for understanding he refused to give. (As she later said, 'I wrote the song "I Will Always Love You," because he wouldn't listen to me. I wrote it to say, "I appreciate what you've done, but if I stay around here, I'm going to be in your way and you're going to be in mine."') She told Presley's publisher to go find another fool. Such a fool could not be found; and instead of being the first to take one of the best-selling songs of all time into the pop charts, Presley preferred to record secret message-songs like 'She Thinks I Still Care' and 'I Really Don't Want To Know'.

By April 1977, Presley had retreated almost entirely into his once-glorious past. The set-list for that spring's tour was almost devoid of songs he'd recorded during the seventies. It was like the man yearned to be back where he started – singing 'That's Alright Mama', 'Trying To Get To You', 'Lawdy Miss Clawdy', 'Mystery Train', 'I Got A Woman', 'What'd I Say', 'Johnny B. Goode', 'C. C. Rider' and those great Leiber-Stoller and Otis Blackwell songs he had made his own, 'Hound Dog', 'Jailhouse Rock' and 'Don't Be Cruel'. In Saginaw, Michigan on 3 May, just six of the two dozen songs performed post-dated those fifties glory days. Three months later, he was dead. For some time he had been making ends meet by selling the soul of his own music.

In fact, for a decade and a half Presley had continued displaying his lack of musical roots, like he was Hill & Range's very own tabula rasa. His personal reservoir of songs, it seemed, barely skimmed the surface of Popular Song. When he sat at home and plonked out a tune for himself, and himself alone, it was invariably a post-war R&B tune, a gospel song or some piece of ersatz tradition, like 'Danny Boy' or 'I'll Take You Home Again, Kathleen'. Only when he was allowed to do a gospel album, as he was in 1966, did he bring something of himself to the welcome table, grabbing arrangement credits on no less than five songs on *How Great Thou Art?* – two of which had been previously composed by

Charles A. Tindley at the turn of the century, 'Stand By Me' and 'Bye and Bye'.*

At no point does Presley ever seem to have been driven to return to the source/s. It was something that always set him apart from his label-mates at Sun, all of whom outlived him. Carl Perkins' criticism of 'the new guys [who] don't go that far back with the music – they go back with the records. We go from the record on down to the cotton patch where it came from,' could be applied just as appositely to Elvis.

But it did not apply to Johnny Cash or Jerry Lee Lewis, the two other artists who kept Phillips' Southern fiefdom going through the fifties. And their *musical* influence on the next wave of song catchers would prove as profound as Presley's *sociological* impact. As Cash proved during his time at Sun, he was not averse to covering (in style) 'Goodnight Irene' or 'The Wreck Of The Ol' 97'. Even after he reinvented himself at Columbia as a man for all seasons, he still tap-danced either side of the sliver-thin divide that separated country from folk. He also knew two of the biggest hits of the fifties had been The Weavers' version of 'Goodnight Irene' and the Kingston Trio's 'Tom Dooley', both songs he heard before either act was a twinkle in an A&R man's eye.

Cash may not have predicted the great folk revival of the early sixties, but he *had* seen that train a-coming, rolling round the bend. And he was right there with 'em – even prefacing the change with a history lesson of his own in the guise of country boogie versions of 'Keep On The Sunny Side' and 'Rock Island Line' – at Newport in 1964, when Dylan changed the very paradigm of popular song for all there to hear.

---

* At the same sessions he recorded his most traditional tune to date, the fifteenth-century 'Westron Wind', but he didn't know it. *He* thought he was covering Bob Dylan's 'Tomorrow Is A Long Time', beautifully, after guitarist Charlie McCoy played him Odetta's album of Dylan covers.

CHAPTER 9

# 1950–65: All's Fair In Love and Theft

*Featuring*: 'Goodnight Irene'; 'Rock Island Line'; 'Hang Your Head Tom Dooley'; 'Where Have All The Flowers Gone'; 'We Shall Overcome'; 'Turn Turn Turn'; 'Blowin' In The Wind'; 'Masters of War'; 'Don't Think Twice (It's Alright)'; 'House of The Rising Sun'; 'Scarborough Fair'

> Folk music is a process. The old is continually being made new . . . Two things play [hell] with the folk process: the copyright and the cult of originality. Some people will change a song, not to improve it but just to get a copyright on it. Originality, or maybe I should say novelty, has come to be so prized that people no longer care whether a thing is any good or not, so long as it's new.
>
> Pete Seeger, in 'The Ballad of Pete Seeger', *Holiday* magazine, 1965

In the second half of the fifties, two parallel streams of popular song vied with rock & roll for the hearts and souls of the young – and both set themselves in opposition to the superficiality of Pop and 'the cult of originality'. One came laced with a heavy dose of socialist rhetoric, seemed to think *der Volk* was shorthand for working folk, and cast the saintly Pete Seeger, a radicalized Woody Guthrie and folkloric ideologue Alan Lomax in Jean Brodie-like roles. This was the American folk revival, holier than thou and proprietorial as hell. The other was viewed by most of the English-speaking world as no more than a harmless fad, but was probably the single most important reason the sixties Beat explosion happened in Britain and not America. Its moniker was Skiffle.

In each case, the spark that lit the 'Trad.' touchpaper was a Leadbelly song, just not the same one. In America's case, it was The Weavers' version of 'Goodnight Irene' which set off fireworks. The Weavers, a singing quartet featuring a young, idealistic Pete Seeger, hardly pushed the song at their first Decca recording session. Rather, they chose for the A-side 'Tzena Tzena Tzena', a Palestinian song sung in Hebrew they were fairly sure was traditional but put in their publisher's name, anyway.

Remarkably, this peculiar little song rose to number two, shortly after Anton Karas's otherworldly, zither-based 'Third Man Theme' spent eleven weeks at number one. However, *Billboard* hadn't seen nothing yet. When DJs flipped the record over, they found Irene's last goodnight, minus the verse about injecting morphine, and with Leadbelly's threat to '*get* you in my dreams' made as corny as The Weavers' vocal harmonies by substituting, 'I'll see you in my dreams'. The record sold over two million copies in the US alone, and within weeks the likes of Frank Sinatra and Doris Day were rushing out their versions of this 'bad nigger' ballad.

Two months later, the song was sitting on top of the country charts, courtesy of Red Foley and Ernest Tubb; the following month it entered the R&B charts, murdered afresh by Paul Gayten. In October 1950, the *New York Times* estimated that the song could be heard 1,400 times a minute across the United States. All of which must have made Joel Newman a happy man, for he was the songwriter apparently responsible for this nineteenth-century minstrel song.

Except, of course, there was no 'Joel Newman'. 'Joel Newman' was a composite of the late Leadbelly (who died the previous year), John Lomax (who had died two years earlier), and Alan Lomax, John's heir and Leadbelly's music publisher. As such the prime beneficiary of a song that was, in truth, as public domain as they came, was Lomax Jnr. The fledgling folk revival's favourite folklorist was doing alright, Jack.

Likewise there was no 'Paul Campbell', another name The Weavers bandied around when covering traditional fare, to ensure they benefited from 'the cult of originality' and got *all* the publishing (a 'Trad. Arr. Weavers' credit would have only entitled them to a half-share on the eighteenth-century 'Blow Ye Winds of The Morning'). Indeed, 'Paul Campbell' covered up a multitude of credit-stealing sins. In 1951 The Weavers would record another of Campbell's classics – 'Wimoweh'. But this was no field recording, or Israeli hora; it was Pete Seeger's mis-transcribed version of an a cappella 78 released in 1939 by a Zulu singer called Solomon Linda.

The record had been released in South Africa as 'Mbube' by an Italian immigrant, Eric Gallo, who started out selling imported hillbilly records to working-class South Africans. Gallo acquired the copyright outright from Linda before, in 1951, the large, grasping hands of Alan Lomax carried a copy of 'Mbube' across the Atlantic and into the apartment of Pete Seeger.

Seeger seemed to simply assume the song was 'traditional', even though by his own admission he had a copy of the original Gallo recording, credited unambiguously to Solomon Linda and the Hummingbirds. Quite why Seeger made his assumption and left it at that, he was never called on to explain, being a past master at deflecting awkward questions about the multiple contradictions his copyright chicanery threw up. Seeger set about transcribing the song, but given his non-existent grasp of Zulu, he managed to turn 'Uyimbube' into 'Wimoweh' and make the song sound not like an African folk chant à la 'Hambone', but a western folksong.

The result was another Top Ten single for The Weavers, and, having asked exactly no questions about the song's provenance, Seeger and co. simply credited the song to their favourite alias, 'Paul Campbell'.

Gallo, to his credit, was aware enough to realize 'Wimoweh' was 'Mbube'. In exchange for not contesting the 'Paul Campbell' credit, he struck a deal with The Weavers' publisher, Howie Richmond, which gave Richmond 100 per cent of the US publishing for 'Wimoweh' in exchange for Gallo administering the song in the English-speaking parts of Africa. Seeger would later claim, 'Originally we were going to send [all] the royalties to Gallo. [But] I said, "Don't do that, because Linda won't get a penny."' (This was the self-same Linda who was named on the 78 Seeger had learnt the song from, before crediting 'Wimoweh' to the apocryphal Campbell.)

Seeger later claimed, 'I understood that the money was going to

Linda.' Actually he never took the trouble to find out. As for Seeger's belated caveat, that he should have made 'sure the publisher signed a regular songwriting [agreement] with Linda', but it was so much self-serving sound and fury. As it happens, Gallo was the legal owner of the song; whatever Seeger liked to say, Linda never saw a dime from The Weavers' 'Wimoweh'.

Meanwhile, in Britain Leadbelly's influence was being felt far more widely. In the coffee bars and basement clubs, a form of 'trad.' consisting of one-third jazz, one-third blues and one-third jive was providing a Britain that still rationed its food with a welcome dose of good-time music. And in 1956, when Lonnie Donegan's version of 'Rock Island Line' went Top Ten both sides of the pond, this particular tinderbox was set to commercially explode.

Needless to say, the success of skiffle meant it soon crossed Alan Lomax's radar, though his version of how this happened stretches the bounds of credulity, given that 'Rock Island Line' was already in the American Top Ten by the latter part of 1956. According to a recent biographer, it was only when Alan was passing a music store window in Piccadilly, London that 'he saw a copy of the sheet music to "Bring Me A Little Water, Sylvie" [sic], composed, it said, by Lonnie Donegan ... [It] sent Alan off on a quest to find Kelly Pace, who had taught Leadbelly the song in Arkansas State Penitentiary in 1934 ... When he finally located Pace, he sent a letter asking him if he was the composer ... so he could see that Pace was properly renumerated ... Lonnie Donegan, he discovered, was copying Leadbelly's songs, along with his performance style and introductory remarks, profiting from both.'

The song Leadbelly actually learnt from Kelly Pace (among others) was 'Rock Island Line', and though Lomax's first impulse was to sue – on Pace's behalf, of course – 'he was advised that it was far more complicated, difficult and expensive than he thought to protect the rights to these songs.' It might prove especially difficult if one couldn't claim actual *authorship*. English courts didn't tend to assign publishing royalties to those who had simply transcribed someone else's song.* Lomax's only recourse – and in keeping with his conflict-driven character, it was one he took – was to bad-mouth Donegan in print, something he finally managed in 1964, when the skiffle craze had given way to the Brit Beat boom. Although no one any longer cared, his entry for 'Rock Island Line' in *The Penguin Book of American Folk Songs* (a book only made possible by the folk boom in Britain that Donegan and skiffle had triggered) read:

> John A. Lomax recorded this song at the Cumins State Prison farm, Gould, Arkansas, in 1934 from its convict composer, Kelly Pace. The Negro singer, Lead Belly, heard it, rearranged it in his own style, and made commercial phonograph recordings of it in the 1940s. One of these recordings was studied and imitated phrase by phrase, by a young English singer of American folk songs [i.e. Donegan], who subsequently recorded it for an English company. The record sold in the hundreds of thousands in the US and England, and this Arkansas Negro convict song, as adapted by Leadbelly, was published as a personal copyright, words and music, by someone whose contact with the Rock Island Line was entirely through the grooves of a phonograph record.

One can almost hear the sound of gnashing teeth as the man choked back those accursed words, 'through the grooves of a phonograph record'. As for Pace – who was just one member of the chain gang Lomax recorded in Gould, Arkansas – and his claim to have written 'Rock Island Line', there was one person who knew, or should have known, this was a lie: Alan Lomax. He surely noticed that his father, and his father's travelling

---

* In fact, the Lomaxes' specific brief when hired by the Library of Congress *as employees* had been to collect songs *from tradition*. Therefore, as Legman says, the material he 'signboarded as private property, under the copyright law, for twenty-eight or fifty-six years, [had been] collected . . . in part on funds allotted by the United States government . . . with the intention of saving *for the American people* some authentic vestiges of its fast-disappearing folklore.' That mission statement Alan had long ago ripped up.

companion, Leadbelly, had recorded a version of the song at another prison in Little Rock, Arkansas, the previous month.[*]

Lomax – clinging to his part-copyrights of the late Leadbelly, who had learnt much of his repertoire this way – was convinced contact 'through the grooves of a phonograph record' was less 'authentic' than oral tradition. Yet the skiffle boom should have been an answer to his prayers. The youth of a nation – and not just any nation, the very nation that served as the font of Anglo-American folksong – was grabbing any musical instrument they could, including even their mama's washboard with which they scratched out a beat, and playing the songs he and his father had been so anxious to preserve before the damnable 'phonograph record' could do its worst.

By the time Donegan's version of 'Rock Island Line' hit the Top Ten, the standard skiffle repertoire was already well in place (as were most of the demobbed players who went from jazz to skiffle; both Donegan and Ken Colyer, frontman for the Colyer Skiffle Group, emerged from Chris Barber's popular 'trad. jazz' combo.) That repertoire reads like a one-stop shop of early twentieth-century Americana: from Handy to Hank, from 'Sail Away Lady' (a.k.a. 'Don't You Rock Me Daddy-O'), first collected in Handy's 1926 blues anthology, to 'Mind Your Own Business'; from 'Mama Don't 'Low' to 'Bring Me A Little Water, Sylvie', 'Midnight Special' to 'Easy Rider', 'Pick A Bale Of Cotton' to 'House Of The Rising Sun'; from 'John Henry' to 'John Hardy'. This was an alternative vision of American popular song, whose lyrical linchpins were Leadbelly and the Carters, Big Bill Broonzy and Josh White. ASCAP artists barely got a look in. And for any British folksong – say, a 'Derby Ram' or a 'Golden Vanity' – to be deemed acceptable it also had to be burnished in American tradition.[†]

---

[*] Cue that hilarious scene in Eric Idle's Rutles mockumentary, *All You Need Is Cash*, where they track down an old bluesman who claims to have written all the Rutles' songs, even as his wife loudly proclaims, 'He's lying. He's *always* lying.'

[†] Skiffle singer Nancy Whiskey seems to have been a rare straddler of the skiffle–folk divide, releasing an album on the folk label Topic in 1957 at the height of the skiffle craze.

A steaming-mad Lomax finally decided to get in on the act himself, not with a collection of authentic Library of Congress recordings but by forming what skiffle historian Chas McDevitt calls a 'pseudo skiffle' combo. Alan Lomax and The Ramblers featured three well-known folksingers: the American Peggy Seeger, Scot Ewan MacColl and that most English lady, Shirley Collins. But their two Decca singles (the second of which introduced MacColl's 'Dirty Old Town' to British audiences) barely registered with 'the kids'. Whereas Lonnie Donegan, whose first two singles had also been on Decca, before he slipped through their hands, was racking up hit after hit. 'Rock Island Line' was followed by 'Midnight Special', 'When That Evening Sun Goes Down', 'Alabamy Bound', 'Cumberland Gap', 'Sally Don't You Grieve', 'Tom Dooley' and 'Darling Corey'. Everyone a winner.

Donegan also had the measure of his source material. When he covered a Woody Guthrie song, as he did successfully with 'Grand Coulee Dam' in 1958, he credited Guthrie with the words, while taking an arrangement credit on the 'traditional' tune himself. He was technically right to do so – Guthrie never having written tunes – but it was simply not done.

What was also never done – save by the blithe Donegan – was taking the best songs from rival skiffle outfits' repertoire and rushing one's own version into the shops first. The Vipers, probably the best live skiffle act in London even before Hank Marvin and Jet Harris joined the combo on their way to The Shadows, had made their versions of 'Don't You Rock Me Daddy-O' and 'Cumberland Gap' famous among skiffle aficionados, but after Parlophone's George Martin signed them to that famous EMI subsidiary they were slow making the cuts available to the public. Donegan was not; so his defanged renderings charted higher and earlier than theirs. To compound any sense of injustice, Donegan took the self-same 'Trad. Arr. Donegan' credit on both tracks.

In fact, Donegan and Lomax were much alike. Both assumed a proprietorial attitude to material that came their way; neither felt any shame presenting others' work as their own (Lomax fell out with the New England folk collector Helen Flanders because he copied and broadcast material of hers, given to him with a strict embargo on dissemination); and they both stood in the line of fire when Pete Seeger aimed his metaphorical musket at those who 'change a song, not to improve it but just to get a copyright on it'. For, as professional curmudgeon Gershon Legman pointed out, by 1960 Lomax was doing exactly as Donegan had, posting a curiously discordant note at the end of the introduction to his collection *Folk Songs of North America*: 'Warning is hereby given that *most of the songs in this volume are protected by copyright*.' Even Lomax's most recent biographer, John Szwed, felt obliged to try and explain away such a seeming contradiction:

> Those who [have] examined the BMI list of songwriters . . . see Alan's name on hundreds of songs. There are many kinds of copyright, however . . . Alan did not himself file for copyright, but signed Popular Songwriter Contracts that allowed publishers to copyright those songs. On those agreements for folk songs Alan's name, along with the singer's, would come under the title 'Writer', but with added language that said, 'Collected, adapted and arranged by'. If the song was original with the singer, it might say that it was 'by' the singer and 'Adapted and Revised by Alan Lomax'. Lomax's actual copyrights read, 'Traditional song, arranger'.

But Alan never *arranged* any of the folksongs he collected – he simply wasn't a competent enough arranger. He did, however, bowdlerize the texts, as he openly admitted – even celebrating his own ingenuity as he created composites which flew in the face of all post-Child folklore. In Lomax's work 'Frankie And Johnny' and 'Frankie And Albert' were one and the same, and Leadbelly's way of doing 'Rock Island Line' could be reconciled with Kelly Pace's with the aid of a red pencil.

Alan did not stop at copyrighting only songs he or his father collected first-hand. In 1958 he was on the receiving end of a second publishing bonanza in eight years when he took a share of the copyright on The Kingston Trio's phenomenally successful version of the traditional murder ballad, 'Hang Your Head Tom Dooley', on the grounds that he knew someone who'd once collected a similar version of the song.

This left Lomax splitting the proceeds on another million-seller with the twee-est of folk trios and folklorist Frank Warner, who had collected the song in 1938 from Frank Proffitt. A well-known local folksinger from North Carolina, Proffitt had learnt the song from his aunt Nancy Prather. Nancy in turn learnt it from her mother, Edy Adeline Pardue, who supposedly knew both Tom Dula (locally pronounced 'Dooley') and the girl he murdered, Laura Foster, back in 1866. (The crime appears to have been carried out as punishment for giving him VD; he transmitted this information to his partner, who was commonly considered complicit in the deed.)

Quite how any of this conferred a copyright, Lord knows. Warner had collected the song from Proffitt after approaching a dulcimer-maker in Beech Mountain looking for folksongs; the man turned out to be Proffitt's father-in-law, Nathan Hicks. Warner, back then, was a respectable folklorist who had studied under Frank C. Brown and Newman Ivey White at Duke University. Which presumably means he already knew about the three versions of the song in the Frank C. Brown collection, all collected by the trusty Mrs Sutton shortly after the Great War.

Sutton was evidently greatly taken with the song. She even provided Brown with copious notes on it, concluding: 'It has all the ballad essentials: a mystery death, an eternal triangle, and a lover with courage enough to die for his lady . . . and in bad verse with a wild minor tune' – a rather magnificent summation of the song's inner power, one which even The Kingston Trio could not wholly dim. Fascinatingly, the lady also put forward the only *credible* name for a possible author, baldly stating, '[It] was composed by an old Negro named Charlie Davenport, and sung to the tune of "Run, Nigger, Run."'

What makes a negro author particularly enticing is the fact that the song is a lyrical redaction of a vulgar ballad, 'The Murder Of Laura Foster', written shortly after the deed by Thomas Land – much as the vulgar ballad of 'Casey Jones' was once manhandled by negro tradition, and came out stronger. Such a thesis was not even mentioned when John and Alan Lomax published Frank Warner's version, collected from (the unattributed) Proffitt, in their 1947 collection, *Folk Song USA*, its sole attribution: 'words and melody adapted and arranged by Frank Warner'.

In the process, the Lomaxes magnanimously conferred on Warner a *partial* copyright. Even after Proffitt recorded the song himself, for Elektra in 1952, the same year Frank C. Brown's multiple versions finally appeared in print, they continued to claim copyright on a song that had actually been first published – by Mellinger Henry – the year Warner recorded Proffitt's version on his primitive portable tape recorder.

As it happens, neither the Kingston Trio, nor Frank Warner, were the first to record 'Tom Dooley'. The honour goes to G.B. Grayson, a blind fiddler from Mountain City, Tennessee. A descendant of the Grayson that arrested the murderer, he recorded the song for Victor in 1929, under the auspices of Ralph Peer.

And when Peer heard The Kingston Trio's 'Tom Dooley', he knew just where they had got it from – the version by Grayson & Whitter, recorded, published and copyrighted by him in 1929. As Frank Proffitt's family was later to do, Peer was seriously thinking about arguing in court when God came to gather this particular jewel. Lomax would almost certainly have met his judicial match had not this potential adversary – someone who would have run circles around him in any copyright case – not gone to meet his Maker, having done a whole lot more for popular song than a man who waged war on 'the phonograph record' even as he collected his thirty pieces of silver.

Had he lived longer, Peer might also have gone after Woody Guthrie, who had plundered more tunes from the Carter Family and Jimmie Rodgers than the rest of the folk revival put together. But when he died in January 1960, songs like 'This Land Is Your Land' ('When The World's On Fire'), 'Reuben James' ('Wildwood Flower'), 'Philadelphia Lawyer' ('The Jealous Lover') and 'Muleskinner Blues' ('Blues Yodel #1') were being sung in coffeehouses and Village clubs, not by rock gods to

American presidents – as Bruce Springsteen would ultimately do with 'This Land Is Your Land' and Dylan with 'Do Re Mi'.

The pioneering Peer barely lived long enough to see the first shots fired by Guthrie's acolytes on behalf of the folk revival. Because in the long term it would not be The Kingston Trio's adoption of 'Hard Travellin'', 'Pastures of Plenty', 'This Land Is Your Land', 'Reuben James' and 'Deportees', but rather Ramblin' Jack Elliott's extensive repertoire of Guthrie covers (including a whole album on Topic) that had the profounder effect.

And when it was not secondhand Guthrie songs that commandered the coffeehouse repertoires of pass-the-hat folksingers, it was the songs of lesser light Pete Seeger, who by his own admission thought 'This Land Is Your Land' 'one of Woody's lesser efforts', but took to heart something Woody often said to him: 'When I get the words, I look around for some tune that has [already] proved its popularity with the people.' Guthrie's attitude to appropriation soon rubbed off on his friend:

> **Pete Seeger**: I didn't really start writing songs till I met Woody Guthrie. And I suddenly learned something that was *awful* important. And that was: Don't be so all-fired concerned about being original. You hear an old song you like but you'd like to change a little, there's no great crime in changing it a little. I saw Woody doing it with song after song . . . One of my first songs ['C for Conscription'] I used the same melody which Woody had copied from Jimmie Rodgers ['Muleskinner Blues'].

It was 1955, soon after Seeger first tried to get the hang of this songwriting lark, when he penned perhaps his most notable 'original' composition, 'Where Have All The Flowers Gone?' He said he didn't notice he'd appropriated the tune 'until about a year later when a friend wrote me and pointed out that it was similar to a lumberjack tune I had recorded from the Adirondacks'. In fact, he got it from a Russian folk melody, 'Koloda Duda', and the idea for the song itself from another Russian folksong,

'Tovchu, tovchu mak', which has the lines, 'Where are the flowers, the girls have plucked them/Where are the girls, they've all taken husbands/ Where are the men, they're all in the army.' (Not quite the same sentiment as Seeger's 'lumberjack tune', which went 'Johnson says he'll unload more hay . . .')

Seeger always remained a less natural wordsmith than Guthrie. (Indeed, he would ultimately require the helping hand of Joe Hickerson to render 'Where Have All The Flowers Gone' circular enough for The Searchers' purposes, convincing enough to qualify as Britpop's first folk-rock foray as early as 1963.) He was far more suited to adaptation. His next oh-so-worthy contribution to the folk(-rock) revolution was little more than a section of the Book of Ecclesiastes set to music. His only two lyrical contributions to 'Turn Turn Turn' – memorably covered by The Byrds, who took it to number one in December 1965 – were the burden/ title-phrase and the final line of the song, which was as one-dimensional as Seeger's political vision: 'A time for peace, I swear it's not too late.'

He had found his real forte: turning psalms of salvation – like the aforementioned passage from Ecclesiastes – into brotherly bonding sessions. He did much the same with 'Jacob's Ladder', an old gospel song usually credited to H.P. Danks, and first recorded by Harrod's Jubilee Singers in 1921. The socialist sinner Seeger transformed its unambiguous, redemptive sentiments ('We are climbing Jacob's ladder [x3]/Soldiers of the cross') into a crass call for unity, 'We are climbing Jacob's ladder [x3]/Yeah, we're brothers, sisters, all', as if universal suffrage was the real reason Moses crossed the Red Sea or Christ died on the cross. But Seeger's most dubious contribution to the art of song catching came when he (and three other 'activists') took the plaintive, yearning beauty of 'I'll Overcome Someday', a song of faith to which only someone with faith could really relate, and made it a secular paean to the triumph of socialism:

**Pete Seeger:** A black preacher in Philadelphia wrote a song, *'I'll overcome someday, I'll overcome someday, If in my heart I do not yield, I'll overcome someday.'* The song became well known in black churches, but Afro-American people carry on a great tradition which says that a song in a book is just a basis to start improvising, and down in the Deep South, they started changing it. In 1926 tobacco workers in Charleston, Carolina went on strike and some pickets who were walking up and down singing old hymns changed it still further. Instead of being 'I will overcome', it became,'*We will overcome, We'll get higher wages, We'll have higher pay, We will overcome someday.*'

They taught this song to a white friend, an organiser of the union who taught it to me, and I took it up north and made up extra verses. I taught it to Guy Carawan who was about 30 years old at the time. He took it back down south in 1960 and taught it to the students who were sitting in restaurants and demanding a cup of coffee, no matter what colour their skin . . . In two or three months, this song went right across the south and it became the theme song of the Civil Rights Movement.

The notes to Bruce Springsteen's 2006 collection of 'Seeger related' songs, *The Seeger Sessions*, describe the result as 'the most important political protest song of all-time'.* When asked about the song in 2010, Guy Carawan stated, 'I was the only one working down [south] for about five years spreading that song. Frank [Hamilton]'s name is on the copyright because he first taught me that song out in California. He'd heard it from Zilphia Horton, who had worked in the south in the labour movement . . . She learned that song from black people.' No mention of Seeger.

Perhaps Seeger got his cut for ensuring 'We Shall Overcome' became the unofficial anthem of the Newport Folk Festivals in 1963 and 1964. That, though, was before the event was famously hijacked in 1965 by a former protest singer from Minnesota he had brought up as his own, tutoring

---

* It was one of just two songs on the thirteen-track 'tribute' which gave Seeger a song-credit, while Springsteen himself took ten.

him to spout the party line in ever more poetic ways, only for the boy to reveal he grew up listening to R&B and wanting to be Little Richard.

The boy-poet called himself Bobby Dylan; though no one in the Village, Seeger included, believed for one minute this was his real name. He had been hanging around the Village dressed as a Chaplinesque raga-muffin for just over a year, soaking up the scene like a sponge, scribbling Guthriesque pastiches on the nearest notepad, waiting for the floodgates of inspiration to burst open. His earliest originals even took their tunes from his hero. 'Song To Woody', one of two originals to survive his debut LP's rigorous culling process, borrowed Guthrie's '1913 Massacre' as both template and tune. The other, 'Talkin' New York', adopted Guthrie's [ie. Chris Bouchillon's] talkin' blues format, 'an obscure Negro blues form . . . perfectly suited to his sense of humour'.

Meantime, Seeger became instrumental in setting up a mimeographed zine dedicated wholly to topical songs. If Sis Cunningham and Gordon Friesen were *Broadside*'s ostensible publishers, Seeger was their campfire cheerleader, writing in its first issue in February 1962, 'We must have an outpouring of topical song. What does it matter that most will be sung once and forgotten?' (His wish was granted.) In the first issue, Sis and Gordon published another of Dylan's talkin' blues, 'Talkin' John Birch'. In the sixth, they published his first earnest attempt to transcend the bonds of topicality. Called 'Blowin' In The Wind', it set a bar for fellow Broadsiders he alone would raise again.

The song, though, had clear antecedents, and at least one grizzled old Commie heard 'em the night Bobby debuted it to Gil Turner at the ever popular Gerde's Folk City. It was an event auspicious enough for Turner to recall it later that summer in print:

**Gil Turner:** One night, two months ago, Bob came flying into Folk City where I was singing. 'Gil, I got a new song I just fin-ished. Wanna hear it?' The song was 'Blowin' In The Wind,' one of his best efforts to date in my opinion. I didn't recognize the tune at the time and neither did Bob, but Pete Seeger heard it and pegged the first part of it as an imaginative reworking of 'No More Auction Block.'

Forty-two years later, Dylan admitted he knew all along what it was he had been reaching for, which was the same kinda effect on listeners as that anti-slave song: '"Blowin in the Wind" follows the same feeling . . . I just did it on my acoustical guitar when I recorded it – which didn't really make it sound spiritual – but the feeling, the idea . . . that's where it was coming from.'

That sense of yearning might have been made explicit had Dylan continued to work on the song's fourth verse, 'How many times have you heard someone say/If I had more money I'd do things my way/But little [do] they know . . .' – one he wisely deleted before it was ever performed. The lines in question are a straight lyrical lift from Jack Rhodes's 'Satisfied Mind', a song Dylan had worked up the previous year for his second Gerde's residency. Thankfully, he decided three verses was enough, sparing himself a potential copyright suit from the notoriously litigious Porter Wagoner. 'Satisfied Mind' was certainly in copyright in 1962; and remained so in 1980, when Dylan opened his second gospel album, *Saved*, with it.

Turner was so impressed by the song Bobby played him that April night, he decided to write a cover-story on the young tyke for *Sing Out!*, the premier folk periodical. The piece unapologetically laid out Dylan's early method of songwriting, one which took the same liberties with copyright that all fledgling folkies brought up on Guthrie, Leadbelly and Seeger had been coached to do:

> His method of writing places the emphasis on the words, the tune almost always being borrowed or adapted from one he has heard somewhere, usually a traditional one. I remember the first night he heard the tune he used for the 'Ballad of Donald White'. It was in Bonnie Dobson's version of the 'Ballad of Peter Amberly'. He heard the tune, liked it, made a mental record of it and a few days later 'Donald White' was complete.

This was not likely to be a problem if the songs stayed as unremittingly topical as 'Donald White', based as it was on a TV show Dylan caught about an institutionalized killer. But 'Blowin' In The Wind' was different, and Dylan knew it. Less than a fortnight after he wrote it, he was already looking to give the song as much artistic elbow-room as he could, introducing it in concert with the statement, 'This here ain't a protest song or anything like that, 'cause I don't write protest songs . . . I'm just writing it as something to be said, for somebody, by somebody.'

He wasn't alone in recognizing early on that this was a song which would change everything, always. Folk entrepreneur Albert Grossman – already angling to be Dylan's next manager – knew it too. The second he heard it, he started to make plans to scotch Dylan's current publishing deal with Leeds Music and grab himself a slice of the pie. Fortunately for him, Dylan had yet to demo the song for the publisher, though he *had* published it in *Broadside* magazine in May 1962, with a copyright notice indicating it was the property of Duchess Music (a Leeds Music subsidiary).

Grossman convinced his protégé to go up to the Leeds Music offices with hard cash and buy back his contract, which Dylan dutifully did. Grossman then cut himself in on Dylan's end of a publishing deal he promptly negotiated with Artie Mogull at Witmark Music. He also – unbeknownst to Dylan – arranged for Witmark to kick back to him personally part of *their* half-share of the publishing in return for bringing them the protestin' poet. As a result, Grossman was at one point earning more in publishing from Dylan's repertoire than the artist himself. Not surprisingly, when Dylan eventually found this out, after his fabled motorcycle accident, he hit the roof. So began a twenty-year battle with Grossman (and, ultimately, his widow) to regain control of his publishing. (And in the final shot he won the war, though only after Uncle Albert was lying in his grave.)

Six whole weeks after it appeared in *Broadside*, 'Blowin' In The Wind' was the first song demoed and copyrighted under the new Witmark deal, signed 13 July 1962. Two months later it was published in tandem with

Turner's glowing cover-story in *Sing Out!*. Which was where New Jersey high-school student Lorre Wyatt saw it, and from where he learnt how to sing it. A member of The Millburnaires, a cheesy folk trio in the Kingston tradition, Wyatt played the song at a rehearsal that October. When asked where he got it from, he claimed to have written it. The other band members insisted they perform it at a high school performance, and all too soon Wyatt found himself telling tall tales for a living:

> Thanksgiving Assembly [1962]. The *one* time we would do the song. My strictest instructions to everyone were not to mention who wrote it, but Don circumvented that by saying, 'Here's a song written by one of the Millburnaires.' At the end of assembly, people streamed backstage . . . Next Monday my homeroom teacher asked to see me after school for a 'just between you and me' chat. She wondered why I didn't want to sing that song anymore. I pulled out the answer I had been toying with all weekend, and told her I had sold it. . . . When she asked, 'For how much?' I blurted out, '$1,000.' . . . The other Millburnaires pressed to know who I had sold the song to. They remember me saying, 'Well, he doesn't really pronounce it Dillon or Dielan. Sort of somewhere inbetween. He talks kinda funny.' . . . In April [1963] the Millburnaires recorded . . . a momento record of 800 copies. My name appeared on three cuts: a love song I had written, a peace song I'd set a new tune to (and implied that I'd written) and '[Blowin' In The] Wind' . . . In June, I wrote a letter to Broadside fabricating a story that people were mistaking a song I wrote entitled 'Freedom Is Blowing In The Wind' for Dylan's. I hoped the letter would be shown to Dylan . . . In late September our high school LP was released nationally by Riverside Records. They urged me to make a solo album. Invariably, the dorm phone seemed to be for me, 'I'm so and so from the Rhode Island Daily Rumor and . . .?' 'No comment.' A researcher from *Newsweek* called persistently, hammering on the disquieting questions.

The *Newsweek* reporter wouldn't take no for an answer. Her name was Andrea Svedburg and she was researching a premeditated hatchet-job on the protest singer, 'revealing' his real name and his middle-class upbringing in the Mid-West. She was even willing to print a 'rumor circulating that Dylan did not write "Blowing In The Wind," that it was written by a Millburn (N.J.) high school student named Lorre Wyatt, who sold it to the singer . . . Wyatt denies authorship, but several Millburn students claim they heard the song from Wyatt before Dylan ever sang it.'

Astonishingly, Dylan did not sue the highly influential weekly, though this act of libel was as cut and dried as the one he simultaneously committed with 'The Lonesome Death of Hattie Carroll' – a song which basically accused William Zantzinger of bludgeoning the poor maid to death. Instead, he wrote a fine retort, 'Restless Farewell', referring only in general to those who sought to cover him in a 'dust of rumours'. He then set the lyrics to a famous Irish drinking song, 'The Parting Glass', he'd heard The Clancy Brothers sing of an evening.*

'The Parting Glass' was hardly the first tune Dylan had learnt from The Clancys, or put to a set of lyrics he could call his own. A lilting lyric called 'Farewell' (featured now in the Coen Brothers' *Inside Llewyn Davies*) lifted the whole arrangement from Liam Clancy's rendition of 'The Leaving of Liverpool', though Dylan was wise to refrain from releasing it until 2010. Where he stirred up a real hornet's nest, though, was in taking their version of an Irish anti-patriot song by Dominic Behan, called 'The Patriot's Game', and rewriting it as the patently superior 'With God On Our Side'. (Various eyewitnesses claim Dylan wrote this after hearing the song in London the winter of 1963, though the first documented performance comes a month after The Clancys played Behan's song at a famous St Patrick's Day Carnegie Hall show which Dylan almost certainly attended.) Despite being namechecked in the sleeve-notes, Behan was furious when the song appeared on the same album as 'Restless

---

* Wyatt himself would not come clean until 1974, when he wrote a long *mea culpa* in *New Times*. Thirty-eight years later, he would record a joint album with fellow songstealer, Pete Seeger.

Farewell', although it was not until more than twenty years had passed that he gave full vent to his dissatisfaction.

Even before Svedburg's *Newsweek* story broke, Dylan was developing a reputation for taking a fair bit from, and giving little back to, his folkie friends, many of whom were struggling to make ends meet. To numerous former friends, he was no longer the same man who had given a co-credit to the late Henry Thomas on his 1962 version of 'Honey Just Allow Me One More Chance', although the only part of the song he took from Thomas was a commonplace chorus collected by Dorothy Scarborough a few years before Thomas's recording. (Of course, Thomas wasn't around to reap any pecuniary dividend, but at least it was recognition of a debt and led many, myself included, to check out Thomas's 23-song recorded oeuvre.)

That, however, was before Grossman took Dylan under his wing. Six months later, when Dylan wrote his masterful 'Masters Of War' to the tune *and* arrangement of 'Nottamun Town', patented – if not copyrighted – by the great traditional singer, Jean Ritchie, no arrangement credit was forthcoming, even after the song appeared on his breakthrough second album, *The Freewheelin' Bob Dylan*, in June 1963.

Where Ritchie first heard Dylan's song is not documented. It could well have been when they shared a stage at a Newport workshop in July 1963. But she would have recognized it immediately as the one handed down in her family since time immemorial; the arrangement was seemingly unique to the Ritchies, although the song itself had been collected in variant forms in Missouri, New Jersey and Nova Scotia. Even if Dylan had claimed he took his arrangement from Cecil Sharp's well-known text and tune, published in 1932 and still in copyright, that version itself originated with Jean's aunts, Una and Sabrina. Ritchie felt no qualms about claiming her share of the spoils; she went after Witmark, who wisely settled the matter quietly (according to one of the more unreliable Dylan biographers, for $5,000). The credit, though, remained 'words and music Bob Dylan'.

Ritchie's arrangement, moreover, continued to be ransacked by rogue folksingers. It was to appear on three important English 'folk revival' records of the sixties: Shirley Collins and Davy Graham's *Folk Roots, New Routes* (1964), Bert Jansch's *Jack Orion* (1966) and Fairport Convention's *What We Did On Our Holidays* (1968) – all without a namecheck, all unquestionably the 'Ritchie' variant. Ritchie responded in kind, noting in the introduction to her 1965 anthology, *Folk Songs of the Southern Appalachians*, 'Because of recent developments in the field of folk music, I have found it necessary to copyright many of the Ritchie family songs.' What ever could she mean?

Dylan and his publishers had meanwhile become embroiled in another dispute over a song found on *The Freewheelin' Bob Dylan*. And this time it was personal. The song in question dated back to October 1962, and was called 'Don't Think Twice, It's Alright'.

Initially, Dylan seemed to be on fairly solid ground, given that the song was clearly based on one dating back to at least the turn of the century, when it bore titles like 'Who Gon[na] Bring You Chickens?' and 'Who's Goin' To Buy Your Whisky?' However, there had been an intermediary stage, a sophisticated adaptation by a young folklorist-singer of Dylan's acquaintance, Paul Clayton, who had recorded a song called 'Who's Gonna Buy You Ribbons?' in 1959. This time it wasn't just the melody Dylan had 'borrowed' from his friend, as anyone conversant with both songs would know instantly. He had taken the 'music lock, stock and barrel and very nearly the words', the first and last verses of which read:

It ain't no use to sit and sigh now, darlin'
And it ain't no use to sit and cry now
It ain't no use to sit and wonder why, darlin'
Just wonder who's gonna buy you ribbons when I'm gone . . .

So I'm walkin' down that long, lonesome road
You're the one that made me travel on
But still I can't help wonderin' on my way
Who's gonna buy you ribbons when I'm gone?

We also have the testimony of at least one eyewitness who was there the day Clayton played Dylan the song. According to fellow folk musician Barry Kornfeld, Dylan's supposed response on hearing it was, 'Hey, man, that's a great song. I'm goin' to use that song.'

Of course, in October 1962 Dylan and Clayton were both scuffling songsters trying to make it, with total sales of Dylan's March 1962 Columbia debut standing at less than five thousand copies. By the following October, though, *Freewheelin'* was in the album charts. And, more importantly, Peter, Paul and Mary had the song lined up as a follow-up to their chart-topping version of 'Blowin' In The Wind'.

Mutual friends found themselves caught in the crossfire as Clayton attempted first emotional blackmail and then legal threats to receive his (partial) due. As his best friend, Stephen Wilson, recalls, 'To a person who was dying of no money, half of the twenty or thirty or forty grand [due] would have been a huge [windfall] . . . ['Don't Think Twice'] wasn't a rewrite [though], it was a very fresh take. But Paul didn't see it that way. He wanted to be associated with Dylan, so that [big falling-out] pained him.'

In the end, Clayton settled for a pittance – supposedly no more than $500 – though he had a far stronger case than Jean Ritchie, and everyone down in Washington Square knew this was no mere happenstance of tradition. The spat soured Dylan's and Clayton's relationship for a number of months and was probably partly responsible for Dylan's decision to leave another early masterpiece, 'Percy's Song', off his third album. The song was another to borrow heavily from a Clayton recording, albeit of the resolutely traditional 'The Wind And The Rain'. Dylan was sequencing the album the week after Svedburg accused him of plagiarism and fraud. Now was not the time to rock the boat, or even row it ashore.

Not everyone was as affronted by Dylan's debt-ridden lyrics. When he returned from Rome to London in January 1963, he played English folksinger Martin Carthy his latest song, which caused more merriment than wonder: 'Bob went away to . . . Italy and in the time he was away . . . he wrote "Girl from the North Country," [then] he came back and he said, "I've got a song to play you." It was at the Troubadour, and he started to play, and he had that little guitar thing that I play in "Scarborough Fair." He was singing . . . and he went into this figure and he just burst out laughing . . . and he wouldn't do the rest of it. He went all red.'

Carthy's rearrangement of the ancient 'Scarborough Fair' was one of his signature pieces, but he let Dylan adapt it with his blessing. He was less happy when, two years later, another East Village refugee, name of Paul Simon, popped up in London and asked him to play his arrangement of the song. The following year it was on a Simon & Garfunkel album named after its memorable refrain, *Parsley, Sage, Rosemary & Thyme*; and the year after that, it was theme tune to the Oscar-winning smash, *The Graduate*.

At the time Carthy kept his counsel. But finally he had to say, 'I resent . . . that he said he wrote it. He took enormous pains to learn it, when I wrote it down word-for-word for him. [Sure,] it's as much his song as it was mine, but his way of getting it wasn't entirely honourable.' Simon would learn – as Dylan had – that a reputation for song snatching, once acquired, can be a hard thing to lose.

It remains doubly ironic that at the precise point when Dylan was starting to transcend tradition, outgrowing the legally questionable practices of his mentor Guthrie, he came under fire for songstealing. By February 1964, with *The Times They Are A-Changin'* barely announced, he wrote his first wholly original work, tune *and* text (though even here he was clearly inspired by a work in the public domain, Arthur Rimbaud's symbolist poem, 'Le Bâteau Ivre' [The Drunken Boat]). The song was 'Mr Tambourine Man', and Dylan insisted on playing it to Carthy that May, to show that he had transcended tradition.

Indeed, Dylan acolyte Donovan was so convinced his mentor utilised only traditional tunes, he wrote his own lyric to the tune of 'Tambourine Man'. Thankfully he played it to Dylan first – as one filmmaker witnessed:

**D.A. Pennebaker**: I used to catch Dylan listening to 'Catch The Wind' . . . so he liked Donovan before he even saw him . . . Well, Donovan was very excited and decided to play something for him . . . a song called 'My Darling Tangerine Eyes'. And it was to the tune of 'Mr Tambourine Man'! And Dylan was sitting there with this funny look on his face, listening to 'Mr Tambourine Man' with these really weird words, and about halfway through the second verse, Donovan realizes that Dylan is cracking up – and Neuwirth and I were fighting it back . . . Then Dylan says, 'Well . . . you know . . . that tune . . . I have to admit that I haven't written *all* the tunes I'm credited with, but that happens to be one that I *did* write!' And Donovan says, 'I didn't know. I thought it was an old folk tune!' . . . I'm [pretty] sure he never played the song again.

Pennebaker (and his 'Eye') was in Dylan's hotel room more than once on that May 1965 English tour, and captured him duetting with Joan Baez on a number of traditional songs. One of these was the lovely 'Wild Mountain Thyme', a song Irish folksinger Francis McPeake was now claiming copyright on, even though the lyrics had been published as far back as 1818. But Dylan himself had moved on. R&B nicks were now his thing, as he showed a couple of days later when he vamped away at his latest song, 'Phantom Engineer' (a.k.a. 'It Takes A Lot To Laugh'), on the hotel piano. At least one verse of it was a stone steal from Leroy Carr's 'Alabama Woman Blues'.

One imagines the subject of song-credits and moral debts may also have come up when Dylan met Alan Price on that trip. The keyboardist had recently departed from The Animals after months of acrimony, a direct result of Price taking sole credit for arranging a song the band (at least in part) copped from Dylan himself. The song was 'House Of The Rising Sun', and one could write a book – as Ted Anthony has – about the roads it travelled in the fifty years before The Animals took it to the top of the charts on both sides of the pond, defining the folk-rock sound into the bargain.

A key question is whether these Geordies really did derive their template from Dylan himself. Or did the N'Orleans lass take another road – via Dave Van Ronk – to Newcastle? Dylan said he had not *really* heard the song until it was performed by fellow New York folkie, Dave Van Ronk, 'in a lonesome hungry growlin whisper [that] any girl with her face hid in the dark could understand' (as he put it in a 1963 poem). Van Ronk admitted he personally learnt the song from a Hally Wood record. However, as he later said, he 'put a different spin on it by altering the chords and using a bass line that descended in half steps – a common enough progression in jazz, but unusual among folksingers'.

Dylan adopted the song, then recorded it (without asking Van Ronk's permission), and suddenly it was 'Dylan's version', not Dave's. In fact, Dylan seems to have been too embarrassed to copyright the arrangement, which went unprotected till 1978. Because of this, The Animals were on fairly safe ground covering it and crediting it to themselves – or even to Alan Price. As Price himself is on record as saying, 'I based our version on the Bob Dylan record. I took his chord sequence and I rehearsed the band.' This was apparently enough to confer copyright.

Yet a clear Dylan influence was already evident on The Animals' first single, an Animalized version of 'Baby Let Me Follow You Down', another song found on Dylan's debut.* What was truly strange about that first single was not so much its chosen title ('Baby Let Me Take You Home') as the song-credits, which changed with the breeze. On demo copies of the original 45, all five Animals were credited as co-authors, which certainly was not the case. By the time the single appeared in the

---

* Nor should the influence of this album on other English rockers be downplayed. Though they may have eventually checked out Blind Willie Johnson's original, Led Zeppelin surely first heard 'In My Time of Dyin' on Dylan's eponymous platter. And Rod Stewart – who covered 'Man of Constant Sorrow' on his solo debut – is on record as saying, 'In 1962 . . . I got to hear Bob Dylan's first album . . . Nothing had altered the air around me like that Dylan album. I would play it over and over on the family radiogram . . . It didn't just broaden my horizon, this record: it drew my horizon.'

shops, it bore the worrying catch-all credit, 'Trad. Arr. Price'. By the time the song appeared on *The Most of The Animals* in 1966, it was being credited to Russell-Farrell.

Both the latter two credits contained a grain of truth, though not the whole truth. Neither Russell nor Farrell were aliases for Memphis Minnie or Kansas Joe (who appear to have recorded the song first, in 1930, as 'Can I Do It For You?'); or even Blind Boy Fuller and/or Reverend Gary Davis (whose 'Mama Let Me Lay It On You' is a closer prototype for Dylan's, and therefore their, version).

Rather, the 1966 credit referred to Bert Russell (a.k.a. Bert Berns) and Wes Farrell, the former of whom had already been responsible for 'Twist And Shout'. And there was no doubt that Russell and Farrell's version – which they had released some month earlier as The Mustangs – was the prototype for The Animals' version, twelve-string intro. et al. In fact, The Animals producer Mickie Most had picked up Berns' original demo of 'Baby Let Me Take You Home' from New York publisher Bobby Mellin on a trip to the city in 1963.

There was equally little doubt Berns himself had copped his song from the first Dylan album, after he had returned raving about Dylan from seeing him at his April 1963 Town Hall concert. This was someone, after all, who had adapted Guthrie's 'Hard Travellin'' into 'Hard, Ain't It Hard', for a Solomon Burke session a month earlier, and whose first single back in October 1960 used Paul Clayton's 'Gotta Travel On' as its flipside. But Berns also knew the publishing ropes, and so added his own distinctive intro., and a Dixonesque middle-eight, and took all the credit. Just as he would later with the fifteenth century 'I Gave My Love A Cherry' when he turned it into the Them classic, 'I Gave My Love A Diamond'.

As for The Animals, they were already showing a surprisingly lackadaisical attitude to song publishing. Fortunately, 'Baby Let Me Take You Home' only dented the lower rungs of the British charts. If they had subscribed to lessons from the 'once bitten, twice shy' school of rip-offs, they'd have been fine. As it was, Price took sole credit for its successor and so, as lead singer Eric Burdon wrote in his autobiography, 'with the stroke of a pen, the rest of The Animals were screwed. Ripped off from the get-go – from inside.' No longer had the band collectively reworked a song found on that first Dylan record. Price, and Price alone, had crafted an arrangement of a song known to *all* American folk revivalists thanks to Leadbelly, Woody Guthrie, Josh White and/or Hally Wood – one Dylan had himself been singing since a student in Minneapolis.

In fact, Burdon went on record at the time to say The Animals had based their version on the Josh White recording, made twenty years before Dylan's and which had formed the basis for at least one English skiffle version back in 1957. White, a bluesman from Greenville, South Carolina, had made his first recordings in 1932 when just eighteen, after spending his adolescence helping blind bluesmen around – including, or so he claimed, Blind Lemon Jefferson. He had recorded 'Rising Sun Blues' *as a blues* at the end of 1941, and as song-historian Ted Anthony writes, 'The deliberate, minor-key version performed by White is the first that carries a melody truly similar to the one familiar today.'

White also sang the song from the vantage point of a woman, as was almost certainly the case originally, though versions released by Clarence Ashley and Roy Acuff, both of which predate White's, changed gender as part of its transition into a rounder's drinking song ('Go fill the glasses to the brim . . .'). A version recorded by The Callahan Brothers in April 1935, even bore the title 'Rounder's Luck'.

White at least had the wit and wherewithal to copyright his arrangement, perhaps to set it apart from the version the Lomaxes had published earlier the same year in *Our Singing Country*. Again, though, strange names appear as co-arrangers – in this instance, Nicholas Ray (the film director, though at this time a minor folk music promoter) and Libby Holman (a singer White sometimes sang with back then). White later stated he learnt the song 'from a white hillbilly singer in . . . North Carolina'; it was a claim his so-called friend, Alan Lomax, refused to take on trust, prompting White to write about how 'he had to "convince" a folklorist that [I] hadn't learned it from one of his books.' A single listen should have told

Lomax as much. But he was unconvinced by White's protestations, and again used the snotty aside – in 1960's *Folk Songs of North America* – to claim primacy: 'I took it down in 1937 from . . . a pretty, yellow-headed miner's daughter in Middlesborough, Kentucky, subsequently adapting it [sic] to the form that was popularized by Josh White.'

Where Lomax had a point – just not one that conferred a copyright – was with White's lyrics, which clearly derive at least in part from those he'd published. He knew these could not be found in tradition because yet again he had 'frankensteined' two of the three versions collected during a 1937 Kentucky field trip – from Georgia Turner in Middlesboro and Bert Martin in Clay County – to 'create' an eight-verse lyric.

In that collection he also alludes to the song's roots in a bawdy English ballad, though he fails to provide the evidence – perhaps because he had failed to collect any of the raunchy versions floating in tradition's cesspool, which a man touring with his new bride, Elizabeth, was unlikely to hear sung. However, versions collected by Vance Randolph in the Ozarks, which seemed to date back to the 1900s, suggest it may well have begun life as a product of the erotic muse:

> There is a house in New Orleans,
> They call it the Rising Sun,
> An' when you want your pecker spoilt
> That's where you get it done.
>
> They drink all day an' fuck all night
> Until your money's gone;
> They kick your ass out in the street
> When the second shift comes on.

In September 1959, when Lomax was in the final stages of putting together *Folk Songs of North America*, he decided he would finally publish Georgia Turner's text and tune intact, all the while insisting it was 'adapted and arranged, with new words and new music', a bald-faced lie.

Growing nervous about the song's increasingly wide dissemination, and the difficulty he might have asserting *his* copyright if another 'Irene' or 'Tom Dooley' came along, he wrote to Turner, sending her a contract with Ludlow Music Inc., his long-time publisher. John A. Lomax, Alan Lomax and Georgia Turner were credited therein for a song called 'The Rising Sun Blues (New Orleans)'.

The contract, alleging that the song was 'collected, adapted and arranged, with new words and new music' by the trio, was the standard one Lomax sent his correspondents. It gave them a mere 25 per cent of the publishing. Half went to Ludlow Music, another quarter to him. When Turner queried the small sums that accrued, at some point in the sixties, Lomax informed her the song had already been 'pirated' (his word); probably a reference to the Dylan version, not The Animals'.

Again, it seemed there was no way Alan could cut himself a slice of a song to which he did not contribute a single note or word, just because he had the 'foresight' to record three versions of it *after* it had already been collected by three other folklorists in the Southern Highlands, the Ozarks and Virginia – and after it was recorded at least three times for commercial labels. To compound his sense of injustice, The Animals' version finally inspired Dylan to take that sound and stitch it to the words now filling his head, from a world kaleidoscopic enough to contain all forms of popular song.

In the process, he was to fuse folk music and electric blues into one. Folk-rock not only drove the final nail into the coffin of traditional song but brought folk back into the fold of popular song, where its many younger brothers and sisters eagerly awaited its return.

Lomax himself never forgave Dylan, or his manager, Albert Grossman. He and Grossman were, memorably, to exchange physical blows after Lomax Jnr introduced Dylan's new backing band at the 1965 Newport Folk Festival with the kind of snide remark that had long peppered his prose.

# CHAPTER 10

# 1941–65: How Many More Times?

*Featuring*: 'Rollin' Stone'; 'I Can't Be Satisfied'; 'Rollin' And Tumblin'; 'I Just Wanna Make Love To You'; 'Hoochie Coochie Man'; 'Mannish Boy'; 'Got My Mojo Working'; 'Sitting On Top Of The World'; 'Smokestack Lightning'; 'Little Red Rooster'; 'Baby Please Don't Go'; 'Surfin' USA'; 'Like A Rolling Stone'

'I think [the young British musicians] are great people, but they're not blues players. Really what separates them from people like Wolf and myself [is that] we're doing the stuff like we did way years ago down in Mississippi. These kids are just getting up, getting stuff and going with it . . . It's not real.'

Muddy Waters

When the worlds of folk and R&B collided at the Newport Folk Festival in July 1965, one might well have expected Muddy Waters to side with Alan Lomax – a man who had recorded him 'on his front porch' back in 1941 and 1942 – as Albert Grossman and the feisty folklorist traded blows after his 'shitty introduction' for the Paul Butterfield Blues Band. But it seems Muddy reserved his disdain for British blues musicians. It was not a matter of colour, but location, location, location.

Paul Butterfield and Michael Bloomfield, the two white Chicagoans who were the mainstays of the Butterfield band, had been sitting in at South Side blues gigs since the early sixties, after Bloomfield got the blues by gatecrashing Waters' long-term residency at Pepper's. As long as Bloomfield remained content to play the shit out of 'Good Morning Little Schoolgirl', 'Spoonful', 'Look Over Yonder Wall' and 'Mystery Train' – bizarrely credited to 'author unknown' on their Elektra debut LP – he was real enough in Waters' eyes.

Just like Waters, neither Butterfield nor Bloomfield were songwriters. Their purism stemmed not just from the sonic immediacy of hearing Chicago's blues *in situ*, but also from a lack of interest in going beyond the blues even when the songs became jam sessions. And yet, Bloomfield was to end up a key figure in the three most important R&B albums to appear in America at the mid-point of a tumultuous decade, one of which was as revolutionary as Elvis at Sun.

At the August 1964 sessions for the first of these – John Hammond Jnr's *So Many Roads* – Bloomfield hooked up with folksinger Bob Dylan again, after last seeing him sixteen months earlier at his club debut in Chicago. The songs Bloomfield, along with Charlie Musselwhite and three members of The Hawks, were putting down constituted a whistle-stop tour of R&B. Muddy Waters' 'Long Distance Call' and 'I Want You To Love Me', Willie Dixon's 'Down In The Bottom' and 'You Can't Judge', Big Joe Williams's 'Baby Please Don't Go' and Bo Diddley's 'Who Do You Love' and 'O Yea!' were all given a spin round the block.

Next up was that Elektra Butterfield Blues Band debut – which took two attempts, months apart and wildly different in scope. A Muddy Waters track ('I Got My Mojo Working') and a Willie Dixon cut ('Mellow Down Easy') sufficed to display their roots. The album that changed it all, though, came out in September 1965 – between Hammond and Butterfield's twin beacons of white electric blues. It was called *Highway 61 Revisited*, and its lead track, 'Like A Rolling Stone', one of the three songs that got Dylan booed off at Newport, was already a number two single by the time the album hit the shops.

Bloomfield was there for the duration. But although almost the entire album was rooted in R&B, this was something else. Bloomfield perhaps realized the music he loved was about to be fused again with folk – especially after Dylan told him he would use him only if he didn't play 'any of that B.B. King shit'. The moment others heard 'Like A Rolling Stone' it became clear it wasn't just folkies and bluesmen who needed to find a new niche. Those in the Brill Building could pack their bags, too. Paul

McCartney's reaction on hearing it the first time says it all: 'He showed all of us that it was possible to go a little further.'

For one man in particular, it was an epiphany that turned him from a flashy, copycat blues guitarist in an R&B covers band, Curtis Knight & The Squires, into the finest American guitarist-songwriter of the rock era. He promptly formed his own R&B band, Jimmy James and The Blue Flames, and started playing the Cafe Wha, where his wound-tight revamp of 'Like A Rolling Stone' was a nightly highlight as was his equally jet-blasted rendition of Howlin' Wolf's 'Killing Floor'. Snapped up by a visiting ex-Animal, Chas Chandler, and whisked away to a happening England, he re-emerged the following January as the frontman and sole songwriter of the three-piece Jimi Hendrix Experience,.

Asked about the impact Dylan had on him the following month, in one of his first press interviews, Hendrix admitted, 'I really dig him. I like that *Highway 61 Revisited* album, and especially "Just Like Tom Thumb's Blues" . . . I could never write the kinds of words he does, but he's helped me out in trying to write, 'cause I got a thousand songs that will never be finished . . . Now I have a little more confidence in trying to finish one.'

Not that the lucky few who caught Hendrix at London's Flamingo Club the same week would have heard the evidence. The set almost entirely comprised covers, save for 'Can You See Me?' and 'Stone Free', two early blues originals. And the highlights were still 'Killing Floor', Dylan's 'Like A Rolling Stone', B.B. King's 'Rock Me Baby' and Robert Petway's 'Catfish Blues'. None of these would feature on the six singles or three studio albums (one a double) issued in his name in the next two years, but each defined the difference a year, a listen to a Bob Dylan album and a change of scenery could make. The last two in particular changed the template of what R&B could be, departing from their ostensible sources almost from take-off and only returning when it came time to land.

Despite the credit to Petway on posthumous Hendrix cash-in CDs,

Jimi's 'Catfish Blues' was a distillation of three songs Muddy Waters claimed as his: 'Rollin' Stone', 'Still A Fool' (often called 'Two Trains Runnin') and 'Rollin' And Tumblin'. As such it was essentially a Waters tribute; Hendrix even sometimes introduced it as 'Muddy Waters Blues'. On the first two, Waters had recast Petway's original 'Catfish' figure; while the third only became synonymous with the electric bluesman twenty-one years after Hambone Willie first laid claim to it. The triple-ply blues suite was dropped from Hendrix's set about the time he wrote 'Voodoo Chile', for the simple reason this classic cut evolved out of 'Catfish Blues' (a solo demo tape shows the raw idea for the latter developing from the former). This only happened after Hendrix found 'a little more confidence in trying to finish' his own songs.

Whereas in New York Hendrix couldn't even get arrested, he found a refreshingly receptive audience for his brand of R&B in London. This was because, since the early sixties, England had been the home of the blues boom, leaving Chicago-based bands like Paul Butterfield's rank outsiders at another of pop's perpetual revolutions. As with skiffle, this was a boom wholly inspired by a handful of crude post-war recordings made a thousand miles from New York and a million miles from the pop charts, transposed across the pond with its prewar antecedents in that melange of folk and blues intact.

Again, it had been English musicians who picked up on American undercurrents of popular song that were being largely ignored by America's young. In fact, the London-based blues boom that allowed Hendrix to bask in its afterglow was another offshoot of the post-war 'trad. jazz' boom which had already spawned skiffle.

When The Rolling Stones – formed from Alexis Korner's rootsy Blues Incorporated – first established a name in the nation's capital in the early months of 1963, they laid their sound down at Ken Colyer's Jazz Club, Studio 51. Back then, before Andrew Loog Oldham dressed them up and Decca's Dick Rowe – still smarting at letting The Beatles slip through his grasp – demanded a poppier sound, the March 1963 demo tape that got Brian Jones and the Rolling Stones the Decca deal comprised two Bo Diddley songs, two Jimmy Reed songs and a Willie Dixon original. At that time the six-piece band were the purest of the pure.

Recalling early pep-talks, guitarist Brian Jones suggested it had been 'Mick [who] usually led the discussions. He'd say that we really had to go for what we believed in. We had this sort of obsession about pushing rhythm 'n' blues across to a wide people here. We wanted *our* idols to be idolized by everybody else.' The singer's early comments to the press certainly suggest someone with a fundamentalist approach to this 'alien' musical form:

> **Mick Jagger:** It's okay for people to holler around about their favourites like Elmore James, or John Lee Hooker, but that won't help these stars get known on a wider level unless groups like us go round the country playing their sort of music. We don't look like a bunch of schoolmasters, I admit, but at least we try to educate people in American blues music.

Of course, when Jagger used the term 'American blues music', he really meant the output of one studio in a specific city: Chess, Chicago, IL. A glance at early Stones set-lists shows a band with plenty of attitude but devoid of originality, plying the works of Chuck Berry, Muddy Waters, Howlin' Wolf and Bo Diddley. Jimmy Reed and Elmore James got a look in – the latter's 'Dust My Blues', 'Blues Before Sunrise' and 'Happy Home' were all part of the Stones' 1962 repertoire – but otherwise it was Chess pieces only.

As Keef later put it, 'Our aim was to turn other people on to Muddy Waters. We were carrying flags, idealistic teenage sort of shit. There's no way we think anybody is really going to seriously listen to us. [Just] as long as we can get a few people interested in listening to the shit we think they ought to listen to.' Such a high-minded goal was to last until the moment their manager Andrew Oldham realized that in music-making, the real money lay in publishing.

In the eighteen months before their own Chess 'audition', the Stones were one of many English R&B bands that were 'getting up, getting stuff and going with it': The Pretty Things, The Yardbirds, The Detours (the early Who) and The Ravens (the early Kinks) in London, The Animals in Newcastle, the Spencer Davis Group in Birmingham, The Monarchs (Van Morrison's pre-Them combo) in Belfast, to name a chosen few. But even when British youth was exposed to Chicago's finest – and the Stones had toured the UK with their idol, Bo Diddley, for six weeks in autumn 1963 – they preferred their own brand, even if it came not from the cotton fields but from dark satanic mill towns. Dartford's rolling renegades were the first English R&B combo to break out – and the first to release British R&B into a marketplace that may not have known 'real R&B', but knew real (gone) music when they heard it.

As Bo could have told 'em, conquering the US would not be such a breeze. When, four months after The Beatles stormed the Capitol, the Stones arrived in America, to make their US TV debut with a Willie Dixon song, the response was decidedly tepid. The Stones picked themselves up, dusted their broom and headed for Chicago where, a week later, they ran into Muddy Waters at Chess studios on 2120 South Michigan Avenue. He had agreed to meet and greet this quintet of cocky Cockney R&B purists that called themselves after one of 'his' classic numbers, 'Rollin' Stone'.

The Stones were at Chess primarily because of the work Waters, Willie Dixon, Howlin' Wolf, Chuck Berry and Bo Diddley had done the decade before. But they had already started dipping their toes in a wider song pool. Of the fourteen songs they cut across the two days at Chess, just two – 'Look What You've Done' and 'I Can't Be Satisfied' – came from Waters' chest, and only the latter, the *ur*-text of Muddy's blues since at least 1941, would be considered suitable for release (though I personally rate their piston-powered version of the former). They were also cocksure enough, in these hallowed environs, to jam their way through two 'original' instrumentals – '2120 South Michigan Avenue' and 'Brian's Blues (Stewed & Keefed)'. If Waters joined in on the loose jam the boys named after the studio's address, his contribution was edited from the version Decca UK ended up releasing.

Meanwhile, the song from the session destined to become the Stones' first UK number one was a Bobby Womack song, 'It's All Over Now'. It was hardly the sort of thing one usually recorded at Chess. But while Waters stayed stuck in the Mississippi mud, the Stones were already moving on.

No one at 2120 traded on their 'authenticity' as much as, or for as long as, 'Muddy' Morganfield. Muddy, as much as Carl Perkins, liked to trace his lineage back to the Mississippi Delta and 'to the cotton patch where it came from'. Perhaps it was why both exhausted their store of song-ideas the day they stopped mining tradition.

In Muddy's case, it all went back to the day Alan Lomax pulled up at his stoop and asked if he had a song to sing. The most enduring song he played that day was one even Lomax knew was not Muddy's own. When he queried the country bluesman about it, he found Waters' explanation for the song's genesis changed with the summer breeze, as Jonathan Lethem highlighted in his important essay, 'The Ecstasy of Influence':

> After singing the song, which he told Lomax was titled 'Country Blues' [sic], Waters described how he came to write it. 'I made it on about the eighth of October [19]38,' Waters said. 'I was fixin' a puncture on a car. I had been mistreated by a girl. I just felt blue, and the song fell into my mind and it come to me just like that and I started singing.' Then Lomax, who knew of the Robert Johnson recording called 'Walkin' Blues', asked Waters if there were any other songs that used the same tune. 'There's been some blues played like that,' Waters replied. 'This song comes from the cotton field and a boy once put a record out – Robert Johnson. He put it out as named "Walkin' Blues." I heard the tune before I heard it on the record. I learned it from Son House.' In nearly one breath, Waters [here] offers five accounts: his own active authorship: he

'made it' on a specific date. Then the 'passive' explanation: 'it come to me just like that'. After Lomax raises the question of influence, Waters, without shame, misgivings or trepidation, says that he heard a version by Johnson, but that his mentor, Son House, taught it to him. In the middle of that complex genealogy, Muddy declares: 'This song comes from the cotton field.'

The answers Lomax received convinced even him to steer clear of claiming a copyright from this legal quagmire. Whatever Waters claimed, 'Country Blues' was a dual homage to House's 'My Black Mama' and Johnson's 'Walkin' Blues', while the other key song he played Lomax that day, 'I'se Be Troubled', had an equally debt-ridden past. Yet it was with this pair that Waters was preparing a path away from the country.

When Lomax returned to Waters again the following year, he learnt that Waters had added a coupla songs to his repertoire, neither very original. He also found out that popular pieces at local dances still included Tommy Johnson's 1928 'Bye Bye Blues' (which Howlin' Wolf would record for Chess as 'I Asked For Water'); and that Waters owned a wind-up Victrola, two records by Arthur Crudup and Tony Hollins' version of 'Crawling King Snake' – but no Robert Johnson records.

Lomax had ended up at Waters' porch only after finding out the king of the delta blues singers, the late great R. Johnson, was dead. He found a repository of rural tradition who fit the Frank Walker model, someone whose 'repertoire . . . consist[ed] of eight or ten things that they did well and that was all they knew'. But like Jimmie the Brakeman, Muddy was convinced it was enough and hopped a train to Chicago some time in 1943, determined to replicate his initial recording experience in a sound-proof studio. He later boasted, 'The blues is tone, deep tone with a beat . . . By itself that sound would never have made it to Chicago. I guess I'm one of the first people who was thinking of that sound, leaning on that sound and when I got here I found people could get close to that sound.'

In reality, a number of blues musicians who worked (when required) for Lester Melrose were already beefing up that country blues sound in the Windy City, when Waters demoed three songs for Melrose and Columbia in September 1946. But Melrose didn't dive in. Waters changed tack, recording two uncharacteristic, commercial-style blues for the Aristocrat label the following year. 'Little Anna Mae' b/w 'Gypsy Woman' fooled no one, not even the new boss Leonard Chess, who was so underwhelmed he held on to the tracks for several months before letting them leak into the world. Fortunately for the future of music, Chess gave Waters a second chance.

In April 1948, Waters came in to cut a second single for Aristocrat. If he had nothing new to say, by then he had at least found a new way to say it. Tired of trying to second-guess his producers, this time Waters gave it to 'em straight, cutting three songs in a single afternoon, two of them the self-same numbers he'd played Lomax seven years earlier. Only they were now called 'I Can't Be Satisfied' and 'Feel Like Goin' Home'. Although he was only accompanied by Big Crawford on slap bass, they rocked like a ship out on the sea.

This was the famous occasion when Chess complained, 'I can't understand what he's singing,' and wondered aloud who the hell would buy this kinda music. He did not expect a reply, but he got one – from the female co-founder of Aristocrat, Evelyn Aron: 'You'd be surprised who'd buy that.' At this stage Aron still had as much say at Aristocrat as Chess, so the record was released. Its impact was immediate. By nightfall on the first day of its release, the price of available copies on the south side of town had doubled, or so the legend goes. Chess had underestimated demand, big-time. The single reached eleven on the R&B charts and gave Aristocrat its first bona fide hit.

It would also be their last hit for two years (meaning a further eight Muddy Waters singles). By that time Chess had ousted the last of the Arons, renamed the label after himself, and Waters had exhausted most of his core repertoire. These included 'You're Gonna Miss Me (When I'm Dead and Gone)', a song Lomax liked so much he recorded it twice back in 1942, 'Rollin' Stone' (Waters's adaptation of Petway's 'Catfish Blues'), and reinterpretations of Robert Johnson's 'Walkin' Blues' and Hambone

Willie's elemental 'Roll and Tumble Blues'. These were the songs and sound which would inspire every would-be British blues guitarist from Keith Richards to Peter Green, Eric Clapton to Jimmy Page. But they failed to generate any chart action outside of Chicago itself, where electric blues was the new rockin' religion.

Waters became convinced it was Chess who stood in his way; and not because he had yet to see a royalty cheque. Chess simply refused to let him record with his live band, a four-piece that at this time included the likes of Jimmy Rogers, Little Walter and 'Baby Face' Leroy Foster. In their pre-rock & roll pomp this lot blasted the blues till the whole South Side heard the news.

Determined to show Chess he knew how to make blues as electric as a trip-wire, Waters recorded 'Rollin' And Tumblin' under the moniker The Baby Face Leroy Trio, and then – to get around his exclusive contract with Chess – released it on his manager's homegrown label, Parkway Records. The bottleneck style Waters unleashed here came from another blue planet, and though the song failed to reignite the R&B charts, it convinced Chess to think again. When Waters followed up a re-recorded, Chess studio rendition of 'Rollin' And Tumblin' with 'Louisiana Blues', a slowed-down version of the same song with different words, he finally resumed residency in the R&B charts.

The problem Muddy found was one common to bluesmen of the Delta school – there were only so many ways to shake the tree of plenty without ripping it up by the roots (as Hendrix would do). By 1950, Waters was struggling to maintain an edge, or keep his band interested. As his guitarist Jimmy Rogers later remarked, 'He never was a very good writer. He'd come up with an idea, and we'd build from that.' Most of the time they were working from pre-existing foundations. 'Rollin Stone', 'Walkin' Blues', 'Rollin' And Tumblin', 'Still A Fool', 'Turn The Lamp Down Low' (a.k.a. 'Baby Please Don't Go'), 'Trouble No More' and 'Rock Me' – all songs Waters recorded between 1950 and 1956 *and* took a song-credit on – all patently derived from pre-existing blues, in most cases ones already copyrighted.

What Hambone Willie would have made of Muddy's modern take on his 'Roll And Tumble Blues' we'll never know, because after recording just six songs for Okeh in 1929, he ended up in jail for murder, where he was murdered himself in a prison brawl. Waters doubtless knew the song's other commercial antecedents – Gus Cannon's 'Minglewood Blues', which actually predates Hambone's, and Charley Patton's 'It Won't Be Long' – but when he was later asked about the song, the only version he deferred to was Hambone's: 'I think I played it better than anybody else I know and I was a Johnny-come-lately. I met Son House, James Smith and all of them people, but I played it better than either one of them – except the one who made it on the [original] record.'

Some debts transferred to the post-war era. Muddy's 'Rock Me' may predate B.B. King's 'Rock Me Baby' by eight years, but it was still six years adrift of the Lil' Son Jackson song, 'Rockin' And Rollin', to which both were equally beholden; while his 'Trouble No More' owed as much to Big Maceo's 'Worried Life Blues' as Sleepy John Estes' 'Someday Baby Blues'. Big Joe Williams's 'Baby Please Don't Go' had been recorded at least three times by its 'author' before Waters wondered whether a change of title might confer a change of copyright.*

In fact, as Benjamin Filene notes in his book on American roots music: 'Waters's hits from the early fifties . . . remain[ed] securely within the traditional Delta blues style. Almost all the songs were slow, twelve-bar blues that followed the A-A-B lyrics pattern. Waters was . . . updating his sound with talented band members, but basically he was resting his commercial hopes on variations of the same sorts of songs he had played for Alan Lomax a decade before.' Once again, it took a (five-single) run of chart failures in 1952–3 to make Waters change his mind, and parameters. When he did, it was at the behest of a big bass man who would ring changes that were to revolutionize R&B.

\* \* \*

---

* According to legend, Williams actually got the song from his wife who, when she heard it on a jukebox playing below her apartment, ran down to see who had nicked it, only to find out it was her husband.

That bass man was Willie Dixon, and unbeknownst to Chess, he was already a secret songwriter. Until that auspicious Muddy Waters session in January 1954, Chess had been content to see Dixon as a musician and session organizer. Already, though, Dixon had a rep. as something of a hustler, with dark mutterings from other musicians about how 'he could get you a date with Chess or one of the smaller labels he also worked for if you were willing to give him a "taste" – that is, willing to kick back some of your session fee.'

When Dixon 'suddenly' transformed himself into a songwriter whilst Muddy was still trying to rework yet another Charley Patton or Son House riff, certain Chessmen were convinced he had 'purchased or stole[n] many of the songs he copyrighted'. However, according to Dixon's autobiography, he had been hiding this light of his until he had amassed 150 songs, the best of which he now drip-fed to Waters and Howlin' Wolf. He had concluded it was all a question of structure, telling Peter Guralnick, 'In dealing with twelve-bar music you could never get a chance to express everything or tell a complete story. And so I started writing introductions to these songs, and also middle [eight]s, and changing ideas within it.'

This was exactly what he now did with 'I'm A Hoochie Coochie Man', 'I Just Want To Make Love To You' and 'I'm Ready', all of which cracked the R&B top five in 1954. And his uncredited reworking of 'Maybellene' also gave Chuck Berry and Chess a top five *pop* hit, turning the blues into a popular craft again and showing others how the form could be updated. As he put it, 'Every time you change the news, you got to change the blues, because the news ain't always the same.' *He* had heard the news – as had Berry, the only other person at Chess reading from the same page.

'Hoochie Coochie Man' – a seemingly standard blues song that broke all the rules – first suggested he was on to something. Ben Filene's distillation of the Dixon method tells it like it is: 'Like most pop songs, "Hoochie Coochie Man" divides neatly into eight-bar chunks. It also borrows from pop tunes the technique of the recurring chorus, an element foreign to most Delta blues songs . . . [And] the song's admixture of pop-influenced blues and juiced-up downhome lyrics proved explosive.' Waters' biggest seller to date, it rose to the top three on the R&B charts in March 1954. Chess promptly cajoled Dixon into writing more songs like it, copyrighting them to his own publishing company, Arc.

Dixon was now the official Chess R&B songwriter, publishing contract pending. Not everyone was thrilled. Jimmy Rogers, Waters' guitarist, suggests those defining 1954 singles were more of a collaborative process: 'Willie Dixon got credit for being a writer on a lot of songs he just played a part in . . . I had enough edge on him there not to let him hook me up that way, but Muddy went for it.' It was an accusation Chuck Berry also sent in Dixon's direction. But if it was that simple, why weren't others following Dixon's lead? After all, as Berry pithily put it, 'Baby please don't go, baby please don't go, I love you so, baby please don't go. What's to that?'

Waters, no shrinking violet, certainly convinced himself he could do the same thing. Indeed, with 'Mannish Boy', 'Got My Mojo Working' and 'Evil' – his three best-known songs from the second half of the decade – he stopped borrowing brazenly from pre-war predecessors and instead filched 'musical techniques from Dixon's work – eight-bar verses, repeated choruses, stop-time', and when that didn't work, took from Bo, too [Filene].

'Mannish Boy' sailed close to the wind, given Diddley's ability to harbour a grudge. However, it was 'Got My Mojo Working' that really got Muddy in deep water. It was another Muddy parody, setting the bravado of 'Hoochie Coochie Man' and 'I'm Ready' to a stock, Dixonesque groove. But the song was not his. It had been released in 1956 on Baton by Ann Cole and the Suburbans, credited to Preston Foster, and with lyrics that might strike a chord: 'Got my Mojo working but it just won't work on you [x2]/I want to love you so that I don't know what to do/I got my black cat bones all pure and dry/I got my four-leaf clovers all hanging high/I got my Mojo working but it just won't work on you.'

This time Waters had no defence, having witnessed Cole regularly perform the song while touring together. Arc Music were obliged to recognize the primacy of Foster's copyright, though only after Waters initially tried to copyright the song to himself.

By the time Waters was passing off 'Got My Mojo Working' as his own, he didn't have Willie on hand to slap that bass or counsel him on copyright. Dixon had quit Chess. He had grown tired of the arm-bending required to get Leonard Chess to come through, and he went looking for another home:

> **Willie Dixon**: I wouldn't say that Chess appreciated what I was doing. I got fed up with money coming out wrong, that's why I started working for Eli [Toscano] . . . Then Eli gambled away all the money he was making, and I had to go back to Chess. At that time I didn't know enough about copyrights – you might get one check from Leonard when he felt like it, then you never knew when the next one was coming. One time Willie Mabon thought he had a big cheque coming from Leonard after he had a hit with 'I Don't Know'; then when the money arrived it came up short. He went into the Chess building with a gun and Leonard had to lock himself in his room. Chuck Berry might have enough clout to go after Leonard with a gun, but not Willie Mabon.

For everyone, save perhaps Berry – whose appeal straddled the racial divide – Chess was for most of the fifties the only game in town. But again, Dixon acted decisively where other labelmates, perhaps with more clout, merely bitched and moaned behind Leonard's back. Unfortunately Cobra, the short-lived label Toscano set up, would always be beset by financial worries, even after Dixon wrote the label its first single, 'I Can't Quit You Baby', which became a top ten R&B hit for Otis Rush (and a veritable moneyspinner all over again when Led Zeppelin covered it on their debut album).

Without Willie, Waters and the Wolf initially floundered. Pre-Cobra, Dixon's role at Howlin' Wolf sessions had generally been to help pick away at the Wolf's pre-war dragnet and tie down that bottom end. Wolf thought he had songs to spare, and Dixon was content playing bass on all of Wolf's Chess sessions from March 1954 through June 1957 as they laid down songs like 'Baby, How Long', 'Evil Is Going On', 'I Asked For Water' and 'Smokestack Lightning'. Each advanced on the sound and sensibility originally displayed by Wolf on 'Cryin' At Daybreak', the single he cut for RPM in 1951, using antecedents as localized in time and place as Waters' equally explosive Chess debut.

Like Waters before him, Howlin' Wolf only turned to Dixon's songwriting after he exhausted the repertoire of 'originals' he had scooped up from the communal pre-war pool. That he had a tranche of them should come as no surprise to anyone conversant with the man's background. Born Chester Burnett in Mississippi in 1910, he was lucky enough twenty years later to meet the great bluesman Charley Patton, from whom he learnt the likes of 'Pony Blues', 'Moon Going Down', 'High Water Everywhere' and 'A Spoonful Blues'. His professional moniker came when he tried to emulate Jimmie Rodgers' blue yodel and discovered, 'I couldn't do no yodelin', so I turned to howlin'.'

He had also evidently heard Tommy Johnson and the Mississippi Sheiks – maybe in person, but if not, certainly on record. Both 'Cryin' At Daybreak' and 'Smokestack Lightning' use the melody and refrain of Johnson's 'Big Road Blues', as well as the falsetto moan found in Johnson's 'Cool Drink Of Water Blues'. The 1956 version of the latter also lifted stanzas two, three and four from the Mississippi Sheiks' 'Stop And Listen Blues', recorded in February 1930. It gave Wolf his first Top Ten R&B hit since his first Chess single, 'How Many More Years' b/w 'Moanin' At Midnight', back in 1951. In 1957, he returned to plunder the Sheiks again with his irresistible take of 'Sittin' On Top Of The World', though only after recording his version of Tommy Johnson's 'Cool Water Blues', the memorable 'I Asked For Water (She Bought Me Gasoline)'. In each case, the song credit read Chester Burnett.

Fortunately for the Wolf, an exasperated Dixon knew by early 1959 he would have to sue for peace and return to Chess, feeding the label's blues behemoth songs which took that sense of braggadocio he had given Muddy's work to a whole other level. Dixon resumed their alliance that summer, donating a taster of how things could be. Written to type,

'Howlin' For My Baby (Darling)' gave Burnett ample opportunity to howl.

In the years before the British blues boom, Dixon and Wolf set about compiling a select but fearsome body of songs whose imagery remained resolutely traditional – in the case of 'Spoonful', coming straight from a Charley Patton Paramount 78 – but had a pop sensibility that conferred copyright on Dixon and kudos on Wolf. It is no coincidence that 'Little Red Rooster', 'Back Door Man' and 'Spoonful' would become big hits for the Stones, The Doors and Cream before the decade was out, though neither Jagger nor Morrison could muster a fifth of the Wolf's menace.

By the time the British blues players started buying up every Chess single they could find, the unholy trinity of Waters, Dixon and Wolf had given a whole generation of electric bluesmen their own set of gospels. And like all good believers, they took everything they read on those Chess labels as the Truth.

Ultimately, it would be the songs Dixon wrote in the three years after his return to Chess in 1959 that would provide a gilt-edged pension plan – though they would have nothing like the same initial impact as Muddy Waters' 1954 triple whammy. And Howlin' Wolf was not the only beneficiary. Waters also now realized he needed to be nice to the three-hundred-pound hulk if he was ever to whiff success again. A pair of songs Dixon gave Waters in 1962 – 'You Shook Me' and 'You Need Love' – fell with a resounding thud, but the aftershock resonated long enough to provide Dixon with his most robust revenue stream, once he set legal Rottweilers on certain credit stealers from across the pond. In the same year, he gave Bo Diddley one last leg-up with the compulsive 'You Can't Judge A Book By Its Cover', a song so catchy the Stones demoed it as a possible first single when Bo's own take had barely reached the import shops.

By 1964, the great unwashed of Great Britain were sending a steady stream of song publishing to the south side of Chicago, the home of Arc Music. Taking at face value Waters' supposed authorship of 'Trouble No More',

'Rollin' Stone' and 'Rollin' And Tumblin', and Wolf's of 'Smokestack Lightning' and 'Sitting On Top Of The World', the Brits were initially oblivious to the sound of cash registers ringing four thousand miles away.

That is, until Lonnie Donegan – of all people – decided he would call the Stones to account on a December 1964 episode of the hugely popular TV show, *Juke Box Jury*, suggesting *they* were exploiting the 'original' blues artists and making money out of 'their' songs. Of the various howls of 'hypocrisy, thy name is Lonnie', one from John Berry in the letter pages of *Record Mirror* would have brought a particularly broad smile to the face of Alan Lomax:

> I've been a blues fan since before the skiffle days. The Stones are very serious about the blues and have done it and its exponents a lot of good – more than can be said for the skiffle craze. As for saying that the Stones are exploiting blues artists and making money out of it, Mr Donegan has got things the wrong way round. When the Stones record a number by a blues artist, the credit is given to him and he gets the royalties. They also seize every chance to make these artists more known here. In Mr Donegan's day, the idea was to take a song of an obscure artist, adapt it to skiffle and record it as 'Trad arr. Donegan' . . . Surely, that's nearer exploitation.

Not only were Donegan's barbs a case of the pot calling the kettle colored, but as Jagger was quick to point out in a letter of his own to *Melody Maker*, 'These legendary characters wouldn't mean a light commercially today if groups were not going round Britain doing their numbers.' The furore may even have helped the Stones' last R&B A-side, Willie Dixon's 'Little Red Rooster', to reach number one in the UK. Meanwhile, Jagger told *Disc*'s Penny Valentine, 'The reason we recorded "Little Red Rooster" isn't because we want to bring blues to the masses. We've been going on and on about the blues, so we thought it was about time we stopped talking and did something about it.'

The single should have provided a bonanza for Dixon. But when

Muddy Waters came up to him one day and impertinently suggested, 'You oughta give me some of that money you're making off these songs I caused them [English] boys to have,' the three-hundred-pound Dixon squared up to Waters and insisted he had yet to see his own share. Evidently, any distaste on Waters' part for the Anglicized version of the blues did not stop him laying claim to someone else's copyrights when he needed a new guitar amp. Maybe all that braggadocio on record was not such an act.

In fact, he significantly overvalued his contribution. Although the Stones had taken their name from Muddy's remake of 'Catfish Blues', the only one of his own songs they covered in their halcyon days was 'I Can't Be Satisfied', for which they had the good grace to give him sole credit. Dixon's songs, on the other hand, always had enough pop sensibility to sit easily either on a B-side ('I Wanna Be Loved'), an A-side ('Little Red Rooster') or an LP side ('I Just Wanna Make Love To You').

Other blues acts with a sense of what made a song perennially popular also benefited from the British blues boom, including Big Joe Williams, whose song (or his wife's), 'Baby Please Don't Go' was a Top Ten hit for Van Morrison's Them. And although Big Bill Broonzy died in 1958, his estate considered 'The Key To The Highway', a song covered by everyone from the Stones to John Mayall's Bluesbreakers, a Broonzy composition, though it was recorded first by Charlie Segar in 1940.

Even the version Big Bill recorded the following year with Jazz Gillum was credited to Gillum. Broonzy's explanation was simple: 'Practically all of blues is just a little change from the way that they was sung when I was a kid . . . You take one song and make fifty out of it . . . just change it a little bit.' In fact, Broonzy laid claim to just about everything in his distinctly familiar repertoire, a patent impossibility, telling Alan Lomax: 'All these numbers I recorded, practically, were mine. Maybe ten or twelve were other guys' numbers, but the rest I wrote . . . Back in those days some of these guys were better musicians than I was . . . so these record people took lots of my numbers and give um to other guys to make.'

Elmore James was another to profit, grabbing a credit on assorted cover versions of 'Dust My Broom' – a song many blues fans presumed he had purloined from the late Robert Johnson, as opposed to, say, Leroy Carr or Kokomo Arnold. James, though, was no pre-war bluesman. He actually learnt the song from Arthur Crudup, with whom he gigged around 1949. He may even have initially believed it originated there. Crudup recorded the song himself in March 1949, and took a song-credit, too. But this time, Crudup did not make or lose millions on a song he had largely appropriated because his own version – with some less effective lyrics – passed everyone by, superseded by the altogether more blistering version James recorded in 1951 with Sonny Boy Williamson.

For now, British bands asked precious few questions as they doled out the publishing on 'Good Morning Schoolgirl' to Williamson instead of Son Bonds, author of 'Back And Side Blues'; on 'Smokestack Lightning' to Howlin' Wolf, as opposed to the Mississippi Sheiks and/or Charley Patton; on 'Boogie Chillen' to John Lee Hooker, not Blind Blake for 'Hastings Street Boogie'; and on 'Don't Lie To Me' to Chuck Berry, rather than Tampa Red. As for Waters, pretty much anything he put his name to was suspect, even when plagiarizing himself.

In fact, the only people the Brits were making rich with their covers of R&B and soul singles were the label bosses themselves. There was even one particularly shameful instance when Berry Gordy, owner of Detroit's Motown Records, arranged to have Barrett Strong's name removed from the song-credits before 'Money (That's What I Want)' was covered by The Beatles and The Rolling Stones. Gordy – whose own name had appeared on 'Money' from the outset, even though no one at the 'Money' session can remember him making a single telling contribution – pocketed the lot.

If there was a 'co-author' it wasn't Gordy. Nor was he 'at' the session. Had Gordy been disposed to surrender his share back in 1959, when the song nearly topped the R&B charts (stopping at number two), it should have been to Ray Charles. Because, as Barrett Strong openly admits, 'We were doing another [Motown] session, and I just happened to be sitting there playing the piano. I was playing "What'd I Say," by Ray Charles, and the ["Money"] groove spun off of that.'

Leonard Chess was never quite as brazen as Gordy, but he was hardly going to win an award for good business practice. All the exposure over in Britain only made Bo Diddley complain loud and hard about Chess's accounting: 'I don't know who they were paying out the money they said they were paying , but it sure wasn't to me.' The label boss even protected one Chess artist's interests when somebody pointed out that the riff to The Beach Boys' first major hit, 'Surfin' USA' in 1963 was a 100 per cent cop from Chuck Berry's 'Sweet Little Sixteen'. The settlement would serve as an object lesson to all-comers to keep their hands off. Arc demanded a 50 per cent share of the Beach Boys' royalties and a song-credit that now read, 'Berry-Wilson'.

Generally, such steals had to be blindingly obvious for Chess to notice; and Chuck Berry riffs by the mid-sixties were almost ubiquitous in popular music. So ubiquitous in fact, that Dylan decided to announce his semi-electric apostasy on his fifth album, *Bringing It All Back Home*, with a homage to Berry's 'Too Much Monkey Business'. The amphetamine-fuelled 'Subterranean Homesick Blues' became his first Top Forty single.

It wasn't Bobby's first cop from Chuck, just the first one pop critics noticed. The little guitar figure he'd used on his 1964 composition, 'I Don't Believe You', came from Berry's Chess version of 'Worried Life Blues' (a.k.a. Sleepy John Estes' 'Someday Baby Blues').* Once again, it was a case of 'interesting people steal[ing] more interestingly'. In fact, Dylan's most interesting cop from the period when he was the wild mercury kid came from such an unlikely source that it took four years, and a highly attuned producer, to point it out. After nearly a year of immersing himself in the kinda R&B he grew up with – and inspired by the commercial impact of The Animals' 'House of The Rising Sun' – Dylan wrote 'Like A Rolling Stone', and thus rewrote the book of pop.

---

* Estes' song had been supplying other songs since the London Blitz, including Muddy Waters' 'Trouble No More', a song Dylan himself would cover in 1992, fourteen years before he revisited Estes' original for his own 'Someday Baby', a recasting of the song with enough lyrical debts to keep blues lexicographers busy till the crack of doom.

What was on his mind is not readily apparent from the finished lyrics, or even the song titles he doodled in the margin of its original draft: 'False Knight On The Road', 'Butcher Boy', 'Pony Blues' and 'Midnight Special'. All were songs in the public domain, none serve as an obvious predecessor. But what was also in the public domain was 'La Bamba', a traditional Mexican folksong adapted by Ritchie Valens for his 1958 hit. Phil Spector commented on the connection in a 1969 *Rolling Stone* interview, where he drily remarked, 'Rewriting "La Bamba" chord changes is always a lot of fun and any time you can make a Number One record and rewrite those changes, it is very satisfying.' Sixteen years later, Dylan owned up to the charge, telling Cameron Crowe, 'It just came, you know. It started with that "La Bamba" riff . . . My wife and I lived in a little cabin in Woodstock, New York, which we rented. I wrote the song there.'

That may not, however, be the whole truth. It seems Dylan actually started the song in London, at the Savoy Hotel to be precise, a matter of days after he had booked a session with England's premier 'authentic' R&B combo, John Mayall's Bluesbreakers, who at this juncture featured a precocious young blues guitarist name of Eric Clapton. The session was a complete disaster. (At one point, Mayall asked the singer if he had worked with bands much.) But 'Like a Rolling Stone', whatever its antecedents, unlocked Dylan's electric muse.

The result was rock music – along with a very angry Alan Lomax and an even angrier Pete Seeger (who later concocted another of his fairytales, claiming he had just been upset by the Newport sound mix!). It also provided the final trigger for (mainly English) songwriters to put all their musical influences into one great big melting pot, and stir. By the end of 1965, Lennon and McCartney did not feel so all alone. Mick Jagger and Keith Richards, Ray Davies, Pete Townshend, Van Morrison, Steve Winwood, Steve Marriott and Ronnie Lane had all picked up pens and begun to do a very British duckwalk.

It was time for blues purists like the Butterfield Blues Band and John Mayall's Bluesbreakers to head back underground and re-evaluate; biding their time, doing drugs and playing the blues, in that order. R&B's time would come again, but only for those willing to follow Hendrix down the path to psychedelic blues. Meanwhile, Britain's songwriters went to work unaware that, at the end of it, many of the pockets they would be lining would be sewn into American pants.

# CHAPTER 11

# 1962–7: Take Another Little Piece

*Featuring*: 'All My Loving'; 'I Feel Fine'; 'Yesterday'; 'Not Fade Away'; 'Play With Fire'; 'Spanish Harlem'; 'The Last Time'; 'You Really Got Me'; 'I Can't Explain'; 'Satisfaction'; 'Substitute'; 'Gloria'; 'Here Comes The Night'

> The record companies [in the early 60s] were on the look out for songs for the likes of Cliff Richard, Adam Faith and Marty Wilde. None of the new British pop or rock stars wrote their own material, so there was always a chance of getting a song published . . . The Beatles revolutionized our business because they didn't need songs – they had their own.
>
> Bill Martin, songwriter, in *Northern Songs: The True Story of The Beatles' Publishing Empire:* Brian Southall (2007)

While the rest of these conjoined isles enjoyed an R&B boom through the early sixties, the port of Liverpool, resolutely separatist, kept itself to itself still spinning off skiffle's axis. Even the new-fangled rock & roll took some getting used to: when John Lennon's Quarry Men played their first concert at The Cavern in August 1957, owner Alan Sytner sent a terse message to Lennon after a raucous 'Blue Suede Shoes': 'Cut the bloody rock.' Preferring a poppier sound to the relentless backbeat of the blues, bands like The (Silver) Beatles, The Searchers, The Big Three and Rory Storm and The Hurricanes coined a new term in pop's lexicon – Merseybeat.

Perhaps the sense of novelty that was forever pop's primary brief came easier to bands like The Beatles precisely because they avoided steeping themselves in American folk and blues. The only Chess act they covered, even in 1961 when they made regular sorties to Hamburg, was Chuck

Berry. As for the quasi-traditional material mined by others, the only such songs in the Quarry Men's repertoire in 1957–9, when still a semi-skiffle outfit, came entirely from secondary sources: 'Freight Train' (Chas Devitt Skiffle Group), 'Maggie May' (The Vipers), 'Cumberland Gap', 'Midnight Special', 'Railroad Bill', 'Rock Island Line' (Lonnie Donegan), 'When The Saints Go Marching In' (Bill Haley) and 'Worried Man Blues' (The Vipers or Donegan).

But what really set The Beatles apart from their contemporaries, even early on, was a willingness to perform, without any sense of shame, their very own pop pastiches – which was everything they wrote at this stage. Even during their first crude attempt to record themselves in 1958, they spent as long on a McCartney-Harrison original, 'In Spite Of All The Danger' (the first and last time Harrison got a co-credit for crafting a guitar solo on a Beatles track), as they did on a cover of 'That'll Be The Day'.* And by 1960, at least four other 'original' songs – 'Hello Little Girl', 'Like Dreamers Do', 'Love Of The Loved' and 'One After 909' – were already mainstays of their set.

By 1962, it was clear Lennon and McCartney had enough songs of their own – even if, on the first day of this auspicious year, they cut a fifteen-song demo which omitted their strongest original song ('One After 909'), and included three embarrassing novelty songs ('Sheik of Araby', 'Three Cool Cats' and 'Besame Mucho').

Six months later, at EMI, they corrected their mistake, playing Parlophone producer George Martin 'Love Me Do', 'P.S. I Love You', and 'Ask Me Why'; though still not 'One After 909', a song they returned to at their third single session. All four McCartney-Lennon compositions – as the credits read then – were good enough to render Frank Ifield and his antiseptic ilk redundant. And by June 1964 The Beatles had released their first all-original album, *A Hard Day's Night*, a thirteen-song masterclass in pop songwriting. In the intervening two years, they had recorded three

---

* Thankfully, they did nothing with the former or they might have heard from Rose Marie McCoy and Charles Singleton, the authors of 'Tryin' To Get To You', the Elvis classic from which 'Macca' copped the tune.

albums, seven singles and thirty-four original Lennon-McCartney compositions which ripped up the rulebook.

Remarkably, this was all achieved without much in the way of obvious plagiarizing, though 'All My Loving', written for the second album, was an exception. For that earnest attempt on McCartney's part to write an MOR standard – something at which he would later excel – he needed a little help from a 'friend'. In this instance it bore a distinct melodic similarity to a 1959 Dave Brubeck Quartet track, 'Kathy's Waltz', hardly a song their caterwauling audience was likely to pick up on. But The Beatles' most blatant 'nick' in the pre-*Rubber Soul* era was probably the riff from Bobby Parker's 'Watch Your Step'. A song that featured in their early live repertoire, it was put to service for their eighth single, 'I Feel Fine' (and was still being pressed into service, more subtly, on 'Day Tripper' and 'Ticket To Ride'). Though he happily admitted to being a teen 'tea-leaf', the bassist preferred talking in generalities whenever the subject of song-stealing came up, as it did in 1974:

> **Paul McCartney**: We used to nick a lot of stuff . . . especially Miracles, early Motown. Those kind of records because nobody had heard of them at the time. Only people, groups in the business like the Stones . . . Just a few hip groups. And the Stones and us used to have a quick wink about who'd nicked what. I don't nick as much as I used to. I've gone clean.*

Fortunately for The Beatles and the Stones, lessons in harmonics and song structure from soul singers were not actionable. Lennon, more magpie than musicologist, insisted in his last major interview that he had a more conscious way of avoiding writs: 'I'd often carry around someone else's song in my head, and only when I'd put it down on tape . . . would

---

* Macca's insistence he has 'gone clean' does not perhaps bear close scrutiny. On his 2013 album, *New*, 'Everybody Out There' takes its chorus lock, stock and two smoking barrels from Lloyd Price's 'Just Because', a song any Beatles fan would know from John Lennon's *Rock & Roll* album.

I consciously change it to my own melody because I knew that otherwise someone would sue me.' Perhaps McCartney did the same with his most famous – and valuable – song. 'Yesterday', he says, was written after waking up one morning with a yearning for scrambled eggs, a gorgeous melody in his head and a deep conviction he had heard it somewhere else. No one has ever isolated the prototype for 'Yesterday', but it is tempting to endorse Spencer Leigh's suggestion – that 'McCartney had heard Nat "King" Cole's "Answer Me, My Love," the mood and the tempo [of which] are similar; and Nat even sings, "You were mine yesterday, I believed that love was here to stay."'

Whatever its inspiration, by June 1964, Lennon and McCartney's songwriting – so fashionable even their detritus supplied hits for The Fourmost ('Hello Little Girl'), Billy J. Kramer ('I'll Be On My Way', 'I'll Keep You Satisfied' and 'From A Window'), Cilla Black ('Love Of The Loved' and 'It's For You') and Peter and Gordon ('A World Without Love' and 'Nobody I Know') – had, indeed, 'revolutionized our business'. The country's non-Liverpudlian bands, raised on R&B, had yet to unleash a single successful, self-composed sortie on the charts.

The Stones, who had 'reluctantly' accepted a Beatles cast-off ('I Wanna Be Your Man') for their second, November 1963 single just to gain a foothold in the single charts, were still some way off a hit formula of their own when they concluded work on their own debut album in February 1964. Jagger was already on record as saying, 'Can you imagine a British-composed R&B song? It just wouldn't make it.' The LP reflected his belief, featuring just two originals, 'Tell Me' and 'Little By Little', and another early group jam, 'Now I've Got A Witness'. As the title indicated, the latter was them riffing on Holland-Dozier-Holland's 'Can I Get A Witness' before (or after) they recorded the real thing.

But if their album was R&B through and through, the Stones' manager, Andrew Loog Oldham – who had already learnt publishing royalties on B-sides were equal in every way to those on A-sides – had begun emulating the old Clarence Williams trick, filling up the flipsides of their singles with 'original' songs. When they didn't have something suitable and time was not on their side, as was the case with 'I Wanna Be Your Man', they simply recorded a group jam and credited the result – in this instance, 'Stoned' – to Nanker-Phelge, a jokey pseudonym usually used when a track was collectively composed by the band. At the same time, Andrew Oldham, fancying himself as another Brian Epstein, was trying to get other bands to record any compositional cast-offs. Imagine his, and their, surprise when one of five Jagger-Richards demos recorded in November/December 1963 – with titles like 'Shang A Doo Lang', 'I'll Hold Your Hand' and 'It Should Be You' – gave Gene Pitney a Top Ten hit. The song was 'That Girl Belongs To Yesterday' – the first in a long line of Jagger put-down songs directed at (a member of) the opposite sex.

Jagger immediately claimed the reason they gave such a catchy song away was 'because it is so different to the material we work on stage with the group . . . We almost had to produce birth-certificates to prove to some people that we'd [written it].' In fact, such was Jagger's conviction that 'a British-composed R&B song' was a contradiction in terms, he had decided to emulate a commercial songwriter. Never short on self-confidence, he set the bar as high as the Brill Building ceiling, revealing that the person 'who really impresses us on the songwriting kick [is] Burt Bacharach. He gets a commercial feel to his work, but it's way, way above most of the normal pop stuff.' In the same 1964 interview, he also hinted for the first time that 'maybe we'll soon get the knack of writing material which would suit the Stones on a single record.'

Oldham knew they weren't quite ready. Should the songs start to flow, they could always test out a couple on the (for now, less important) US market – as they did with 'Tell Me' and 'Heart of Stone'. Baby steps, boys, baby steps. Meantime, there were plenty of Stones B-sides to fill.* The UK B-sides of singles three to seven ('Not Fade Away' to 'Satisfaction') juxtaposed Jagger and Richards' impressive growth as songwriters against

---

* He reserved pastiches like 'Oh I Do Like To See Me On The B-Side' for the strictly fun-time Andrew Loog Oldham Orchestra.

their waning R&B purism. 'Little By Little', 'Good Times, Bad Times', 'Off The Hook', 'Play With Fire' and 'The Spider And The Fly' charted this incremental ascension into Britpop's firmament.

Yet Oldham always felt it was their third A-side, a song we've already encountered in multiple guises, which was their real breakthrough. Through Oldham's eyes, 'Not Fade Away' may have been a Buddy Holly song, but he 'considered it to be like the first song Mick and Keith "wrote," in that they picked the concept of applying that Bo Diddley thing to it. The way they arranged it was the beginning of the shaping of them as songwriters. From then on they wrote.'

They still needed an 'original' B-side, for which they turned to a songwriter with proven pedigree. 'Little By Little' was apparently written mid-session by Jagger and a guest Oldham had invited along, perhaps because Regent Sound Studio was still strictly mono. A faintly embarrassed Phil 'Back To Mono' Spector suggested to Oldham, 'I guess it'd be better if you didn't say too much about me being here on the session. After all, you don't want people saying that I was the guy responsible – you know how people talk.' Oldham was happy to make his boys guilty by association, giving Spector his first Stones song-credit a month after the Andrew Loog Oldham Orchestra gave his doo-wop classic, 'To Know Him Is To Love Him', a treatment it wouldn't forget.

Did Spector expect a co-credit on this innocuous track? He'd had his share of non-credits in LA back in the rock & roll era as he learnt the recording ropes: 'I made a lot of records that were hits that I didn't put my name on, because I couldn't. I took my three hundred dollars and ate for a month and some other guy got the producer credit.' He even claimed to have written for the biggest name in showbiz, telling Richard Williams, 'I was writing songs for Elvis Presley, and I wasn't getting any credit, but I didn't care, because people in the business were finding out, and that's what was important – getting a reputation.'

By the time he landed a production gig with Leiber-Stoller, though, he wanted to see his name on the label. In the end he browbeat Jerry Leiber into putting some words to a melody he had. It became 'Spanish Harlem', a Top Ten hit for Ben E. King. It was the only time Stoller didn't share a credit with Leiber, even though he claimed in their joint oral biography that when Leiber played him the song, 'I was sitting at the piano and started to play a fill between the phrase. The fill fit perfectly . . . I've never heard the song played [subsequently] without that musical figure . . . but I also knew that Phil didn't want to share credit with anyone but Jerry, so I kept quiet.'

By 1964, the shoe was on the other foot. With any song Spector produced, he expected, nay demanded, a co-credit for his creative input at the studio. To his mind at least, this was a form of composition, even if the song was given him by writing partnerships as prolific as Goffin-King and Mann-Weil. In fact, the next time he crossed paths with the Stones in the studio, he provided just exactly this kind of input. The result was the Stones' first original masterpiece, 'Play With Fire'.

The jury remains out as to whether the right person got the cheque. When 'Play With Fire' came out as the B-side of the Stones' first all-original single – and their first 45 to chart both sides of the Atlantic, having been recorded at a Hollywood session in January 1965 – it was credited to Nanker-Phelge. (On 'Little By Little', the credit had read, 'Phelge-Spector.') To muddy the water further, the Stones continued to credit their B-sides to Nanker-Phelge up to 'The Spider And The Fly' (B-side to August 1965's 'Satisfaction'). But the credits for 'Off The Hook' and 'The Spider And The Fly', the B-sides either side of 'Play With Fire', were later amended to Jagger-Richards; those for 'Play With Fire' were not.

However, given that the only members of the Stones present at the recording were Jagger and Richards – the latter on acoustic guitar, the former banging a tambourine, reciting his own deliciously spiteful lyrics – a band composition seems rather unlikely. Spector played bass, and Jack Nitszche, Spector's preferred arranger, provided that distinctive harpsichord arrangement and tamtams. But Nitszche was far more than just an arranger. A producer and songwriter in his own right, he would co-write the Oscar-winning 'Up Where We Belong' in 1982. And – along with middle-class Michael's misogynistic lyrics – the arrangement of 'Play With Fire', far too sophisticated for the Stones themselves at this stage, is what makes the song.

Moreover, if 'Play With Fire' really was a Jagger-Richards composition, it seems slightly surprising Oldham chose as the A-side the other song recorded that day. Because 'The Last Time' was not wholly theirs. Only a few months earlier, Jagger had suggested to the band's first biographer, 'Sometimes we come up with an idea only to find that it's a dead pinch from something that's been done before. You know how it is, some melody sticks in your mind and you get it all mixed up and think it is your own invention. Still, there's always someone around to tell us when we go wrong.' Well, Oldham didn't hear anything wrong with 'The Last Time'. In fact, he was quietly ecstatic. Yet he must have known (or soon discovered) it 'was basically re-adapting a traditional Gospel song that had been sung by the Staple Singers . . . Luckily, the song itself goes back into the mists of time.' Their probable source, on the other hand, didn't.

Even though the Staple Singers' version dated back to 1955, James Brown had done his own secularized recasting of the song just six months earlier. His 'Maybe The Last Time' ended up B-side to the ultra-dynamic 'Out Of Sight', a song the Stones had seen the hardest working man in showbiz perform on the famous *TAMI Show*, a film special the two outfits recorded in October 1964. At the same time, Richards might even have heard a stray horn riff from Brown's backing band, The Famous Flames, which gave him the germ of an idea for their next A-side.

Putting 'The Last Time' out as the follow-up to 'Little Red Rooster' had not only put the Stones' songwriting duo on the starting blocks, but a gun to their heads:

**Keith Richards:** We didn't find it difficult to write pop songs, but it was *very* difficult . . . to write one for the Stones. It seemed to us it took months and months and in the end we came up with 'The Last Time' . . . I think I was trying to learn [the Staple Singers version] on the guitar, just to get the chords, sitting there playing along with the record . . . At least we put our own stamp on it, as the Staple Singers had done . . . It gave us something to build on to create the first song that we felt we could decently present to the band to play. . . 'The Last Time' was kind of a bridge into thinking about writing for the Stones. It gave us a level of confidence; a pathway of how to do it. And once we had done that . . . there was no mercy, because then we had to come up with the next one. [2003]

It also changed the dynamics of the band forever, as the power base shifted. The Stones stopped being a democracy and became an oligarchy of two. The axis of the band had already started to tip that way; with Oldham driving the plane, it turned ever faster. Bassist Bill Wyman quickly realized 'the Stones was going to be a hard barrier to crack with my own compositions, since the "Unholy Trinity" controlled what was recorded'. He did not have to look far to find the evidence. A Wyman original called 'Goodbye Girl', recorded at the band's second Chess session in November 1964, remains unreleased to this day, not even accorded B-side status. In fact, as he suggested in his Sixties memoir, *Stone Alone* (1990), it was really all over now:

**Bill Wyman**: The reshaping of the Stones' role came directly from the songwriting posture of Mick and Keith. Hit singles like 'The Last Time' had been just that: solid commercial records that hadn't strayed too far from the popular music paths and were vehicles that allowed us to get our act together. From our formation, the group was the Rolling Stones with a five-way split in money. It was never Mick Jagger and the Rolling Stones. But the extra money they made from songwriting and publishing effectively made Mick and Keith more the leaders than Brian, Charlie and me – their names carried the weight. They'd bring a song in, suggest a style and what the bass line and drums might do, and then we'd play around with it, perhaps, and throw in our own ideas.

That the Stones were starting to feel the pressure by January 1965 is not entirely surprising. Two days before 'The Last Time' was recorded and the same day they released their second album (15 January), the simultaneous release of two singles – both 'original' compositions – gave notice the Britbeat Sweepstake might not be a two-horse race, after all. At the time, the one that really concerned Oldham was The Kinks' fifth single, 'Tired Of Waiting For You' – though it was actually The Who's 'I Can't Explain' which would signal the emergence of the Stones' long-term rivals for the tag, 'Greatest rock & roll band in the world'.

In The Kinks' case, 'Tired Of Waiting For You' was the fourth A-side authored by frontman Ray Davies, the third consecutive single to reach the top two, and the second Kinks 45 to hit the top spot in the past six months. This was Beatles-like success. And The Kinks' pop peak.

Just nine months earlier, Davies' first A-side had been released to the stores. 'You Still Want Me' was neither a concerted assault on Merseyside's domination of the pop charts, nor representative of The Kinks' R&B repertoire. In fact, as *NME* noted in its review, 'Although they are not a Northern group . . . The Kinks have learned much from Mersey trends.' A shameless attempt at a Thameside version of Merseybeat, it deservedly sank without trace. But by the time The Beatles were top of both singles and album charts in August 1964, Ray Davies had written, recorded, re-recorded and released the first song to seriously challenge the Merseysiders' hegemony of UK Pop in eighteen months.

The inspiration for his breakthrough had been a most unlikely one. As Davies said in 1998, 'I'd written "You Really Got Me" as tribute to all those great blues people I love: Leadbelly and Big Bill Broonzy.' However, the released version (recorded that July) with its slashing guitar intro. and adrenalin-rush beat, sounded nothing like either Leadbelly nor Broonzy, let alone a version cut the previous month, which producer Shel Talmy recalls 'was a slower and much bluesier version, but . . . an extremely good recording. It would [still] have gotten to number one.' (There is no way of knowing, because the 'bluesier version' has never seen the light of day.)

Talmy had the wit not to fuck with the formula on their follow-up, 'All Day And All Of The Night', which although stalling at a creditable number two – held there by The Supremes' 'Baby Love' – hardly suggested Davies' songwriting streak was at an end. 'Tired Of Waiting For You' became a third three-minute classic in a row; and this time Davies, having 'learned much from Mersey trends', created a Merseybeat masterpiece from up on Muswell Hill. Unfortunately, Davies had already tied himself to record, publishing and management contracts that would still haunt him – and his brother, Kinks guitarist Dave – fifty years later.

But everybody around the two brothers seemed convinced this whole Britbeat thing was nothing but a flash in the pan, and proffered the same advice – enjoy it while you can. As Dave Davies admitted: 'We happily signed whatever agreements were placed in front of us, not wanting to jeopardise in any way the willingness of the publisher and the record company to work on our songs and recordings. It was [rather] unfortunate that we were so naive in regard to copyrights, the publishing and performing rights of our original material.'

At least they hadn't signed away their publishing to the American producer responsible for their early hits, the cocky Shel Talmy. Their 'little brother' band, The Who, were less fortunate.

But then the song Townshend had sent Talmy, hoping to persuade him to produce his band, was a pretty shameless cop of The Kinks' first two hits, as the guitarist-songwriter admitted in *Rolling Stone* six years on: '"Can't Explain" can't be beat for straightforward Kink-copying.' Talmy suspected an ulterior motive: 'He specifically wrote "I Can't Explain" to get my attention because I had done The Kinks.'

In fact, according to the producer, what Townshend actually sent him bore little relation to the song they released that January:

**Shel Talmy**: 'Can't Explain' I heard . . . as a one minute thirty seconds demo. [It was] just a collection of chords stuck together. I rearranged the whole thing . . . It was a conscious advance on The Kinks . . . [though] 'Can't Explain' is certainly the format, the same general ballpark as The Kinks. I'm the connecting link [between The Kinks and The Who]. It's basically my sound. I rest my case on the last record The Who did when they were The High Numbers ['I'm The Face']. A piece of crap . . . I had a sound in my head, so when The Kinks came along it was a way of getting it . . . We formed a team. [1976]

That 'one minute thirty seconds demo' has not appeared on any of the three double albums of Townshend demos released in the past twenty-five years or on bootleg, so we may have to take Talmy's word – never a great idea.

Townshend himself sent up Talmy's exalted view of his contribution to 'I Can't Explain' in that 1971 *Rolling Stone* article, suggesting, 'Dear Shel got us our first single hits. So he was as close to being God for a week as any other unworthy soul has been. Of course it was a short week; I quickly realized that it was really the brilliant untapped writing talent of our lead guitarist . . . that held the key to our success.' Extracting themselves from the clutches of the immodest producer, though, would prove easier said than done. Perhaps The Who should have read the agreement they made with the fast-talking American before signing; or noticed that he made the B-side of their 24-carat debut a leaden blues called 'Bald Headed Woman' which had already featured twice! once as itself, and then again as a blues jam called 'I've Been Driving On Bald Mountain' – on The Kinks' debut LP, credited to a certain S. Talmy.

Even Talmy wasn't sure whether he had simply stolen or adapted this 'old gospel blues'. But he knew that on top of a hefty slice of the 'mechanical' royalties from the A-side, he had cut himself in on half the publishing from the singular success of 'I Can't Explain'.*

None of these British bands seemed to have the slightest sense of the value attached to such publishing – that is, until The Beatles let everyone in on the secret by floating their 'own' publishing company, Northern Songs,

---

* As it happens, both songs could be found – and doubtless were by Talmy – on a 1959 Odetta LP called *My Eyes Have Seen*, gratifyingly credited to our friend, Trad. Arr.

on the Stock Exchange in February 1965, with a startling valuation of £4 million. Having revolutionized the art of songwriting, it seemed The Beatles were about to reinvent the publishing business – by making the biggest mistake of their young lives,

The division between songwriters and performers that had held for most of the post-war era had now been sundered by the four Scousers; but whereas the sharks that swam around London's Denmark Street knew the money was in publishing, to a band from Liverpool, it was all about performing and recording. They needed a businessman they could trust, and they placed theirs in a man who ran a retail outlet in Liverpool. He placed his in a man called Dick James, who had no fins on him. But Brian Epstein was out of his depth the minute he met the smiling, balding businessman with the lyin' eyes.

The story of Epstein coming to James's office to discuss switching the Beatles' already potentially lucrative publishing to his organization is well known and oft-repeated. Epstein turns up early, James ushers him in, hears an acetate of The Beatles' second single ('Please Please Me'), as well as Epstein's heartfelt complaints about EMI's lack of promotional work for 'Love Me Do' (which had actually done rather well for a debut single by an unknown band, peaking at seventeen).

James nods understandingly, makes a phone call to *Thank Your Lucky Stars* producer Phillip Jones in Birmingham, plays him the acetate over the phone and the band are promptly booked for the show. Epstein is so impressed he fails to hear the sound of Scott Joplin's piano in the background. Because it was a scam all the managers and publishers in the early sixties used. They had the TV producers in their pockets and they knew it. In all likelihood, James had prearranged the call to Jones; but even if he hadn't, there was no prospect of Jones refusing him. In this scenario, Epstein was the rube. Now, to seal the deal. Because, as Beatles insider Peter Brown recalled, in his revealing *The Love You Make* (1982):

[James] offered Brian a clever deal. John and Paul would form a songwriting partnership called Northern Songs. They would each own 20 per cent of this company, and Brian, in lieu of a 25 per cent management fee, would own 10 per cent. Dick James, in return for his responsibilities as a music publisher, would get 50 per cent of the earnings. In literal terms Brian signed over to Dick James 50 per cent of Lennon–McCartney's publishing fees for *nothing*. It made him wealthy beyond imagination in eighteen months.

In fairness to James, 50-50 deals with publishers were the norm in those days. As songwriter and plugger Bill Martin has remarked, 'Publishers . . . paid for the demos, took the song to record companies, sub published it and plugged it. They worked hard in those days and that was worth 50 per cent. Every song writer in those days signed a contract like that.' But that was all pre-'Please Please Me'. The Beatles almost single-handedly dismantled this outmoded business model. And if they hadn't signed their publishing away in perpetuity, they would now be enjoying the 80-20 split their groundbreaking contribution to songwriting made the norm.

But in November 1962, they were as babes in Childwall Woods. Sensing that all he needed now was the signatures of John Lennon and Paul McCartney, and he would own half of potentially the most valuable songwriting partnership in sixties pop, James dispatched a Savile Row suit to do the deed, a day still etched in McCartney's mind forty-three years later:

**Paul McCartney**: John and I were taken for a ride. No doubt about it. We were in a little mews in Liverpool one morning and there was this lawyer, who we later found out was [supposed to be] ours. He didn't look like ours and he certainly didn't do a deal like he was ours. We'd signed the whole thing away one morning before getting on a train and we didn't understand what it was. Later, when we tried to readjust it, [Dick James] said, 'I can't'. I know now through having a publishing company that you can, at any point . . . We really thought that [setting up our own publishing company] meant 100 per cent owned. But of course it turned out to be 49 per cent to me and John and Brian and 51 per cent to Dick James and [his partner] Charles Silver. [2005]

That last sentence is potentially significant. It strikes me as unlikely that at almost 64 McCartney, wouldn't know the difference between a 51-49 split and a 50-50 split after running a valuable publishing company of his own for quarter of a century. If Epstein really did sign away 51 per cent of The Beatles' publishing, he had also signed away *control* of Northern Songs, a crucial factor in all that was to come. And James wasn't done with the northern naif.

At the end of 1964, James came up with another of his scams, intended to tie The Beatles' publishing to him with ribbons of steel. He would float Northern Songs on the Stock Exchange, giving the two songwriters an immediate windfall they didn't need in exchange for a future indentured to Dick James Music. Again, Peter Brown witnessed Epstein all at sea as he gave James the lion's share of an asset he had played almost no part in creating. Perhaps there was some underlying reason Mr James had been asked to sing the theme tune to a TV version of *Robin Hood* back in the late fifties:

[In 1965] Northern Songs, the Beatles' song publishing company that had been established in 1963, was turned into a public company and floated on the London stock exchange. It had become clear that . . . John and Paul could at least save a great deal of money by turning highly taxed income into capital gains. Northern Songs was the obvious asset to use, but no-one had ever sold what was basically a songwriting partnership as stock before . . . The man who [thus] deserved most of the credit for convincing the City that Northern Songs was a valuable commodity was Dick James, the Beatles' music publisher. Dick James knew the value of Northern Songs best of all, because the Beatles music had made him into a multimillionaire . . . Three years later, five million shares of Northern Songs were being offered on the stock market. In the flotation John and Paul retained 15 per cent of the stock ... NEMS retained 7.5 per cent, and in an act of largesse, George Harrison and Ringo Starr were given 1.6 per cent between them. Dick James and his business partner, Charles Silver, were left with 37.5 per cent, valued at $1,687,000 ... Dick James became for the Beatles a symbol of the music business. He was a balding, Jewish uncle to the boys, a man with a big cigar and a sly smile, who taught John and Paul one of the biggest lessons in their lives.

By now, the two Liverpudlian songwriters had become a little more savvy about the business, and a lot less trusting of their manager – even if they were still unaware of the fiasco he had presided over in 1964 with Seltaeb. This was another Joplinesque sting in which, rather than the usual 90-10 split on marketing official merchandise, Epstein had agreed to a 10-90 split; he was forced into a protracted lawsuit to get the agreement terminated.

If that deal cost The Beatles millions in the short term, the Northern Songs deal would cost them hundreds of millions in the long term. As McCartney told his official biographer, 'We just signed this thing, not really knowing ... that we were signing our rights away for our songs, ... and that is virtually the contract I am still under.'

In order to sell the pair on going public with their song publishing, James and the blinkered Epstein convinced them the deal would circumvent the punishing 98 per cent tax rate they were paying on income, because the money would come to them as a dividend. Rather than set up a sensible tax shelter, Epstein took advice on tax planning from his music publisher.

The Beatles had fallen prey to a misconception common among so many sixties British bands. Based on a misunderstanding of why American rock & roll had proved so short-lived and the status quo had been so promptly restored, they had misread the tea-leaves of pop culture, and imagined that their current level of fame and fortune was going to go away some day soon.

It was a misconception The Beatles shared with the Stones, who were also about to sign their publishing away, even after they sought advice from an accountant. Unfortunately, that accountant was Allen Klein, a man who had taken on Morris Levy and bested him, and someone who made Dick James look as fearsome as Flipper.

Dick James knew The Beatles wrote songs, and hit songs at that. It didn't take Benny Spellman to realize 'Please Please Me' was chart material. It is not so clear Allen Klein knew what or who he was signing up.

Throughout July 1965, while Klein was negotiating with Oldham to take over the Stones' publishing and renegotiate their contract with their UK and American labels, the Stones' successor to the derivative 'The Last Time', '(I Can't Get No) Satisfaction', was climbing the US charts and – at least for now – cementing their position in pop. By 10 July it could climb no higher – destined to stay at the summit for four more weeks. By the time it started its descent, Andrew Loog Oldham and the five Rolling Stones had put their names to two contracts with Klein. One would cost them around $15 million to extricate themselves; the other they were released from only at its expiration in 1970.

Bassist Bill tried to explain the skewed logic underlying the transfer of the Stones' entire song publishing to an entity run from New York by a man with all the charm of a boa constrictor and known for squeezing every last dollar out of his victims:

> **Bill Wyman:** Significantly, the several record and songwriting advances Klein had secured for us from London Records and Decca had been skilfully structured so that he received the advances and paid the money out to us in small amounts over many years. We had been convinced by him that we would, through this system, not fall victim to the problem of making a huge sum of money over a two- or three-year period, paying 83–93 per cent in tax and then finding we'd got absolutely nothing if we weren't successful in the future. It was a 'steady income'.

Klein, willing to play along with the Stones' 'rebel' image, had originally presented himself as a caped crusader come to do battle with the suits on their behalf. At his initial meeting with Oldham he had assured the manager he would get them £1 million for their publishing rights, which he did by going straight to David Platz at Essex Music – who, in 1966, bought Immediate Music, the Stones' publisher. Klein required no great negotiating skill to do this, just a shrewd understanding of how publishing had worked since the days of Ralph Peer. But for Oldham's outfit, and particularly the newly galvanized song-team, Jagger-Richards, it seemed like money for old James Brown riffs.

Again, Klein proffered a deferred payment scheme that appealed to anyone gullible enough to think Pop – in the post-Newport era – was a passing fad, and that 'the boys' would have need of a 'steady income' when all this went away. The day the Stones issued their fourth US album, their manager signed a letter drafted by Klein that surrendered *control* of the Stones' song publishing for the forseeable. It read, 'For our mutual benefit and in order for all of us to participate in a proposed capital gains transaction [I have] assigned all masters of your performances for the USA and Canada to a corporation that we jointly own named Nankerphelge.' They must have been out of their heads!

It would be some years before The Beatles and the Stones realized just how monumental an error they had each made – by which time they would both be clients of the Klein corporation, like it or not.

Nor was Klein content to leave his repatriation of Pop's intellectual property there. In 1966, The Kinks' manager, Robert Wace, brought him in at the suggestion of Peter Grant, then the Yardbirds' manager, 'because we weren't making a lot of money . . . His real job was to get a hell of a lot of money from [Reprise] in the States. And he never really brought it off.'

It is debatable how hard Klein tried to renegotiate the Kinks' US record deal. When he realized Ray Davies's publishing was not on the table – and was the subject of acrimonious litigation with former managers, Larry Page and Eddie Kassner, that meant Davies would not see a red cent from his publishing until 1970 he seemed to lose interest. Perhaps, by the summer of 1966 – after Davies having suffered the first of two very public nervous breakdowns in May – he thought The Kinks had just about burnt themselves out.

If so, Klein was proven wrong. Davies came back even stronger. 'Sunny Afternoon', 'Dead End Street' and 'Waterloo Sunset' would all go Top Five in the UK in the next twelve months. (The latter two would be recorded by Davies behind Shel Talmy's back; he knew their production deal with Talmy was about to expire and was determined to take over himself, dispensing with the royalty cut Shel had previously been receiving.) In the case of 'Dead End Street', Davies actually 'waited until Talmy had gone [home] and recorded it again', according to coalman and stand-in Kinks bassist, John Dalton.

The Who were not so lucky – with either Talmy or Klein. They had tied themselves to the mast with Talmy at the helm, as guitarist/writer John Perry explains:

Signing a production deal directly with Talmy put the band straight into the studio, and removed at a stroke the problem of how to find a record deal. Talmy would take care of it! This probably appeared a wonderful shortcut to everyone in The Who camp for a week or two, until all the implications were properly appreciated. Broadly, the terms of Talmy's standard production deal (by no means atypical of the time) gave him: Control over the recording and production process; ownership of the tapes (thus control over their placement); a five year term (as a producer). Once a track was cut, he would 'use his best endeavours' to sell it to a company (no massive effort being required, since he had a standing arrangement with Decca in the US) and guarantee to pay the band a royalty of [2½ per cent]. What Lambert and Stamp initially failed to appreciate was that Talmy might be getting a royalty of anywhere between 6 per cent and 10 per cent from the record company – and was free to pocket the balance . . . Lambert and Stamp's

inexperience caused them to agree to too long a term – five years
– and too low a percentage: 2.5 per cent, renegotiated after 'I Can't
Explain' to 3 or 4 per cent.

Though Townshend retained his publishing, they pretty much signed
everything else away. And five years was an awfully long time on the vol-
atile planet of pop, especially as Townshend had just written yet another
three-minute mini-masterpiece. 'Substitute' would be The Who's follow-
up to their teen anthem 'My Generation', and was another song where,
Townshend admits, 'several key changes [were] pinched, again, from The
Kinks'.

Pete was also learning to diversify the debt-pool, even taking 'the
stock, down-beat riff used in the verses . . . from a record played to me
in [*Melody Maker*'s review column,] 'Blind Date' . . . The record I said
nice things about wasn't a hit, despite an electrifying riff.' (That single,
'Where Is My Girl?' by Robb Storme, had indeed died a death.) His other
acknowledged lift came from a fellow chart act, though again he appropriated 'interestingly'. He had been played in rough mix form The Rolling
Stones' '19th Nervous Breakdown', which he openly aspired to emulate
in *feel*. For fellow guitarist John Perry, though, 'the clearest cop I hear is
a Motown bass line, [though] not from a Miracles record [as Townshend
later claimed] but from The Four Tops. "Substitute" follows Pete's demo
faithfully. All the components are present in the demo, including the
looping bass riff that drives the verse . . . This riff . . . is very closely related
to The Four Tops' "I Can't Help Myself." Take Jamie Jamerson's bass line,
iron out the syncopation, and you have the bass line of "Substitute."'

None of these debts were ever called in; but he was not so sure
this subtler, poppier kind of song suited Shel. And when Townshend
decided *he* would produce The Who's auto-destruct version of another pop classic, he set them on a collision course with a man who
believed his contribution to the cause was as great as the guitarist.
Once again, Shel Talmy set about claiming he was responsible for
The Who's sound – which anyone who had witnessed them at 'The

Railway', pre-Talmy, knew to be patent nonsense – and this time it became a legal matter:

**Pete Townshend:** Shel responded by bringing legal action . . . claiming that he deserved the lion's share of the royalties because he had contributed significant musical guidance. I had worked from my own demo . . . and in my own affadavit claimed that if the court compared my demos with Shel's [band demo] they would see that all the creative work had been done by me before Shel even heard the song . . . My demos were disallowed as evidence, and Shel was informed that his contract stood. This meant that we were still tied to Shel and the feeble royalty he paid us. I turned for guidance to Andrew [Loog] Oldham who . . . told me he thought his friend Allen Klein might be able to exert leverage to break Shel's grip, but to do that we might have to break with Kit and Chris.

Once again Klein was looking to insinuate himself into an A-list Britbeat band's affairs, keeping his eye on the real prize – Townshend's publishing. After their defeat in court, Klein reminded Townshend they had only lost in the UK and asked for another meeting. And so, as Townshend writes in his recent autobiography, 'On 27 June 1966 I went back to New York once more, this time with our lawyer, Edward Oldman . . . Ted Oldman [then] reported to Kit and Chris that Klein was trying to take over the band, and they quickly brokered an out-of-court settlement with Talmy. He would no longer produce The Who and we'd be free to make a new deal with any record company we chose.' Not for the last time, Klein had overplayed his hand. The deal Stamp and Lambert struck with Talmy gave him a royalty override of 5 per cent on everything they produced in the next five years. It was an expensive lesson, but at least it kept The Who free of Klein's malevolent maw, even as further doors closed on Talmy.

By 1966, freelancers like Talmy were finding it harder and harder to get British bands to sign away their creative lives for twiddling a few dials one afternoon in a studio. Maybe Talmy needed to look further afield. At year's end Australian band The Easybeats charted with their first UK single, after Talmy succeeded in removing their preferred producer, Ted Albert, who had been responsible for a string of number-one singles in their homeland. But, as Talmy told the *NME* in 1976, 'As soon as "Friday On My Mind" became a hit, the [Easybeats'] manager came to me and wanted me to take a reduction in royalties . . . I told him up which orifice he could stick his group.'

Talmy was not alone in finding these British-based upstarts ripe for the picking. If he had followed Phil Spector's tailwind across the pond, others followed. In March 1965, Bert Berns arrived in England with a production pedigree that might not have ranked with Spector's, but still put Talmy's to shame.

As a songwriter, Berns only ever really had one idea, but it was a good one. As fellow Atlantic producer Jerry Wexler opines, '[Berns's] feeling for Latin rhythms was right as rain. His affinity for the Cuban *qua-jira* was deep, and he practically made a cottage industry on the chord changes of "Guantanamera," written in the 19th century by Jose Marti, the Cuban revolutionary hero. He used those identical changes in "Twist and Shout," "A Little Bit of Soap" and "My Girl Sloopy" (an R&B hit for The Vibrations in 1964), plus a slew of similar songs.'

In fact, according to Wexler, Spector had been partly responsible for denying Berns a near-certain number one with the first of these: 'The scene was Bellton Studios, where Phil and I were recording The Pearls, an epicene male duo, singing a song I thought had hit potential . . . Bert Berns, the composer was there [as] Phil and I went at it with unrestrained ferocity. In the end we managed to fuck up a natural hit. When Bert objected, I invited him to shut up.' Despite Spector, 'Twist And Shout' would become a lucrative earner, just not for The Pearls. Ditto The Vibrations and 'My Girl Sloopy'. Berns got over the experience, while continuing to rewrite the same key changes. But what he really wanted was to cross (the) Atlantic.

Bert had been brought over in spring 1965 by another of Britain's hustler-managers, Phil Solomon, because he (thought he) needed a producer-songwriter for his latest young charges – a quintet of Belfast bruisers called Them, whose singer, Van Morrison, had already turned surly belligerence into an art-form on and off stage. Solomon told me he met Berns in New York, 'through the publisher Bobby Mellon . . . He was recording with The Drifters . . . I thought that Bert knew the American market from beginning to end. I was a newcomer . . . I thought the answer was to bring Bert over to record Them.'

Quite why Solomon thought he needed songs from this third party, even he never could explain. At Them's first London session with Decca's Dick Rowe, on 5 July 1964 – when Ray Davies was still playing with the structure of 'You Really Got Me' – their singer had produced no less than three top-notch R&B rabble-rousers of his own: 'One Two Brown Eyes', 'Philosophy', and a riff for all seasons named after a dead cousin, 'Gloria'. Solomon issued none of these as A-sides – not even 'Gloria', a garageband classic from that first, insistent chord change.

Like Berns' 'Twist And Shout', even the stupidity of strangers would not stop 'Gloria' from becoming one of the sixties' most valuable songs, covered by everyone from Hendrix to The Doors. But, according to the musical members of Them, someone else in the band – aside from Morrison – lost out on the publishing bonanza. Billy Harrison, Them's lead guitarist and leading bruiser, suggests all those early songs were 'written' in a way familiar to many a band who let their frontman take the credit:

> **Billy Harrison**: Van didn't write songs – he wrote ideas and then the song came as he was performing. He never had a song written down – maybe words here and there on cigarette packets – but you'd start to diddle around between numbers with some riff and he'd put something on top of it and gradually it would evolve.

And as Them organist Eric Wrixon has said, 'If I were a hard-nosed barrister, I would argue that some of the royalties from that song ['Gloria'] should be shared with Billy Harrison. It was [he] who came up with the riff.'

Though it was recorded at their first Decca session, 'Gloria' was neither the A- nor the B-side of Them's debut. Even when it was released, in November, after the band's first 45 flopped, it was left to prop up their startling reinvention of Big Joe Williams' 'Baby Please Don't Go' – for which Harrison again failed to receive a part-credit even though all parties agree it was his compelling guitar intro., more than the sentiments of (Mrs) Williams's familiar lament, which made it a Top Ten hit.

Solomon clearly didn't have much of a clue about what constituted a likely hit, or what songs to hide on B-sides. (According to Solomon it was Pat Campbell, then in charge of promotion, who chose 'Baby Please Don't Go' as the A-side.) But he knew the value of publishing, and made damn sure 'we signed a deal [for] music publishing, everything'. Stuart Cromie, who had produced the five-track demo ('Gloria' included) that got the band their record deal, was handed the contract Solomon had given Them and recalls, 'I looked at it and said, "I wouldn't sign that. I think you could negotiate a better deal." It was 50 per cent to Phil [Solomon], 50 per cent to the group – and they paid all the expenses. It was . . . a three-year contract . . . They, needless to say, signed it.'

When 'Baby Please Don't Go' proved a solid smash, Solomon began wondering where was he going to find another hit song. After all, Them was only fronted by the greatest white R&B singer-songwriter the British Isles has yet produced, a man whose publishing he controlled. Having wasted 'Gloria', he brought in Berns, who offered the band 'Here Comes The Night'. It was a terrific pop song, but hardly 'them'. Which is why Berns had already cut the same song with Lulu as a pop ballad with strings. However, it was Them's burly bruiser at the mike-stand who was now given his chance to wail, and seized it.

Predictably, it was an even bigger hit, halting just one shy of the top spot. Yet it also set a dangerous precedent. It suggested Them was a pop band, and they were not. When Morrison started refusing to play ball – after a self-composed follow-up, 'One More Time', confirmed pop was not his forte – Solomon brought in another tame songwriter-producer. And this one would do it for the bus fare. Only one problem – Tommy Scott, in the words of Them's new guitarist, Jim Armstrong, 'would come in and say, here's a wee song I wrote on the Tube on the way in this morning. Whatever was number one last week, he wrote [again].'

The policy derailed the band just as Morrison was finding his feet as a songwriter and Them as great improvisers. Their most radical statement would be one group composition even Morrison seemed (initially) embarrassed to take sole credit for, telling an American journalist: '"Mystic Eyes" just happened. We didn't plan a note. It was during the first recording session for the LP, and we were just busking around. Someone started playing a fast riff and we all just joined in. The lyrics I sing at the end were just words from a song I had been writing at the time.' ('Mystic Eyes', like 'Gloria', was a minor hit Stateside, where Solomon did not have the final say on Them A-sides.)

By the time 'Mystic Eyes' charted Stateside, Billy Harrison had already quit, disgusted at the way Solomon ran the business side. By the summer of 1966, the rest of Them were equally mutinous. When Solomon refused to release another Morrison classic, 'Friday's Child', as a single and sent them on a US tour with just enough funds to live on bread and water, the Belfast boys went to war. Solomon's response was to cut the band adrift, after reminding them they didn't have a direct contract with Decca, 'they had a contract with Hyde Park Music.'

Morrison, forced to return to Belfast penniless and pissed off, had at least made contact with Bert Berns while stranded in America, and agreed to send him tapes of the songs he was now writing, some of his very best. In the meantime Berns had set up his own record label, tired of seeing little in the way of return from Ahmet Ertegun's Atlantic for crafting and producing The Drifters ('Under The Boardwalk') and Solomon Burke ('Everybody Needs Somebody To Love'). He almost immediately struck gold, releasing The Strangeloves' 'I Want Candy' and the song he had co-written (with Wes Farrell) and recorded at Atlantic, as 'My Girl Sloopy', back in 1964. Now recast as 'Hang On Sloopy', it was given to The McCoys, whose version topped the US charts and – licensed by Loog Oldham's new label, Immediate – went Top Five in the UK at the end of 1965.

It seemed Berns really did have the success recipe; and Morrison, for all his professed distaste for pop aesthetics, wanted a taste. For now, though, he would have to bide his time as Them's legal ties to Solomon slowly unravelled. Solomon kept a hold of 'Gloria' et al., but he lost out on a share of Morrison's lucrative four-decade solo career, proving he was more Polk Brockman than Ralph Peer.

Morrison was not the only fortunate son to have witnessed Berns' gifts as a producer in that brief window Bert spent in London studios. Guitarist Jimmy Page, who allegedly played lead on Them's 'Baby Please Don't Go', having previously sat in on several of Talmy's sessions with The Kinks and The Who (it is his rhythm guitar behind Townshend's slashing lead on 'I Can't Explain'), was a quick learner. And although he didn't need any guitar lessons, he was anxious to learn the ropes when it came to publishing. A brief liaison with the multi-talented singer-song-writer Jackie DeShannon, another émigré from across the pond who had arrived in London looking to sell her songs to the mother country's pop bands, whetted Page's appetite for doing things his way. In fact, the next time Page was in New York – on his way to L.A. to renew acquaintance with DeShannon – he was invited to use Berns' spare bedroom; and duly contributed a song he co-wrote with DeShannon to Berns' next project, a Barbara Lewis album.

Thanks to Berns' tutelage, Page saw just how the game was played and returned home full of ideas about forming his own supergroup – a studio entity based around The Who's rhythm section and wunderkind keyboardist Nicky Hopkins, with himself and Jeff Beck on guitars. In May 1966 the outfit, minus bassist John Entwistle, recorded Page's first notable instrumental composition, 'Beck's Bolero', a song that ended up on the Jeff Beck Group's debut LP, *Truth*, and (more lucratively) on the B-side of that disco favourite, 'Hi Ho Silver Lining'.*

When it became clear this supergroup was never going to get off the ground, Beck asked Page if he would like to join him in The Yardbirds, and in the summer of 1966 Page formally joined a band who seemed to go through guitarists like other Britbeat bands went through guitar picks. Over the next two years he would do the usual crash-course in music industry travails, while the supergroup idea remained on the backburner, until autumn 1968 when he assembled a band who made Cream sound like lightweights. Thanks to Keith Moon, they even had a name: Led Zeppelin. Now all they needed was some songs they could beg, borrow or steal.

---

* Initially called 'Bolero' and credited to Beck on the single, it was reissued with 'Page' listed as composer but the title amended to 'Beck's Bolero'. When Beck later claimed the guitar-melody line was actually his, Page responded by saying, 'I wrote it, played on it, produced it . . . and I don't give a damn what he says,' establishing a pattern for blustering his way through any counter-claim for credit that would hold throughout his lucrative career.

# CHAPTER 12

# 1967–80: Loved In Vain

*Featuring*: 'Babe I'm Gonna Leave You'; 'Black Mountain Side'; 'Dazed And Confused'; 'Whole Lotta Love'; 'Bring It On Home'; 'Gallows Pole'; 'When The Levee Breaks'; 'In My Time Of Dyin'; 'Nobody's Fault But Mine'; 'Love In Vain'; 'Dust My Broom'; 'Hellhound On My Trail'; 'Crossroads'; 'Statesboro Blues'

> The Yardbirds allowed me to improvise a lot in live performance and I started building a textbook of ideas that I eventually used in Zeppelin.
>
> Jimmy Page

Jimmy Page was hardly the only figure at the end of 1968 who was looking to turn years of session fees and peer-respect into a Surrey mansion and a Swiss bank account. Ritchie Blackmore was equally tired of having his feedback-strewn guitar workouts drowned out or cut short by Screaming Lord Sutch; while Robert Fripp was looking to trade in the cheerful insanity of Giles and Giles for the schizophrenia of King Crimson. In Page's case, he simply felt recycling riffs had barely made him a living, and it was high time it did.

There seems a cold calculation to the way Page put Led Zeppelin together, a sense it was a jigsaw he had to complete and John Bonham, John Paul Jones and Robert Plant (after first choice vocalist Terry Reid passed) were the right pieces. But there was still a piece missing – a songwriter. Although Page had been planning this for two and a half years, when Zeppelin entered Olympic studios in October 1968 original songs were in short supply. Page brought to the sessions three songs ultimately copyrighted by him, but not one of them was his.

The first, 'Babe, I'm Gonna Leave You', though credited as 'Trad. arr. Page', had been composed in the late fifties by a fledgling folksinger. On the other hand, 'Black Mountain Side' – credited simply to Page – was as traditional as they came. And Page knew it, because he had learnt the song from Bert Jansch's classic album of traditional songs, *Jack Orion*, where it was identified (correctly) as 'Black Waterside'. He even admitted, 'I was absolutely obsessed by Bert Jansch. His first album had a great effect on me. It was so far ahead of what anyone else was doing. That was what got me into playing acoustic.'

Nor was 'Black Mountain Side' the first time Page had plundered Jansch's store of songs. 'White Summer', a song included by The Yardbirds on their final studio album, *Little Games*, was essentially his pseudo-psychedelic take on Jansch's unique arrangement of the Irish folk ballad, 'She Moved Through The Fair'. The song would carry over into the early Zeppelin set.

So would another song introduced into the live Yardbirds repertoire at the end of 1967, 'I'm Confused'. In fact, this would become the centre-piece of most Zeppelin shows. Now called 'Dazed And Confused', this was the third song he brought to that first London session, and apparently it was now a 'Jimmy Page' composition.

His previous band knew better. They had been on hand when the sup-port act at a Yardbirds New York show in August 1967 had been a certain Jake Holmes, who had just released his debut album, *The Above Ground Sound of Jake Holmes*. As Holmes later recalled, 'That was the infamous moment in my life when "Dazed and Confused" fell into the loving arms and hands of Jimmy Page.'

All of the Yardbirds were blown away by this extraordinary slice of psychedelic folk, particularly the way Holmes took off into uncharted territory with some of the wildest riffing this side of an Echoplex. As the band's drummer Jim McCarty subsequently confirmed, they went to a record shop the next day to buy a copy of Holmes's album, having 'decided to do a version . . . We worked it out together *with Jimmy contributing the guitar riffs in the middle* [my italics].' And that is the key phrase. Page had unilaterally decided it was intrinsically unfair that guitar improvisations by a man like himself, around an existing tune, did not confer any, let alone sole copyright on the improviser. Essentially, with 'Dazed & Confused', he took copyright law into his own hands. The song that provided the raw outline of this Zeppelin stalwart would be replaced by one which primarily comprised 'the guitar riffs in the middle'. And as those guitar riffs got longer and longer, Page's own memory of where the bare framework came from grew hazier and hazier until, asked outright by Matt Resnicoff, 'I understand "Dazed" was originally a song by Jake Holmes. Is that true?', in a 1990 *Musician* interview, he went all coy:

> **Jimmy Page** [sourly]: I don't know. I don't know. [Inhaling] I don't know about all that. I'd rather not get into it because I don't know all the circumstances. What's he got, the riff or whatever? Because Robert wrote some of the lyrics for that on the album. But he was only listening to . . . We extended it from one that we were playing with The Yardbirds. I haven't heard Jake Holmes so I don't know what it's all about anyway. Usually my riffs are pretty damn near original [laughs]. What can I say?

It would take a belated suit by Holmes in 2010, and headlines around the world, for Page to even consider admitting that Holmes might have authored the song's theme, lyrics, title and structure.

By then, the success of the scheme Page cooked up in 1968 – to concoct a band that blended Muddy Waters and Cream – had seemingly gone to his head. Such was certainly the view of Glyn Johns, the engineer he cut out of a production credit on that seminal debut album: 'Jimmy [Page], since [that first album], has been proved to have the most extraordinary attitude to anything he's involved with, which is that he will take credit for pretty much everything and never allow anyone else to have credit for *anything*.'

Even when caught dead to rights, Page would insist on retaining a share of the credit; as he would with his interpretation of the 'traditional' song, 'Babe I'm Gonna Leave You', taken from Joan Baez's 1962 album, *In Concert Part 1*. Unfortunately for him the song, though credited as traditional on early pressings of the Baez record, was actually composed by Californian student-folksinger Anne Bredon some time in the late fifties. Baez herself acknowledged the fact as early as 1964, in *The Joan Baez Songbook*, where she introduces the song by noting, 'restlessness is rarely expressed so well in modern urban blues as in this song by Anne Bredon of San Francisco'.

Five years later, Page remained apparently unaware the song had an author; and as luck would have it, Bredon – who now preferred basket weaving to music weaving – remained unaware of Led Zeppelin's cover version until the late 1980s, when Page was called to account. He still refused to yield full credit. On the 1990 CD remaster of that influential LP – another cash bonanza for him and the kids – the song-credits read, 'Bredon, Page and Plant'. Page's contribution was to change the key to A minor. What, pray tell, was Plant's?

The Zeppelin singer's song-credit is particularly bizarre because it was the first one Plant received on an album that had been cast entirely in Page's image. The three 'group' compositions on *Led Zeppelin* – 'Good Times Bad Times', 'How Many More Times' and 'Communication Breakdown' – were credited to Page/Jones/Bonham. Plant was even excluded from 'How Many More Times', a song where Page later admitted cutting his two instrumental cohorts in on the publishing of what was clearly a 'live-in-studio' workout involving all *four* band members: '["How Many More Times"] has the kitchen sink on it . . . It was made up of little pieces I developed when I was with The Yardbirds . . . It was played live in the studio with cues and nods . . . I initiated most of the changes and riffs, but if something was derived from the blues, I tried to split the credit between band members.'

In fact the song may have another Yardbird-related debt. A group called the T-Bones, fronted by Gary Farr, recorded a rather similar tune called 'How Many More Times' at the height of the (first) British blues boom in 1964–5. Although the album sleeve gives no writing credits, its liner notes were written by none other than original Yardbirds manager, Giorgio Gomelsky. Nevertheless, Zep's – and the T-Bones's – 'How Many More Times?' actually comprised large chunks of Howlin' Wolf's 1951 recording, 'How Many More Years', with elements of The Yardbirds' arrangement of 'I'm A Man' and Page's 'Beck's Bolero' (another part of which bassist Trevor Bolder later nicked for the intro. to Bowie's 'Jean Genie') thrown in for good measure.

Then, just as the song begins to lose its way, Plant launches into Albert King's 'The Hunter' as if it was his idea – which it probably was. They were lucky to get away with 'The Hunter', which Free (who did credit King, thus identifying the source) were soon making their own. If Page thought he had done his homework on copyright, he had forgotten to brief his chosen singer. This would not be the last time that Plant would throw in a snatch of some old blues song or the last time the guitarist bel-lyached about it even as Zeppelin went to that great balloon farm in the sky:

> **Jimmy Page:** Well, as far as my end of it goes, I always tried to bring something fresh to anything that I used. I always made sure to come up with some variation. In fact, I think in most cases you would never know what the original source could be. Maybe not in every case – but in most cases. So most of the com-parisons rest on the lyrics. And Robert was supposed to change the lyrics, and he didn't always do that – which is what brought on most of the grief.

In fact, the most grief centred on another song composed in that first year of Zeppelin's existence, the centrepiece of a second album where Plant came into his own and the cops became cleverer, but still visible. It was called 'Whole Lotta Love'; and this time Page – who later told *Rolling Stone* he felt he 'was under pressure to come up with my own riffs . . . on the first LP, [though] I was still heavily influenced by the earlier days'

– invented a riff of his own. However, a riff does not a song make. And 'Whole Lotta Love' had more debts than your average Florida homeowner.

It started with 'You Need Loving', a song included by The Small Faces on their 1966 debut LP. Again, Page's ears pricked up when he heard it at a Small Faces/Yardbirds gig. According to singer Steve Marriott, 'Jimmy Page asked me what that number was, that we did . . . I said, "It's a Muddy Waters thing." Which it really is . . . After we broke up, they took it and revamped it . . . They just put a different rhythm to it.'

It transpired Marriott and Lane were not immune to a li'l credit stealing themselves, impertinently taking a joint song-credit on 'You Need Loving' even though, as Willie Dixon biographer Don Snowden points out, their version 'is almost identical to the sound of the Muddy track with the organ – not to mention throwing in a verse's worth of "Land of a Thousand Dances."' Unfortunately for Zeppelin, 'You Need Love', the song the Small Faces had copped theirs from, was not only a 'Muddy Waters thing', it was a Willie Dixon song. And though Dixon had (in theory) done very well out of the first Zeppelin album – which already included 'I Can't Quit You Baby' and 'You Shook Me' (the latter already covered by The Jeff Beck Group) – neither got the airplay generated by 'Whole Lotta Love' when Atlantic released it as a US single in November 1969. By April 1970, it had been certified gold for a million sales. Again, when Zep got that writ they settled out of court; again, the original song-credits remained. Page still wanted the world to know it was *his* riff.

Which was not the case with 'The Lemon Song', another track on *Led Zeppelin II* where Page had again taken 'something . . . derived from the blues, [and] tried to split the credit between band members' (which now included Robert Plant). The song had audibly evolved out of the band's early live interpretations of Howlin' Wolf's 'Killin' Floor', and just like their previous lift from the Wolf, they threw in a chunk of Albert King (in this instance, 'Cross Cut Saw') and a new name for good measure. The ruse had worked last time, but evolved or not, 'The Lemon Song' wore its debt on its sleeve and Jewel Music sued. This time Page was required to give up any co-credit.

One doubts Page was stoical enough to think win some, lose some. But such is assuredly the case. Jansch never sued, and Holmes' suit was so belated a large herd of horses with gold in their saddles had long bolted. And there was another song on *Led Zep II* where he got off scot-free. On 'Bring It On Home', Page had the temerity to actually recreate Sonny Boy Williamson's 1963 recording of the same name, note for note, with his guitar intro, even if after that, the song took off into more original territory. At least this suggested an awareness things could not continue this way, and fortunately for Page, Plant had finally started to come into his own as a lyricist. Meanwhile, the guitarist decided to wise up:

**Jimmy Page**: Well, we started writing our own blues songs, didn't we? After the first album [sic], I was really conscious of the fact that we had to start carving our own identity . . . In the early days, I was quite happy to borrow from Otis Rush [sic] for 'I Can't Quit You'. It was a pleasure. But after a while I started realizing that that wasn't what I should be doing. I felt I had to start developing my own thing.

That quote may suggest a change of heart. In fact, it was really more of a change in approach on Page's (and Plant's) part, one that others from the great late sixties blues revival had already anticipated. It was called doing your homework on public domain folk-blues.

After all, Wolf and Waters were near-contemporaries of bluesmen upon whose giant shoulders *they* regularly stood. They had actually known the likes of Charley Patton, Tommy and Robert Johnson – but that didn't make them their legatees. Nor did it transfer copyright their way. As Plant pointed out in a 1990 interview, 'If you read *Deep Blues* by Robert Palmer, you'll see that we did what everybody else was doing. When Robert Johnson was doing "Preaching Blues," he was really taking Son House's "Preacher's Blues" and remodelling it.' This was what he thought the band should be doing as and when they weren't adapting another Page song-idea. And by the third album, even if Page was no longer inclined to let the improvised blues which still dominated the live set fill up their later albums, Plant was increasingly chipping his name into the band's edifice.

Their battle for the band's soul would inform their next six albums, beginning at the sessions for the third long-player, where a long blues medley saw Plant improvise various blues and early rock & roll lyrics over a slide guitar riff from Page. When it appeared on *III* as 'Hats Off To (Roy) Harper', it had undergone radical surgery which pruned some of its more problematic lyrics, but it still bore 'a strong lyrical resemblance' to Bukka White's 'Shake 'Em On Down', and White was not yet dead. Fortunately for them, he wasn't paying attention.

The infusion of this folkier strain on that third album did not entirely reflect Page's obsession with folk guitarist Bert Jansch. He loved Jansch's guitar work, not his folkiness. Plant, though, loved his electric folk and wanted to take the band in a direction more akin to the one ploughed by the *Full House* line-up of Fairport Convention, using songs so traditional they were *never* copyrighted and giving them the rock treatment. Despite convincing Page to join him for an onstage jam with the *Full House* Fairport at LA's Troubadour club in September 1970, he had only partial success in his mission. *III* was only a demi-acoustic affair. But it did include Child ballad #95, 'The Maid Freed From The Gallows', a song Francis Child himself noted had been found in Sicily, Spain, the Faroe Islands, Iceland, Sweden, Germany, Russia, Denmark and Slovenia, as well as Britain and her ex-colonies.

However, Zeppelin's 'Gallows Pole' came from a distinctly twentieth-century source: Leadbelly. His 'Gallis Pole', an unexceptional American variant with none of its traditional cante-fable elements preserved, had been recorded for Moe Asch's Folkways in 1948.* Zeppelin, though, were

---

* The summer before, he had recorded 'Cotton Fields', a quasi-traditional song transformed by his estate into a Leadbelly original (as it perhaps was). Covered by both The Beach Boys and Creedence Clearwater Revival shortly before Zeppelin revived 'Gallis Pole', 'Cotton Fields' had not been copyrighted until 1962, but it would become the estate's best earner, surpassing the contentious 'Irene'.

not about to cut him in on a medieval ballad they had slowed back down, rearranged and made part of their one-sided folk-rock fusion.

By *Four Symbols*, Plant managed to cajole Page into recording the traditional-sounding 'Battle of Evermore' and the semi-traditional 'When The Levee Breaks' – a reworking of Memphis Minnie's song of the same name, from which the quartet bought the whole bottle and gave her a fifth, which she had just two of her seventy-six years left to enjoy – but otherwise Plant was back to improvising assorted blues and early rock & roll snatches on the rarer occasions when lyrical inspiration failed him.

The rock & roll sensibility, on hold for most of Zep's folk-rock third, was back with a vengeance for this, their hard rock fourth. At least two songs at the sessions developed from rock & roll medleys worked up with ex-Stone Ian Stewart on piano. 'Rock And Roll', as the title suggested, was the product of such a medley, this one based around Little Richard's 'Keep A Knockin'', a song that already had a troubled past.

But by now Page had learnt the art of 'developing my own thing' and the ghost of Clarence Williams let him be. Less of a departure, more like an impromptu jam was 'Boogie With Stu', which was based on Ritchie Valens' 'Ooh My Head'. That one was put on the backburner, appearing only in 1975, when they had need of half a dozen outtakes from albums three, four and five to plump up *Physical Graffiti* to a double. This time they attempted to head off trouble by giving a part-credit to Valens' widow. However, for Mrs Valens a part was never quite good enough:

> **Jimmy Page:** Curiously enough, the one time we did try to do the right thing, it blew up in our faces. When we were up at Headley Grange recording *Physical Graffiti*, Ian Stewart came by and we started to jam. The jam turned into 'Boogie With Stu', which was obviously a variation on 'Ooh! My Head' by the late Ritchie Valens, which itself was actually a variation of Little Richard's 'Ooh! My Soul'. What we tried to do was give Ritchie's mother credit, because we heard she never received any royalties from any

of her son's hits, and Robert did lean on that lyric a bit. So what happens? They tried to sue us for *all* the song.

Aside from this hiccup, the sprawling double set was largely trouble free, despite devoting fifteen minutes of time to two songs with rather obvious debts to first-generation bluesmen. 'Custard Pie', the album opener, was another case of Page writing a tune based around one he knew well and expecting Plant 'to change the lyrics'. In their released form, however, they were almost word for word those found on 'Drop Down Daddy' by Sleepy John Estes, recorded at the same July 1935 sessions as his more famous 'Someday Baby Blues'. Plant also requisitioned Sonny Terry's 'Custard Pie Blues' to fill in any gaps.

Plant was becoming quite adept at riffling through country blues' back pages, and he seemed a whole lot less apologetic about it than Page. When he was asked about such songs by *Melody Maker*, as *Physical Graffiti* rose to its preordained top spot around the world, he simply pointed out, 'There are so many classics from way, way back which we can give a little of ourselves to take them through the years.' And with 'In My Time Of Dyin'', an old Blind Willie Johnson song he presumably first heard on Dylan's debut (he uses Dylan's chosen title, not Johnson's, which was 'Jesus Make Up My Dying Bed'), he imposed eleven whole minutes of Zeppelin bombast over Johnson's magnetically understated original.

Content that the long-dead blues believer wouldn't mind, he also returned to this lesser-known Johnson for 'Nobody's Fault But Mine', the highlight of *Physical Graffiti*'s weak successor, *Presence*. Page continued insisting the song, as Zep recorded it, 'was nothing to do with the original. Robert may have wanted to go for the original blues lyrics, but everything else was a different kettle of fish.' The fact that Plant segued between the two Johnson songs on the 1977 tour suggests the singer felt otherwise.

This particular Johnson had died in mysterious circumstances after recording just thirty songs for Frank Walker's Columbia between 1927 and 1930. Only one photo of the singer has survived, and details of his hard life are sketchy, though these two songs had endured to serve these British blues musicians. The irreligious Tommy Johnson recorded even fewer songs and died even more mysteriously, also leaving behind a single publicity photo; while his 'Big Road Blues' became a direct precursor to 'Smokestack Lightning' and 'Sitting On Top Of The World', two stand-ards all blues revivalists knew, albeit in the proto-electric guise patented by Howlin' Wolf, the one bluesman to best Page.

But the one Delta Johnson who bequeathed the greater mystery, and the greatest legacy of songs ripe for appropriation, was Robert Johnson, another act who recorded for ARC/Columbia when its race division was pretty much the last label standing.

Surprisingly little of this iconic bluesman can be found in Zeppelin's work, though Plant used the lust-filled line about the 'juice running down my leg', from one of Johnson's lesser efforts, 'Travellin' Riverside Blues' – a song Zeppelin toyed with in the early days, but only ever put down at a BBC session – in 'The Lemon Song'. By the time the session version was eventually released on a four-CD retrospective in 1990, how-ever, Zeppelin's previous liberties with blues copyrights were common knowledge. And the now-active Johnson estate demanded full credit even though, aside from the title and some of its commonplace lyrics, the song bears only a nominal resemblance to Johnson's version, itself a recasting of Charlie Patton's 'Banty Rooster Blues'.

In not releasing anything else of Johnson's at a time when his work was a public domain free-for-all, the English band missed their chance. Here was another bluesman who had died young, wherea-bouts unknown, in circumstances unknowable, without a will, having recorded twenty-nine songs that were largely hybrids of former blues. Not only that, but when the producer of the first official collection of Johnson songs, Frank Driggs, put out 1961's *King of The Delta Blues Singers* – an album whose impact is still being felt – he discovered none of the songs had yet been copyrighted, making them fair game. There was another problem. Nothing Johnson wrote was wholly his, either lyrically or musically, every single song having definable antecedents found in someone else's grooves.

Far from being an innovator, Johnson was the last of a dying breed, born too early to trip the light electric in sweet home Chicago, and too late to participate in the birth of the blues record industry. Rather, as Francis Davis suggests, Johnson was 'the last *great* performer . . . to sing and play the blues in the style originated by Tommy Johnson or Son House or Charley Patton or Big Bill Broonzy . . . As a self-accompanied country performer, he was a throwback.'*

Johnson was not a songster like Henry Thomas or Leadbelly, or even Blind Willie McTell. But like them, he was a walking sponge who liked to soak up songs, and adapted at will existing tunes and transposed lines and verses from other songs. Unlike them, he was not a traditional singer. He was a one-man jukebox. The jukebox was his muse.

At any point in the continuing story of popular song, Johnson's work would have been a legal minefield. He was the first post-modern blues-man, which is a polite way of saying he was a natural-born thief in a way that would have made Jean Genet blush. He couldn't even claim his lyrics merely drew from the same traditional imagery as those of his mentors, because they didn't. As Stephen Calt has shown, of the hundred-plus verses found on his recordings, just three relied on blues commonplaces ('The woman I love took my best friend/Some joker got lucky, stole her back again'; 'My mama dead, papa went out to sea/Ain't got nobody to love an' care for me'; 'I went to the mountain, looked as far as my eyes could see/Some other man got my woman, and the lonesome blues got me').

Yet so ubiquitous has Johnson's work become that it seems almost sacrilegious to suggest he stole more than he originated, embellished more

---

* He could even have been considered the last of the great songsters, had it not been that by the time he was recorded white record producers had very little time for interpretations of 'Casey Jones', 'White House Blues', 'Make Me A Pallet On The Floor', 'East St Louis Blues', 'You Can Mistreat Me Here, But You Can't When I Go Home', and 'Black Gal, Whyn't You Comb Your Head?' All were traditional songs Johnson apparently liked to play in his decidedly non-traditional way.

than he ever penned, and that the brilliance of his guitar/vocal delivery disguises a very unoriginal auteur. If John Lennon could be sued for using a single line from a Chuck Berry song, imagine the litigation which would have ensued if Blind Lemon Jefferson had lived long enough to point out that the couplet, 'The train's at the depot with the red and blue lights behind/Well, the blue light's the blues, red light's the worried mind', came from his 'Dry Southern Blues' (1926), not Johnson's 'Love In Vain'. Or that 'She got el'gant movements from her head down to her toe/An' she can brake in on a dollar, man, most anywhere she go', came from his 'Change My Luck Blues' (1928), not Johnson's 'Walkin' Blues'. (The fact that Johnson actually sings the nonsensical 'Elgin movements' suggests he misheard another exemplary Paramount pressing.)

Kansas Joe, too, might have been inclined to wonder where little Robert got the line, 'A woman is like a dresser, some man always ramblin' through its drawers', in 'From Four Till Late', if it wasn't from his 'Dresser Drawer Blues' (1932). As for what is probably Johnson's most famous line, 'I believe, I believe I'll dust my broom', it originally constituted a couplet which ended, 'So some of you lowdown rounders, Lord, you can have my room.' Kokomo Arnold had used both on 'I'll Be Up Someday' – and we know Johnson paid mighty close attention to what Kokomo did.

Which is perhaps why first-generation blues enthusiast H.C. Speir was less impressed by Johnson than his latterday brethren. As Speir's modern mouthpiece, blues researcher Gayle Dean Wardlow, put it, 'Speir had heard . . . Charlie Patton, Skip James and Tommy Johnson. So Robert Johnson was just an unknown blues singer trying to make a buck . . . The first-line singers of the Twenties weren't influenced by records, they were influenced by people they heard playing live. [Whereas] Robert Johnson heard a hell of a lot of good records somewhere.'

Anyone who knew this stuff well would have recognized Johnson's frames of reference in a minute. Indeed, Dylan tells a story in his 'liar's autobiography', *Chronicles*, about playing a white label of Johnson's 1961 album to Dave Van Ronk, who 'kept pointing out that this song comes from another song and that one song was an exact replica of a different song. He didn't think Johnson was very original . . . I thought Johnson was as original could be.'

Johnson certainly gave Dylan a notion of how much easier it might be to stitch songs together, rather than write them (a notion Dylan would return to extensively after hitting sixty). By September 1962, Dylan was performing a version of Johnson's 'Kind Hearted Woman' that was as beholden to Leroy Carr and Skip James as Johnson, one on which he sometimes segued into Blind Lemon Jefferson's 'See That My Grave Is Kept Clean'.

By then Dylan had figured out how Johnson put it all together, having begun his own plundering of the blues. Johnson had a laissez-faire attitude all of his own, convinced his predecessors all worked from the same handbook. And like Dylan, he rarely learnt his melodies in person; they came mostly from playing records over and over again, as Jimmie Rodgers had. Which perhaps explains why he disappeared for a time in his teens to re-emerge as a guitarist with a golden touch; he had not gone to the crossroads at midnight, he had called on some of his women 'friends' and riffled through their record collections for 78s by Johnny Temple, Leroy Carr, Kokomo Arnold, Memphis Minnie, Peetie Wheatstraw, Son House, Charley Patton, Skip James, Hambone Willie, Blind Blake and/or Lonnie Johnson. Because he was nothing if not thorough. By the time he returned to the Southern juke joints he was a one-man Anthology of American Blues Music.

Johnson especially liked Leroy Carr and Peetie Wheatstraw. The list of musical cops from the former runs to a quarter of Johnson's 29-song canon: 'I Believe I'll Make a Change' ('Dust My Broom'); 'My Woman's Gone Wrong' ('Rambling On My Mind'); 'How Long Blues' ('Come On In My Kitchen'); 'Prison Bound Blues' ('Me And The Devil'); 'When The Sun Goes Down' ('Love In Vain'); 'Straight Alky Blues' ('Cross Road Blues'); and 'Mean Mistreater Mama' ('Kindhearted Woman'). Meanwhile, Wheatstraw's work directly influenced the likes of 'Terraplane Blues', 'Steady Rollin' Man' and 'Little Queen Of Spades' (courtesy of his 'So Long Blues', 'Johnnie Blues' and 'King Of Spades').

Johnson was nothing if not judicious in his choice of sources. If Hambone Willie's 'Roll And Tumble Blues' gave him the basics for two tunes ('If I Had Possession' and 'Travelin' Riverside Blues'), Johnnie Temple's 'Lead Pencil Blues' and 'Evil Devil Blues' inspired two equally memorable melodic cops, 'Sweet Home Chicago' and 'Hellhound On My Trail'. This man had trawled the output of twenties race record divisions till he had the style *down*.

There was nothing hit and miss about Johnson's methodology, for his was hardly the usual cut and thrust of contemporary song-copping, but something else – a conscious distillation of an already dying art form. Because, as Calt writes in his unpublished biography, 'A fair number of the blues lyrics Johnson annotated in a notebook he kept for that purpose and later committed to wax were drawn from obscure, outmoded blues records.' Such a notebook, seen by witnesses, confirms Johnson was no illiterate folkloric songster.

By the time Johnson was scooped up by Columbia's Don Law, records like Papa Charlie Jackson's 1924 'Salt Lake City Blues' or Ma Rainey's 1923 'Moonshine Blues' – which between them provide the memorable couplet in 'Walkin' Blues', 'I'm leavin' here tonight if I have to ride the blinds/ Take a freight train special, tell the engineer lose no time' – were relics of a bygone blues. In fact, as Calt points out, only two of his assorted lyrical borrowings were lifted from recordings still current by the time Johnson entered the studio in 1936; and those came from Leroy Carr's 'Hurry Down Sunshine' (1934) and the already-mentioned Kokomo Arnold's 'I'll Be Up Someday'.

It is almost as if Johnson was trying to capture the pure Delta blues before it was too late, not just for his own sake but for the sake of music itself. And that perhaps is what we hear in his most fearful songs, like 'If I Had Possession Over Judgement Day' and 'Me And The Devil Blues'. Not a fear of perdition, but of posterity's lack of interest, a voice left unheard.

So what did Don Law think when he first heard such lyrical larceny? By the time of Johnson's first session, in November 1936, Law was experienced enough to have known the difference between bluesmen who plundered tradition and those who cherry-picked from records and fellow recording artists. Yet no one did it quite like Johnson.

Usually, bluesmen would take a leaf out of Big Bill Broonzy's book and 'take one song and make fifty out of it . . . just change it a little bit'. Johnson was unique, a master craftsman, using materials that were invariably already captured on record. Thankfully for him, at this time A&R men simply wanted songs they could claim the two-cents publishing on. They did not file musical notation with the US Copyright Office. So as long as a song was not an exact copy of a recent hit, they were happy as Larry. But in this strange halfway house created by the US 1909 copyright law, a song had to be 'fixed' if it wanted full protection, and that meant notated. Otherwise, it remained fair game for anyone inclined to cover it – as long as they 'just change[d] it a little bit'.

It was into this twilight world of intellectual property that Johnson's talents were flung, and where they began to take root. By the time Led Zeppelin flirted with the Johnson legend, his work had already been picked apart by blues dynamos like Muddy Waters and Elmore James, and then more thoroughly pillaged by John Mayall's Bluesbreakers and the two commercial combos, Cream and Fleetwood Mac, subsequently formed by Mayall's former guitarists, Eric Clapton and Peter Green. For all three, *King of the Delta Blues Singers* had become a black vinyl bible. And each was determined to take Johnson's work into commercial realms he can only have imagined.

Clapton would prove to be the key disciple and commercial conduit; Green's use of Johnson's work was less reverential. This was partly because Clapton continued to present himself as a blues purist bringing coal-black blues from Boulder to Birmingham. However, there was nothing pure about Cream's sources, as evidenced by the song-credits to 'Crossroads' and 'Four Until Late' (Johnson), 'Rollin' And Tumblin'' (Muddy Waters, not Hambone Willie) and 'Sitting On Top Of The World' (Chester Burnett, not Walter Vincent of the Mississippi Sheiks). Johnson had purloined both former tunes. Two decades later the Wolf and Waters did the same with the latter two. So to give them credit in 1967–8 suggests a surprising ignorance of country blues almost a decade after Sam Charters published his influential overview of the field.

For 'Rollin' And Tumblin' one could perhaps excuse the power trio's ignorance of Hambone Willie, but the Mississippi Sheiks' 'Sitting On Top Of The World' was the second most oft-recorded blues tune in the years before Johnson set 'Come On In My Kitchen' to it.*

Peter Green, though, knew a rogue from a rookie. On the first Fleetwood Mac album, the credit for his rearrangement of Johnson's 'Hellhound On My Trail' to a blues tune of his own making read, 'Trad. arr. Peter Green', even though the lyrics were mostly Johnson's. When the band joined in for a blues masterclass, 'Dust My Broom', on the second Mac album, *Mr Wonderful*, Green called it right, crediting it to 'Johnson Arr. [Elmore] James'.†

The Stones had also wised up about song-credits by the time they thought about recording two tributes to Johnson in 1969–70. The first of these, a dramatic reinterpretation of 'Love In Vain', was credited on *Let It Bleed* to 'Woody Payne', a close cousin of Nanker-Phelge. A song not found on the 1961 *King of The Delta Blues Singers*, it actually came from a pirate album of rare Johnson 78s Keith Richards had discovered. He immediately fell in love with the song.

However, he also realized 'if we were going to record it there was no point in trying to copy the Robert Johnson style.' By this point Richards was heavily 'into country music – old white country music, '20s and '30s stuff, and white gospel . . . I'm trying to figure out some nuances and chords, and I start to play ['Love In Vain'] in a totally different fashion. Everybody joins in and goes, yeah, and suddenly you've got your

---

* Apparently, when its creator Walter Vincent first showcased the song to the Sheiks' fiddler, Lonnie Chatmon, in Greenwood, Mississippi in 1930, Chatmon asked him, 'What kind of song is that?' Vincent's response was, 'It's a blues – you can one step to it.'

† Green soon outgrew his blues mentors in the studio, reserving his Delta outings for informal BBC radio sessions and/or late-night club dates. It would require the 1995 release of BBC recordings before his incendiary versions of 'Preachin' Blues' and 'Sweet Home Chicago' took the CD stage; by then every Johnson song bore a copyright notice.

own stamp on it.' Imagine his surprise, having rearranged Johnson's jigsaw, when the Johnson estate came after the Stones in the late nineties for Woody Payne's interpretation of a song Johnson wrote very little of himself.

They also wanted a piece of another Johnson song the Stones had tackled the same year *Let It Bleed* and CBS's second instalment in the *King of The Delta Blues Singers* series appeared. Recorded in October 1970 with ex-Bluesbreaker Mick Taylor, 'Stop Breakin' Down' was released (with a new vocal) on 1972's *Exile On Main Street*, credited to all five Stones. Again, the Stones had drastically reinterpreted one of Johnson's most derivative pieces, which itself incorporated parts of at least two Memphis Minnie songs – 'Caught Me Wrong Again' and 'You Got to Move' – as Johnson, short of songs at what was to prove his final session, sought to imitate the spirit of a 1935 Buddy Moss blues called 'Stop Hanging Around'.

But at the time the Stones paid dual tribute to Johnson – thereby greatly expanding general awareness of his work – the Johnson legend was only just starting to build a head of steam. It would take a visit to Commerce, Mississippi in 1973 by a blues fan called Steve LaVere for that legend to resound to the sound of cash registers ringing.

It was from a childhood friend of Johnson's that LaVere obtained the address of a half-sister, Carrie Thompson, who had moved to Baltimore from Memphis around 1940. And much to LaVere's delight, she had two photos of the half-brother she barely knew.

With these photos, recordings of her reminiscences and a signed agreement that he would act as her agent, LaVere contacted the legendary Columbia producer John Hammond, and succeeded in persuading him to not only instigate a full-scale reissue of Johnson's work but to sign over the copyrights to LaVere, copyrights Hammond did not have the right to assign. Hammond took LaVere at his word that he would pay Johnson's family in turn.

Given that the only Johnson recordings not covered by the albums

Columbia had already issued in 1961 and 1970 were a dozen or so alternate takes ('safety takes' made in case the glass master should be damaged), it was hard to see what the appeal of such a set might be. And whatever appeal it had diminished as soon as LaVere insisted Johnson's half-sister (via himself) receive royalties from any resultant set.

By 1976, *Rolling Stone* was reporting that 'the album is currently being held up by a disagreement over royalties with LaVere.' It would be 1990 before it appeared. By that time the (late) half-sister's claim had been challenged by an illegitimate son, whose first question, when another blues archivist came calling in the late eighties, was depressingly predictable: 'Is there anything coming from my daddy's records?'

The answer was, not as much as you might think – at least at the time. As Sam Charters wrote in a disclaimer at the front of his Robert Johnson songbook, published the same year LaVere found his living link to the king of the delta blues: 'Robert Johnson died without copyrighting any of his songs, and there was no copyright claim made by any of his family; so the songs are what is called "public domain," meaning that they cannot be claimed or copyrighted by anyone.'

But that would be the case only until a new US copyright law came into effect. Which was just around the corner – 1976, to be exact – at which point US law finally recognized that a recording conferred copyright. For most of the old bluesmen any such inadvertent bounty from their plugged-in successors came too late, but not for Johnson's 'heirs'.

Not every black man recorded in the twenties and thirties by white A&R men was left without the requisite protection. Anyone captured by the late Ralph Peer could be confident that somewhere in the archives of Southern Music was a royalty statement gathering dust. One potential beneficiary had not passed away until 1959, five months before the man who recorded him in Atlanta back in 1928 and 1929. But Blind Willie McTell had no expectation any cheque awaiting him at Southern Music was going to amount to a hill of beans. It would take a 'various artists' sampler compiled by Sam Charters the following year, as companion to his *Country Blues* book, to make one of McTell's songs, 'Statesboro Blues', a staple of the blues revival.

Not that he was any more entitled than Johnson to claim said song as an original work. As his modern biographer, Michael Gray, writes:

[McTell] would say of his methods of composition: 'I jump 'em from other writers but I arrange 'em my way.' And it's true that [on 'Statesboro Blues'], he drew on early records by the female 'classic blues' singers. Most obviously he drew from the Texas-born Sippie Wallace . . . [the first verse of whose] 'Up The Country Blues', made in Chicago in late 1923, . . . runs: 'Hey, hey, mama, run tell your papa/Go tell your sister, run tell your auntie/That I'm going up the country: do you want to go?', and its last verse has the repeated use of '[so-and-so]'s got 'em' – all of which McTell reworks into the teasing catalogue of piled-up people suddenly introduced into the middle of 'Statesboro Blues' . . . He also uses Bessie Smith's 'Reckless Blues', twisting her 'My mama says I'm reckless, my daddy says I'm wild' from parental complaint to parental death . . . Finally, he also seems to have used an April 1927 recording by the Alabama-based Ivy Smith, whose 'Cincinnati Southern Blues' includes the couplet, 'She leaves Cincinnati at five o'clock/You oughta see that fireman gettin' his boiler hot.' Willie transforms this into, 'Big 80 left Savannah, Lord, and did not stop/You oughta saw that colored fireman when he got them boiler hot.'

Nonetheless, the song was copyrighted by Peer, just in case McTell's musical alchemy might eventually turn to gold. And after the groundwork laid by recordings of Dave Van Ronk and Taj Mahal in the sixties, lo it came to pass: The Allman Brothers opened their double live album *At The Fillmore East* (1971) with this exemplary slice of Southern boogie. The album, certified platinum in 1992, almost single-handedly generated six figures in back royalties for McTell's estate.

Yet it would be fifteen years before a claimant would step forward to claim his prize. Ernest Bernard McTell, the *adopted* son of Blind Willie's wife, Kate McTell, had never known his foster father and his only interest in his stepfather's work was the kind that accrued from a lump sum. After a spell in prison, he finally got his hands on Willie's back royalties at the end of 2007, after the publisher had grown increasingly concerned it might end up in state coffers because of a threatened change in the law. Bernard would be found dead the following June, just forty-three, his internal engine broke beyond repair.

His stepfather's last commercial release from a lifetime without due recognition, 'Broke Down Engine' b/w 'Kill It Kid', had appeared on the newly formed Atlantic Records in 1950 after McTell recorded an album's worth of familiar blues and gospel fare for Atlantic's founder, Ahmet Ertegun, in October 1949. When Ertegun found a more marketable song snatcher in Ray Charles he left the McTell tapes in the bottom drawer.

Just as Bernard was getting his hands on McTell's publishing, Ertegun's most successful song snatchers, Led Zeppelin, were playing a one-off reunion as a tribute to their late friend and label boss. Plans were already afoot for a double live album of the event. The multi-disc set would include interpretations of two Blind Willie Johnson songs and the now-familiar Jake Holmes psychedelic blues called 'Dazed and Confused'. Yet every song was copyrighted to one or more members of the modern musical monolith Jimmy Page formed in his own image back in 1968, when he was still waiting for the last fair deal to go down.

# PART THREE:

# I FOUGHT THE LAW AND THE LAWYERS WON

# CHAPTER 13

# 1967–82: I Me Mine

*Featuring*: 'Boris The Spider'; 'Paint It Black'; 'Jumpin' Jack Flash'; 'Death Of A Clown'; 'A Whiter Shade of Pale'; 'Taxman'; 'While My Guitar Gently Weeps'; 'Badge'; 'Something'; 'Come Together'; 'Golden Slumbers'; 'My Sweet Lord'

> At first it was great [to get a song on an album]. It was like, 'Hey, I'm getting in on the act too!' After a while I did [start to resent it], especially when I had good songs. Sometimes I had songs that were better than some of their songs and we'd have to record maybe eight of theirs before they'd listen to one of mine.
>
> George Harrison

Once Lennon and McCartney had lit the way, it wasn't just fellow Beatles who wanted a share of the songwriting spoils. A whole generation of Britpop bands burnished by American R&B took a long, hard look at themselves and began to write about what they saw in the mirror, at the clubs and on the street. Between 1964 and 1966, chastened in part by the initial failure of English R&B to sell itself to the cash-rich youth of America, the bands trailing in The Beatles' wake produced an R&B/pop fusion that was as rhythmic as the former and fizzy as the latter. Their understanding of the craft of song publishing, though, trailed some way behind their grasp of song writing.

Also put at risk was the camaraderie that had bound British bands together through the long hard slogs in places like Hamburg, and on package tours the length and breadth of the British Isles, where even headliners were expected to play their hits and eff off. By 1966, the package-tour approach was dying faster than the Dodo, just as the power-base of the leading English bands – The Beatles, The Rolling Stones, The Who and The Kinks – had shifted inexorably in favour of their supposed songwriters. Just about all song ideas from constituent members became grist for the creative mills of Lennon-McCartney, Jagger-Richards, Pete Townshend or Ray Davies. Not surprisingly, the end product sometimes reflected its fair share of bad blood, and tensions inside these close-knit bands occasionally spilled over into violence.

Prior to May 1966, The 'Oo's rhythm section would have seemed an unlikely breeding ground for seething resentment (unlike the battle Roger Daltrey and Townshend fought for leadership of the band, which also came to blows but once Townshend became sole songwriter was only ever going to have one outcome). Townshend and John Entwistle had been the band's axis since the skiffle era, each arsenal of sonic assault perfectly complementing the other. And though it was the latter who was the classically trained musician, when the band's own captains of industry began to push for a songwriter from within the ranks at the end of 1964, it was Townshend who put himself forward.

After the success of 'I Can't Explain' any contributions to the creative process from the others were far more limited than in other bands, simply because Townshend produced solo demos for all his songs. By 1966 these were more than mere skeletal outlines, and the others were expected to adhere to what was laid down. Perhaps the first sign of mutiny, appropriately, had come during the 'My Generation' sessions – when bassist Entwistle broke out.

As Townshend relates the song's composition in *The Decade of The Who*, right from the pre-stutter first demo he had always included 'a spoof bass guitar solo (later improved upon by John)'. But not only did Entwistle essentially write his own part, he later claimed to have 'sabotaged' the recording by turning his bass up midway through the master take (the bass sound having already been beefed up by engineer Glyn Johns' judicious use of a concrete paving slab, on which he mounted the bass amp). In those days, there was no way of recalibrating the bass level, and so the solo explodes from the speakers. And, as John Perry writes, 'The break is a nicely judged mixture of taste and flash, rhythmic subtlety and blindingly fast runs using all four fingers of the right hand.' The Ox was demanding a greater say in the *songs*. But Townshend wasn't listening.

It would take the possibility of The Who losing their rhythm section, perhaps to Jimmy Page and Jeff Beck, after a fracas on 20 May 1966 – the result of Keith Moon and Entwistle's belated arrival at the Corn Exchange in Newbury, fresh from a party at *Ready Steady Go!* – for Townshend (and Daltrey) to sit up and take notice. But when they did, all hell broke loose. Townshend swung his guitar not at Moon's drum-kit during the usual 'My Generation' auto-destruction, but at Moon's head. Daltrey joined in, wielding his mike stand in Moon's direction. The mêlée continued even into the dressing room.

A week later, Moon was telling anyone who would listen he had quit The Who, as had Entwistle. Things were patched up by the end of June but the rift was real. As Townshend told *Melody Maker*'s Chris Welch, 'I saw myself writing film scores while Keith and John saw themselves forming a group called Led Zeppelin.'

What may have finally brought things to a head was another Who recording session, to which only Entwistle and Moon turned up. They responded by writing their only joint composition, 'In The City', a fun song which also signalled a realignment of the band's creative identity. After a five-month hiatus brought on by legal matters and band disagreements, the full quartet had earlier recorded 'I'm A Boy' b/w 'Disguises', the successor to 'Substitute'. And no question, 'Disguises' beats 'In The City' hands down in The Who pantheon. But when 'I'm A Boy' appeared, it had the Entwistle-Moon composition on the B-side.

And from here on, for the duration of the five-year Talmy settlement, B-sides – save when it was Moon's ('Dogs Part 2') or Daltrey's turn ('Here For More') – would be allocated to John Entwistle, who quickly developed a style all his own. It seems likely that Townshend felt obliged to split the publishing revenue from The Who's hits – and at this stage that was every UK 45 – with Entwistle in order to achieve détente and restore unity. And giving him the B-side was a way of doing that without sacrificing their chart prospects.

Daltrey and Moon would also get a piece of the publishing on the next album, *A Quick One*, but the pieces they contributed were so pitiful and/or strange that this would be a one-time concession. Entwistle's two contributions, however – 'Boris The Spider' (a song Townshend admits only band 'politics or my own shaky vanity' stopped from being a single A-side) and 'Whiskey Man' – proved he was no slouch as a songsmith. Future Who albums would usually reserve a slot or two for Entwistle's mordant worldview. And when even this did not suffice, he got to make four woefully underrated solo albums for the band's own Track label during the first half of the seventies.

Another stone-faced bassist in an even more successful British outfit, The Rolling Stones' Bill Wyman, had long given up hope of such a gesture on his own frontman's part. Essentially, this was because Mick Jagger was no democrat. Once he assumed de facto leadership of the Stones, Jagger deferred to one man and one man only – guitar sidekick Keef – even then thriving on powerplays, while Richards just wanted to enjoy the ride. And confirmation that both Wyman and Brian Jones were fast becoming second-class Stones – an ironic status, given the obsession with class found in so many of Jagger's mid-sixties lyrics – came the day in March 1966 they cut 'Paint It Black'.

Jagger-Richards had been coping with the increased level of expectations remarkably well, following 'Satisfaction' with their most singalong single, 'Get Off Of My Cloud' and the A-side all those previous B-sides had been working up to, '19th Nervous Breakdown'. But it was 'Paint It Black' that laid down a marker, saying the Stones were no longer an R&B band with delusions of pop grandeur. It was also a track Wyman thought should have been credited to Nanker-Phelge, and not just because of his own suggestion – a brilliant touch – to use Hammond organ pedals to play a second bass riff in double-time.

It was Jones's contribution on sitar and acoustic guitar that made the

track stand out in an era awash with great British 45s. His inventiveness
even drew rare praise from manager Andrew Loog Oldham, who noted
how 'you can hear his colour all over "Lady Jane" and "Paint It Black."
It was more than a decorative effect. Sometimes Brian pulled the whole
record together.' However, as Wyman observes, even though 'Mick and
Keith knew that Brian's flexibility and prowess as a musician helped give
many tracks a touch of magic, there seemed an unwritten rule that he was
kept down, made to feel like simply a contributor.'

Nor was Jones a Stone alone. As Wyman recounts, 'It happened frequently that basic ideas and middle bits by Brian, Charlie and me went
into the melting-pot during long studio sessions, but over a period of
hours or days the origins of our suggestions disappeared. I'd say something like, "That thing I did in the middle really worked, didn't it?" And
Mick would reply: "That was my idea!"'

Wyman's reaction was typically stone-faced: 'I'd dismiss it with a
laugh rather than argue at the time – [after all,] who wants a disagreement
in the studio when you are all trying to be creative?' But given Jones's
fragile sense of self, the consequences for him were bound to be telling.
Musician–friend Dave Thomson later recalled an incident at this time,
where 'we were going to write a song together and he chopped it, saying,
"If I take it into the studio, they'll just mock it, won't use it "' No prizes
for guessing who the 'they' were.

Jones was to become ever more self-conscious, abandoning himself to
the hedonism that would ultimately immerse him. Wyman was not such
a pushover; even though, of all the frustrated songsmiths locked in bands
with room for only one song-partnership, his abiding resentment would
prove the most deep-rooted and least catered for. So, starting in 1965, he
began to produce and compose for other outfits. Throughout the period
1965 to 1968, he supplied a steady stream of largely forgettable singles for
the likes of Bobbie Miller, Moon's Train and The Cheynes, culminating
in two singles (and an album) with The End in 1968, the A-sides of which
he composed with Peter Gosling.

They both sank without trace – unlike another song Wyman claims he co-composed that spring, after a catastrophic 1967, creatively and commercially, for the Stones. They desperately needed a single that made a statement. But Jagger didn't expect it to be the bass player's statement:

**Bill Wyman:** The crucial riff for ['Jumpin' Jack Flash'] was mine, and it evolved in the unorthodox way that some of the best ideas do. One night, during rehearsals at Morden, I was sitting at the piano waiting for Mick and Keith to arrive. Charlie and Brian came in as I began playing the electronic keyboard, messing around with a great riff I'd found. Charlie and Brian began jamming with me and it sounded really good and tough. When Mick and Keith walked in they said, 'Keep playing that, and don't forget it – it sounds great.' A few weeks later when we were in the Olympic studio[s], out came my riff, the backbone for Mick's terrific lyrics, 'I was born in a crossfire hurricane . . .' And we all worked on the music. The part I'd composed worked perfectly – but the credit for this, one of our best tracks ever, reads Jagger-Richards. I knew the important riff was my idea and so did the band, but I'd forgotten to do anything about it. Even Keith admitted in interviews that I wrote that song.

This was to be the hand of fate dealt Wyman for the twenty-five years it took him to say, sod this. In that time he would be allowed to make two mid-seventies solo albums, neither in his fellow bassist John Entwistle's league. As for Stones song-credits, Wyman would get one, 'In Another Land', on their long-playing psychedelic breakfast, *Their Satanic Majesties Request*. As if that particular dog's dinner was somehow his fault, he was not asked to bring anything else to the table.

As for Jones, he quit the band in June 1969, tired of Jagger's mind games, finally realizing that the only way to build his sense of self-esteem was to make a clean break. It was sink or swim; sadly, it was the former. He was found dead in his own swimming pool shortly after midnight on 3 July 1969. The Stones' then producer Jimmy Miller was the first to suggest he 'never quite adapted to the commercial and image aspects of the

Stones', which now involved thirty pieces of silver. Brian's contribution to the Stones – which included any number of memorable riffs he'd made his own – would henceforth be downplayed in the Gospel According to Mick 'n' Keef. And the solo album he had often promised, but never delivered, became another stick with which to beat down memories of the man's stellar contribution.

Nor was Jones the only second-rung songwriter in a band that had original songs to spare whose failure to deliver an oft-reported solo album became 'evidence' he was not up to the task. Dave Davies of The Kinks had been talking about his own album since July 1967, when his first solo single, 'Death Of A Clown', had reached the Top Three. And yet, it singularly failed to appear.

In the end, Dave held his hands up and admitted the album he slung together at sessions from 1967 through 1969 was just a collection of songs (and even then, two were his brother's leftovers), and that he 'was much happier within the structure of The Kinks'. It would be 1980 before he would release his first solo album and 2011 before that aborted sixties effort saw the light of day. He would just have to be content with being the brother with the looks.

Once his younger sibling became the Great Songwriter, it seems brother Dave lost heart – though it was he who had provided the few originals the pre-Kinks Ravens included in their set; and barely had Ray written his first A-side when Dave was donating one of his own ('One Fine Day') to Shel Naylor, another act their managers rated. The importance of Dave's contribution to The Kinks' breakthrough single, 'You Really Got Me', has also been argued about ad nauseam. The riff, as with any riff, was all about execution – and in that Davidian moment, Leadbelly and Big Bill Broonzy were nowhere to be seen.* But like Jimmy Page, who was

---

* The Davies brothers are still squabbling over credit for the 'You Really Got Me' riff fifty years on. When Ray took the credit himself in the version told in current West End musical, *Sunny Afternoon*, brother Dave threatened to bring an injunction unless the story was changed.

in the studio that day, notebook in hand, Dave soon learnt a riff was not a song. His follow-up to 'Death Of A Clown' confirmed it. 'Susannah's Still Alive' had the great piano intro., played by the redoubtable Nicky Hopkins, but without the lyrical contribution his brother had provided on the previous 45, the song merely meandered towards the 180-second mark.

Nonetheless, any three-minute rock single needed such a riff. It provided the fuel injection which made the song's engine hum. And it has remained the most contentious part of the process, simply because if the riff in question wasn't played by the song's author, it usually meant the lead guitarist, or keyboardist, had taken a raw melodic idea and run with it. Was this composition? The most protracted dispute involving a British single from the sixties would revolve around exactly this point. The song they were still squabbling about four decades later was the defining chart-topper from the summer of love and – according to evidence given in the three trials it took to decide who wrote what – the most played song on radio – ever.

Procol Harum's 'A Whiter Shade of Pale', credited for forty-two years to Gary Brooker and Keith Reid, had an absolutely distinctive Hammond organ intro, courtesy of Matthew Fisher. The irony at the heart of all this litigation is that it boiled down to the fact that Fisher had copped a different part of Bach's oeuvre to the one appropriated and arranged by Gary Brooker ('Air On A G String' and 'Sleepers Awake' as opposed to *Ich steh mit einem Fuß im Grabe*, a.k.a. 'I am standing with one foot in the grave'), throwing in elements of the intro to Percy Sledge's 'When A Man Loves A Woman' for good measure. But the essential point – ultimately proven in a court of law in the face of Brooker's belligerent insistence that the song was his alone – was that the intro was Fisher's idea.

As such the 2009 Law Lords' verdict was a triumph for all band members who ever took a rudimentary three-minute song and gave it an intro that made it immortal. As the judge in the original case stated in his written verdict, 'It is clear that, at the time at least, . . . [Keith] Reid considered that it was Mr Fisher who wrote the organ part.' The result, six weeks at number one, speaks for itself. As did Fisher who said, on hearing the verdict, 'I can assume that from now on I'm not going to be on Gary's and Keith's Christmas card lists, but I think it's a small price to pay for finally securing my rightful place in rock & roll history.'

Not surprisingly, given their stature, it has been The Beatles's booty which has been the one most prone to disputes, then and now. Such disputes arose as the inevitable by-product of working out songs live in the studio, a practice that only really started to be abandoned when The Beatles decided to take three months creating an album where studio effects and 'thematic coherence' disguised a diminution in song-craft on the part of one of the most dynamic duo in British pop.

By then, the public die was cast: Lennon was the intuitive genius whose flights of imagination lit up their LPs, while Macca could hum a good tune and good ol' George, well, he might get the odd bone thrown his way. But as of 1967, not only were the days when Lennon matched McCartney lick for lick, lyric for lyric long gone, but Harrison was starting to get the hang of this songwriting lark. It was this shift in the pop paradigm that set the biggest band in the world at loggerheads, and led Harrison for the first time, in the summer of 1966, to threaten to quit.

The most privileged of the 'lesser' songwriters from the great Britbeat era was determined to get his fair share of album-time, or die trying. When the Beatles were finally laid to rest, it was to Harrison's 'I Me Mine', at the end of a four-year struggle for a share of songwriting spoils which began the year George told the others he would not tour again and that he wanted more than the token track to his name on the next LP.

Harrison had been serious about the business side of songwriting for some time, cutting his own deal with Dick James shortly after Northern Songs went public in February 1965. He had already formed his own company, Harrisongs, but was contracted to give any songs that appeared on Beatles albums to Northern Songs until 1968. However, whereas Lennon and McCartney allowed James to make as much as the two of them put together, Harrison negotiated himself 80 per cent of the monies from

275

record sales, 70 per cent of the receipts from overseas publishing and 66 per cent of all performing and broadcast fees. What a shame he wasn't also managing the band's affairs.

Now all he needed to do was convince the others they should put more of his songs on those multimillion-selling Beatles albums. But there was a seemingly insurmountable psychological barrier, the nature of which insider Peter Brown made plain: 'As far as John and Paul were concerned, George was only a third-class Beatle, and there was nothing he could do about it. His music was summarily dismissed at recording sessions, and his few songs to appear on Beatles' albums were relegated to filler positions.'

The situation only began to change in 1966, and not just because Harrison started to produce a handful of songs of real quality, but because Lennon was failing to produce enough songs. Those he did produce, moreover, needed more work to become a Beatles song – work which usually devolved to McCartney, but which on one notable occasion at the end of the *Revolver* sessions required Harrison's input.

Lennon had first taken LSD in 1965, and had gone on to consume the drug regularly, believing it would aid his muse. It was not that Lennon's personality had been changed by his consumption of LSD because in the words of Beatles publicist Tony Barrow, he had always 'had a MTV-level concentration-span. He got bored very quickly and pushed things aside.' Now, though, that lack of concentration had spread to the very core of his and the band's identity – his songwriting. And as his drug consumption rose, the energy spurts that would still enable him to produce work of the stature of 'Strawberry Fields Forever', 'A Day In The Life', 'I Am The Walrus' and 'Happiness Is A Warm Gun' would become less frequent, and frustratingly fleeting.

Lennon may have been slouching at the *Revolver* sessions, but what he did finally deliver – notably 'Tomorrow Never Knows', 'I'm Only Sleeping' and 'Rain' – kept everyone believing he was still the leader and the others mere followers. 'She Said She Said', another telling contribution, was a song he had been inspired to pen after taking LSD in August

1965 in the company of The Byrds' Roger McGuinn and David Crosby; but as was becoming a pattern in his songwriting, he had faltered at the altar of melodic variation. As with 'Rain' and 'Tomorrow Never Knows', he initially thought if he made the song sufficiently strange it would disguise a lack of basic song-structure, just as six months later McCartney would add the necessary bridge to 'A Day In The Life', another song Lennon seemed willing to leave one-paced and two-dimensional.

But when Lennon turned round at the session on 21 June 1966, his usual saviour was not there. As McCartney later recalled, 'I think we had a "barney" or something and I said, oh, fuck you!' Lennon was obliged to ask for help from the kid in the corner fiddling with his guitar. Harrison later said this involved putting together two separate 'bits' to construct 'She Said She Said'. These two fragments presumably connected the main part of the song, written in the Mixolydian mode, to the brief but powerful bridge – in 3/4 time and the wholly alien Dorian mode – recalling a childhood reverie ('When I was a boy . . .'). And it seems it was Harrison who figured out how to make that change.

Lennon could still turn a phrase, especially if allowed to display his biting wit. He even provided reciprocation of sorts for Harrison's (uncredited) contribution to 'She Said She Said' with input to Harrison's standout track on *Revolver* – one of two lyrical Lennon contributions to Harrison's nastiest songs (the other being 'Piggies' on *The White Album*). As he informed *Playboy* in 1980, 'I remember the day [George] called to ask for help on 'Taxman', one of his first songs. I threw in a few one-liners to help the song along . . . I didn't want to do it . . . I just sort of bit my tongue and said okay.'

This tells us much about Lennon, from the begrudging nature of his help to the extraordinary comment that Harrison's biting attack on British government policy was 'one of his first songs'. This was eight years after the band's first demo, which included a McCartney-Harrison composition, and five years after Lennon wrote *his* first song with Harrison, the instrumental, 'Cry For A Shadow'.

In fact, it would appear Harrison stopped writing songs shortly after this because he had little expectation anything he wrote would be recorded. The next song he brought to the band was, according to legend, the direct result of a local Liverpudlian journalist, Bill Harry, recalling how much he liked 'Cry For A Shadow' and asking George why he didn't write more. The response was 'Don't Bother Me', another song which showed the abiding influence of The Shadows. And because, by September 1963, the initial store of self-composed McCartney-Lennon songs, compiled over the previous half-decade, had just about run dry, it would end up on *With The Beatles*. But when Lennon and McCartney got a second creative wind, Harrison was once more out in the cold. It would be eighteen months before he was let in again, and as head-revolutionary Ian MacDonald suggests, the 'sketchy arrangement and murky recording [of 'I Need You'] suggest that he got little help' from the others.

If he wasn't going to get any tutoring from his so-called friends and bandmates, Harrison would look elsewhere. If Lennon wasn't willing to share his songwriting secrets, the two of them did share their first acid trip, when a society dentist thought it a wheeze to 'spike' their drinks at an April 1965 party. The experience opened up the pair to a different point of view, and in October 1965 Harrison wrote his first notable Beatlesong. 'If I Needed Someone' took its guitar figure from his friend Roger McGuinn's recasting of the traditional 'Bells of Rhymney', a conscious cop Harrison asked Beatles publicist Derek Taylor to acknowledge on his behalf to the party concerned. McGuinn already knew, was happy for his friend, and loved what he had done with that Byrdsian guitar figure. Harrison's other, more didactic contribution to The Beatles' first real masterpiece, *Rubber Soul*, 'Think For Yourself', also held up.

Unlike Lennon, Harrison's acid experience had not resulted in him becoming 'psychologically addicted to LSD, taking it daily and living in one long, listless chemically altered state'. Nor had it made him lighten up, or see the world through rose-tinted shades. All three Harrison songs on *Revolver* – a contribution that highlights the lack of songs Lennon was producing, or finishing, in his psychotropic state – display a healthy cynicism about 'being a Beatle', whether it be the deceptive 'Love You To', the admonitory 'I Want To Tell You' or the tart 'Taxman' (a song which MacDonald insists owes melodic debts to James Brown's 'I Got You' and Spencer Davis Group's 'Somebody Help Me').

By *Sgt Pepper*, Harrison had turned his increasingly sceptical eye in the direction of the band's song publisher, the obscenely well-off Mr James. As he later said, '"Only A Northern Song" was where I was starting to get a bit of an idea that this bloke [James] would always show up. You'd only written half a song and he'd be trying to get you to assign it.' This loaded message suggested Harrison was not long for Northern Songs (sure enough, he did not renew their agreement in 1968). And yet, when McCartney came to sequence an album with more padding than its predecessor, and was still only twelve songs, he overlooked Harrison's distinctly psychedelic offering in favour of barnyard noises. Perhaps it was because he still imagined he might need James's help some day.

McCartney (and Lennon) were starting to pass over Harrison-composed outtakes at the very time he needed all the help he could get. 'It's All Too Much', a song that made the summer of love a cautionary tale even as Lennon spouted the cliche-ridden 'All You Need Is Love', didn't even make the *Magical Mystery Tour*, a project which, aside from the magisterial 'I Am The Walrus', was desperately short of insight or inspiration.

Both Harrison's song and Lennon's anthem for the aegis seemed to delight in 'sampling' the works of others, expecting The Beatles' status alone would protect them. And in Harrison's case, he was right. Richard Gottehrer and The McCoys were flattered that he had lifted a verse from 'Sorrow' as 'It's All Too Much' went into its extended coda (one McCartney consciously emulated on 'Hey Jude' the following year). Whereas the snatch of Glenn Miller's 'In The Mood' on 'All You Need Is Love', accompanying similar fragments of 'La Marseillaise', Bach and 'Greensleeves', brought a threat of legal action from Miller's estate and an out-of-court settlement. A legal challenge on the band's behalf might have been the wiser course of action: the snatch of Miller was barely noticeable and had no bearing on the song's success, and anyway he didn't write it. More importantly, the signal sent to the world at large by such a challenge might have saved both Lennon and Harrison much subsequent legal grief. But the cult of originality and the escalating price of Northern Songs stock demanded the problem be made to go away.

Unfortunately, the debts of the world's most popular band were mounting even as their own percentage of their income was diminishing, thanks to the legacy of their late manager. Brian Epstein's last significant act for the band he discovered was to renegotiate their EMI recording contract, due up at the end of 1967. Honourable, trustworthy Mr Epstein wrote into the new EMI contract a clause whereby his own company, NEMS, would collect all monies due to The Beatles, from which he would continue to deduct a gouging 25 per cent – even though his contribution to a band who had stopped touring, and who if they needed publicity made a phone call, verged on the non-existent. As for any creative input, Lennon had already told him to keep his trap shut when recording. What he did not point out to 'his boys' was that the new contract would run for nine years – a full eight years longer than the duration of his management contract. And then he died.

Lennon, having slowly surrendered leadership of the band, all but gave up producing single A-sides – or B-sides, leaving McCartney to reel off three Beatles singles in close succession: 'Hello Goodbye', 'Lady Madonna' and 'Hey Jude' – only one of which warranted its worldwide number one status. If Lennon contributed the flipsides to the first and last of these, purchasers of 'Lady Madonna' were surprised to find on its B-side 'The Inner Light', a George Harrison song which spoonfed them chunks of the Taoist holy book, the *Tao Te Ching*, for its lyrics.

By January 1969 it finally dawned on the two ostensible bandleaders that their previous song selection process had been fostering dissension in the ranks. When Lennon insisted on recording his 'Ballad of John and Yoko' as a Beatles single, Harrison decided to sit this one out, 'because it was none of my business. If it had been "The Ballad of John, George and Yoko," then I would have been on it.' A conciliatory Lennon agreed to give Harrison the B-side, 'Old Brown Shoe', which this time beat the A-side hands down.

The thrashing out of Harrison's status had already taken place on camera, a conversation between all three Beatle guitarists at Apple studios captured by documentary maker Michael Lindsay-Hogg, as McCartney drew a biting retort from the elephant in the studio:

> **Lennon** [to McCartney]: We always carved the singles up between us. We have the singles market, [George and Ringo] don't get anything. I mean, we've never offered George B-sides. We could have given him a lot of B-sides, but because we were two people, you had the A-side and I had the B-side.
>
> **McCartney**: Well, the thing is, I think that until . . . this year our songs have been better than George's. Now this year his songs are at least as good as ours.
>
> **Harrison** [interjects]: That's a myth, because most of the songs this year I wrote last year or the year before, anyway. Maybe now I just don't care whether you are going to like them or not, I just do 'em.

This telling conversation came just days after Harrison walked out on the band for real, and again on camera. Only after much cajoling did he agree to return.

Harrison had a point – and he knew it. The songs he 'wrote last year' but only now offered for band consumption included 'Something', written during the *White Album* sessions. Again, it came about after thinking about someone else's song, this one by Apple's latest signing, James Taylor. 'Something' took its first line from Taylor's 'Something In The Way She Moves' before moving into Harrison's immaterial world. Once more, the cop merely flattered the source songwriter, who later said he 'was pleased to think that I'd had an impact on The Beatles. Anyway, the end of my song was just like "I Feel Fine." So I didn't think of what George had done as plagiarism, because I had already stolen from them.'

Again the Scouse songwriter had got off scot-free, even if 'Something' was not a song he was able to hold onto entirely; as McCartney, displaying some Scouse wit of his own, commented at the time: 'That was . . . George's first big effort, and everyone covered it and it was lovely and it made him lots of money that he could give away . . . Well, it turns out [Allen] Klein has got himself into that company.' The song still became Harrison's one and only Beatles A-side, when it was paired with 'Come Together'. And it enjoyed an even more lucrative afterlife, being covered by everyone from Frank Sinatra to Elvis Presley.

It seems Harrison always envisaged giving the song to someone else to cover. Initially, he gave it to the quintessential English soul singer, Joe Cocker, figuring if he could salvage 'With A Little Help From My Friends', he could raise any lyrical platitudes from the dead. But he always said that when he wrote it, he 'heard Ray Charles singing it' because on his best-known Beatle song, Harrison was hedging his bets.

It was indicative of a remarkably business-like attitude to his work, one reflected in the fact that the two best songs he completed in 1968 were donated to those outside the band – neither even being recorded by The Beatles, though in the case of 'Sour Milk Sea' (recorded by Jackie Lomax) it had been one of four Harrison songs demoed for *The White Album* in a concerted song-swapping session at Harrison's Esher home.* Harrison was becoming increasingly philosophical about (or simply resigned to) McCartney's mystifying preference for a 'Bungalow Bill' over 'Sour Milk Sea'. As he told the court where their disagreements ended up, 'To get a peaceful life I had always let [Paul] have his own way, even when it meant that songs I had composed were not being recorded. At the same time I was helping to record his songs and, into the bargain, I was having to put up with him telling me how to play my own musical instrument.'

---

* 'Not Guilty', another fine Harrison Esher cut, would have to make room on the album for Lennon's recording of a sonic hedgehog being run over by the number nine bus.

He at least enjoyed his first hit single, and Cream's last, co-writing 'Badge' with 'best friend', Eric Clapton, who also added some terrific lead guitar to his one major contribution to *The White Album*, 'While My Guitar Gently Weeps'. And just to prove he could write with the best of them, Harrison spent a happy Thanksgiving in the company of the Dylans at their Woodstock home, where he and his host discussed the art of songwriting and co-wrote 'I'd Have You Anytime'.*

By 1970, Harrison planned to put all this songwriting in a single triple-weave basket, and call it *All Things Must Pass*. At least these songs were his to have and hold. Even if he was still legally tied to his fellow ex-Beatles, he had managed to extract himself from the talons of the ever-grasping Dick James. In fact, he took it upon himself to tell James just what he thought of him when he called to see the man – on behalf of John and Paul – in the spring of 1969. James had decided to sell his share of Northern Songs, to Lew Grade of all people, at the very point when The Beatles were at their most vulnerable, and when cashflow was heading almost entirely in one direction – outwards. Harrison was ostensibly there to ask him to forestall the sale until John and Paul could return from Amsterdam and New York respectively, and make him a counter offer.

One suspects if it had been Lennon doing the talking that day, he may well have done so with his fists, à la Bessie Smith. But James was confident he could handle Harrison, and told him straight, 'he had no intention of waiting for John to get out of bed; he said he had to move his shares quickly or the price might fall. "It's a very serious matter," he told [Harrison] solicitously. George lost his composure, jumped up and began to scream, "It's fucking serious to John and Paul is what it is!"'

The incident served to confirm to a shaken James that holding onto the shares would be more trouble than they were worth. Having brought his supercilious son Stephen into the fold, he left it to him to claim that

---

* Harrison may also have met fellow guitarist Robbie Robertson, who like Harrison had taken his time flowering into a songwriter of the first water, but in the years 1968–71 would become just that, beginning with the just-released *Music From Big Pink*.

the real reason his father sold Northern Songs 'without giving them the chance to buy it' was that, 'at the time there was no way that they could have bought it, because they weren't talking to each other.' That is simply not true. Lennon and McCartney were even united enough to mount a serious campaign to try and stop the public shareholders selling their shares to the new interest, a campaign that would have ended in them regaining control of their own publishing if they could have raised the money to match Grade.

The disintegration of Apple, The Beatles and Lennon's first marriage in the previous two years put paid to that dream. But what they really needed at this juncture was a good legal scandal, preferably combined with a double dose of sheer bloody-mindedness from both Lennon and McCartney. Opportunities resided deep in the small print of their publishing contract, if only they had not been sleepwalking to the brink of financial ruin. After all, a plagiarism suit, even one that came to naught, could have set the Northern Songs share-price plummeting.

Lennon certainly did his bit, by plagiarizing the works of others on songs copyrighted to Northern Songs; indeed, such was his sense of disassociation from all he had wrought that he no longer seemed bothered to disguise such larcenous acts. His contemporary comment about the last Beatles album the former Fab Four recorded says it all: 'The Beatles can go on appealing to a wide audience as long as they make nice albums like *Abbey Road*, which have nice little folk songs like "Maxwell's Silver Hammer" for the grannies to dig.'

This withering remark was clearly directed at McCartney, who had included the aforementioned song and indeed 'Octopus's Garden' (written by Ringo) on the album as a salve to his troubled conscience (and perhaps to further disguise the self-evident disintegration of a once-formidable four-way partnership in song). But if it hadn't been for McCartney's ingenious solution to the problem of how to utilize half a dozen Lennon song-scraps by creating a fifteen-minute song-suite, there never would have been an *Abbey Road*.

And if it wasn't for Harrison's 'Something' and 'Here Comes The Sun', there wouldn't have been any obvious hits 'for the grannies to dig' on *Abbey Road*. Nor would there have been a Beatles 45 with enough cross-generational appeal to reach number one, on which Lennon could piggyback his own 'Come Together'; which had itself come together after messing about with an old Chuck Berry riff ('You Can't Catch Me'), a debt he foolishly thought he could leave explicit and then subsequently deny:

> **John Lennon**: 'Come Together' is me – writing obscurely around an old Chuck Berry thing. I left the line in, 'Here comes ol' flat-top'. It is nothing like the Chuck Berry song, but they took me to court because I admitted the influence once years ago. I could have changed it to, 'Here comes old iron face.' But the song remains independent of Chuck Berry or anybody else on earth. [1980]

(He was probably baffled by all the fuss. It wasn't like he hadn't done this before, i.e. taking the opening line to a rock & roll classic and running with it. *Rubber Soul*'s 'Run For Your Life' kicked off with, 'I'd rather see you dead, little girl, than to be with another man', a line made famous by Elvis's rendition of 'Baby Let's Play House'. But Morris Levy did not own that song and so Lennon got away with it.)

It would take another court case, in July 1975, before the origins of 'Come Together' were resolved (largely in Lennon's favour). The debt to Berry – via Morris Levy – would be valued at a paltry $6,795, somewhat less than Levy's legal bill, and a hundred thousand less than Levy had to pay Lennon for bootlegging his *Rock & Roll* album.

Lennon had simply become increasingly blasé about taking liberties with someone else's songs. When critics lauded his first post-Beatles solo album, *Plastic Ono Band*, in 1970, few noticed that the tune of 'Isolation' was stolen wholesale from an obscure 1959 Barrett Strong track. The original, 'Oh I Apologize', may have been hidden away on a Motown B-side, but it was on a single Lennon had certainly heard – Strong's original R&B hit, 'Money', covered by The Beatles on their second album.

He should have taken his cue from his estranged partner-in-song, who when he needed a little help with the words – as he did during the fraught framing of The Beatles' farewell platter – turned to anthologies of dead poets. Thomas Dekker's seventeenth-century 'Golden Slumbers' had its own tune, which as McCartney recalled, 'I thought . . . was very restful, a very beautiful lullaby, but I couldn't read the melody, not being able to read music. So I just took the words and wrote my own music. I didn't know at the time it was four hundred years old.' He was, however, fairly confident it was out of copyright. And that was the nub. Dekker's descendants got nowt. Lennon got half.

Harrison would not be as judicious as McCartney, or as lucky as Lennon. But then, like Lennon, he had not only made his own bed, but – to spite McCartney – had chosen to lie in it with the most uncuddly man in Christendom, Allen Klein. As someone who professed to believe in karma, one might have expected the events of 1968-69 to make Harrison a changed man. But Harrison could fume and feud with the best of them, and no sooner had he got McCartney out of his life than he was locking horns with Klein.

Klein, for all his faults, was a master at locating 'lost' song royalties and other accounting 'oversights' – he had even succeeded in getting Morris Levy to pay rock & roll singers Buddy Knox and Jimmy Bowen some belated royalties. So when Klein convinced three of The Beatles he could straighten out the financial morass at Apple and renegotiate a new deal with EMI, he wasn't jiving. What he didn't make explicit was that *he* would thus control the purse strings, and they would have to come to him metaphorical cap in hand to get their mitts on their own money – a case of, you never give me *my* money.

Also, no matter how much Klein liked to play up to his bullyboy image, the fact that his name put fear in the hearts of associates, friends and enemies alike was often unproductive – i.e. bad business. He may have read Machiavelli's *Il Principe*, but he clearly hadn't understood it. Fearful folk do desperate things. Klein's involvement with three of the Fab Four convinced one party that he needed to jump overboard – as

Peter Brown put it, 'Dick James had seen the writing on the wall; it was written in Allen Klein's handwriting, and James was determined to pull out.' Lennon meets Klein, signs with Klein, convinces Harrison and Starr to do the same, James sells Northern Songs. 1-2-3, easy as ABC.

The other problem with Klein, one that concerned McCartney most, was that he enjoyed setting people against each other. He fed antagonisms and he fed on insecurities. With a powder keg like Lennon this was a recipe for indoor fireworks. Though professing to be an accountant, Klein was really the divorce lawyer from hell. He also took a casual attitude to leaked documents and legal privilege – which led one London high court judge to describe his testimony as having 'the flavour of dishonesty'.

Simply put, Klein had form. When Bob Dylan was about to sign with MGM, post-motorcycle accident, for a whopping million dollar advance, Klein was given Dylan's 'true' sales figures by CBS lawyer, Clive Davis, confidential documents he promptly took to the MGM board to convince them not to sign Dylan for what he deemed a foolishly large sum. Klein, convinced Dylan was a spent force, got his way.

He also got it hopelessly wrong. Demand for Dylan product had actually grown since he became Woodstock's favourite mystery tramp. When he did return in 1968 his records sold better than ever. And MGM would have had the two most important acts in American rock on the same roster. Instead, they never signed Dylan, and in 1969 they lost The Velvet Underground to Atlantic.

When McCartney took as his own counsel his new father-in-law John Eastman, a high-powered New York lawyer, Klein took the gloves off. Eastman simply washed his hands of the man. His version of events suggested 'we cooperated with Klein for about two weeks. It was agreed that both of us would see all The Beatles' documents, but Klein took out all the important stuff and sent along a huge bundle of documents containing nothing of importance.' Klein expressed open contempt for such legal niceties: 'I ripped off those documents, damn right! But Eastman and McCartney had already gone behind our backs buying Northern Songs shares.' Here was a man who equated criminal obstruction with

McCartney's prudent business decision to buy (back) shares in what was essentially his own songwriting.

Fortunately for Klein, Lennon and Harrison's time in India had not made them any less susceptible to fake gurus – of both faith *and* finance. Harrison, who felt betrayed that McCartney had invested in his own songwriting, wasn't about to renegotiate his own contract with Northern Songs, by which he received a greater percentage than his fellow Beatles. Because he only put on his business head when so inclined, while petty enmity had long coloured his judgement where Paul was concerned.

As for Lennon, his perceived rivalry with McCartney was all that mattered. Between 1970 and 1973, when he could have stayed at home with Yoko, let the clock tick down on the Northern Songs contract and convinced McCartney to do the same, he was writing more songs than he had in the last four years of the band, most of them about the latest cause to capture his wayward attention. Yet all he needed to spike the Lew Grade/Dick James deal was to come together with Paul and agree to call their bluff. They had already delivered the minimum number of songs stipulated in their 1968 agreement. Indeed, as Peter Brown suggests, the notion had reared its head as the Northern Songs battle was heating up:

> John and Paul's first tactic was to imply that if the sale to ATV went through, they would stop composing together and not ful-fill their six songs a year minimum stipulated in their Northern [Songs] contracts. An exasperated Lew Grade felt it necessary to reassure the stockholders in a statement to the *Financial Times* saying, 'I have every confidence in the boys' creativity. They would not possibly be able to sit still and write only six new songs a year. Apart from that, songwriting plays an important part in the boys' income.'

But Grade's 'confidence' was as thin as the paper he signed when he bought James out. Here was Lennon and McCartney's chance to put an end to the Northern Songs farrago. Simply stop writing – or more accurately, stop publishing – their new songs for three years and watch Northern Songs stock plummet.*

This was one spat Harrison was content to sit out. He had his own songs back, or at least the ones he'd written since 1968. He may already have done what Lennon and McCartney chose not to, holding back songs written in 1967–8 until the Northern Songs deal expired. (It certainly seems that way; and Harrison's comment to Lennon and McCartney, see previously, seems to confirm it.) And if he needed someone to get nasty, he now had his pet Rottweiler in New York to bite legal legs.

However, Harrison failed to consider that such animals invariably end up biting their supposed owners. He didn't realize this until he found Klein snapping at his heels from across the courtroom as he argued that 'My Sweet Lord' and The Chiffons' 'He's So Fine' were different songs, as opposed to a suit waiting to happen.

Even if The Chiffons' publisher, Bright Music, had not brought suit against Harrison, it seems probable Delaney Bramlett would have. Bramlett told any old rock writer he had come up with the raw idea for 'My Sweet Lord' backstage at a 1969 Delaney & Bonnie show: 'I grabbed my guitar and started playing the Chiffons' melody from "He's So Fine," and then sang, "My Sweet Lord, oh my Lord, oh my Lord."' Harrison apparently joined in, but did little to develop it any further.

An early studio version, later bootlegged from acetate on *Songs For Patti*, presents the song in similar form, minus Harrison's later embellishments and backing vocals. And in this form, the debt to the 1963 US number one 45 is even more obvious. Indeed, when he heard the song on the radio, Bramlett claims he called Harrison up and said he hadn't meant for him to use the exact same melody. His main reason for calling, though, was to discover the whereabouts of his co-credit (and attendant royalties). He later asserted, 'I was never given credit on that song, but he

---

* In his ill-informed *Rockonomics* (1993), Marc Elliott suggests this is what Dylan did between 1971 and 1973 to ensure Albert Grossman did not get his hands on more of his song stock; in fact Dylan simply had writer's block.

did admit that the song, to a large extent, was mine, and I never saw any money from it.'

However, Bramlett chose not to pursue his own claim when the writs started flying. Indeed, although he was called in The Chiffons' case, he found himself 'unable to give evidence'. A friend indeed.

Perhaps he thought George had it coming. Others certainly did; when the subject of songstealing came up in John Lennon's last interview, he displayed little sympathy for his old friend George, and the mess he had got himself in over 'My Sweet Lord', suggesting, 'He walked right into it. He knew what he was doing.' Harrison certainly had a history of nods and winks towards other songs. Ian MacDonald suggests 1968's 'Long Long Long' based its 'triple-time changes' on Dylan's 'Sad Eyed Lady of the Lowlands', while the debts incurred by 'If I Needed Someone', 'Taxman', 'It's All Too Much', 'The Inner Light' and 'Something' were there for all to hear. But the one person who would have spotted 'He's So Fine' in 'My Sweet Lord' immediately was Phil Spector, the producer whose records The Chiffons sought to emulate. And where was Spector the day Harrison unveiled the song in the studio? Behind the console.

Nor did it take long for more dispassionate parties to notice the similarities. The *Rolling Stone* reviewer noted it, as did the judge in the original 1976 court case. In fact, Judge Owens' summation was damning. He decided it was 'clear that "My Sweet Lord" is the very same song as "He's So Fine" with different words and [that] Harrison had access to "He's So Fine." This is, under the law, infringement of copyright, and is no less so even though sub-consciously accomplished.'

As for the idea it had been 'sub-consciously accomplished', the judge lacked all the evidence: Delaney Bramlett's testimony, if produced, would have made a case for 'intentional plagiarism'. If that case had been made, Harrison stood to lose the entire gross earnings for 'My Sweet Lord', a number one single everywhere, calculated already at $2,133,316 – as well as both sides' court costs. Judge Owens gave the ex-Beatle the benefit of the doubt, telling Harrison afterwards, 'I actually like both songs.' To which Harrison derisively retorted, 'What do you mean *both*?! You've just ruled they are one and the same.' But, even with all the judge's evident goodwill towards the ex-Beatle, he judged three-quarters of the success of the song as down to its plagiarized tune; and only 25 per cent to Harrison's name and the incantatory words.

This, though, was hardly the end of the matter. Because back in 1971, when Bright Music first filed suit, Allen Klein met with Seymour Barash, the company's president, on his client Harrison's behalf, to try to resolve the dispute. Klein offered to purchase the entire Bright catalogue, again on Harrison's behalf; while Barash countered with the suggestion that Harrison surrender the copyright to 'My Sweet Lord' and Bright would pay Harrison 50 per cent of net receipts.

Negotiations continued even as the case moved towards litigation. The case was further delayed when Bright, which had been teetering on the brink of bankruptcy for a while, was placed in receivership. In January 1976, Harrison offered the company $148,000, supposedly representing 40 per cent of the US royalties on 'My Sweet Lord', an offer which Bright's own attorney described as 'a good one'. But an almost-bankrupt Bright Music unexpectedly responded by demanding a patently unreasonable 75 per cent of worldwide receipts and surrender of the song's copyright. Something or someone had changed their minds.

Frankly, having recently terminated his contract with Klein, Harrison should have smelt the whiff of mendacity. True to form, Klein had responded by attempting to buy Bright Tunes himself, confident (like everyone, save Harrison) that they would succeed in their suit. As part of his offer, Klein furnished Bright with information regarding the domestic royalties the song had generated, and his own estimate of overseas earnings as well as the future value of the copyright. Such was his arrogance, he thought he would get away with this clear breach of his fiduciary duty to his former client. He had overplayed his hand – and Harrison had the means (and the necessary backbone) to make him pay.

When Bright Tunes sold its copyright and rights in the litigation to Klein's ABKCO, they consigned Klein to five more years of litigation. At the end of it, the district judge and appeal court judge both agreed Klein had acted improperly in purchasing Bright Tunes, and was not entitled to profit from his purchase of their rights in the original Chiffons song. Klein was ordered to hold the rights in trust for Harrison, to be transferred upon payment of $587,000, plus interest, the exact amount Klein had paid for Bright Tunes.

Klein had been weighed in the balance and found wanting. At last, Harrison was free of Klein; free of the song that had made him the first solo Beatle to top the singles and album charts both sides of the pond; and free of having to share mechanical royalties from all things past and present with the other Beatles. The last of these – which held until October 1974 – had been part of the agreement all parties had signed at the dissolution of the band, meaning Harrison had to share the success of *All Things Must Pass* with his less productive ex-brethren. Harrison could now start rerecording unused songs he had demoed for Spector back in 1970 – having finally heeded his own original title for 'Beware of Darkness', prophetically called 'Beware of ABKCO'.

The Rolling Stones only learnt to beware of Allen Klein and ABKCO after Mick Jagger consulted titled accountant Prince Rupert Loewenstein as their Decca deal expired. They had decided to break free of Klein whatever the cost. Loewenstein's advice was 'straight, direct – and dangerous'. According to Bill Wyman:

> [Lowenstein said] We should drop Klein and drop out of England . . . Klein said that many of the songs we had said were completed after 1970 were in fact written previously – and claimed a slice of them. It [got] very ugly. To this day, the Kleins own the pre-1970 Rolling Stones masters, and administrate the publishing of the Jagger-Richards songs of those early years, as well as those of our group songwriting name, Nanker-Phelge . . . Our [other] advisers led us to believe that Klein owed us a minimum of $17 million, maybe more. Mick and Rupert told me we should get rid of him and settle for $2 million.

The Stones had a new motto – Let it loose. They had seen what had happened to The Beatles once they'd become ensnared in Klein's corporate net, and it wasn't gonna happen to them. Now was the time to make those American arenas pay their way back to Blighty, via the south of France, where they would stop off for a short holiday and to record the greatest rock & roll album ever. Hell, they were feeling so generous they gave new recruit Mick Taylor his first – and, as it happens, his last – co-credits, on 'Stop Breaking Down' and 'Ventilator Blues'. (The former he had to surrender in 2000, when another slubberdegullion demanded its return in the name of Robert Johnson.)

Meanwhile, the other A-list British pop bands who came through the ranks at the same time finally extracted themselves from the equally catastrophic publishing and recording agreements *they* had made between 1963 and 1965. Ray Davies regained all his frozen publishing by the end of 1970, though only by agreeing to a lower royalty than he was truly due. The Who were also free and clear of Talmy and his 5 per cent override by autumn 1971, at which point they released *Who's Next*, the album that pushed them into the same firmament as the Stones and onto every classic rock station. It was a brave new world for Britain's songwriters. And its copyright lawyers.

CHAPTER 14

# 1967–86: Sweet Honesty And Bitter Fingers

*Featuring*: 'Skyline Pigeon'; 'Your Song'; 'Brown Eyed Girl'; 'Madame George'; 'Born To Run'; 'Because The Night'; 'Suspicious Minds'; 'I Will Always Love You'; 'Yesterday'

'Sure, people are still being screwed, but mainly because of old contracts.'

Elton John, *NME*, 8 March 1975

By March 1975, Elton John – who had been personally responsible for almost 2 per cent of music sales worldwide in 1974 – was convinced he could see light at the end of the tunnel. After producing two albums a year for Dick James Music over the past five years, he was but a single album away from extracting himself from the figure mercilessly lampooned – by ex-Python Eric Idle in his Rutles mockdoc, *All You Need Is Cash* – as Dick Jaws.

In Idle's words, Jaws was 'an out of work publisher of no fixed ability, [who] signed them up for the rest of their lives: "Just lucky, I guess."' If Dick James was similarly blessed, it was not with a pair of ears. Though Elton John had literally landed in James's lap, he had been resolutely mishandled, under-capitalized and under-promoted, forced to boost his subsistence-level existence with anonymous session-work only to finally break big, despite everything Dick failed to do. Just lucky, I guess.

Elton was now talking about a future without James, albeit couching his criticisms of the way his copyrights had been handled in code. As he told his *NME* interrogator, 'Once I'm free of all contracts I've got so many ideas concerning how to give back something to the public . . . I've got two more albums to deliver to DJM at the moment.' One of those was the already-completed *Captain Fantastic & The Brown Dirt Cowboy*, an album which he fully admitted 'is all about ourselves . . . it's very open and it's very honest about our personal relationship and also, it's very honest about all the business things we went through.' In particular, there was one song intended to bite the hand that once fed him scraps. The grasping Shylock figure with snakes for fingers portrayed alongside 'Bitter Fingers' in the lyric booklet may not have been one James recognized, but in tandem with Taupin's caustic lyrics, it was one Paul McCartney certainly would have.

The fact that James had no sooner sold The Beatles' publishing to Lew Grade than he found a second money-making machine in Elton John surely suggests a rare gift for talent-spotting. After all, he had been telling financial journalists since 1967 that he was 'trying to build the company up so that it does not rely too heavily on Lennon and McCartney'. And by 1969, DJM had indeed moved on, or so his son Stephen recently claimed: 'I wasn't involved with The Beatles or Northern Songs, because I was working with a guy we'd signed called Elton John.'

Not according to John, he wasn't. No one at DJM was. John, and his lyricist Bernie Taupin, were simply left to their own devices, expected to churn out chartbusters according to a brief that came from the top – and the early fifties:

**Elton John**: To give [Dick James] his due, he did give us a lot of freedom. But on the other hand he did keep on saying, 'You've got to write Top 40 material for Cilla and Engelbert,' which we wasted two years of our lives trying to do. And it lasted until Steve Brown joined the company as a plugger and told us that our stuff was all right but not quite there as yet. It wasn't as good as we could do and he asked us the reason why; so we told him that half of us wanted to write things that we really wanted to write while the other half had to do what Dick wanted us to do – and that was write hit songs. For the life of us, we couldn't write a hit song. So in the end Steve said 'Fuck Dick' and told us to write what we liked. The first thing we wrote after that was 'Skyline Pigeon' and then 'Lady Samantha'. [1975]

Even these two songs John and Taupin could not hang on to. James had such little faith in the pair he felt the need to bribe another of his acts – albeit not with his own money – to get him to record one of their songs.

Roger Greenaway, whose own publishing company, Cookaway, was administered by James, recalls going into the DJM studios and hearing John complain that nothing was ever going to happen: 'So I asked him to play me some of his songs. He played me "Tealby Abbey" and "Skyline Pigeon" . . . Dick said if we were going to record them, we could have the songs because we were taking such an interest in Reg and Bernie.'* Funnily enough, this was not how Bernie Taupin remembered it in his notes to *Rare Masters* (1992): '"Skyline Pigeon" was the first really good song that we ever wrote . . . There was a guy called Roger Cook that wanted to record it, and in order for him to record it, Dick James gave part of the publishing to him.'

How terribly old school. Because James was as old school as they came. How fortunate he had a son brought up with the Denmark Street set of values. Stephen James, or so he would like us to believe, was so hands-on with Elton he was responsible for signing him in the first place, after he found John had been using the DJM studios surreptitiously to record dozens of demos:

**Stephen James**: After listening to the [demo] tapes, I thought the lyrics were pretty awful, but the melodies had something quite different, original and interesting. I told Caleb [Quaye] to arrange for Reg to meet me as I wanted to talk to him about the demos, so

---

* Greenaway gave the latter song to his partner Roger Cook, who duly murdered the poor bird.

he came round . . . and that's when I told him he couldn't use the studio [anymore] unless he signed to DJM, or he paid for the time. I knew he couldn't afford to pay, so instead he signed.

That last sentence suggests Stephen was a chip off the ol' block. But again, Elton himself has absolutely no recollection of James Jnr's intervention. Elton was quite clear about how he ended up with Dick Jaws' first cousin, and it was DJM studio engineer Caleb Quaye not James Jnr who went to bat for him: 'A lot of groups were going in there and cutting demos for nothing without Dick ever knowing about it. When Dick eventually discovered what was happening he had this great purge. Caleb more or less went into Dick's office on his knees and said Reg and Bernie are worth fighting for, and so Dick signed us to a [direct] contract.' Just lucky, I guess.

Just as with another deal James cooked up six years earlier, signing John did not mean the publisher was about to put his hand in his now-deep pockets – or be any more hands-on. As DJM employee Lionel Conway recalls, 'Although [Elton] was recording for hours in the studio with . . . Caleb and others, Dick wasn't really interested in what he was doing . . . [But then] it wasn't costing him anything because he was doing everything in-house. [It's not like] there was a vast amount of money going into Reg's pockets. He was on £20 a week.' (The publishing contract John and Taupin signed gave them a joint advance of £100, and a weekly wage of £10 each, deductible against future royalties. The agreement ran for six years.)

James' masterplan was to get the pianist to write a song for the Eurovision Song Contest, an annual event whereby the whole continent could express its disgust that Britain had consistently produced the catchiest pop in the world by imitating it, and then voting that year's closest non-English imitation the best pop song in Europe.* The song Elton came up with, 'I Can't Go On Living Without You', was so awful he had to write the lyrics as well, 'because Taupin wouldn't have anything to do

---

* The year Elton nearly got in, the Spanish winner ('La La La') was sued for nicking its melody from the Kinks' 'Death Of A Clown'.

with it'. And Taupin wasn't the only one investing in Elton's career who thought both father and son clueless:

> **Caleb Quaye:** There was a real artistic dichotomy going on [at DJM], because we were not interested in [writing] that commercial sort of stuff. We were listening to The Beatles, the Stones and Hendrix, and all the rock stuff, and Reg had no interest in writing more of the 'stupid stuff' as we called it. It was really difficult because most of us at DJM were listening to the American singer-songwriters, such as Joni Mitchell and Laura Nyro . . . So we had our artistic vision but the company was saying it wanted more songs for people like Cliff Richard. It was out of that sort of pressure that 'I Can't Go On Living Without You' came from.

Clueless or not, Dick James was nothing if not an opportunist. Even he had realized by the end of the sixties that there was as much money to be made in putting out records as in publishing. So he decided to set up a label.

His first venture, Page One Records, established in partnership with ex-Kinks overseer Larry Page, didn't last long: 'When [Dick James and I] formed Page One Records,' said Page, 'it was a sort of handshake deal, no contract or anything like that. We signed some artists and had some big hits. One day I read in the *Record Retailer* that Dick James had formed his own record label. For me, that was the beginning of the end.'

The label James had 'formed' was called DJM (Dick James Music), and he not only signed Elton John to the label, but held on when an offer with no strings came his way – courtesy of Steve Winwood's brother, now an A&R man for Island Records:

> **Muff Winwood:** I was travelling back to Pinner one evening . . . when this guy came and sat down next to me . . . He said he had been the piano player with . . . Bluesology, who had supported [the Spencer Davis Group] a couple of times at the Marquee . . . We got talking and he said . . . he had a deal with Dick James to write songs.

He [said he] wanted to make an album, but Dick James wouldn't let him . . . The next night he and Bernie came round to the house and . . . played me some of their songs. I thought they were really good, and . . . we both went in to see Dick and tried to negotiate to sign Elton for Island Records . . . We would do all the recording, promotion and selling for the album and Dick could have all the publishing. This meant that Lionel [Conway] and I would do all the work and Dick would earn a lot of money with the publishing, without doing anything. But he still wouldn't have it.

The album Winwood heard in prototype that night was to be Elton John's second. He had already made *Empty Sky*, a syrupy concoction that was far too middle of the road to reach the kids playing by the kerb. Now Quaye was being told that if this new album 'didn't work, then they would cut Reg and the Elton project from the label'. And still, James refused either to fund the project properly or ship it off to Island. In fact, so desperate was Elton's situation that he spent most of the year separating *Empty Sky* from *Elton John* doing covert session-work to make ends meet.[*]

It was back to the drawing board, and the penny-pinching publisher in whom Elton still placed his trust; even though, as he was already aware in 1971, 'Dick's very, very aware of money.' By then, Elton's live shows and the Laurel Canyonesque vibe of the next two albums, *Elton John* and *Tumbleweed Connection*, had turned him into a Stateside phenomenon and Dick Jaws could go back to his counting-house again.

---

[*] Much of this material has slipped into the world in recent years. His contributions to the hugely successful *Top Of The Pops* budget albums have been collected as *Reg Dwight's Piano Goes Pop*, as has the Witchseason demo-acetate of Nick Drake, Beverly Martyn and Mike Heron songs he recorded with Linda Thompson (née Peters) just before *Elton John* appeared. He also played piano on a Hollies session, coming up with a beautiful part for the chart-topping 'He Ain't Heavy, He's My Brother'. And when Ian McDonald left King Crimson, he found himself booked to add lead vocals to the band's second album, an alliance that might have changed the future course of contemporary song – though not necessarily for the better – had not Fripp given *Empty Sky* a spin and realized 'Reg was clearly not the voice for King Crimson.'

Meanwhile, John and Taupin found themselves tied to James at every turn: recording, publishing; domestic, international. It would be 1975 before they could cut themselves free – that 1969 contract still held good – at which point the fun really could begin. Just as James's relationship with The Beatles broke down the minute they actually read their contracts, so John now realized he had taken a number of trips to the cleaners. James had not so much skimmed off the top as sheared away at the sums until there was nothing left. At which point, John's manager, John Reid, concerned at the 'unreasonably high' percentages James's US publishing subsidiary was retaining, sent in forensic accountants to find the song-publishing equivalent of the smoking gun.

It took them six years, but in 1981 James was served papers. John and Taupin asked the court to return their song copyrights, to have their original publishing and recording agreements set aside, and to order James to make restitution on the underpayment of song royalties. The assets at stake were valued at around £30 million.

In what was a landmark case, James's whole process of burying the publishing in the percentages was laid bare. What he had done was create a network of shell companies all around the world, operating under the umbrella of Dick James Music and ostensibly sub-licensing DJM's songs. With the exception of the US subsidiary – where even James had to pay for staff – 'they had no premises, no staff, nothing.' And yet, they were retaining 50 per cent of the publishing from sales in these territories – the rest being sent to James in London, who took his cut before passing the residue onto John and Taupin. (The norm for such sub-licensing deals was 10–15 per cent.)

James had cleverly found a way to pay himself 50 per cent of the publishing, plus commission, after the days of 50-50 splits were long past, due in no small part to his former charges, The Beatles. The clue came when DJM's own counsel, George Newman QC, insisted in court, 'There is simply nothing unreasonable at all about [the subsidiary] retaining 50 per cent.' When a defending barrister uses a term like 'nothing unreasonable', it's a fair bet he means patently unreasonable.

The judge in the case realized it was a highly lucrative scam, and ruled that James's company was guilty of 'deliberate concealment' as well as a clear breach of its fiduciary duty. Setting the 'normal' rate for a foreign sub-licensee at 25 per cent (a good 40 per cent higher than the norm for such seventies million-sellers), he ruled that DJM should pay John and Taupin the backdated difference, estimated to run to at least £2.5 million.

Stephen James claimed it as a 'victory', but if so it was a pyrrhic one. His father had tried his luck one time too many. Dick died of a heart attack just two months after the judge ruled him guilty of 'deliberate concealment'. It was a form of poetic justice: he had spent the last years of his life justifying previous practices under oath (even after the conciliatory John asked James to 'settle this' over lunch) determined to deny a man he had been robbing for a decade and a half his due.

The son of the father sold DJM later the same year to Universal Music for £12 million. By then, he had reached some kinda rapprochement with Paul McCartney, who continued to hanker after the Northern Songs catalogue Stephen's father had sold from under him back in 1969. In the autumn of 1977, McCartney and Lennon jointly instructed a firm of London accountants to carry out a royalty audit on both ATV Music and Northern Songs. Unsurprisingly, their work revealed a substantial shortfall in royalties and a series of 'accidental' accounting errors, every one of which was to the benefit of ATV and at the expense of the creator/s. Two years later Macca admitted he was still brooding about events from seventeen years earlier:

> **Paul McCartney**: It is funny to think that somebody owns 'Yesterday', and that it's only to do with me as far as the royalties are concerned. It's funny to think of some of the things that went down. In fact, it's more than funny, it's crazy, because companies were sold behind our backs, and we always had [such] a tiny share of everything. And all the big businessmen always advised us to sell everything. They never said, 'Hold onto your paintings because one day they might be valuable.' [1979]

In 1982, another opportunity arose to buy Northern Songs back as ATV Music ran into financial difficulties and was put up for sale. And this time McCartney had money in the bank. Oddly enough, he turned to the son of his nemesis for advice. A sanguine Stephen 'told him that he should buy it, but [Paul] said they wouldn't separate it out from ATV Music and that he was [only] prepared to pay £25 million for Northern Songs. I told him he was mad and that he should go for the whole of ATV, strip Northern Songs out and then sell the rest.'

It was the first piece of good business advice a James had ever given James Paul. Yet McCartney refused to move without the other copyright-holder, who was now the prickly Yoko Ono. His brother-in-song was dead, senselessly gunned down by a disturbed fan in December 1980; and Lennon's executor did not share his romantic attachment to this incomparable body of work, fearing another costly miscalculation over her late husband's copyrights.

But if Ono did not want to deplete her cash reserves, there was one pop star who had more cash reserves than he knew what to do with. In August 1985 Northern Songs (and its parent publisher) was acquired by none other than Michael Jackson, who at the time considered himself 'a musician who is also a businessman . . . [who has] learned the hard way about business and the importance of publishing and royalties and the dignity of songwriting'. McCartney, who knew all about 'the dignity of songwriting' was appalled. Having complained to *Rolling Stone* about some faceless suit owning 'Yesterday', he found another former friend had taken his place, to which he could only say, 'It's a bit galling now to find that I own less of "Yesterday" than Michael Jackson. It's a thorn in my side.' And a stab in the back. The little punk.

At least James Jnr had seen the writing on the wall. The singer-song-writers his father and friends had spent the sixties fleecing were by the 1970s armed with enough financial muscle to launch a volley of writs and countersuits, sometimes burying their adversaries in privileged paper. The seventies would be the decade of publishing lawsuits – and in almost every case it was, as Elton said, 'people [who we]re still being screwed . . . because of old contracts'.

The names of those marshalling their forces in this publishing war were already familiar to most *NME* and *Rolling Stone* readers: Bob Dylan, Bruce Springsteen, Dolly Parton and Paul McCartney being just four of the writers turned fighters. But the first combatant to start the fight back was the artist who had been on the receiving end of the worst legal advice of all – his own.

George Ivan Morrison had certainly not learnt his lesson from his time in Them. On 9 January 1967, waiving the right to legal representation, he signed two separate contracts with Bert Berns for publishing and recording. The two in tandem tied him to Bang Records for five years, during which time all his songs would be published by Berns. In the last generous mood of his life, Morrison threw in 'ownership of the masters', and gave Berns 'the right to add to, delete from, change, modify or amend the performances of [the] Artist by any and all means, including new or different instrumentalists, vocalists, sound effects, orchestrations &c.' All this from a compulsive control-freak. What, pray tell, was he thinking?

The answer is, he wasn't. As he admitted in 1997, when he agreed to talk about the inspiration behind 'Bigtime Operators', hardly the first (or best) song he had written about the great Berns rip-off, 'I'd signed a contract with Bert Berns for management, production, agency and record company, publishing, the whole lot – which was professional suicide as any lawyer will tell you now.' (They'd have said the same even back then, Ivan.) Instead, he let his rancour fuel his art, most obviously in 1973 when he wrote the sardonic 'Drumshanbo Hustle', which recalled 'the day . . . they were trying to muscle in on the recording and the publishing . . . [But] when you read the standard contract, you just signed.'

What prompted this recriminatory reverie on events from five years earlier was another flurry of legal threats to and from Berns' widow, Eileen, after she dug up an album's worth of 'lost' recordings Van had made with Berns. Recorded before *Astral Weeks*, they included prototypes for two of his most cosmic songs, 'Beside You' and 'Madame George'. The war between the pair, which began the day Bert died in December 1967, has raged ever since.

Before Berns' burial, Morrison was at least working with someone who seemed to know how to make pop songs, even if he had had to surrender half the publishing to sign that devil's pact. Their first collaboration had been 'Brown Eyed Girl', the song that to this day remains the one most identified with Belfast's moodiest bugger. And for all of Morrison's chops as a songwriter, what he was not – at this stage, anyway – was an arranger. Whereas Berns had already proven, with and without Van, that he knew how to craft hits; as Jerry Wexler said, his 'feeling for Latin rhythms was right as rain'.

As soon as Morrison played Berns this delightful lovesong to his muse, Janet Planet, Bert began to shape the sound. The result was not music to Van's ears; as he said, three years later, 'Bert made ["Brown Eyed Girl"] the way *he* wanted it, and I accepted the fact that he was producing it . . . But it was *my* song, and I had to watch it go down.' If only it were that simple. In fact, as Planet herself recalls, 'Bert really wanted to completely orchestrate and completely mould what [he] was going to do and what he was going to be, and after a certain point Van just bridled at that, . . . want[ing] to have more input into how the music was going to go.'

Tough shit. He had already handed Berns complete control. The extent of Morrison's disenchantment only really came out when he recorded a number of 'revenge' songs to escape from his publishing contract in the winter of 1969, one of which consisted entirely of him mockingly chanting, 'Yeah, we'll get a guitar . . . we'll get three guitars/No! No!! we'll get four guitars/and we'll get Herbie Lovelle to play drums/and we'll do the sha-, sha-la-la bit.' Another was called 'The Big Royalty Check', in which Morrison sang of 'waiting for my royalty check to come, and it still hasn't come yet. It's about a year overdue. I guess it's coming from the Big Royalty Check in the sky.'

The result of such truculence – as the pattern of his character became more intricately woven – was that Morrison became ever more morose, difficult and stubborn. He even passed up the opportunity to exchange the half-share he'd given Berns on 'Brown Eyed Girl' for a cut of another highly lucrative pop classic. Berns had been writing the song and got stuck, so he asked Morrison to help. But Morrison demurred, and his excuse was a doozie, 'I just didn't *feel* that kind of song.' Co-written with Jerry Ragovoy instead, 'Piece Of My Heart' originally went to the 'wrong' Franklin sister, not Aretha but Erma, who still did enough to make it an R&B hit. Then Janis Joplin claimed it for her own on her million-seller, *Cheap Thrills*. It would end up being sung by three of the greatest female soul singers of all time: Joplin, Etta James and Dusty Springfield.

Of his own volition, Morrison had missed out again. And still he continued to place his trust in Berns – a man whose business methods and associates allegedly drove Neil Diamond to try buying a gun – until the dark December day when Berns died of a congenital heart condition. Thereafter, Morrison's publishing contract was suddenly the property of a man called Carmine, a man you did not mess with unless you had a death-wish.

**Janet Planet:** One of the memories I'll take to my grave is Carmine pounding on our hotel-room door at the St George Hotel in Times Square going, 'Van, you're finished in the business. D'you hear me?' . . . Carmine was said to have [already] broken a guitar over Van's head . . . He was a scary guy, and Van has this lifelong ability to forget that he can't act out.

Meanwhile, the Bang royalty statements – coming on the back of a major pop hit like 'Brown Eyed Girl' – continued to arrive. But, as Planet says, 'It was absolutely amazing how the numbers just seemed to add up so there was never any money there.' Morrison needed help or he was only ever going to be a footnote to the story of pop.

Fortunately for the man, his most recent record and a series of won-derful acoustic gigs in Boston had impressed some people with clout, among them Boston DJ and musician Peter Wolf, jazz producer Lewis Merenstein and Warners A&R man, Joe Smith. The latter two cooked up a deal with the Berns estate by which Morrison was released from his Bang contract and any future obligations under his publishing contract, Web IV Music. The agreement they signed on 2 September 1968 involved a settlement of around $75,000 (from Morrison's Warners advance). All that was required of Morrison were three obligations:

(a) submit to Web IV for publication three original compositions per month, written by Morrison, for a period of one year, totalling 36 original and publishable songs. Web IV reserve the right to accept the musician compositions as submitted.

(b) to assign to Web IV one half of the copyright in any composition written and recorded by him and released on a 45 rpm single within one year from September 12, 1968.

(c) to include two compositions owned or controlled by Web IV in any 33⅓ rpm long-playing phonograph record recorded by Morrison with one year from the date of the release and containing at least two musical compositions written by Morrison.

But this agreement did not mean Merenstein, Morrison and Warners were free and clear to start building Van's career. There was the small matter of Bert Berns' mobbed-up friends. It devolved to Joe Smith to solve the problem – using the 'brown paper bag' method preferred by the mob-handed:

**Joe Smith**: The word was there was some mob money involved [with Berns]. Van was sitting in Cambridge, Mass., at the time, destitute . . . [but] a friend of mine who knew some people said I could buy the contract for $20,000. I had to meet somebody in a warehouse on the 3rd floor on 9th Avenue in New York. I walked up there with twenty thousand-dollar bills – and I was terrified . . . There were two guys in the room. They looked out of central casting – a big, wide guy and a tall, thin guy. They were wearing suits . . . I said, 'I'm here with the money. You got the contract?'

. . . I took that contract and ran out the door and jumped from the third floor to the second floor, and almost broke my leg, to get on the street, where I could get a cab and put the contract in a safe place back at Warners.

The agreement with Web IV still needed attending to. Clause B was managed by the simple expedient of not releasing a single that year. Duh! Clause C, more significantly, forced Morrison to include 'Madame George' and 'Beside You' – two songs of real vision he'd copyrighted to Web IV – on *Astral Weeks*. Fortunately for Van, though this masterpiece sold poorly in its first year, it would go on to sell year on year. Ms Berns was obliged to content herself with the $75,000 and the steady drip-feed of beer money from radioplay on 'Brown Eyed Girl' (a drip, drip, drip which would ultimately run to millions).

Now all Morrison needed to do was record the thirty-six songs required to satisfy condition A. Instead, he gave Eileen three dozen non-sense songs, none of which were remotely suitable for release (although they have been). As Merenstein states, the session at Mastertone Studio allowed Van to get 'all his grievances out at Bert Berns and Bang'.

By the next time Berns and Morrison locked horns, Morrison could afford legal advice and was a far more worthy adversary; or would have been were it not for some old familiar character defects, like a 'lifelong ability to forget that he can't act out'. When Morrison went after Berns in January 1973 for a 'failure to account and pay royalties' in a way that was 'wilful and deliberate', demanding 'the return to plaintiff of the owner-ship of all musical compositions written or co-written by plaintiff', Eileen responded with a countersuit.

In it, her brief pointed out that the 'plaintiff submitted thirty-two musical compositions to Web IV, all of which are completely unpublish-able because they contain vulgar and coarse language, and are entirely devoid of any substance of originality or artistic merit'. And here was the kicker: 'By reason of the foregoing, Morrison remained obligated under the aforementioned exclusive writer's contract during the five-year period stipulated therein.' Berns, who had taken four years to raise this matter, was never going to win what would have been a protracted legal spat, but the threat was enough to get Morrison to back down and content himself with control of his post-1970 publishing – the part without 'Gloria' and 'Brown Eyed Girl'.

However, for a man like Morrison, controlling 80 per cent of his own publishing was never going to be enough. And when it came to *his* publishing, it seemed like Morrison was forever destined to repeat the same mistakes. In 2008, having basked for four decades in the praise consistently heaped on *Astral Weeks*, he decided to recreate the album at a series of live shows on the fortieth anniversary of the original recording. Mr Morrison's interest in the project was not wholly nostalgic.

His was a twofold mission: to reclaim the album from its original producer, Lewis Merenstein, and to reclaim part of the publishing from Warners Music. The way he intended to do this was by placing the album in its 'correct' sequence, not the order Merenstein had devised back in 1968 – a contribution some noisome rock biographer highlighted in his 2002 Van biography, *Can You Feel The Silence?*[*]

This new sequence would re-establish the album as the work of a single-minded auteur called Van, man. However, the great plan went pear-shaped from the start. The bandleader at the original sessions, the great jazz bassist Richard Davis, whose inspired accompaniment had been such an integral part of the original *Astral* experience, took umbrage when, at rehearsals for the 2008 reincarnation, Morrison instructed him to play off a score. Davis told him where he could stick his recreation and the gig proceeded with exactly one member of the original studio line-up – guitarist Jay Berliner – in a twelve-piece band supposedly replicating the feel of the original, inspirational jazz trio.

But Morrison wasn't done with his act of reclamation. The eight-track album now boasted two further pieces, neither of them part of

---

[*] Lewis Merenstein: 'I sequenced the album – totally . . . I don't think he even saw the album cover before it came out.'

the original sessions nor, as it happens, his original Warners publishing contract: 'Listen To The Lion', and something called 'Common One', which was only ever an album title, never a song. By making such a move, he could assign himself a further fifth of the publishing on *Astral Weeks* Mk. 2.

There was more. Three of the eight original *Astral Weeks* songs – the title track, 'Slim Slow Slider' and 'Cyprus Avenue' – received additional, semi-improvised scat sections, of the kind that had peppered Morrison's live sets for years. According to the sleeve, these short verbal riffs qualified as distinct compositions in their own right, entitling him to a half-share of these 'two-part' songs. (He had pulled this stunt before, on 1979's *Into The Music*, where he claimed that a similar embellishment at the end of an extended cover of 'It's All In The Game' qualified as a separate song, 'You Know What They're Writing About'.)

Unfortunately, the 'songs' now listed as 'I Believe I've Transcended', 'Start Breaking Down' and 'You Came Walking Down' merely made the new work a great big melting pot of gloop. The result was an album on which Van may have owned a third of the publishing outright, but it was most certainly not *Astral Weeks*. As a result, sales of *Astral Weeks Live At The Hollywood Bowl* replicated the minimal initial sales of the original. The difference was, *Astral Weeks* kept right on selling – and will still be selling long after Morrison mouths off to his Maker – while *Hollywood Bowl* began its slim slow slide into obscurity, thanks to its creator's insistence that he wanted *his* fucking album back.*

\* \* \*

---

\* Morrison was not alone. A rash of live versions of classic albums appeared at the start of the twenty-first century – as if to say, I may not be able to get my publishing back, but at least I can rewrite history. The most extreme example would be Richard Hell's second album, *Destiny Street*, where new vocals, new guitar parts and a new sequence made for an unnerving experience for anyone familiar with the original. Again, the idea was partly to raise a great big digit to Marty Thau, whose label the original LP appeared on. The most controversial revamp, though, would be The Beatles' *Let It Be . . . Naked!*. McCartney's belated attempt to reclaim 'his' album – and in particular his song, 'The Long and Winding Road' – from Phil Spector's instrumental impositions was all part of a prolonged plan to reinforce McCartney's role in that part of pop history.

At the turn of decade the most prolific songwriter of the sixties, Dylan, could also finally look forward to full control of his publishing after brokering his own agreement with ex-manager Albert Grossman, which confirmed the formal dissolution of their business relationship on 17 July 1970. Though it left Grossman with a share of the publishing until the end of 1971, Dylan knew he was about to deliver the last album under their agreement (*New Morning*), and he had no intention of adding anything significant to post-war pop until both his deals with Grossman and CBS Records had expired (which in the latter case would be August 1972).

Grossman had done rather well out of their previous agreement/s, having 'signed [Dylan] up for ten years, for part of my records, for part of my everything' (as Dylan described it to his old journalist-friend Robert Shelton, in May 1971). Even after the Witmark deal had expired at the end of 1965, he had set up Dwarf Music on Dylan's behalf, cutting himself a slice of *Blonde On Blonde*, *The Basement Tapes* and *John Wesley Harding*. Only then did Dylan start to look at the books. By the time Dylan formed his new company, Big Sky Music, in 1969, Grossman was no longer calling the shots, and the smaller slice he now received would no longer be delivered by sleight of hand. Dylan had learnt the hard way, if you want somebody you can trust, trust yourself.

He would not make the same mistake again. Which makes his 1973 decision to sign a record deal with David Geffen, founder and overseer of Asylum Records, seem quite mystifying. Geffen, the master of cross-collateralization, could make any deal sound like a dream till it became a nightmare, and was already known to be as cavalier with his artists' artistry as he was with his lifestyle choices. His most fabled three-card trick pre-Asylum came when he renegotiated Laura Nyro's record contract in such a way that CBS acquired her publishing company, Tuna Fish Music, in exchange for CBS stock worth around $3 million. As is detailed in Fred Goodman's *Mansion On The Hill*, this meant that, 'as co-owner of Tuna Fish, Geffen received 50 per cent of the money. If the deal [had been] a simple contract extension, his share as Nyro's manager would have been a standard commission, normally 15 per cent.'

However, once it was *his* own label on the line, Geffen introduced the novel notion that record advances should be cross-collateralized against the publishing.* It was a practice no self-respecting entertainment-lawyer would agree to. Indeed, in the modern era, no manager in their right mind would put publishing as 'a guarantee' against record sales. But when the manager was Geffen himself or a business partner, the problem went away – no one in the Californian Asylum was about to say a word against the practice. In fact, when it was put to The Eagles, Glenn Frey recalls, 'There were no questions asked; we didn't think anything of it. We didn't even have lawyers. It was simply put to us that the insurance against a shitty record was publishing.' No wonder Geffen always wore a smile, whether he enjoyed the sleep of the just or not.

Dylan, though, was no rube. And Geffen needed Dylan more than the artist needed him. So Geffen agreed to license the next Dylan album for seven years (and, if he was lucky, the one after that), in return for providing support on the biggest tour in rock history – the Dylan/Band 1974 tour – and printing, pressing and selling the new Dylan album, *Planet Waves.*†

Dylan had a gameplan that involved playing Geffen off against Clive Davis, now president of CBS. By August 1974, CBS had got Dylan back again, but for a whopping increase in his album advances and the reversion of unreleased masters. It seems Uncle Albert had taught him how to win the war after losing every battle. Geffen learnt not to trust a man just because he once wrote a song he liked. In future, his own musical taste (such as it was) would play no part in business.

Even as Dylan was returning to CBS in the summer of 1974 – they wiser, him richer – the latest 'new Dylan' was in serious danger of being turfed

---

* Though successive albums on a recording contract are routinely cross-collateralized, meaning losses on early, less successful albums could be offset should success subsequently come, to cross-collateralize the 'publishing' and 'recording' advances was an 'innovation' only a Geffen would dare introduce.

† In direct opposition to *Planet Waves* was the first of a threatened series of CBS 'revenge' albums, *Dylan*, wholly comprising cover versions, most of which did not pay publishing to their erstwhile artist.

off the label after just two disappointing sellers to his name. He was saved by a jaundiced rock critic who claimed he had 'seen the future of rock and roll and its name is Bruce Springsteen'. CBS finally stumped up the money to turn this 'new Dylan' into The Boss, and *Born To Run* became the first seventies chartbuster to suggest the spirit of the sixties was not entirely dead. But no sooner was that difficult third album storming the charts than His Bruceness was being told to dump his manager, Mike Appel, and sign instead with his saviour, critic Jon Landau.

Landau desperately wanted his piece of the pop pie. But Appel still had a finger in every aspect of Bruce's career: manager, publisher, producer, booking agent and publicist. And the deal Springsteen had originally signed with Appel's publishing arm, Laurel Canyon, was effectively for the once-usual 50-50 split. (Another contract, with Columbia, he signed in an unlit parking lot at midnight, so business-savvy he wasn't.)

Up until 1975 Appel made it clear he was prepared to talk about changing the terms 'but it was not a pressing concern, because there was no money'. Until suddenly there was. Only now Springsteen was considering his options, even though Appel was prepared to give him 75-25 on the publishing *retroactive to 1972*, as well as stock in the publishing, production and management companies he had set up on his client's behalf.

Someone, though, had got to Springsteen, and he wielded a hyperbolic pen. A remarkably ungrateful Springsteen now wanted what was his, and was prepared to burn bridges with the man who had been foreman to his master-builder for the three years it had taken to raise Cain. Another rock artist who had signed first and worried later, Bruce now found the 'rinky-dink' contracts he had put his name to back when he was a nobody held up. His response was to rail at the injustice of it all in a way that was both irrational and counter-productive, ranting at counsel during a 1976 deposition in language more befitting the Asbury Park boardwalk than the halls of justice:

**Bruce Springsteen**: There was money floating all around the office, all the fucking time, that is. I don't know where it went. I

don't know who got it, and I don't know who paid what to who
. . . Yes, he gave me any fucking thing that I wanted – that I paid
for with my own money. You know, that's exactly what he did, and
when the big dollars rolled in, they rolled right into his pocket. So
he ain't doing me no favours . . . I have been cheated. I wrote 'Born
To Run', every line of that fucking song is me and no line of that
fucking song is his. I don't own it . . . I have been cheated . . . My
management contract was stolen from me. He told me, 'Trust me,
trust me,' and I signed the goddamn thing. And the first thing he
did was to go to CBS and he made his deal twice as good, his own
personal deal twice as good . . . And it wasn't until I fought to have
Jon Landau on *Born To Run* that we had any success recording
whatever. On the publishing, he stole my songs . . . Five hundred
thousand dollars comes in and Mike slaps it in his pocket, and now
he is going to give me half of my own song. Thanks a lot, Bob. I
don't live that way . . . It is like this, man, somebody stabs you in
the fucking eye and you stab them in the fucking eye . . . You got
a lot of fucking balls to sit there [and talk] about my breaking my
fucking word when he did [this] to me, he fucking lied to me up
and down. [1976]

Springsteen would eventually get his way, mainly because his record
label wanted him out of the contract Appel had wisely signed on his
behalf – a licensing deal which put Appel's production company between
the artist and the record company – and tied directly to CBS. As such,
even though the judge in Springsteen's case ruled that CBS had no rights
in the dispute, they made sure that Springsteen – who remained, on
paper, bankrupt – had a well-funded legal team. The deal Springsteen
signed – and CBS funded – gave Appel $800,000 and a reduced produc-
tion royalty of 2 per cent (from 6), while still leaving him with a 50 per
cent interest in the twenty-seven songs Springsteen had recorded and
released in the past three years. Given that the stroppy singer only owed
Appel two more albums (one of which could have been a live one), and

his publishing contract had just a year left to run, it was the deal of the century for Appel.

Springsteen, having bought his freedom – at a helluva price – duly turned it into a license to dither. The next three E Street Band albums would take eleven months, eighteen months and twenty-four months respectively to record. Not surprisingly, there were a fair few leftovers in the song department – many superior to what he was releasing in his own name – and in 1978, as he toured North America remorselessly, his biggest single hits were 'Because The Night' by the Patti Smith Group (a song he had initially demoed, then given to Patti, who in rewriting the lyrics claimed a co-song-credit and a share of the publishing) and 'Fire', covered by Robert Gordon and The Pointer Sisters.

Springsteen had always written far more songs than he could use himself. But he would never be quite as prolific – or as profligate – as in the months before he recorded his first album, *Greetings From Asbury Park*, when he was simply a songwriter for Laurel Canyon Music, Appel's publishing house. Even if titles like 'Visitation At Fort Horn', 'Saga Of The Architect Angel', 'Ballad Of A Self-Loading Pistol' or 'Balboa Versus The Earth Slayer' suggested he'd swallowed a rhyming dictionary, by 1998 Springsteen's sophomoric efforts were of interest to tens of thousands of fans all around the world.

Springsteen, perhaps the most prolific American songwriter of the seventies, doubtless now wishes he had been a bit more quality conscious in those years. Because as he said on the stand during a 1998 case in London's High Court, attempting to stop the release of a double CD of his Laurel Canyon demos, 'The music that you come up with when you are sitting in your room alone with your guitar late at night is one of the most personal things in your life.' Especially, if it happened to be 'Eloise', a weird little song about a nun holding a priest in her sexual thrall that was promptly recast as 'Growin' Up'.

Elton John knew just how he felt, after one Dutch bootlegger with money to burn and a Sotheby's account released three CDs' worth of

Dick James demos in the early 1990s. They'd been recorded when Elton was earning a pittance for writing songs with titles like 'Tartan Coloured Lady', '71–75 New Oxford Street', 'When I Was Tealby Abbey' and 'Regimental Sgt. Zippo'. As he said in 1975, 'In those days we'd do anything for our ten quid a week.' Even after Elton okayed the release of his anonymous *Top of the Pops* recordings, he refused to present a selective official archival diary of his lost juvenilia.

For both Bruce and Elton, being signed to a company who thought publishing first, recording second, left quite a body of work to disown before record sales took them down a different road. In each case, they had left a plentiful supply of publishing demos behind – well behind, they hoped.

In this they were following a familiar path, one which their mutual hero trod first. As a result, Dylan had unwittingly presided over the birth of rock bootlegs in 1969–70. The demos he made for Leeds Music in 1962, Witmark Music between 1962 and 1964 and Dwarf Music in 1967 (the fabled 'basement tapes', always intended as publishing demos), had all been extensively bootlegged on albums with cryptic titles like *Great White Wonder, Troubled Troubadour, Poems In Naked Wonder* and *Ceremonies of the Horsemen.*

No matter how much Dylan tried to keep a lid on songs he did not consider finished, or copyrightable, some resolutely refused to go away. 'I'm Not There', a 1967 Dwarf Music demo he did not even copyright until 1970, proved particularly problematic. As far as Dylan was concerned, it was never finished. (When Cameron Crowe asked him why it had never been released, Dylan snorted, ''Cause it wasn't there!') But such was the song's allure that in 2007 it became the title (and title track) of Todd Haynes' fictional biopic of Dylan – at which point Dylan finally allowed his 1967 demo into the world, thirty years after the bootleggers beat Bob to it.

Shortly afterwards, Dylan okayed the release of the forty-seven extant demos he had recorded for Leeds and Witmark in his pre-electric days. But still songs from 'the simple years' kept popping up – a chunk of them at auction-houses in manuscript, most of them written at the kitchen table of his friends, the MacKenzies, in the spring and summer of 1961, when he was still struggling to unlock his muse and reliant on some guy called Trad R for his tunes.

Inevitably, some songs got lost along the way – not all of them insignificant. 'I Was Young When I Left Home', a song he recorded in Minneapolis in December 1961, was for a number of years viewed as simply a reworking of the traditional '900 Miles'. But it was so much more, and in 2001, it was finally released and copyrighted. Other potentially interesting songs from the period, like 'Talkin' Hypocrite' and 'Liverpool Gal', were taped but remain uncirculated. As were a bewildering number of basement tape originals until November 2014, when the whole kit'n'caboodle appeared as the eleventh Dylan *Bootleg Series*. Whether or not Dylan would prefer they remain under wraps may ultimately be beside the point. In today's digital free-for-all, it seems unlikely they will stay that way (certainly if the masters continue to reside outside his possession).*

Not surprisingly, the copyright free-for-all has meant a great number of works in progress have come into the public domain; not only early demos, but also non-classic prototypes of classic songs lacking that 'x' factor. The roots of one of David Bowie's biggest-ever hits – and the *Billboard* breakthrough for which he'd been waiting five years – were stripped bare in 1995 when *Rarestonebowie* appeared, a collection of rarities authorized by Bowie's ex-manager Tony Defries *against Bowie's express wish*.

On it was a 1974 TV performance of a song called 'Footstompin'. Ostensibly a 'cover' version of a 1961 single by The Flares, Bowie's version segued into 'I Wish I Could Shimmy Like My Sister Kate', the old New Orleans folk song our friend Clarence Wiliams copyrighted to himself back in 1922. But it also used a guitar riff that was the work of

---

* Already changes in European copyright are freeing all recordings of American artists that are more than fifty years old from any 'exclusive' right to reproduce; allowing anyone with a pressing plant within easy reach to release their version of Dylan's early demos as long as they pay the publishing. Not surprisingly, some have carped the diem.

Bowie's guitarist, Carlos Alomar. That riff would form the basis for a famous studio jam that as Alomar has recalled, Bowie subsequently 'cut up . . . [until] he had the form of the song he wanted'. Onto this Bowie grafted 'all . . . the high-pitched singing', a suggestion of John Lennon's which would entitle him to the same share of the resultant song, 'Fame', as Alomar – the man whose riff defined the number-one song. Lennon, who once opined, 'Music is everybody's possession. It's only publishers who think that people own it,' was happy to take his piece of this particular lucrative pie.*

Bowie had feared for a while he had missed his chance to write a standard. Asked, in 1968, to supply an English lyric for a French pop song called 'Comme D'Habitude', he had written a new set of words rather than trying to adapt the French lyric. He not only cut a demo of the result, 'Even A Fool Learns To Love', but also shot a crude early video of the song with his then-girlfriend, Hermione Farthingale. But the English publisher decided David's song didn't do the necessary, and commissioned another lyricist to have a go. This time he struck platinum. The lyric Paul Anka wrote was 'My Way'.

After Sinatra had the biggest hit of his career with Anka's song, the now-famous Bowie responded by writing 'Life On Mars', placing a cryptic note next to the title on the sleeve to 1971's *Hunky Dory*, 'Inspired by Frankie'. It would take the Bromley-born chameleon twenty years to admit what that inspiration was. Finally, in 1993, he owned up to nicking parts of the original Claude François tune: 'There was a sense of revenge because I was angry that Paul Anka had done "My Way." I thought I'd write my own version. There are snatches of melody in "Life On Mars" that are definite parodies.'

Like Elton and Springsteen, Bowie simply hoped this slip of the pen

---

* Perhaps this largely unwarranted credit for Lennon was belated karma for being denied a co-credit on Darren Young (aka Johnny Gentle)'s 1962 Parlophone single, 'I've Just Fallen For Someone'. As Gentle later confessed: 'I couldn't work out a middle-eight and John came up with something that seemed to fit, (sings), "We know that we'll get by/Just wait and see/Just like the sun tells us/The best things in life are free." It flowed well but . . . there was no question of him getting a songwriting credit.'

would go away. He never bothered to revive, or re-record, 'Even A Fool Learns To Love' – as he would do with a number of 'lost' songs from the same period – because it was, to his mind, juvenilia; one of a number of early songs he wished he'd never written. Another of these was 'Little Toy Soldier', an April 1967 demo of which took two lines from The Velvet Underground's 'Venus In Furs'. Bowie has obstinately refused to release it to this day, even after putting pretty much everything else out from the pre-*Oddity* period on an archival two-CD set in 2010.

Not that it is the lifting of Lou's lyric which ensures the continuing absence of 'Little Toy Soldier' from the canon; it is probably embarrassment – at the subject matter, not the execution. For the song tells of a girl called Sadie who winds up a toy soldier so that it whips her, and one day she overwinds it and it whips her to death. Bowie was similarly concerned about a song which had disturbed his mother (presumably because of the line, 'wear the dress your mother wore'), 'Let Me Sleep Beside You'. That, too, he held back. Even the bisexual Bowie disowned lyrics which might keep a team of psychiatrists hard at work for five years.

Likewise, Van Morrison all but disowned a late Them composition of his, which the post-Van band then released themselves. Called 'The Queen's Garden', it featured Van's first transvestite-in-song (anticipating 'Madame George'): 'See the Duke in drag, waving a yellow flag/Walking in the Queen's garden.' He also made sure a Them reissue programme omitted both the full version of his first paean to paedophilia, 'Little Girl' (with Morrison's audible cry, on the fadeout, 'Little girl, I wanna fuck you!'), and another song about a girl growing up too soon, 'Mighty Like A Rose', with its references to drug-pushing teachers that 'teach you how to roll a joint . . . Oh, you're only fourteen summers, but God knows/ Child, you're getting mighty like a rose.'

In neither case did Bowie or Morrison have anything – artistically, anyway – to be ashamed about. 'Little Toy Soldier', 'Let Me Sleep Beside You', 'The Queen's Garden' and 'Mighty Like A Rose' were four of the better songs inspired by the psychedelic cauldron of (and about) London town and its increasingly casual attitude to societal taboos. But all these songs had been written and demoed at a time when there were no rock bootlegs by a generation of post-Beatles songwriters who hoped fame and fortune was just around the corner. And as it happens, it was; only for the first battalion of bootleggers to discover there had been a lot of detritus cast aside on the way to dreamland, and the punters wanted it all, and wanted it now.

# CHAPTER 15

# 1967–82: Musical Differences (Parts 5–9)

*Featuring*: 'Time Waits For No-one'; 'Moonlight Mile'; 'Burn'; 'Supper's Ready'; 'I Know What I Like'; 'The Lamb Lies Down On Broadway'; 'Speak To Me'; 'Wish You Were Here'; 'Shine On You Crazy Diamond'; 'Comfortably Numb'; 'Bohemian Rhapsody'

> The way that we claw each other's eyes out over the credit and wealth is quite ugly.
>
> Roger Waters, Pink Floyd

As the idealism suffusing the sixties turned to the harsh cold glare of the seventies, established bands for the first time had to face up to the destabilising effect song-credits could have on group equilibrium. As psychedelia gave way to 'Prog', discontent in its many guises (whether over the percentage of songs on an album, the share of a credit or the publishing itself) claimed several bands expected to lead British rock into this brave new world of progressive sound – even those opting for an even-handed distribution of song-credits.

Cream, the original rock power-trio, contained one serious songwriter (Jack Bruce), a blues purist and a drummer with a business head but no actual songwriting talent. Indulgent jams credited to all three instrumentalists suited Eric Clapton and Ginger Baker just fine. But Bruce, who co-wrote all their early hits with poet Pete Brown, soon tired of sitting out drum and guitar solos. In 1969, all three announced 'solo' projects, in Clapton's case as part of supergroup Blind Faith with ex-Traffic officer, Steve Winwood. A Traffic that had included both Winwood and Dave

Mason had lasted just two albums, before Mason decided he had spent long enough crying to be heard. Jethro Tull and King Crimson didn't even last that long before Mick Abrahams and Ian McDonald went on their merry way, leaving their former partners, Ian Anderson and Robert Fripp, as overseers of these bands' increasingly grandiloquent direction. Meanwhile, Page-Plant had become the default credit on Zeppelin tracks, much to the annoyance of the rhythm-section.

Even the Jimi Hendrix Experience had an unhappy second songwriter in its midst. After being given a song apiece on *Axis: Bold As Love* and *Electric Ladyland*, bassist Noel Redding decided by spring 1969 to pump up his own Fat Mattress. Meanwhile, Pink Floyd, the one psychedelic band who owed it all to their lead songwriter, were left in the lurch when Syd Barrett became too hot to handle, and the songs he wanted 'his' band to record were too weird for words. 'Scream Thy Last Scream' was not what the others had in mind as a follow-up to 'See Emily Play'. Whatever was Barrett thinking?

Fast-forward to November 1974, and a reconstituted Pink Floyd, now one of the two or three biggest bands in the world, are touring the British Isles playing not only the whole of *Dark Side Of The Moon* (a concept-piece that had begun life as *Eclipse: A Piece For Assorted Lunatics*), but a 25-minute song about Syd Barrett's descent into madness called 'Shine On You Crazy Diamond' and two variations on a theme, pointedly enti-tled 'You Gotta Be Crazy' and 'Raving and Droolin'.

The years 1974–5 stand as the period of British Prog's pomp. Led Zeppelin's *Physical Graffiti*, Pink Floyd's *Wish You Were Here*, King Crimson's *Red*, Queen's *A Night At The Opera*, Genesis's *The Lamb Lies Down On Broadway* and Deep Purple's *Burn* were the cream of a bumper crop – every one of them featuring a cooperative of composers. But all was not as it seemed. The song-credits for all six bands had become a bat-tleground, with Crimson the first to be caught in the crossfire.* But what really set the cart rolling in a year of headlines about band break-ups,

---

* *Red* was not only released posthumously, it was recorded posthumously, with the split agreed in advance.

'musical differences' and recriminations on song-credits was the departure in December 1974 of the newest, youngest member of the 'greatest rock & roll band in the world', The Rolling Stones.

Though Mick Taylor had only joined the Stones towards the end of sessions for their 1969 masterclass, *Let It Bleed*, he had been on hand for the remarkable run of albums that followed their escape from Allen Klein: *Sticky Fingers* (1971), *Exile On Main Street* (1972) and *Goat's Head Soup* (1973). But by *It's Only Rock 'n Roll* (1974) tensions were mounting, especially when the Glimmer Twins (Jagger and Richards' new co-production tag, ensuring band decisions became yet more centralized) included the six-minute 'Time Waits For No One', complete with an exquisite two-minute lesson in mellifluous guitar soloing from Taylor. It was credited to Jagger-Richards, a point made by NME journalist Nick Kent to Taylor in an October 1974 interview.

Taylor seemed surprised, 'Do they? I haven't seen the finished article.' In the course of that conversation, Taylor also revealed that he had 'made creative inserts into other tracks', specifically 'Till The Next Goodbye' and 'If You Really Want To Be My Friend'. Pressed by Kent as to whether he was 'pissed off', Taylor finally admitted, 'Well, I was rather annoyed when I wasn't credited with one song [on *Sticky Fingers*] – "Moonlight Mile." I wrote that with Mick at Stargroves and we both recorded it with Charlie . . . [Also] "Hide Your Love" [on *Goat's Head Soup*]. Mick and I did that together as well.' Six weeks later, Taylor tendered his resignation.

His five-year battle for song-credit, largely between him and Jagger, was over. Indeed, Taylor later claimed that Jagger broke his word – just as he had with Brian Jones: 'We used to fight and argue all the time. And one of the things I got angry about was that Mick had promised to give me some credit for some of the songs – and he didn't.' Jagger may even have left his co-songwriter in the dark, as Keith Richards claimed in his autobiography that 'Mick [Taylor] could never explain why he left.'

According to one insider, Richards not only remained unaware of the *cause* of Taylor's departure, but was openly apologetic about his treatment;

and when the ex-Stone ran into Keith a couple of years ago, the Glimmer twin supposedly saying, 'Oh, we really owe you man. We really owe you.' But, predictably, nothing came of it. Such was Jagger's unswaying self-belief it never even occurred to him that Taylor's presence had helped give the Stones a second bite at the creative cherry; or that from now on they would spend most of their stage time spitting out the pips.

If the lack of a co-credit could breed discontent, there were others in the rock pantheon convinced one could have too much of a good thing. By 1973, Deep Purple and Genesis were starting to sell records in the hundreds of thousands. But even as Mick Taylor was packing his bags, Purple's explosive lead guitarist Ritchie Blackmore and Peter Gabriel, the main vocalist and visual focal point of Genesis, were looking for outlets away from the bands they fronted.

In Blackmore's case, his first threatened rebellion came after the success of *Machine Head* and the double live album, *Made In Japan*, in 1972, had put Purple among the big boys and made a 1968 agreement to split song-credits five ways look decidedly ill-advised. Back then, Deep Purple Mk. 1's two biggest hits ('Hush' and 'Help') were both covers. But Blackmore had now been forced to resort to a little blackmail to recalibrate song-credits: '[*Machine Head*] was a great LP, I thought. We had ideas. Ian Gillan, myself and Roger, it began to be a trio writing then. Jon started stepping back . . . [But] on *Who Do We Think We Are?*, everybody refused to write with everybody else. I was even holding back ideas. I was saying, "I'm not giving you these ideas because they're going to another thing."'

Blackmore, essential to the band, was granted his wish. An agreement was reached with the others that future song-credits would reflect only the contributions of the parties responsible. But it came at the expense of the Mk. 2 line-up – vocalist Ian Gillan decided to leave while the going was good, which only further strengthened Blackmore's position, especially as he quickly developed a rapport with Gillan's replacement, David Coverdale. The others, however, were starting to lose interest:

**Jon Lord**: What we lost after the Mark II split was the ability to cross-communicate. By this time the band was a disparate thing . . . Ritchie was the first to say that he who writes gets. I think that was a mistake, and that's not economic sour grapes . . . The band simply worked better when everyone had an interest in all the songs. When somebody now came up with a completed song, the others would think 'there's nothing in it for me' and become disinterested. Ritchie [also] produced less and less good ideas than in the past.

And no sooner was Blackmore seemingly vindicated by the excellence of the first Deep Purple Mk. 3 studio album, *Burn* – largely composed by himself and Coverdale – than he lost interest, too. Lord duly admitted, in 1975, 'My forte lies in developing the initial ideas. I find it very difficult to write a convincing riff, for instance, because I don't play guitar and the kind of rock & roll we play is very much a guitar-oriented entity.' So once Blackmore was producing 'less and less good ideas', the organist found he had very little to work with.

In fact, Blackmore had started stockpiling song-ideas and riffs for a solo project he was planning to complete before the next Purple album. A venture founded on the back of 'Black Sheep Of The Family', a cover Blackmore wanted to record as a single, the Rainbow debut platter also included a Yardbirds song ('Still I'm Sad') and an extemporization around the sixteenth-century 'Greensleeves' – appositely called '16th Century Greensleeves' – which Blackmore had written with Elf's Ronnie James Dio. It was when this track, in Dio's words, 'turned out to be better than the A-side . . . [that] Ritchie decided to do an album'. The result, *Ritchie Blackmore's Rainbow*, was quite a departure – and one he controlled from concept to credits:

**Ritchie Blackmore**: I didn't want any virtuosos, because it was going to be a singer-cum-guitarist thing. I didn't want organ solos and drum solos . . . That's what I was getting away from . . . [The material] hasn't been [about] some gigantic riff which it's all rested on, it's been an actual melody and chord progression which can stand on its own, without a great riff going all the way through it. [1975]

Indeed, by the time Blackmore returned to Purple to begin work on *Stormbringer*, he really didn't want to know. As producer Martin Birch recalls, 'It wasn't going the way Ritchie wanted and by the time it came to the mixing stage Ritchie seemed to have lost interest completely.' Blackmore's own account of the sessions suggested an insurmountable problem: 'In the studio we'd be five egotistical maniacs, pushing the faders up so each of us would be progressively louder than any of the others. It wasn't a team effort any more, the songs seemed to have been forgotten.'*

Blackmore quit shortly after the release of *Stormbringer*, announcing that his solo album would now be the first release of the band Rainbow. Jon Lord's explanation was simple: 'He found he couldn't express his ideas with people who wouldn't bend to his will.' First and foremost, though, the guitarist wanted quality songs, even if it meant reverting to the aesthetic of the outfit he had co-founded back in 1968: 'Everybody wants to write their own material. They say it's got to be original shit instead of copied good stuff. I think there are too many bands doing their own stuff, and it's bad [if] they can't write.'

If Blackmore had grown tired of sharing publishing on tunes he largely wrote himself, Peter Gabriel's departure from Genesis a matter of weeks later came as more of a shock. Genesis seemed on the verge of great things, and the band's public image had always suggested a real unity of purpose. But within Genesis the division of labour had never been clear-cut. As Gabriel himself said in 1974, 'Genesis initially consisted of four members. There was Tony Banks, Michael Rutherford, myself and Anthony

---

* The one exception was another Blackmore/Coverdale track, 'Soldiers of Fortune', from which Dire Strait Mark Knopfler would take subject-matter and feel, but not the soul, when he recast it as 'Brothers In Arms'.

Phillips. The four of us were songwriters. Mostly, Mike and Anthony would write together, and Tony and I would write together. Eventually, we banded together and started working on a general basis.' This republic of public schoolboys soon gave way to more imperial tendencies.

Each Genesis artefact, from *Trespass* (1970) to *The Lamb Lies Down On Broadway* (1974), pushed at Prog's already extravagant envelope. The double concept album in which that sequence culminated may well be the genre's high watermark, with scale of conceit for once matching ambition and execution. But it was also an album which drew a line between Gabriel and the others, and the battleground was song-credits.

The resultant power clash had been coming a while – ever since the major songs in the set became ones conceived lyrically by Gabriel, even if the music continued to be a five-way collaboration. Even after Gabriel produced the finished lyrics for most fans' favourite live set-pieces, such as 'The Knife' or 'The Musical Box', the others had remained convinced theirs was an equal partnership. But the lyrics they – and especially Mike Rutherford – really wanted from Gabriel were ones like 'Get 'Em Out By Friday' or 'Harold The Barrel', 'which were like mini operettas'. Such songs gave the rest of the band room to move musically, and provided some of the pomp post-*Pepper* audiences demanded.

But although the usual publishing split on lyrics and music was 50-50, Genesis split all publishing five ways, which was hardly fair when Gabriel almost single-handedly conceptualized the magnum opus which would take up the entire side of their fourth album, *Foxtrot*. The whole impetus for this piece, 'Supper's Ready', came from the man at the microphone:

**Peter Gabriel:** The first sequence [of 'Supper's Ready'] was about a scene that happened between me and [my wife] Jill . . . It was one night at Jill's parents' house in Kensington, when everyone had gone to bed . . . we just stared at each other, and strange things began to happen. We saw other faces in each other, and . . . I was very frightened, in fact. It was almost as if something else had come into us, and was using us as a meeting point . . . Anyway, that's how I got into thinking about good and evil, and forces working against each other. That's the sort of thing that 'Supper's Ready' . . . fed on . . . Often I felt that I could talk to the audience through the band's material, and the audience would understand what I was trying to say, and I would have a release, and a conversation with the audience through that.

At the same time as expressing a desire for 'a conversation with the audience', Gabriel was cutting down lines of communication with others in the band. He would note, on his departure, 'I've always written the pop-song type things . . . Now I can fiddle about with more poppy things that couldn't come out with the band'. 'Willow Farm' was one such piece, wholly Gabriel's, but inserted into 'Supper's Ready' as light relief. The musos in the band wanted to jam out, to indulge themselves instrumentally (which makes what they would become doubly ironic). And at the forefront of this ideological spat was keyboardist Tony Banks. For Banks, 'it seemed just luck that "Supper's Ready" turned out the way it did . . . We sort of just threw together all these various bits that we had.'

In fact, the only part that indisputably derived from the instrumentalists (perhaps as Gabriel's sop to majority opinion) was what Banks calls 'the "Apocalypse" section [which was] an improvisation thing which Mike, Phil and I did together'. As an instrumental jam, 'Apocalypse in 9/8' was hardly the natural culmination of such a complex combination of moods. Sensing this, and behind Banks' back, Gabriel wrote a vocal coda which he sang over the finale, resolving the struggle between good and evil from which the song had grown, and presaging the next all-embracing concept, England as the 'new Jerusalem'. It made the song whole and propelled the band into the higher echelons of British Prog. But as Gabriel later observed, 'Tony was outraged that I'd gone over his sacred solo. [Thankfully,] the rest of the band were really excited by what I'd done, and the popular vote was always the deciding factor.'

Gabriel also got 'the popular vote', inside and outside the band, for Genesis's first hit single, 'I Know What I Like', the one single-length track which could be pulled from their next ambitious artefact, *Selling England By The Pound*. Gabriel based his lyric on a painting, working in tandem with a visual artist (and non-band member) for the first time: 'The original Betty Swanwick drawing, which later turned into our *Selling England By The Pound* album-cover painting, didn't have a lawnmower on it. She added it later. We talked about the characters pictured in the painting, and then I worked the lyrics around her ideas of the piece and the group's interpretation of it.'

When the song became their first pop hit, Gabriel felt vindicated, even if the Prog mantra insisted only albums mattered. This would be the contentious backdrop for Genesis's epic, *The Lamb Lies Down On Broadway*, a work surely inspired – in scale and singular vision, if nothing else – by Pete Townshend's equally remarkable *Quadrophenia*, released the previous December. But whereas Townshend was the undisputed creative arbiter of The Who's direction, Gabriel was compelled to play the game of band politics to get his way after a bout of follow me, follow me:

> **Peter Gabriel:** I persuaded the band to go for a concept – I really had something in mind, which was *The Lamb* – but we had to go through this democratic procedure of saying, 'Let's all submit ideas and let's work on the best one.' . . . I probably was getting difficult and obstinate, as I tend to get if I'm put in a corner. We were all unfair manipulators. But Tony Banks and I were better at it than the others . . . The [*Lamb*] story had a lot of faults, but there aren't many books written by committee. I think you need leadership in a lot of artistic work because committees spend a lot of time not being bold and going for compromise solutions. You need singular vision.

And that 'singular vision' would be *his*, even though Banks plainly did not approve of the band decision to go along with Gabriel, later insisting,

'We gave in more than we should have done at that point.'* For perhaps the last time, artistic vision would get the casting vote at a Genesis board meeting.

Having won the day, Gabriel still felt obliged to keep the collective will onside in the months it took to realize *Lamb*. It would be an ongoing struggle, especially when Banks and Hackett renewed their battle for the band's soul by asking to contribute some lyrics of their own:

**Peter Gabriel:** To try and keep everybody happy, there would be parts of [*The Lamb* . . .] where we'd be discussing lyrics and throwing some words around for different bits. [There was] 'The Lamia', which was Tony's musical piece, or 'Supernatural Anaesthetist', which Steve had brought in. So then they would discuss lyrical stuff with me, because they'd got 'the writer's ticket'. But I was pretty anal about hanging on to some lyrical flowthrough, and being able to put a stamp on it. I really wanted a tougher edge to this record . . . and I didn't think there was anyone else in the band who was going to deliver that. [2007]

While Gabriel shut himself away writing the lyrics and libretto, the rest of the band concentrated on writing (most of) the music. Even here, though, Gabriel provided significant input. Banks credits the vocalist with all of the music to 'Counting Out Time', 'and most of "Chamber of 32 Doors," and then the odd bit here and there on other tracks.'

In fact, Banks was growing increasingly frustrated at the way the media focused on Gabriel and ignored the contribution of other band members like, well, himself. Group credits on all the songs didn't help, making it almost impossible for any critic to glean who contributed what. The keyboardist tried to set one scribe straight in the middle of the *Lamb Lies Down On Broadway* world tour:

---

* If *Trick Of The Tail*, their first post-Gabriel effort, was the alternative, rock aficionados the world over can be grateful Banks did not get his way.

**Tony Banks:** The only thing I do object to is when [the press] credit Peter with more than he actually does. I don't care who they want to talk to in the band . . . but when it comes to the writing of the music and lyrics and the stage presentation and everything, we all work on them together. It's a pity if Peter gets the total credit for that. It sort of evolves over long periods of time, our music. Sometimes you start off with bits you've had with you for three years, and you develop them as a group into much longer things. [1975]

'Lilywhite Lilith' was a reworking of an early Genesis track, 'The Light', that was wholly his own work. But 'Lilywhite Lilith' was not 'The Light', and his assertion that 'normally, in the past, the lyrics have been split between all of us', was misleading at best, disingenuous at worst. Gabriel had been the band's primary lyricist since at least *Nursery Cryme* (1971), his increasing grasp of this sphere coinciding with Genesis's growing success.

What made the whole process of transferring Gabriel's vision for *Lamb Lies Down* to vinyl and stage particularly fraught was the fact that he had already informed the others he would be leaving after they completed this six-month promotional drive. If his own motivations were mixed up in his mind, the issue of songwriting remained paramount – not so much from the financial side as from the vantage point of artistic autonomy. His creative direction and theirs were increasingly pointing in diametrically opposite directions. As Gabriel told his biographer, Spencer Bright, 'I was trying to give it a street slant . . . [even] before punk happened. I felt an energy in that direction, and it seemed that prancing around in fairyland was rapidly becoming obsolete.' He wanted to focus on self-expression, not chart stats, 'to make albums important to me and those who buy them, however many it is'.

A brave face was required from the four-piece Genesis as they said goodbye to the only first-class lyricist the band would ever have. In fact, they seemed positively ebullient about the future. Tony Banks was telling *Sounds* the week after Gabriel's resignation, 'Everything Genesis has written has been created by the five of us. One person leaving will change that one fifth. The songs will carry on the same.' Phil Collins had also convinced himself Banks and Rutherford wrote 'nearly as much [of the lyrics] and very much in the same style [as Gabriel] – it's a band style of writing, not Peter's alone; it's a product of all of us'. Evidence to the contrary did not take long to manifest itself. The ingredients in their next pop confection would include the likes of 'Squonk', 'Robbery, Assault And Battery' and 'Mad Man Moon'. Whereas Gabriel's solo debut included 'Solsbury Hill', 'Modern Love' and 'Here Comes The Flood'.

While Gabriel remained remarkably diplomatic in the interviews he gave shortly after his departure, he did raise for the first time the issue of the equal split on publishing: 'This democratic thing – it didn't really work like that. In fact, there was a playing of politics. One would pretend that things were someone else's ideas to get them through . . . With the writing thing, royalties were shared out five ways when generally three people in the band did the words.' And although his letter of resignation, published by all four UK music papers, was written in the same code as recent lyrics, one part cut to the chase:

> The vehicle we had built as a co-op to serve our songwriting became our master and had cooped us up inside the success we had wanted. It affected the attitudes and the spirit of the whole band. The music had not dried up . . . but our roles had set in hard. To get an idea through 'Genesis the Big' meant shifting a lot more concrete than before.

The others' continued insistence that they were a musical collective – despite all evidence to the contrary – had ultimately set singer against band. But having driven out the man at their creative wheel, those who had previously benefited from the singer's surges of inspirational speed decided he had been right all along: a change was in order. Barely had

Gabriel vacated the room than Mike Rutherford was telling the papers, 'You end up saying well *I* wrote this and that. We don't want it to be that way. the band will focus more on the individual now, but . . . working within the band set-up.' After giving their former singer the thin end of the royalty wedge for at least three albums, the quartet of survivors had now decided song-credits would no longer be collective. Pushed to explain the change, Rutherford showed why he should perhaps have continued to remain the quiet one:

> **Musician**: Why did you suddenly start splitting up the songwriting credits since previously all the material was credited uniformly to Genesis?
> **Mike Rutherford**: Two reasons: (a) the songs were written more by individuals this time. It was different on the *Trespass* album, for instance. On that album we all added our own bits. Someone would lead with an idea and the rest would blend in; (b) because in the past the rest of the group were still looking for a singer 'cause we got a bit overlooked. I think if on the older albums people could have seen who wrote what, and seen that most of the writing was done by us and not Pete, then when Pete split people wouldn't have thought that the remainder of the group would be in a bind, 'cause creatively we're not. [1976]

Most Prog bands had already eschewed the egalitarian model, so the decision to credit songs individually, not collectively, returned Genesis to rock's centre ground. Pink Floyd were also becoming less democratic just as they became one of the biggest bands in the pop world.

As a result an entire bookshelf has been devoted to describing the single-minded way Roger Waters not only assumed the Floyd's leadership but cut away each and every contribution the other members tried to make until only his monomaniacal version of the band remained. Such was his determination to see Floyd cast in his image, and his image alone, that by

1983 Waters, a vocalist with the range and emotion of balsa wood, would find himself without a band.

When Pink Floyd reformed – without Waters – in 1987, *Rolling Stone* wanted to know what happened. Guitarist David Gilmour was in no doubt that all that power had gone to Waters' head: '[Roger] forced his way to become that central figure. That's what he really wanted . . . I felt, and I'm sure Nick [Mason] did too, that it was not the best thing to happen. As productive as we were, we could have been making better records if Roger had been willing to back off a little bit, to be more open to other's people input.' They finally realized they were better off without all his egomania.

It was the unexpected global success of Waters' grand gambit, *Dark Side of the Moon*, in 1973 that had made him more bitter than grateful, and more determined than ever to do things his way. Being rich was not enough – he wanted the credit, the whole credit and nothing but the credit. As he insisted in 2003, '[*Dark Side of the Moon*] is my baby . . . They were my ideas and I wrote them.' But this was not really true. Richard Wright rejoined, '*Dark Side* is essentially Roger on lyrics and Dave and me on the music.' What Waters called 'important contributions' from Gilmour and Wright was actually the art of collaboration.

In fact, the raw outline of the project called *Eclipse: A Piece For Assorted Lunatics* came together at group rehearsals in December 1971, a full year and a half before it became *Dark Side of the Moon*. Gilmour's description of those sessions confirms a four-way collaboration: 'We went to a warehouse in Bermondsey, which belonged to The Rolling Stones, and we were there for a little while, writing pieces of music and jamming . . . You jam, you knock stuff about, you plunder your old rubbish library.'

If Waters had plenty of ideas he had just one finished song, 'Money', which he brought to these sessions in demo form. He also provided lyrics for a long piece Wright had written himself in 1970 for the *Zabriskie Point* soundtrack, but which director Michelangelo Antonioni in his not-so-infinite wisdom left on the cutting-room floor. 'The Violence Sequence' duly became 'Us and Them'.

Waters' scathing view of Dave Gilmour's contribution in particular never deviated, 'Dave likes to think that his lack of contribution has to do with laziness . . . [but] he's not really a writer. However conscientious or hard-working Dave was, he would never actually write anything.' Gilmour fully admits he 'didn't actually bring anything of mine into those rehearsal sessions . . . [However,] it's not something I'm wracked with guilt about . . . Most of the melodies that I sang I made up in the studio at the time of doing them, or in the rehearsal room. That's the way we tended to work.'

Actually, it was Gilmour who came up with one of Floyd's best-ever songs, which would have fit perfectly the 'concept' with which Waters claimed to be framing the material (it being an album 'about the pressures we personally feel that drive one over the top'). In the early months of 1972 – before Waters himself added 'Eclipse' to the *Dark Side* equation – Gilmour wrote the atmospheric 'Childhood's End', but it was promptly wasted on another soundtrack album, *Obscured By Clouds*, and dropped from the live set after just two performances despite being Floyd's most Barrettian piece in years.

Such became the pattern whenever Waters felt threatened by another band member's compositional contribution. He alone was allowed to be the wordsmith, fully believing the lyrics he was now writing qualified him for some major literary award. In reality what had once been sub-Barrettian ('Corporal Clegg'), was now just as likely to be overwrought and overthought. Drummer Nick Mason challenged Water's belief the lyrics were the key to the album's success: 'It depends upon how the listener feels. If they think the lyrics are the absolute crux of the whole [*Dark Side*] record, then Roger was under-credited . . . but the music is important as well; and so are the sound effects, the voices, the concept, the fact that these ideas are rolled into one.'

None of this would matter much if *Dark Side* had not become such a stupendous success, selling over ten million copies worldwide over the next two years. Convinced his genius had been belatedly recognized, Waters gave himself up to 'many years when I really regretted having given away half the writing credits, particularly "Speak To Me." I gave it to [Mason]. Nobody [else] had anything to do with it at all.'

The credits given Mason on 'Speak To Me' and 'Any Colour You Like' were likewise intended to keep vital components of the former cooperative happy. As Wright wistfully recalled, 'It was quite honestly . . . the end of that era of the band working very closely and creatively together . . . [even if] we had a few disagreements on the publishing when we were close to finishing it – well who get's what?'

Nor were members of the group alone in finding their contribution largely unacknowledged. The engineer at all the *Dark Side* sessions was Alan Parsons, later to work under the moniker of the Alan Parsons Project. He certainly was responsible for many of the album's sound effects, notably the one on 'Time' where all the clocks circle the (in the case of Quad, four) speakers until they all start chiming together. It was a loop he had recorded himself for a sound effects record. The Floyd co-opted the idea and then closed ranks. And Parsons knew he would have a hard time claiming such input qualified as composition. Twice shy, he declined to engineer *Dark Side*'s successor; instead he produced his own Floydian concept album, the baroque *Tales of Mystery and Imagination* (1976).

Meanwhile, the scale of Floyd's success was making it nigh on impossible for the collective to decide on a direction forward. Or as Waters later put it, 'We'd achieved what we set out to achieve together and the only reason we stayed together after that was through fear and avarice.' If no one else was going to guide the band through rocky seas, he decided he was going to grasp the helm. And not let go.

After *Dark Side*, Waters no longer seemed inclined to even go through the motions of consulting the others, all of whom had invested just as much emotionally and personally in the band. Gilmour bridled most at Waters' presumptuousness, knowing that he was as integral a part of the 'Floyd sound', 'It creates a feeling that you have to defer to him on [all] matters – and on musical matters, I didn't feel I should.'

Waters meanwhile decided he didn't like the way the publishing was divided up. He decided a rebalance of the publishing, and in turn, the resultant revenue streams was in order. From 1974 on there would be a new Floyd order:

**David Gilmour**: In later lyrics, the lyric came to count for half, so the lyricist would get 50 per cent of a track and the musicians would get 50 per cent. So if we wrote a piece of music, all four of us jointly, Roger would get 62.5 per cent of it, 'cause he'd written the words and a quarter of the music, and the rest of us would get 12.5 per cent [each]. That wasn't the case at the time of *Dark Side of the Moon*. [2003]

Waters still didn't feel the publishing on the already-previewed three-song successor to *Dark Side of The Moon* reflected his new vision.

Gilmour was due a co-credit on two of the three songs, and Wright on one of the three (the epic 'Shine On You Crazy Diamond'). For Waters, that would have meant giving up two-thirds of the publishing on one song, and half of the publishing on another. So he informed the others he didn't think the album as previewed at two dozen shows worked, and they would therefore be making a different album – one which would contain two new all-Waters songs, 'Have A Cigar' and 'Welcome To The Machine'.

Gilmour still came out of *Wish You Were Here* well rewarded, splitting 'Crazy Diamond' into two parts giving him and Wright perennial paydays. They would not be so lucky next time. For Mason, there would be no second 'Speak To Me'; and he spoke out, leading Wright to recall, 'Our fights at the end of making a record to decide who had what percentage of each song were always the worst arguments we ever had . . . I still don't know exactly how one works out the credits and percentages. It's always been a cause of much argument and bad feeling.'

On the next album, *Animals* (1976), Waters sequenced the record to ensure the largest wedge of publishing went his way. After he wrote a throwaway guitar doodle, to which he put a single verse of doggerel – by splitting the doodle in two, and calling it 'Pigs On The Wing (parts one and two)' – Waters instantly acquired 40 per cent of the album's publishing.

**Nick Mason:** Towards the end of recording [*Animals*] Roger created two pieces called 'Pigs On The Wing' to open and close the album, designed to give the overall shape of the album a better dynamic and enhance the animal aspect of it. An unwanted side effect was that it opened up the question of the share-out of publishing royalties (which are based on the number of tracks, not their length) since it gave Roger two additional tracks, and meant that the longer piece 'Dogs', co-written with David, was not split up [as originally intended], but left as a single track. This was the kind of issue that would ... prove contentious.

Ineluctably, the Floyd were becoming one man's conceit, even as *Animals* was lapped up with almost Pavlovian intensity by Prog fans around the world. But Waters was not done. Anything Peter Gabriel could do, he could do grander. He now announced a double-album concept piece called *The Wall*, based in all seriousness on what Waters considered to be the 'sado-masochistic relationship between audience and band ... an audience being bombed and the ones being blown to pieces applauding the loudest because they're the centre of action, even as victims'.*

The response of the others was guarded. Wright, for one, thought, 'Oh no, here we go again – it's all about the war, about his mother, about his father being lost ... [and] every song was written in the same tempo, same key, same everything ... But Roger had this material, Dave and I didn't have any.' In a financial jam after some bad financial advice, the other three felt they had little choice but to accede to Waters' grandiose scheme, even if they were sanctioning their own destruction:

---

* Given the friendship between Floyd and The Who in the early seventies, when Townshend was developing a similar idea for his aborted *Lifehouse* project, a conscious debt by Waters cannot be discounted.

**Roger Waters**: [The others] would like to believe, for whatever reasons, that the making of *The Wall* was a group collaboration – well OK, they collaborated in it, but we were not *collaborators*. This was not a co-operative. It was in no sense a democratic process. If somebody had a good idea I would accept it and maybe use it, in the same sense that if someone writes and directs a movie, he will often listen to what the actors have to say . . . Dave played the guitar and wrote the music for a couple of songs, but he didn't have any input into anything else really . . . There was really only one chief, and that was me . . . If you read the programme of the show it says on the inside page, 'The Wall, written and directed by Roger Waters, performed by Pink Floyd,' and that's what it was. I was no longer interested in working in committee. [2003]

*The Wall* (1979) in all its grandiosity single-handedly justified Punk, three years after the fact. Credited to Roger Waters, it could just as easily have borne the name, E.J. Thribb. But even with 'Written By Roger Waters' plastered across the double-sleeve, in small type was a begrudging admission that three of the songs were co-written with Gilmour. Indeed the one really memorable track from the whole indulgent smorgasbord, the corrosively catchy 'Comfortably Numb', as Gilmour says, was 'really the last embers of Roger and my ability to work collaboratively together – my music, his words. I had the basic part of the music done. I gave Roger the bits of music, he wrote some words.'

Waters could not bring himself to admit he had 'merely' added a few words to what was essentially Gilmour's song, ranting at *Melody Maker*'s Karl Dallas for suggesting 'it was Dave who wrote one of the most compelling songs in the thing, "Comfortably Numb." That's just not true . . . What happened is Dave gave me a chord sequence . . . I wrote the melody – and all the lyrics, obviously.' Unfortunately for Waters, the producer drafted in to arbitrate between auteur and backing band was Bob Ezrin. And he remembered rather differently the circumstances by which the song ended up on *The Wall*:

**Bob Ezrin:** 'Comfortably Numb' started off as a demo of Dave's – a piece in D with a lovely, soaring chorus and a very moody verse. At first Roger had not planned to include any of Dave's material, but we had things that needed filling in. I fought for this song and insisted that Roger work on it. My recollection is that he did so grudgingly . . . He came back with this spoken-word verse and a lyric in the chorus.

The working title for *The Wall* could just as easily have been *The Last Straw*. As it happens, there was still *The Final Cut*. By then, Waters had summarily sacked Rick Wright, who co-founded the band with him and Syd Barrett back in 1965.

At least Peter Gabriel called the three landmark records he made immediately after leaving Genesis, *Peter Gabriel*, *Peter Gabriel* and *Peter Gabriel* – or I, II and III, if you prefer. As for Blackmore's Rainbow, it would go through almost as many line-up changes as Deep Purple before Blackmore reformed Deep Purple Mk. 2, the band who always agreed songs should be split five ways in 1985. The Gabriel-era Genesis would also reform in 1982, though only for a single open-air gig. The set-list that heady day essentially comprised pre-1975 songs, the one exception was 'Solsbury Hill', a song Gabriel wrote about his reasons for leaving the band in the first place.

By the time Genesis sold out the Milton Keynes Bowl, Queen were back with their first group number one, 'Under Pressure'. That year, 1982, they were the one band to buck the general trend and go from individual to collective song-credits. It came about after drummer Roger Taylor had been showered with riches thanks to the long-standing anomaly whereby the publishing on both sides of a single were equally divided.

Having written the inconsequential 'I'm In Love With My Car', Taylor had the good fortune to have the song chosen as the flipside of 'Bohemian Rhapsody', an A-side which would stay at number one for an unprecedented nine weeks in the autumn of 1975, cementing Queen's status (over the likes of Thin Lizzy, Bad Company and Mott The Hoople, all superior live acts) as leaders of mid-seventies British hard rock. Piggybacking the success of 'Bohemian Rhapsody' made Roger Taylor a right royal mint, but it also created bad blood, which coursed through the regal system, putting the whole band's equilibrium under pressure:

> **Brian May**: At the time, we'd always work on each other's songs, but when it came to credits, the person who came up with the original idea would go, 'I wrote the fucking song, so I'm taking the writing credits.' A lot of terrible injustices take place over song writing. The major one is B-sides. 'Bohemian Rhapsody' sells a million and Roger [Taylor] gets the same writing royalties as Freddie . . . There was contention about that for years.

From 1982, Queen at least would operate as a cooperative. Not coincidentally, they were also the last original British Prog band standing.

Meanwhile, the man they called Macca, from the act who kick-started Prog back in 1967 with their six-month sojourn in Pepperland, continued brooding about the order of credits on Beatles songs since 1963. The decision he and John Lennon had made to credit each other's songs jointly, even when they had been composed (almost) entirely by one or the other, was, as Lennon told *Playboy*, 'never a legal deal between Paul and me, just an agreement when we were fifteen or sixteen, to put both our names on our songs'. However, what through 1962 had been credited as McCartney-Lennon – which was the case on their first two singles and the self-composed tracks on their debut LP, *Please Please Me* – became, by an agreement cooked up between Epstein and Lennon early in 1963, Lennon-McCartney. And it still rankled sixteen years later:

> **Paul McCartney**: I do [want credit], and not just out of a personal thing for me; I sometimes feel it for John, things getting called

Lennon and McCartney, things like 'Strawberry Fields Forever', 'Norwegian Wood', certain ones John wrote and I just helped a little bit. And there are certain ones I wrote. There's probably only . . . twenty that are really our own. On the rest there's quite a lot of collaboration. [But] I suppose you do get a little niggled; you wish people knew that [song] was mine. [1979]

By then, Paul had already started trying to redress the balance, or so he thought, with the release in 1976 of his first-ever live album, *Wings Over America*, on which all five 'Beatles' tracks were credited to McCartney-Lennon. But if Lennon cared one way or the other, he said nowt. He even offered to deconstruct the various Lennon-McCartney song-credits song by song during his last major interview. He, at least, had let go of the past, secure about his place in pop history. What Lennon had not considered, because he was still a young man, was what would happen to his songs after he was gone. Who would decide that some noodle he had been play-ing around with on a home-tape constituted a *song*?

The answer was Mrs L, a.k.a. Yoko Ono. Indeed, it seemed with Yoko in charge there was almost no limit to the scraps which could be credited as Lennon songs. She even deigned to allow two 'lost' unfin-ished Lennon originals – 'Free As A Bird' and 'Real Love' – to be worked on by the other members and presented as new Beatles record-ings in the mid-nineties, an exercise closer to grave snatching than song catching.

And it wasn't just the songs of Paul McCartney that Lennon was now lead author on. There were also some songs by ex-Bonzo Neil Innes. Back in 1977, ATV Music had threatened to bring suit, 'on behalf' of Lennon, McCartney and Harrison, against Innes for sending up his old friends with a series of razor-sharp satirical skits-in-song written to accompany Eric Idle's 1976 Rutles mockdoc *All You Need Is Cash*.

Innes had made a career out of caricaturing pop, but the publishing on 'I'm The Urban Spaceman' was not about to provide the means to fight ATV. So Innes ended up having to share the publishing with Lennon and

McCartney on songs like 'Cheese And Onions', 'Goosestep Mama' and 'Piggy In The Middle', titles perhaps silly enough for McCartney to have recorded with Wings, but never with The Beatles. Much to the profound embarrassment of Paul, John and George – all inveterate fans of Python, and in George's case, an unacknowledged contributor to the satirical soundtrack – they were now parties to this pathetic act of primetime credit stealing.

Though Lennon was still alive when this went down, there was little he could do: ATV owned The Beatles' songs, for now. But at least he left McCartney's bicentennial act of rebellion on those co-credits well alone. His widow would not prove so obliging. In 2002, when Paul (again) credited nineteen Beatles songs to McCartney-Lennon on his latest live album, *Back In The U.S.*, reflecting the primary contributor in each case, it brought the wrath of Ono down upon him. When she was reported to be considering legal action, McCartney made a public plea for understanding that was pointed enough to remind the lady just whose songs they were:

> **Paul McCartney**: [I] was in an empty bar flicking through the bar pianist's music book [and] I came across 'Hey Jude', written by John Lennon. If there is an argument for 'correct labelling', this is probably the best one . . . It seems to be harmless to me, after more than 30 years of it being the other way, for people like Yoko who have benefited, and who continues to benefit from, my past efforts to be a little generous. [2002]

The gentlest of reminders, it evidently hit its target and the furore died down. Yet Ono, who had been born with a sense of entitlement, never lost it. The idea that she was entitled to speak on her dead second husband's behalf not only on a financial but on a creative basis continued to irk everyone not in the pay of Ono Inc. Even when her late husband's erstwhile songwriting partner just wanted to set the record straight, she reacted like a scalded cat. As far as she was concerned, John's name came first, even when his contribution was negligible. She wished to assert John's primacy in the process – even on songs he loathed. And like many in this sister-hood, she could certainly afford to be difficult in the new golden age for legacy-litigants.

# CHAPTER 16

# 1976–93: Living Off A Chinese Rock

*Featuring*: 'Blank Generation'; 'Pretty Vacant'; 'Anarchy In The UK'; 'God Save The Queen'; 'Shot By Both Sides'; 'Start'; 'Holidays In The Sun'; 'Sonic Reducer'; 'Chinese Rocks'; 'Blue Monday'; 'Smells Like Teen Spirit'; 'In The Pines'

I can't afford to sue you/But I'd just like to clue you . . . FUCK YOU!

Richard Hell, 'Memo To Marty', 1992

At the exact instant that British Prog was betraying some of the high ideals with which it started out, there came a righteous roar from the nether regions of the self-same sceptred isle. And its name was Punk. Punk was a back-to-basics brand of pop that took as its musical template pre-psychedelic Britpop, and borrowed its attitude and aesthetics from the American vanguard of underground rockers: The Velvet Underground, The Stooges, the MC5 and the New York Dolls; all of whom had been spectacularly unsuccessful in their own lunchtimes.

But if the idea took hold of the collective unconscious of youth almost simultaneously in Britain, Australia and on the coasts of America, downtown New York was the first place where Punk became more than an attitude, more like a movement. Barely a year old in the spring of 1975, New York's self-professed originators of the style, if not the sound, had already torn themselves apart over whose songs got recorded.

In early March, Television's Richard Hell was forced to find a new home when co-founder Tom Verlaine revealed a monomania no less profound than Roger Waters', even if it purported to come from a more rarefied place. Verlaine didn't want the songs of Hell, which had quirky titles like '(I Belong To The) Blank Generation', 'Love Comes In Spurts' and 'Fuck Rock & roll', besmirching *his* TV set of high-flown lyrics and languid guitar-work.

Yet Verlaine had evidently forgotten every movement needs an anthem, even a mock ironic one. '(I Belong To The) Blank Generation' was a self-conscious bid to emulate a former attempt from 1959 to speak for one's contemporaries in the style of the times. Whereas, in Bob McFadden's sardonic 'The Beat Generation' he 'belong[s] to the beat generation/I don't let anything trouble my mind', Hell could 'take it or leave it each time'.

'Blank Generation' cleaned the slate even as it tipped its hat 'with [its] new bubblegum-punk words and a dumbed-down production'. Too dumbed down for Verlaine, it seemed. But the very idea of a _____ generation had enough resonance to sail across the pond, where a bunch of would-be punks from Shepherd's Bush saw the song-title on an early Television poster. That was enough for the Sex Pistols bassist to take New York's punk anthem and give it a 'London's burning with boredom' twist:

**Glen Matlock:** 'Pretty Vacant' [is] the only [Pistols] song I wrote entirely by myself. The first idea for it came from a poster that Malcolm had brought back from the States, a small handbill for a Richard Hell[-era] Television gig with the titles of several songs scattered across it. One of the songs was … '(I Belong To The) Blank Generation' … As soon as I saw that I thought: that's the kind of feeling that we want to get across in our songs. Not long after that I was sitting around during a soundcheck at The Nashville. I was wondering what to do with this Blank Generation idea. It certainly summed up how we – and a lot of other people – felt at the time. There was a blank, vacant kind of feeling going around which pervaded the scene … The Blank Generation idea also linked to discussions we'd been having around the band. There was a lot of talk around that time about nihilism and Dadaism. Some of the music press stories on us stressed that aspect quite heavily. And I'd come across some of it doing my reading for the 20th century art section of my art college foundation course. So what I was trying to do was take those kind of ideas and make them really simple . . . From the beginning, the important thing was to get across the idea of the band in the songs of the band. We had to turn meaning into sound. So I wrote the lyrics to 'Pretty Vacant'.

Matlock had also unwittingly written a riposte to New York's claims for punk primacy. In fact, he would be largely responsible for all three of the Pistols' A-sides that acted as audio sticks of dynamite lobbed into the self-satisfied citadel of Rock. As he noted in his memoir of life as a member of punk's first firing squad, '"Anarchy [In The UK]" is all my music with John's lyrics. As is "God Save The Queen." And "Pretty Vacant" is entirely mine, apart from John's update of the second verse – which as I've said earlier was far better than the original.'

But his share of the financial rewards was the same as his portion of the received glory – a quarter – because the Pistols had voted to split all songs four ways, and although Matlock himself 'voted against it . . . I'd been outvoted and I'd agreed to abide by the [others'] decision. In some ways it came out in the wash. "No Feelings" has my name on it but it's nearly all Steve's music and John's lyrics, I had very little to do with it.'

But 'No Feelings' was never a single cut – though it was almost B-side to their one chart-topper 'God Save The Queen'. And among the band-members only Matlock knew an anthem when he wrote it. (Or copped it.) Because, as he fully admits, 'Pretty Vacant' still might not have amounted to anything if he hadn't found the perfect intro. And the place he found it was somewhere he knew he could not admit to the rest of the band, wrapped up as they were in the whole 'Year Zero', anti-Pop dogma. It was an Abba record that made number one all around the world:

**Glen Matlock**: Although I quickly wrote a tune of sorts [for 'Pretty Vacant'], it was never quite right. What I needed was one particular musical idea which would echo the lyrical idea. Finally that riff came to me in Moonies, an upstairs bar in Charing Cross Road, across the street from The Cambridge Theatre. I was in there one lunchtime drinking my way through that week's dole money when Abba's 'SOS' came on the jukebox. I heard the riff on it, one simple repeated octave pattern. All I did was take that pattern and alter it slightly – putting in the fifth, to be technical . . . The next stage was to fit that Abba riff to the chord sequence for the chorus. That came straight from The Small Faces' 'Wham Bam Thank You Ma'am' because it fitted so well . . . I'm amazed that no one has yet noticed that 'Pretty Vacant' is borrowed from 'SOS'. But that's what songwriting is all about. Everything is nicked from something else. Only later, years after you've written the song, do you usually let on. The trick is always the same, to make it sound original.

It helped that the version of 'Wham Bam Thank You Ma'am' from which Matlock copped the chorus-riff was only then available on an obscure German import LP. But this was hardly the only such cop. The Pistols took an awful lot from the beat-group generation, especially The Kinks, The Who and The Small Faces. By the time they had dropped from the set the two Small Faces covers they liked to rehearse, 'Understanding' and 'Whatcha Gonna Do About It' (its lyric changed from 'I want you to know I love you' to '. . . hate you'), the attitude had seeped into the very marrow of their being. As had Kinks klassics like 'I'm Not Like Everybody Else' and 'All Day And All Of The Night', the former of which would inform the lyrics of 'I Wanna Be Me', while the latter would provide the opening riff to 'Submission' after slowing it down and cutting it in half.

The Kinks tracks were a little too well-known for Johnny Rotten's liking, and they were dropped shortly after Rotten joined the short-lived Swankers and all four became Sex Pistols. As Matlock recalls in *The Filth And The Fury*, 'We used to play some covers . . . most of which when we started rehearsing with John he didn't like.' But they still formed the basis of the band's musical identity, no matter how much Rotten preferred the Nazz and Natty Dread. The choice of covers played live was another joint decision, part of the 'all for one, one for all' consensus that lasted as long as the first record and the first use of the f-word on tea-time television. Even the spittin' singer initially talked in terms that smacked of a collective will:

> **Johnny Rotten:** I make sure that if I put words in a song they are what everyone thinks – that it's not just me bullshitting to my heart's content. All [of] our songs will be credited to the Sex Pistols. We don't want any of that 'he wrote this so he gets more money'. That's disgusting. No song is ever written entirely on your own. It's always slagged off by the others so by the time it's been slagged, other people have put their ideas into it. We've all made it what it is. [1976]

For now, the idea rubbed off on a few punk bands who followed the Sex Pistols' star from the outset. The 'share and share alike' ethos of the Punk vanguard even operated when one co-founder took his ball and went home. Howard Devoto had already quit Buzzcocks, the band he had formed with fellow Bolton Technical College student, Pete Shelley, but was at Shelley's shack when 'Pete played me what he would end up calling "Lipstick." And I said, "I really like that riff," and he said, "Okay, I'll give it to you." I just took that riff and constructed another song around it.' The song was 'Shot By Both Sides', Magazine's debut single and their signature tune. Devoto reciprocated by letting Buzzcocks kick off their own singles career with a witty leftover from the Devoto-Shelley era, 'Orgasm Addict'.

And the closer a band was to the white heat centre of this musical movement, the more likely they were to go along with the Pistolean ideal. The Slits were one all-girl outfit of non-musicians who shared and shared alike in the two years it took them to learn to tune their instruments well enough to record them. As was perhaps inevitable, there was one Slits song which got picked for every punk compilation CD going. It was one Viv Albertine wrote, 'Typical Girls'. Their most productive pen-person, however, was the personable drummer:

> **Palm Olive:** I really enjoyed writing the songs: I wrote 'Shoplifting', 'Number One Enemy' and 'New Town'. The way [The Slits] worked, someone would go write a song – like Ari wrote 'Slime' and Viv wrote 'Typical Girls', and then we'd work [on it]. For the royalties and the business side of things, there was an understanding between us that if everyone worked on the music, it belonged to everyone. But I actually wrote those songs . . . The last two I wrote [before I left] were 'FM' and 'Adventures Close To Home'.

After Palm Olive was fired in 1978, The Slits fell apart, their public persona defined by a smutty single album of punk-ska (*Cut*) that was a belated footnote to the years of anarchy in the UK – and lots of press generated because they were anything but typical girls. The songs, though, never flowed again.

The Sex Pistols' penchant for purloining elements of their punk anthems from snot-nosed sixties precursors found equal favour among both punk fraternities and sororities. Elvis Costello was one figure saturated in sixties sounds, largely because of his access to records from his bandleader-father. He also knew what he was doing, and in later years – when the punk madness had passed – would happily dissect each and every track. His description to the redoubtable Spencer Leigh of how he came to pen his breakthrough single, 'Watching The Detectives', showed just what it was that set him apart from his punk brethren, and ensured his career numbered in decades, not – as with some brighter flames – in days:

> **Elvis Costello:** I used to read a lot of Raymond Chandler's books, and I was trying to write a mystery story in a song . . . [incorporating] certain spooky Bernard Herrmann themes for [Alfred]

Hitchcock's films, and the music for *The Twilight Zone*! I was trying to incorporate all that, but I didn't have access to an orchestra and it was done with a combo band. That's the way a lot of pop music works, you're trying to evoke things that are done with much grander sounds, and you end up doing them with old tin cans and elastic bands . . . 'Down By The River' by Neil Young is [also] in there somewhere, in terms of the rhythm guitar part. There's also the guitar theme for 'Man Of Mystery'.

Among other cops Costello owned up to in meticulous notes to two-CD 'deluxe' versions of his classic sextet of albums (1977–1982) were 'Goon Squad' with its 'guitar figure that seems to imitate a very early record by . . . Television' and 'Busy Bodies' whose own guitar figure was 'related to Roy Orbison's "Oh, Pretty Woman,"' both found on *Armed Forces*. 'Dr Luther's Assistant', a 1980 EP track, owed a 'melodic debt to both The Byrds' *5D* and some of Roy Wood's psychedelic songs for The Move', while *Trust*'s magnificently misogynistic 'You'll Never Be A Man' 'borrowed some musical ideas from The Pretenders' 'Brass In Pocket'. And so on. The most gifted magpie in modern music, Costello flitted from genre to genre, riff to riff, in order to feed his own mercurial muse.*

Fortunately, subtlety was the name of the game with our Elvis. After all, in the Year Zero of punk it was bad enough admitting one listened to dinosaur bands, let alone copping a riff or two from them (or, indeed, Them). Siouxsie And The Banshees took great pleasure deconstructing parts of The Beatles' [sic] 'Twist and Shout' and Dylan's 'Knockin' On Heaven's Door' for their anti-rock rendition of 'The Lord's Prayer', but long before they had respectable hits with Dylan's 'This Wheel's On Fire' (a.k.a. the *AbFab* theme) and The Beatles' 'Dear Prudence', they were

---

* Costello's own fascination with the process itself even led him in recent years to compere two series of the TV shows, *Spectacle*, in which he interrogated some of his favourite singer-songwriters, Elton John, Lou Reed and Bruce Springsteen among them, about the tricks of the trade.

spinning both sides of their sixties singles (and all four sides of *The White Album*). The follow-up to their debut smash, 'Hong Kong Garden', was called 'Staircase (Mystery)', but the only mystery was how they got away with recrafting the riff to John Entwhistle's Who 1966 B-side, 'Dr Jekyll and Mr Hyde'.

The proto-psychedelia of 1966 seemed to hold particular appeal to punks. The Jam returned to plunder their favourite mid-sixties Who, Kinks and Beatles tracks again and again. Not content with demoing the likes of 'Rain' and 'And Your Bird Can Sing' – two songs originally cut during the *Revolver* sessions – for *Sound Affects* (1980), the intro bass line from George Harrison's 'Taxman' was deemed to be fair usage when it came to the album's number-one single 'Start'. Even more blatant was Weller's appropriation of Adrian Henri's poem 'In The Midnight Hour' for the first two verses of 'Tonight At Noon', a track on the second Jam album. Though credited solely to Weller, it took its title from one Henri poem and most of its lyrics from another, both found in the 1967 collection, *The Mersey Sound*.

Harrison, who needed neither the money nor the publicity, did not sue Weller. Nor did Henri, though he needed both. And Weller himself chose not to take counsel when the leader of the punk gang, the Pistols, ran out of ideas and copped his 'In The City' riff for their fourth A-side, 'Holidays In The Sun'.

They were less than subtle about it, almost rubbing his jammy face in it with the way 'his' riff leapt out of the murky mix. In fact, the week 'Holidays In The Sun' came out in October 1977, the *Sounds* singles reviewer noted, 'You can't tell me that they don't know they're ripping off The Jam's "In The City" riff. I like the Pistols so much that I'd love to believe that it was a completely unconscious lift, but even if was, the very first person they played it to would surely have pointed it out to them.'

By this time, the Pistols had a problem, one entirely of their own making. They had fired their main songwriter – Matlock. And already the critics Rotten had lampooned in 'I Wanna Be Me' were noticing that their two new songs – 'Holidays' and 'Bodies' – had 'no chewn, my babe, no chewn'. When the eagerly awaited *Never Mind The Bollocks* appeared, just three songs were credited to the Vicious-era Pistols, and of those, only 'EMI' had any chops – for the very good reason that Glen Matlock (co-)wrote it. And demoed it, and then departed with a cheque for £2,000, his payoff for fifteen months propping up the Pistols.

The credits on 'EMI' would soon be revised, and the Vicious account depleted of 33 per cent of its unwarranted spoils. In fact, so non-existent was Sid's musical contribution that he wasn't even trusted to play bass on the tracks he purportedly co-wrote. He did, however, bring one song to the band, an embarrassing one-verse screed of anti-semitic bile he evidently considered funny. 'Belsen Was A Gas' was a leftover from his first attempt at a punk combo, The Flowers of Romance, so named after an atonal instrumental with which the Pistols sometimes opened shows to make a point to those critics convinced they couldn't play.

Once they recruited Vicious, the Pistols finally had someone who genuinely couldn't. The band, though, needed the songs, the bass lines and general pop sensibility of their erstwhile bassist. But they had fired him, according to another of Malcolm McLaren's Situationist press releases, for liking The Beatles; a sackable offence in the new musical order.

Meanwhile, back in the USA, the issue of who wrote what, and who got to help themselves to ex-members' songs, was infecting its own punk politic. When Cleveland's original punk combo, Rocket From The Tombs, split down the middle after sharing two nights with Television in July 1975, the songs were also equally divided. Rabble rousers like 'Sonic Reducer' and 'Down In Flames', the song-credits to which should have read simply David Thomas and Cheetah Chrome,* were donated to the Dead Boys, who gratuitously added the names of Stiv Bators, Johnny Blitz, Jeff Magnum and Jimmy Zero.

If 'Sonic Reducer' enjoyed its status as a punk standard even before Pearl Jam covered it, the RFTT songs that actually broke the mould of

---

* As they would again when an archive CD of RFTT recordings was finally released in 2004.

modern music and unsprung the lock on a sound for the seventies went to Pere Ubu, the outfit Peter Laughner and David Thomas formed in the wake of RFTT's dissolution. Ubu's first two singles would prove to be the perfect epitaph for a band that garnered little credit outside Cleveland and Mancunia for kickstarting punk-rock. 'Thirty Seconds Over Tokyo' and 'Final Solution' also acquired myriad co-creditors from the extended Ubu family.

'Final Solution' would never make a mint – the original picture sleeve pressing now commands four figures – but its pre-eminent position on a various artist collection of bands who played Max's Kansas City would signal a second beginning, as a perennial on punk anthologies. And at least RFTT bassist Craig Bell got his name on the Ubu credits for coming up with the song's immense opening bass riff. Bell liked to lift famous rock riffs and tweak 'em; and not just any riff – only riffs already indebted to another riff. On 'Muckraker' he took Bowie's 'Jean Genie' riff, itself a recasting of the riff from 'I'm A Man'. And on 'Final Solution' he took a bass riff west-coast hard-rockers Blue Cheer had applied to Eddie Cochran's 'Summertime Blues' to steal the thunder of The Who (who were about to issue *their* version).

If Laughner's key contribution to the songs of both spin-off bands would be lost in translation, the equally jaded Richard Hell would also be on the receiving end of the short straw when a song he'd written one afternoon with his friend, Dee Dee Ramone (who told Hell 'he had an idea for a song that he didn't think The Ramones would wanna do'), was co-opted by Johnny Thunders and fellow Junkies as their very own anthem of 'devil may care' drugginess.

For Hell, the song 'Chinese Rocks' was always meant to have an edge of despair ('I shoulda been rich/But I'm just lyin' in a Chinese ditch') that Thunders never acknowledged or conveyed. For Thunders, 'I'm living on a Chinese rock' was a statement so close to home, he felt like he and side-kick Jerry Nolan should have a half-share of the Heartbreakers' anthem just for performing it and re-recording it ad nauseam.

Both would be dead from Chinese burns, aged thirty-nine and

forty-six respectively. Long before then, Hell had moved on to greener pastures and new pleasures, forming his own band, Richard Hell and The Voidoids, with the redoubtable Bob Quine. Unfortunately, he had become convinced he was running out of time to make his mark. It had been two and a half years since he announced the punk onslaught at Television's Townhouse Theater debut in March 1974. As such, he foolishly allowed himself to be persuaded to sign a one-time co-production deal with Richard Gottehrer and Marty Thau, two figures who had seemingly stepped out of a record industry version of *The Time Machine*.

Thau himself had previously presided over the dissolution of the New York Dolls, having cut his teeth in the industry of human happiness as Buddah Records' favourite bubblegum producer, from which vantage point he had witnessed a lot of other people becoming rich from the unceasing labours of Marty the mule. Gottehrer had also become fully versed in the ways of the pop world by associating with Bert Berns, whose Bang label had given Gottehrer and friends a nice nest-egg from their remake/remodel of 'Bo Diddley', 'I Want Candy', back in 1965.

Gottehrer and Thau felt New York punk was ripe for cherry-picking. The pair formed a joint production company, Instant Productions, with a view to signing up the talent before it could afford a lawyer. Their first target was actually The Ramones, with whom they recorded a provisional single, 'I Wanna Be Your Boyfriend' b/w 'Judy Is A Punk'.

However, it turned out the boys from Queen's weren't quite as dumb as they looked, and when Thau showed the contract to Tommy Ramone, he recognized 'one of those 50-50 deals. I said to myself, "What is this? Colonel Parker."' When Ramone recoiled, the predatory pair turned to Hell, a figure they recognized as responsible for at least three of the nascent new wave's defining anthems. In late June 1976, Hell thought he had signed a 'contract with Instant Records to produce and sell my tapes in exchange for 50 per cent of record royalties'. But it proved to be so much more, as Hell recently revealed in his vivid memoir, *I Dreamed I Was A Very Clean Tramp*:

Instant [Productions] offered me a deal in which they'd finance my band's demo tape and pay me $100 a week and a lesser amount to each of the other band members. Once the tape was complete, they'd have four months to get me a contract for an LP. In return for these services and investments, Instant would get approximately 50 per cent of all royalties paid the band by our future label . . . Instant would recoup all their investment (our salaries and the cost of the demo production) from off the top – the advance – of whatever record deal they could get us. I would have approval of any such prospective deal. I didn't have any management or legal advice when considering this offer. It sounded OK to me. I figured how could I lose, given that Instant only had a few months to find me a deal or our agreement would expire . . . I think the chances are pretty good that [Gottehrer] knew all along that Sire, the label he'd cofounded with his friend Seymour [Stein], was pretty much a sure thing for us . . . He even ended up sharing with Seymour Stein half the publishing royalties he was due, by my contract with Instant, from all the songs I wrote that are on my Sire album, *Blank Generation*. Since song-composition (as opposed to performance/recording artist's) royalties are divided equally between the writers and publishers, that means that the pair of them were and are paid a combined total of 25 per cent of the songs' royalties, for the entire life of the songs' copyrights.

Hell's naive view was that 'all of these papers I was signing were limited in their duration anyway. They covered only the first few records and I figured I'd bring out a new record every year indefinitely.'* But there was nothing limited about the duration of the publishing copyrights. Gottehrer and Thau probably thought that (ex-)junkie Hell would not live long enough to throw any rocks at them. In fact Hell cleaned up his

---

* Hell's 1979 single 'I'm Your Man', a self-conscious remake of an old gospel, 'Seated At The Kingdom', suggested the songs were already drying up.

ways in the early eighties, at which point he realized he had been cleaned out by 'record business gangsters'. He would later pursue both Gottehrer and Thau for lost royalties. He also went after the latter in song, with no attempt to spare his feelings, in the hilarious 'Memo To Marty' on 1992's *Dimstars*: 'You're such a parasite fuck/Your soul's a slimy half-buck . . . You oughta be in prison/Drinking manly jism.'

By then, Thunders had gone to meet his personal hellhound, an event memorialized by Hell and Quine at a Tim Buckley tribute concert with a rewritten version of 'Chinese Rocks'. Hell was reclaiming *his* song.* Not that Johnny's sister was taking any notice; she claimed her share of her brother's publishing, even as she sold every shitty cassette of a Heartbreakers show she could find.

Meanwhile, the manager who had presided over the demise of the Dolls and Sid's rush to final judgement released a steady stream of product for punk's plentiful ghouls. However, Vicious was no songwriter. His greatest contribution to the words and music of popular song were the two rewrites he inserted into his ironic incantation of Paul Anka's 'My Way', showing off both his homophobia and a foul tongue. 'I'm not a queer' and 'There were times when there was fuck all else to do' entitled him to no bounty, dead or alive.

What wives and girlfriends, mothers and sisters really needed was a stiff songwriter. In this sense at least, Deborah Curtis was not left holding the baby when husband Ian decided life was but a joke and he was the village idiot. He had even bequeathed Joy Division their next single, 'Ceremony' b/w 'In A Lonely Place', issued under their next nom de plume, New Order. The widow, meanwhile, wrote her own memoir of the man, including at the end of it seventeen Ian Curtis lyrics to songs Joy Division never recorded, perhaps as a hint to others that they could finish them (as others later would with the 'lost notebooks' of Hank Williams and Woody Guthrie).

---

* Ten years later, he finally released his original mid-seventies demo, credited to just the *two* songwriters.

But the only band capable of doing so were no longer living in the past. No sooner had Joy Division issued their double-album epitaph to their former leader, *Still* – as in a bootleg still – than they were on the receiving end of a most unlikely worldwide hit (and a new direction home). 'Blue Monday' was to chart twice in the UK, selling over a million copies domestically while also topping *Billboard*'s Hot Dance Club Play charts. What no one in the band could agree on is where the song actually came from.

According to Peter Hook, 'We stole it off a Donna Summer B-side.'* Keyboardist Gillian Gilbert believed 'Peter Hook's bassline was nicked from an Ennio Morricone film soundtrack,' while the song itself was 'meant to be robotic, the idea being that we could walk on stage and do it without playing the instruments ourselves. We spent days trying to get a robot voice to sing "How does it feel?"' The most famous line in rock music, claimed Gilbert, 'came about because [Bernard Sumner] was fed up with journalists asking him how he felt'. Only it was Bob Dylan who wrote the line, for the very same reason.

Sumner also claimed to have taken elements of the arrangement from 'Dirty Talk', by Klein + M.B.O., and the signature bassline from Sylvester's disco classic, 'You Make Me Feel (Mighty Real)'; while the long intro was sampled from a Kraftwerk song, 'Uranium'. Quite a list. In fact, the one and only original part of 'Blue Monday' seems to be the drum pattern – though even that part was apparently mere serendipity:

**Bernard Sumner**: Steve [Morris] had bought a drum machine, but we couldn't get the sequencer to talk to it. Through [producer] Martin Hannett, we'd gotten to know this scientist called Martin Usher, so I took the sequencer and drum machine to him, and he designed a circuit that could make them speak to each other. The day that we wrote ['Blue Monday'] was the day that we brought the circuit in, hooked it all up and pressed 'GO' on the drum

---

* He meant 'Our Love', actually a 1980 A-side, just not one that charted.

machine, then the synthesiser started chattering away, and some-how it all worked.

Seemingly, the only song on their Walkmans from which Sumner and co. didn't admit taking elements was eponymous indie single, 'Gerry And The Holograms'. But if 'Blue Monday' had a specific starting point, it was this obscure Mancunian slice of electronica, released on Absurd Records in 1979, when Joy Division were still a Buzzcocks support act. The similarities pass the single-listen test with ease (hence various internet postings with titles like, 'New Order Stole "Blue Monday" from Gerry and The Holograms').

Except there was a key difference – 'Gerry And The Holograms' was a piss-take, a send-up of the New Electronica by arch satirist of sound C.P. Lee, of Albertos Y Los Trios Paranoias, and his friend, John Scott. All the members of Joy Division knew the man from Albertos – and his sense of humour. (For those who didn't get the joke, the second Gerry And The Holograms single was called 'The Emperor's New Music'. The record was deliberately unplayable, being a mis-pressed Slaughter And The Dogs single glued to the inside of the sleeve.)

Even after the Pistols' January 1978 dissolution in the hippy hellhole that was Winterland, Rotten's initial idealism had still not been tainted to the point where he was prepared to abandon his belief 'no song is ever written entirely on your own . . . By the time it's been slagged [off], other people have put their ideas into it . . . [and] made it what it is.' The songs of Public Image Limited, the band he formed with two friends and an expat Canadian drummer, would be credited first to 'PiL' (1978–80), then to whoever was in the revolving-door band at the time (1981–2), and finally to whoever John Lydon (né Rotten) was speaking to at the time.

By 1985, he was crediting most songs to a wholly unmusical individ-ual – himself – and his producer, Bill Laswell. The members of the band he had toured the world with – as a plastic PiL – for the past two years were given just two three-way splits and two 50-50 splits on the resultant *Album*. As a result, the nth incarnation of PiL split.*

The change did not go unnoticed among the post-no wave US bands who had taken early post-punk statements from PiL at face value, and were equally inspired by Joy Division – whose credits for both albums read 'words and music by Joy Division', even though Curtis was the band's solitary wordman. In fact, the three biggest rock bands to emerge between post-punk and Grunge – REM, U2 and Nirvana – all consciously adopted the egalitarian model of the Pistols and early PiL, as would the band whose subatomic approach would prove almost as pervasive as these populist purveyors of punk's verités: Sonic Youth. Only one of the above would break the golden rule when success came, and they would be the most short-lived.

After 'Blue Monday', Joy Division's surviving trio got on with making music that would have had fellow Factory-worker Curtis revolving in his cottonspinnin' grave. But New Order would still serve as an inspiration to one survivor of another band whose frontman had a proclivity to try to top himself when the women in his life became too much to bear. David Grohl would show hidden depths in the song department with the Foo Fighters, while protecting the legacy of Nirvana from those who would pick apart its bones. And he would do so despite surrendering 80 per cent of his share of the song publishing after the band had come up with the *Dark Side of The Moon* of Grunge, *Nevermind* (1991).

In April 1992, in what must rank as one of the worst business decisions of the post-punk era, Grohl and Krist Novoselic reluctantly agreed to let Kurt retrospectively renegotiate the three-way split on Nirvana's publishing. The sword of Damocles that he hung over their heads was a threat to break up the band if he did not get his way. In fact, as with any teenage brat, the only way to play this game was to call his petulant bluff.

Cobain's so-called punk ideals counted for naught when the records started selling. He even turned on the band's lawyer, Alan Mintz, for

---

* After writing the first history of PiL back in 1988, I received letters from two ex-members from this era bemoaning the lack of credit.

being there when the trio had reached their original agreement to divide the publishing equally à la the Pistols, and for drafting that agreement in legalese. (Mintz's own privileged view was that 'once [the success of] *Nevermind* was playing itself out, Kurt began to realize that [publishing contracts] weren't just theoretical documents; that this was real money.') Rosemary Carroll, the lawyer who replaced Mintz, believes, 'Kurt decided afterwards that he wrote all the songs – the music, the lyrics, everything. Once it became clear to him how significant the publishing money was, he wanted what was his.' I me mine, times three.

On the face of it, Kurt's stance was fair enough. He *did* write the songs, even if the band as a whole arranged them. Except he was looking to change the past as well as the future. And the revised split, leaving aside any element of blackmail, verged on extortion. Grohl and Novoselic went from equal shares of 33 per cent to Cobain claiming 100 per cent of the lyrics and 75 per cent of the music. They were left with just 12½ per cent of the publishing to divide between themselves. Which means they each gave up 25 per cent of the publishing on an eighteen million-seller, with added *Bleach* – in exchange for a 6¼ per cent share of the publishing on 'I Hate Myself And Want To Die'.

Grohl and Novoselic knew it was a gamble. And they nearly did call Cobain's bluff. For much of spring 1992 it was touch and go whether Nirvana would carry on. But when the pair agreed to a deed which would empty both their bank accounts, they imagined there would be plenty more green bills to come.

Cobain, though, was already driving ninety miles an hour down a dead-end street. And unlike Curtis, he was fast running out of quality songs about the experience. In fact, his next career move was to turn the ear-splitting volume down and play some of his favourite tunes by David Bowie, Meat Puppets and Vaselines, before climaxing an hour-long MTV *Unplugged* with a coruscating version of what he described as a Leadbelly song.

Except 'In The Pines' (a.k.a. 'Where Did You Sleep Last Night?') was never a Leadbelly song. It was not even a song he had cleverly tweaked from its traditional source. Not only did Huddie do the famous folksong straight, but the first recovery of 'In The Pines' had been by Cecil Sharp from Lizzie Abner in 1917; while Frank C. Brown obtained a long text from Pearl Webb in North Carolina that included both the 'in the pines' couplet and the 'longest train' couplet just half a decade later. The first commercial recording using the 'longest train' phrase in the title was the Teneva Ramblers' 'The Longest Train I Ever Saw' 78 in 1927, by which time 'In The Pines' had already been recorded by Dock Walsh, Darby and Tarlton and Clayton McMichen.

Cobain nonetheless gave all the credit to Huddie Ledbetter, proving considerably more generous with the publishing of a dead songster than with his so-called bosom buddies, even if such generosity was down to ignorance, not any inbuilt moral compass. In 1989, having discovered the recordings of Leadbelly – as the likes of Dylan and Van Morrison had done before him and taking Folkways' fanciful song-credits at face value – he began to believe he had found the raw core of contemporary song. However, as was revealed to English journalist Everett True, his impression of the singular songster was as confused as his vision of Punk:

> **Kurt Cobain**: Leadbelly was this poor black man in the early 1900s who went to jail a few times for wife beating and robbery and getting into fights and bootlegging liquor. While he was in prison, he started playing the guitar, and he sang so well that the governor started to like him and let him out of jail. Leadbelly became an apprentice with Blind Lemon Jefferson and started recording songs, but none of the commercial recordings he made ever captured his true essence, except for his last sessions. [1992]

Cobain may have imbued Leadbelly with the combined mystique of every Delta bluesman he could name, Jefferson included, yet in describing a singer prone to 'wife beating and robbery and . . . bootlegging liquor', he seemed to be talking more about himself. If his own journals are any indication, he only ever heard *The Last Sessions*, a 1953 Folkways collection from 1948 home tapes, one of just three pre-punk LPs (along with the US-only *Meet The Beatles* and The Stooges' third best album, *Raw Power*) included in his personal Top Fifty.

Kurt decided to stop at Huddie. His investigations into the fifty years of recorded song B.P. (before Punk) started and stopped with an ex-convict songster who, great as he was, was only the tip of a veritable iceberg of Anglo-Americana.

Even Leadbelly's *Last Sessions*, which he was played by Mark Lanegan of the Screaming Trees, and then recording with him 'Black Girl (Where Did You Sleep Last Night?)' (as Leadbelly called it) in August 1989, was hardly primo Ledbetter. Punk was not originally about deleting all reference points. It was about getting back to basics, to roots as real as a Robert Johnson 78, and – contrary to the norm in an industry of jackals and magpies – being honest in all of one's dealings. But the impressionable Kurt couldn't see through the Year Zero schtick, so he never heard the echo of yesteryear in everything The Stooges, the Sex Pistols, The Clash and the Velvets did. And because he never learned to dig below the surface, his songs were never going to till the land of song long enough to form a dynasty of Grunge. Hence, his (and his spouse's) determination to get the publishing back at any cost.

He still took someone else's teen spirit with him into the next set of Nirvana sessions (along with a copy of The Pixies' *Surfer Rosa*, hoping 'to write the ultimate pop song . . . [by] trying to rip off the Pixies'). But if 'Smells Like Teen Spirit' fused pop and grunge, any further exploration of Americana was short-circuited by success. So much so that when he returned to the inspirational Leadbelly song for his desolate 'howling at the moon' finale to that November 1993 *Unplugged* performance – a raw wail of pain probably directed at an absentee (Courtney) Love, the ultimate beneficiary of Cobain's double-dealing – he found the well was dry and life stinks.

That version would be released with almost indecent haste after Cobain's suicide, still credited to Ledbetter. And when Grohl, Love and Novoselic okayed the release of three more 'Leadbelly' covers on a 2004 Nirvana boxed set, all of them – even 'Ain't It A Shame', a song recorded by Uncle Dave Macon in 1926 – were credited to Blind Lemon's 'apprentice'. It seems Cobain's estate – overseen by the woman the other two blamed for Cobain's change of heart and song-credits in 1992 – had no problem paying a dead song snatcher (or, more accurately, the estate of Moe Asch, head bootlegger at the Folkways family of labels) the publishing on a traditional song. In truth, Cobain was paying his posthumous dues for learning how to howl like Huddie – the original punk.

CHAPTER 17

# 1953–2013: A Thief Can Only Steal From You . . .

*Featuring*: 'Black Waterside'; 'Hey Joe'; 'No Woman No Cry'; 'You Send Me'; 'Caldonia'; 'Let The Good Times Roll'; 'Band Of Gold'; 'Fever'; 'Rubber Ball'; 'Why Do Fools Fall In Love?'; 'Another Day'; 'Mansion On The Hill'; 'The Boxer'; 'Bridge Over Troubled Water'; 'My Way'; 'Life On Mars'; 'I'm Not There'; 'Wanted Man'; 'Ballad Of Easy Rider'; 'Love In Vain'; 'Stop Breaking Down'; 'This Land Is Your Land'

> 'It didn't bother me. It still doesn't *really* bother me. There's the effort of doing these things – you'd get diverted from your normal course of events. You'd be as well to give up music and start suing people! If you want to make your living that way, it's what beckons you.'
>
> Bert Jansch, on why he never sued Jimmy Page for utilising his arrangement of 'Black Waterside'

Leadbelly would have been mystified to find himself listed as the author of 'Black Girl (Where Did You Sleep Last Night)', a song he recorded first for Folkways in the forties and which was initially credited as 'Trad. Arr. Leadbelly'. *He* certainly knew it was an old folksong handed down from time immemorial. But fifty years after his death it had been transmuted into a Leadbelly original by Folkways Music Inc., who duly collected on Kurt Cobain's coruscating cover.

Even in its heyday there still existed a certain honour among folk revivalists, a code as regards credit which most everyone adhered to. It meant both Bert Jansch and Martin Carthy were reluctant to claim 'ownership' of their arrangements of 'Black Waterside' and 'Scarborough

Fair', even though one or the other would serve to replenish the already-ample coffers of Jimmy Page or Paul Simon. By the nineties – now all songwriters could read and write – credit stealing from living artists had become increasingly difficult. But one could still lay claim to a chunk of the continuum of song. If the folk memory has always been an unreliable witness, certain music publishers of the post-oral era happily staked a right to material the actual author had been too uninterested, too poor or born too long ago to copyright. There was always an Alan Lomax or Pete Seeger waiting in the wings.

Lomax knew full well how authors attached themselves to old songs that appealed to the folk. The process was nothing new; nor was it exclusive to the New World. The likes of Henry VIII ('Greensleeves'), Anne Boleyn ('O Death Rock Me Asleep') and James V of Scotland ('The Gaberlunzie Man') had all received credit for songs they almost certainly did not pen but which seemed to fit with the character of these historical figures.

Nor were the Guthries or the Seegers first to apply a broadside moralism to all they found in tradition, placing a political spin on an earlier lyric, hoping to receive credit for songs they had simply manhandled. Any list of beneficiaries from posterity's largesse should include the most notorious blackletter balladeer of all, the seventeenth century publican Martin Parker, a figure well-known for putting his name to almost anything.

And yet the only one of 'his' songs to survive the centuries appeared anonymously, at the height of the English Civil War. 'When The King Enjoys His Own Again' was not perhaps the wisest sentiment for an ex-publican living in London in the 1640s to express in song. If he did write it, Parker certainly wasn't about to take credit, which is why we may be beholden to a passing reference in a 1647 tract for the suggestion – now universally adopted – that it was Parker who 'penn'd that sweet ballad'.*

There have always been literary figures who take delight in penning

---

\* The song's appearance in the Skene manuscript, a Scottish musical collection generally considered to predate the Civil War, casts doubt on such an attribution.

(or adapting) a song, but then go out of their way to deny authorship. A number of snatches in the plays of Shakespeare may well be his, or at least rewritten by him, but he attached no more proprietorial claim to them than he did to the rest of his oral canon. And though James Johnson gave Robert Burns no less than twenty namechecks in the credits for the fifth of the six-volume *Scots Musical Museum* (1787–1803), he did not put his name alongside 'Auld Lang Syne'. Indeed, in Burns's interleaved notes to a copy of the *Museum*, he described the words now attributed to him as 'the original and by much the best set of words', his way of distinguishing them from Allan Ramsay's botched rewrite.

The first published version of 'Black Waterside', the song Bert Jansch revised and restored to vibrant oral tradition, also dates back to Burns's folk-collecting, appearing in the fourth volume of the *Scots Musical Museum*. The song in question, here entitled 'As I Went Out Ae May Morning', was 'communicated to [the editor James] Johnson by Burns, in the poet's own handwriting [and] *some of the verses seem to have been retouched by our bard*' (my italics), or so John Stenhouse asserted in his five hundred pages of 'notes' to the 1853 edition.

Ballad scholars are still arguing about how much Burns retouched the likes of 'Tam Lin' – perhaps the greatest of all Scottish ballads and a lynch-pin of *Liege & Lief*, Fairport's 1969 folk-rock foray – before he passed it on to Johnson; but his is the one Fairport adopted. Or how much Bishop Percy (or his Scottish literary correspondent, Lord Dalrymple) tinkered with (the ending to) 'Edward', a ballad of fratricide that in Percy's version alluded to a heinous motive, incest. Perhaps because such songs lend themselves to being reapplied to current events (cf. the earlier discussion of 'Frankie and Johnny'), murder-ballads in general seem to have undergone more anonymous reworking than any other genre in popular song.

As a matter of fact, a song covered by sixties luminaries like Jimi Hendrix, Arthur Lee's Love and The Byrds is little more than a clever rewrite/update of the traditional 'Edward' murder-ballad Percy published. That song is 'Hey Joe'.

'Hey Joe' is generally credited to Billy Roberts, a California-based folksinger, guitarist and harmonica player from the West Coast coffee-house circuit. But it has been asserted by Scottish folksinger Len Partridge that he helped Roberts write the song when both were playing Edinburgh folk clubs in the mid-fifties. Certainly, somebody with a hand in its composition knew their Scottish murder ballads. As it happens, Roberts may not have benefited greatly from its subsequent success. He reportedly assigned his rights to the singer Dino Valenti – to whom the song is mysteriously attributed on both The Byrds' and Love's 1966 recordings – and who was then languishing in jail in need of funds.

Hendrix's version, though learnt from Tim Rose – who promptly claimed a co-credit, just as he had for Bonnie Dobson's solo composition, 'Morning Dew', on the same eponymous 1967 debut LP – restored the Roberts credit. He – or more likely, his manager Chas Chandler – evidently knew 'Hey Joe' was originally copyrighted (back in 1962) to the otherwise anonymous West Coast folksinger. And ex-Animal Chandler was probably heartily tired of those people who knew the price of everything and the roots of nothing claiming something in the public domain.

For it is not only in the oral era that questionable attributions of authorship have been asserted from the other side of the grave. The stakes in today's 'life plus seventy' era of publishing copyrights couldn't be higher, and some of the claimants' moral fibre couldn't be lower.*

Even Bob Dylan eventually found himself bad-mouthed by another (ex-) songwriter who felt twenty-two years was not enough time to forgive and forget. In January 1986, Irish songster Dominic Behan instigated a lengthy correspondence with *The Guardian* and the readers of its letters page by once again raking up the past, after learning 'that Bob Dylan

---

* The copyight term of seventy years after author's death, introduced into the 1976 Copyright Act, is only supposed to apply to works created after January 1, 1978. All pre-1978 works – *if* still under copyright – were copyrighted for a fixed term of seventy-five years, arbitraily extended by a further twenty years in 1998 in memory of Sonny Bono, of spousal-Cher fame. Still wonderin' why the US has more lawyers per head of population than any similar country?

thought bootlegged work was "outrageous." Bob should know about such piracy . . . [His] "God On Our Side" takes music lock, stock and barrel and very nearly the words [of my song in what] is a complete parody of "The Patriot Game."'

Behan went so far as to insist, 'It is . . . an original tune – as original as any of Ewan MacColl's.' It wasn't 'original'. It was a straight steal, as Dylan's was. But far from being a 'complete parody' of Behan's, Dylan sought 'to broaden the subject matter from the specific to a wider scrutiny of jingoism and imperialism in the name of sectarian religion', as one part-time poet pointed out.

This can of worms would be Dominic's diet for the next six weeks as assorted readers pointed out Behan's song was itself set to a version of 'The Grenadier and the Lady', or, if he preferred, 'The Nightingale'. Both sprang forth from tradition's tree. That part-time poet Roy Kelly found it 'interesting that Dominic Behan's appropriation of a traditional tune places him [to his mind] in the folk process, whereas Bob Dylan becomes a mere plagiarist'. Dylan cared not a jot.

By 2006, Dylan was less inclined to cast himself as a 'thief of thoughts', even though he found himself on the receiving end of another copycat charge when another broadsheet with an even more liberal readership, the *New York Times*, one September day asked the question, 'Who's · This Guy Dylan Who's Borrowing Lines From Henry Timrod?' It seems Dylan had been dipping into the poetry of that second-rate Civil War wordsmith on his recent chart-topping collection, *Modern Times*. Having in recent years been accused of plagiarizing the works of Jack London and an obscure Japanese gangster memoir, *Confessions of a Yakuza* (1991), one would have expected such an accusation to be as water off a drake's back. But for once he talked back, to *Rolling Stone*:

> **Bob Dylan**: In folk and jazz, quotation is a rich and enriching tradition. That certainly is true. It's true for everybody, but me. There are different rules for me. And as far as Henry Timrod is concerned, have you even heard of him? Who's been reading him

lately? . . . Ask his descendants what they think of the hoopla . . .
It's called songwriting. It has to do with melody and rhythm, and
then after that, anything goes. You make everything yours. We all
do it. [2012]

One thing that could be said in Dylan's defence was that ever since his
difficulties at the end of 1963 he had been careful – real careful. Almost
everything he thought out of copyright *was* out of copyright, almost all
he considered traditional was in the public domain. Almost all. He still
had to lock legal horns with Alan Lomax and Ludlow Music in 1970,
when he recorded 'The Days of '49'.

Another song from the 1870s (being published in 1872), 'The Days of
'49', like 'Tom Dooley', had been recorded in April 1928 by Ralph Peer, on
one of his legendary field trips (this one to El Paso, Texas) from another
'Singing Cowboy', Jules Allen. Still, Ludlow Music insisted that the version included on *Self Portrait* was their property, and initially they got
their way: in 1975, the song was re-copyrighted to those two song snatchers, Alan Lomax and Frank Warner.

However, the very idea evidently offended Dylan and/or his manager, because when the song was re-released on *Bootleg Series 10* (2013)
in stripped-down form, from the same 1970 session, it restored the original copyright credit, 'Traditional Arranged Bob Dylan'. And on the
same collection, Dylan also took back 'Wild Mountain Thyme', a song
the McPeake family had been claiming since the mid-fifties on behalf of
Francis McPeake.

When Van Morrison had recorded the song in 1973, he gave the
McPeakes credit. But when the Irish clan threatened to sue Rod Stewart
for his arrangement in 1990, they found that the gravel-voiced singer had
done his homework and knew it dated back to at least 1818, when it was
published under the title, 'The Braes of Balquhidder'. In fact, the only
part that appeared to originate with McPeake was the bridge, 'If my true
love she won't come, I will surely find another . . .', and even that was reliant on the lexicon of general tradition. Stewart's publisher was also able to

show an impressive list of previous artists, The Byrds included, who had recorded the song as 'traditional'.

Meanwhile, Dylan seemed determined to 'return to tradition' songs that had never been traditional, even as he wrote sleeve-notes which blatantly contradicted any such attribution. As writer's block came round again in the early nineties he once again took certain liberties with tradition itself, setting about recording two albums of 'traditional music' in 1992 and 1993. Each included songs by known authors, some of them still technically in copyright.

The Mississippi Sheiks were particularly hard done by. Dylan recorded three of their songs, 'World Gone Wrong', 'Blood In My Eye' and, most impertinently of all, 'Sitting On Top Of The World', crediting all of them as 'traditional'. Yet in the sleeve-notes to 1993's *World Gone Wrong* he gave the credit for the latter two to the Sheiks – whom he described as 'a little known de facto group whom in their former glory must've been something to behold'.

In the same notes, 'Broke Down Engine' was called 'a Blind Willie McTell masterpiece', as indeed it was, having been recorded by the man at least four times in 1930, 1933 and 1949, though it was first recorded by Lonnie Clark in 1929. But it was still copyrighted as a traditional arrangement, and as such helped fulfil the terms of Dylan's recording contract while giving him a half-share of the publishing.

A few diehard folkies did more than bat their eyelids at Dylan's wanton temerity, complaining loud and hard that he had 'stolen' the arrangements of 'Arthur McBride' and 'Canade-I-O' from Paul Brady and Nic Jones respectively. But the only song from these two well-received collections to catch out Dylan was the broadside ballad, 'Jim Jones'; here, a tune he had assumed was traditional turned out to be entirely the work of Aussie folkie Mick Slocum, who had wisely rejected the traditional dirge for one he could call his own. Dylan held his hands up and paid up.

He seemed less inclined to take on the Robert Johnson estate. The one Johnson song ('32-20 Blues') he recorded for *World Gone Wrong* was left off the album, and when it did finally appear on 2010's *Tell-Tale Signs* was credited to Johnson, not Skip James, the true author of '22-20 Blues'. By then, he and his publisher knew all about the way first Steve LaVere, and then Johnson's bastard son Claud, had set about claiming Johnson's copyrights for their own.

It would take Claud Johnson nine years of shuttling between the Chancery Court and the Supreme Court of Mississippi before it was decided he was 'the biological son and sole heir' of the blues singer, and thus entitled to an estate valued in 1998 at an estimated $1.3 million. As *Vanity Fair* feature-writer Frank Diacomo incredulously revealed in a 2008 article on the squabbles over Johnson's estate: 'The decision was based not on DNA evidence but on an unusual bit of sworn testimony by the elderly Eula Mae Williams, a childhood friend of Claud Johnson's mother, Virgie Jane Smith Cain . . . [who] testified that she had watched Cain and Robert Johnson having sex in a wooded area in the spring of 1931, which, nine months later, led to the birth of Claud.'

Even before this Robert Johnson, a magnificent reworker of third-hand tradition, had become the *auteur* and copyright-holder for unauthorized reinterpretations of the works of near contemporaries like Skip James, Leroy Carr and Bo Chatmon. Now, some fifty years after Robert drank the wrong strange brew, the real winner of this misbegotten lottery was the son of someone he barely knew (except in the biblical sense), raising afresh the whole issue of who 'owns' any composite of communal compositions.

Predictably, in the world's most litigious society, that was a conversation for the courts, where layers of obfuscation and opportunism could sully the name of the most righteous song snatcher. Johnson's ostensible publisher – King of Spades Music, a moniker chosen by the WASPish LaVere – was determined to see in the new millennium by claiming all twenty-nine of Robert's recordings as original works under the definition of the latest US Copyright Act. LaVere intended to enforce 'his' rights, too. As he himself said, 'Now . . . that CBS recognizes that my publishing company is the legitimate copyright owner . . . we have a chance at going after some of the other big dogs.' So it was that a US appeal court decided in June 2000 that The Rolling Stones had 'improperly borrowed' two Robert Johnson songs, 'Love In Vain' and 'Stop Breakin' Down', among the most valuable songs in the 'Johnsonian' oeuvre.

The underlying irony of all this is that because LaVere copyrighted Johnson's songs under the 1976 Copyright Act, and not the 1909 act they should have been copyrighted under, most if not all of Johnson's twenty-nine songs actually qualified as 'unauthorized derivative works', if only the estates of Skip James, Leroy Carr, etc. had beneficiaries willing to pursue it. This 2000 judgment should actually have resulted in suits by the estates of Blind Lemon Jefferson, whose 'Dry Southern Blues' provided the final verse of 'Love In Vain', and Buddy Moss, whose 'Stop Hanging Around' was the Stones' true template. But neither Jefferson nor Moss *had* estates. Instead it was Johnson who had become posterity's poster-boy. As Robert Gordon put it, in an authoritative *L.A. Weekly* account of the Johnson shenanigans, 'Leroy Carr, Kokomo Arnold, Tommy Johnson and people whose names we don't even know have weeds instead of memorial stones on their graves. But Johnson has the myth.'

In fact, when ABKCO's attorney Donald Zakarin strenuously argued both songs were 'part of a common musical library used by many artists working in the Depression-era South', and that, 'virtually none of the blues music then was copyrighted by *anyone*', he was using the right legal argument but the wrong approach. He may have known his law, but he knew not his folklore.

Johnson had used the same method as those artists who were 'part of a common musical library', but 'his' lyrics and melodies had already been modified and rendered as individual property by the commercial blues artists who came before him, making them 'unauthorized derivative works'. Nonetheless, the Ninth Circuit Court of Appeals, in its infinite wisdom, decided ABKCO Music were wrong to assume songs by Johnson were in the public domain – which they indubitably *were* when both songs were released – simply because his record company failed to register the copyright in the 1930s.

The illegitimate Claud, who promptly founded the Robert Johnson Blues Foundation to 'honour' the memory of the one pre-war bluesman every music fan already knows, wasn't greatly concerned about honouring the bluesmen who came before. He wanted to separate his presumed father from a unique milieu when performers were authors of the moment they recorded on disc, while the songs stayed the common property of a constant continuum of creativity. It was all about a man called Johnson.

If Johnson Senior unmistakably shaped the songs he appropriated, and perhaps should be entitled to a part-share even fifty years after the fact, it should never have been one rule for his estate and another for every other great Delta bluesman. Likewise, Woody Guthrie indisputably wrote the words to 'This Land Is Your Land', which made him entitled to 50 per cent of the publishing. But his beneficiaries – and the publisher that administered his work – wanted it all. And when this song took on a life of its own, the ever-avaricious Ludlow Music sought to ensure the original king of protest enjoyed his own again, and again.

Bruce Springsteen, who had been playing the song at his shows since reinventing himself as a man of the soil in 1981, released the song on his monstrous five-album live set, *Live 1975–85*, and gave Guthrie's estate its due and then some. Dylan also coughed up when using 'This Land Is Your Land' on a 2005 'soundtrack CD' to the *No Direction Home* film even though the tune was part of the continuum, and as such not copyrightable. (Lonnie Donegan had already set a legal precedent by taking an arrangement credit on the tune/s, giving Guthrie just the words.)

Guthrie never claimed to have written the tune to 'This Land Is Your Land' – or anything else. He was a poet of the proletariat, content to mine his forefathers' songs to his socialist core. As it turned out, no one needed to pay his estate a penny. And no one knew, until Ludlow were hoist by their own pettiness after 'This Land Is Your Land' became the shuttlecock in a lawsuit between Guthrie's greedy publisher and a popular satirical website.

Its public domain status only came to light because during the 2004 presidential campaign the website JibJab featured a parody of Guthrie's song in which Senator John Kerry sang 'You're a right wing nut job!' and George W. Bush sang, 'You're a liberal sissy!', before both sang, 'This land will surely vote for me!' As *CNN* noted at the time:

> The bit is hilarious. Unless you are The Richmond Organization, a music publisher that owns the copyright to Guthrie's tune through its Ludlow Music unit. 'This puts a completely different spin on the song,' said Kathryn Ostien, director of copyright licensing for the publisher. 'The damage to the song is huge.' TRO believes that the JibJab creation threatens to corrupt Guthrie's classic – an icon of Americana – by tying it to a political joke; upon hearing the music people would think about the yucks, not Guthrie's unifying message.

Ms Ostien's self-righteous response suggested she not only knew diddley-squat about the song's origins, but did not seem to have bothered reading Guthrie's lyrics. A song that began life as a satire on Irving Berlin's 'God Bless America' now had a 'unifying message' that could be 'damaged' by an act of satire. The greatest song-satirist this side of the folk revival would probably have coughed up his lungs at the absurdity of it all. But the po-faced Ms Ostien was deadly serious, just not much of a music historian.

As we know, Ludlow, part of TRO (The Richmond Organization), had no claim on the tune to which the website satirist had set its lyrics, it not being Guthrie's in the first place. As for the lyrics, satire has its own exemption under copyright law, covered by the umbrella commonly called 'fair usage' or fair dealing. But it now turned out Dylan and Springsteen didn't need to pay the posthumous piper either; because, when JibJab looked into the matter, it turned out the copyright to the original 1945 publication had expired in 1973 and had not been renewed, as was then required under US copyright law.

TRO now had to fight a rearguard action to claim *any* copyright, which they did by asserting that although the 1945 version was now public domain, subsequent versions from 1956 and later were not. (All were self-evidently the same song, and therefore not entitled to separate publishing copyright.)

Having long specialized in asserting copyright on songs which they claimed were in 'the public domain' when they self-evidently were not, TRO found themselves in an unfamiliar position. After all, for many years their founder's most famous lawsuit, back in 1954, had been that concerning 'Tzena Tzena Tzena', the supposedly traditional A-side of The Weavers' 'Goodnight Irene', brought by Mills Music on behalf of its actual author, Issachar Miron.

TRO founder Howard Richmond didn't merely defend the suit, he counter-claimed that 'Tzena' 'was in the public domain for many years prior to [Miron's] alleged composition . . . [that its author, Miron] first learned of the musical composition when it was broadcast extensively over the radio . . . [and that he] conspired with [his] attorney to enter into agreements . . . for the purpose of asserting claims against defendant [i.e. Richmond] for the profits defendant earned as a result of defendant's exploitation of the song'.

In fact, the mendacious Richmond knew all along the song had been written by Miron, an ex-Israeli soldier, back in 1941 and had been first published Stateside in *Songs of Israel* (1949). So did the New York district court judge who heard the case. He soon saw through Richmond's tissue of lies, deciding the case in favour of Miron; after which the published opinion on the case delivered one of the most damning portraits of a music publisher in the dusty annals of US copyright law:

> Howard Richmond is the general manager of the defendant corporation, Cromwell Music Inc. The [copyright] infringement by the defendant was deliberate. Its own claim to the copyright of 'Tzena' was conceived in fraud and was presented to the music publishing and recording world in the double fraud of concealing the name of the real composer of 'Tzena' and asserting a claim of

authorship in the name of a fictitious person, Spencer Ross, under which the corporation's general manager, Howard Richmond, was masquerading.

TRO – a publisher still evidently cast in its founder's image – would also be party to one of the most protracted, and lucrative, suits of the new millennium. It centred around just how much one particular pop hit was beholden to a semi-traditional, nominally authored 'folk song' from which Pete Seeger, on behalf of The Weavers, had (also) taken a motif or three.

But before that matter could be adjudicated, another kangaroo court sat to decide if copyright could be applied to another 'folk song' with a folk author. In this case it was 'Kookaburra (Sits In The Old Gum Tree)', a five-bar snippet of which appeared in the 1981 (ninety-three-bar) pop song 'Down Under' by Australian combo, Men At Work.

'Kookaburra' was assumed by most Aussies to be as much communally theirs as 'Waltzing Matilda'. The global number one had quite self-consciously lapsed into this little motif in order to amplify the song's underlying message, 'I come from a land down under.' What better way to do that than to 'reference' this well-known Aussie folk tune?

Except, inevitably, it turned out that this old folk tune had actually been written in 1937 by a Girl Guide leader, Marion Sinclair, and under Australian law was still in copyright. The copyright-holder, Larrikin Music, was determined to seize the day – unlike Ms Sinclair, who lived until 1988 but did nothing about the 'melodic homage' – after it had been purchased by Bob Wise's Music Sales, ever looking for another payday and with a deft disregard for moral rights. Only at this juncture did Larrikin Music decide to pursue the matter, finally winning the legal argument in February 2009.

However, much to Wise's chagrin, having petitioned the court for 40 per cent of the song's total publishing revenue, Larrikin were awarded just 5 per cent. The judge realized this snatch of melody was hardly instrumental in the song's success. It could have been worse. Larrikin could and perhaps should have had their case thrown out on the grounds that 'Kookaburra' may not have been a traditional Australian folksong, after all. It sure sounded like a Welsh folksong, 'Wele ti'n eistedd aderyn du?' Fortunately for them, no one could prove said song existed prior to 1937, because it had only been transmitted through oral tradition; while Marion Sinclair was conveniently dead, and could not be questioned on the matter.

Also conveniently dead was Solomon Linda, the Zulu singer from South Africa who in 1939 – two years after Sinclair 'wrote' 'Kookaburra' – had recorded what appeared to be a traditional Zulu chant about hunting lions. Since Linda had signed away all rights to the song and its publishing the day he recorded it for the label of Eric Gallo, he gave very little thought as to how much of 'Mbube', if any, was 'his' and how much his people's.

Having become a Top Ten hit for The Weavers under the name 'Wimoweh', the song was covered a few times over the next decade, once by Jimmy Dorsey, and Gallo's agreement with TRO held (see earlier). 'Wimoweh' entered 'Kookaburra' territory only in 1961, when George Weiss put a new set of words to the Zulu chant, gave it to doo-wop group The Tokens and called it 'The Lion Sleeps Tonight'. Though what Weiss came up with was later dismissed by Phil Margo, a member of the group, as 'thirty-three words of doggerel', only then did Solomon's snatch of Zulu lore play its part in a genuine worldwide pop phenomenon. 'The Lion Sleeps Tonight' was a number one smash for The Tokens in 1961, and was to do the same for Karl Denver and, twenty years on, for Tight Fit. In the meantime, another Token, Jay Siegel, paid a visit to New York's South African consulate, where he was told 'Wimoweh' 'was derived from a traditional folk song that was used as a hunting song'.

The question is, or was about to be, how much of Solomon Linda's creative juices had leaked into 'The Lion Sleeps Tonight'? Because, as even the most partisan voice in the Linda camp, journalist Rian Malan, admitted in his 2000 *Rolling Stone* piece on the song: '[Weiss had] dismantled the [Weavers'] song, excised all the hollering and screaming, and put the rest back in a new way. The ["Mbube"] chant remained unchanged, but the melody . . . moved to center stage, becoming the tune itself, to which the new words were sung, 'In the jungle, the mighty jungle. . .'"

Unquestionably, the 'Mbube' chant was an integral part of 'The Lion Sleeps Tonight' – as 'Kookaburra' was not when inserted into 'Down Under' – and was still an integral part when Tight Fit repeated The Tokens' trick by taking the song back to number one in 1982. What was still unclear, given that it had not even been registered for copyright in the US, was whether the song properly belonged to Linda or Gallo.

Solomon Linda cared not, having left this world behind in 1962 – still without challenging the copyright or attribution of the song's worldwide copyright. Only in 1989 did details emerge about how Weiss and his co-authors had avoided a suit from the notoriously litigious TRO over 'Wimoweh'; and once again it showed Howie Richmond, the then-boss of TRO, to be as untrustworthy as he was unscrupulous. He had agreed a deal whereby Weiss and co. kept 100 per cent of publishing for 'The Lion Sleeps Tonight' as long as the song was published by TRO, meaning he got his usual 50 per cent for administering it. Richmond had thus cut The Weavers and Gallo out of the equation, while keeping his own share intact, and even increased it by gaining the publishing on 'The Lion Sleeps Tonight', which soon replicated The Tokens' success in England at the hands of Karl Denver.

But in 1990 TRO found itself outmanoeuvred when the song reverted to its ostensible authors under the US 'twenty-eight year rule', and Weiss smartly elected not to renew with TRO. Richmond's house now began 'to depict themselves as the righteous defenders of Solomon Linda's heirs', claiming Weiss and co. were 'seek[ing] to deprive Mr Linda's family of royalties' when it was actually Richmond's family that Weiss was seeking to disenfranchise.

As with TRO's role as 'righteous defender' of Guthrie's patriotic words, the crown of concern sat uneasily on Richmond's head and the arbitrators of the dispute awarded the royalties for 'The Lion Sleeps

Tonight' to Weiss and Co., 'with the agreed proviso that they send 10 per cent of writers' performance royalties to the [Linda] family'. What was less clear was how they were supposed to do this, since the South African copyright at this juncture unequivocally lay with Eric Gallo.

In fact, Linda had never provided the slightest evidence the song was actually his (because legally speaking, it never was). His was a similarly impossible legal position to the one Moon Mullican found himself in after Hank Williams and Fred Rose, the only people who could vouch for his co-authorship of Hank's most valuable copyright, 'Jambalaya', both died. And these are hardly isolated examples.

When Bob Marley got into a dispute with his Jamaican publisher, Cayman Music, in the mid-seventies, he began to attribute some of his most valuable songs to trusted confidants like Leghorn Coghile, the Wailer football coach Skill Cole and the wheelchair-bound Vincent 'Tata' Ford. He was then able to place these songs – which include the likes of 'Natty Dread', 'War', 'Rastaman Vibration' and, most tellingly, 'No Woman No Cry' – with his own Tuff Gong Publishing.

Marley's close friend, rock journalist Vivien Goldman, believes the most famous of reggae songs, 'No Woman No Cry', 'may very well have been a conversation that [Marley and Tata] had sitting around one night. That's the way Bob's creativity worked. In the end it didn't matter. The point is Bob wanted him to have the money.' But whatever arrangement Marley came to with Tata, it wasn't one his widow was about to maintain, and in 1987 she and her husband's former manager, Danny Sims, successfully sued to obtain all royalties and rights to the various songs Marley had put in the names of friends and relatives.

Albert Grossman's widow, Sally, may also have had a claim against Dylan for two songs that he seems to have deliberately disavowed, both written around the time their joint publishing set-up, Dwarf Music, was coming to an end in early 1969. The more famous of the two was Roger McGuinn's 'Ballad of Easy Rider', which Dylan chose not to claim a co-credit on, though that lovely bridge ('The river it flows, flows to the sea . . .') was his, and the song itself became the title-track to an Oscar-nominated movie.

The other song, 'Champaign Illinois', Dylan donated to Carl Perkins and allowed his music publisher, Cedarwood, to administer even though he took a co-credit. Two more songs written in 1968 – 'I'd Have You Anytime' (co-written with George Harrison) and 'Minstrel Boy', a song dating from 'the basement tapes' – which should have been copyrighted to Dwarf Music, were instead assigned to the new company Dylan set up in 1969 on far more advantageous terms, Big Sky Music.*

In fact, throughout the recording era, when there has been at least the prospect of financial reward at the end of the rainbow, successful songwriters have sometimes proven coy about taking credit for all they wrote. And although none of these feared for their head – as the authors of 'Bonnie Earl o' Moray' and 'When The King Enjoys His Own Again' might have – some refused a credit simply to stop another song snatcher in his tracks. The practice of putting one's own song in the name of a relative, a friend or a lover, to stop a predatory publisher from staking a claim goes back to the days of Edison. It was a ruse that soul stirrer Sam Cooke adopted in order to retain ownership of songs when still under contract to Specialty. Using friends' and lovers' names on songs he himself had written, Cooke told these trustees in no uncertain terms he would be keeping every penny, it being 'my fucking money'. Perhaps he made an exception for his own brother, L.C., who was credited with writing the song that made Sam a star, 'You Send Me', when every note was brother Sam's. Cooke put his trust in his brother and was rewarded in kind.

Those who put their trust in their wives were not always so fortunate. Perhaps the most famous instance of a songwriter cuckolded with his own cash was the great fifties jump-blues bandleader, Louis Jordan, who in order to divert funds away from his then-publisher put a number of his more commercial songs in wife Fleecie Moore's name. These included

---

* One suspects Dylan might have been happy to let Harrison take the credit for the former, but Harrison doubtless insisted on the co-credit, if for no other reason than to wind Lennon and McCartney up.

'Let The Good Times Roll' (for which she gets a co-credit) and 'Caldonia', perhaps the two songs for which he is now best remembered. Needless to say, the appeal of these songs lasted a lot longer than the Jordans' rocky marriage, leaving Louis to complain, 'Fleecie Moore's name is on ["Caldonia"], but she didn't have anything to do with it. That was my wife at the time . . . She didn't know nothin' about no music at all. Her name is on this song and that song, and she's still getting money.'

At least Jordan got some good material out of the experience. One imagines Fleecie flashed across his mind the day he penned 'Ain't That Just Like A Woman (They'll Do It Every Time)' or worked up his arrangement of 'I'll Be Glad When You're Dead (You Rascal You)'. Jordan's experience also served as a wider warning. When the great Motown songwriting partnership, Holland-Dozier-Holland, broke away from Motown and set up their own labels, Invictus and Hot Wax, they simply invented an apocryphal songwriter, Edythe Wayne, to whom they assigned the likes of 'Give Me Just A Little More Time' and 'Band of Gold' while a $22 million suit with the ever-grasping Gordy played out.

If Holland-Dozier-Holland were by then experienced songwriters and businessmen who knew their way around a BMI contract, Otis Blackwell was still a little-known R&B singer with a yen to become a songwriter in 1956, when a fellow singer called Eddie Cooley came to him with an idea for a song called 'Fever'. Blackwell and Cooley completed the song together but when Little Willie John took it to the top of the R&B charts, Blackwell had already tied himself to another publisher, Joe Davis. The song was credited to Cooley and Blackwell's stepfather, John Davenport.

In fact, the ongoing feud between ASCAP and BMI through the fifties – which ultimately led to the payola scandal at the end of the decade – meant all songwriters had to nail their colours to the mast of one or the other, so it was generally considered wise to keep one foot in each camp by registering different names, setting up two publishing agreements – one with BMI, the other with ASCAP. This led to quite a few misleading song-credits. Clyde Otis, who was a BMI member, became ASCAP artist Cliff Owens when he co-wrote 'Any Way You Want Me' for Elvis.

An equally cryptic alias was put on the label of 'Rubber Ball'. Bobby Vee's breakthrough hit was (co-)credited to Ann Orlowski, the mother of a better-known songsmith:

**Gene Pitney**: A songwriter in the States affiliates himself with either ASCAP or BMI. When you sign with one of them, you state that you will not belong to the other, but everybody did because publishers always had separate ASCAP and BMI publishing companies. I had two or three hits with BMI, but the publisher wanted to shift some money into an ASCAP firm because of the tax rates on the money that was coming into the different firms. He said, 'We're going to put "Rubber Ball" into my ASCAP firm but we can't put your name on it.' I didn't understand what he was talking about as I was just a songwriter at the time. He said, 'Who do you want to be?' and I said, 'Any name at all?' He said, 'Yes', so I said that my mother's maiden name was Orlowski and it could be [credited to] Ann Orlowski. She got a big kick out of having her name on a hit record but I told her that, in case these people ever came from ASCAP, she was going to have to play 'Rubber Ball' to prove that she wrote it. She had a tremendous ear for music and she could play it on the piano. It was the funniest thing to see my mother sitting down and singing 'bouncy, bouncy' and all the parts to 'Rubber Ball'. She was ready for that knock on the door.

Nor was Ann the only mother of a rock & roller to offer her (pseudo-) songwriting services. According to biographer Ellis Amburn, Buddy Holly's mother, Ella, 'was always writing songs, but Buddy found her lyrics too sweet. She came up with "Maybe Baby" and he worked on it, turning it into what many consider his best song. She refused any credit as her fundamentalist Christian background made her look on rock & roll as the devil's music.' Or perhaps his agent on earth, Norman Petty.

If Mrs Holley didn't need any coaching from her son, only Mrs Orlowski seemed to think she might be called on to explain how she wrote a catchy pop song. Yet this was precisely what at least one name appearing on a major doo-wop hit had to do *under oath*, with hilarious consequences. When Morris Levy was sued by Frankie Lymon's widow in 1984 for back royalties on 'Why Do Fools Fall In Love?', he was pressed to explain on the stand how exactly he made such a telling contribution: 'You get together, you get a beat going, and you put the music and words together. I think I would be misleading you if I said I wrote songs, per se, like Chopin.' Not for the first time, Levy was not taken at his word, and his name was removed.

On the other hand, when Paul McCartney was taken to court by Lew Grade, on behalf of ATV Music, over the shared song-credits he gave to his wife Linda on his second post-Beatle album, *Ram*, and the hit single 'Another Day', Grade found himself wholly unable to prove Paul wrote those songs alone. This mattered because, as Peter Brown states:

> 50 per cent of the publishing rights . . . would go directly into Linda's pocket, bypassing Northern Songs. Lew Grade was furious at what he saw as a deception on Paul's part, for Linda had not been and was obviously not now a musician capable of composing with Paul . . . The essence of Grade's lawsuit was that Linda had no musical ability . . . Paul's lawyers maintained that Linda's musical ability was not the point of the case, and that it was his privilege to compose with absolutely anyone he wanted to compose with, regardless of their musical experience . . . To everybody's surprise and delight . . . Paul and Linda won the suit.

Predictably, no sooner had Paul started 'writing' with his wife than ex-Quarry Man, John, felt compelled to do the same. The difference was that the classically trained Yoko had long considered herself a composer and wanted 'to make my own music'. (In fact, for much of the seventies she was the more prolific partner.) But 'Commercial' was not this lady's middle name. On the one album where husband and wife split the songs equally – 1972's *Sometime In New York City* – sales were so bad Allen

Klein had to negotiate with EMI to ensure the album did not count as a solo Lennon project, because of (well-founded) fears its US sales would fall below the 500,000 mark that had been a condition of the solo Beatles' expansive new EMI royalty.

The experience failed to dissuade John and Yoko from working together again. When Lennon returned to the fray in 1980 to start work on his first album of original songs in six years, *Double Fantasy*, it was once again conceived as a joint project – and this time it was Yoko's songs propping up the weaker ones from the pen of the ex-Beatle. In fact, the song the two of them were working on the night he was shot, a Yoko original called 'Walking On Thin Ice', suggested she might soon outstrip him in the song department. Thankfully for Ono, she had never accepted she was 'less than' Lennon, just because he was once a Beatle.

Others were not so fortunate. Beverly Martyn, the gifted wife of singer-songwriter John Martyn, had started out as a songwriter in her own right, penning the powerful 'Sweet Honesty' (duly covered by Elton John) and contributing as many strong songs to the Martyns' first joint record, *Stormbringer*, as her wifebeater of a husband. But by the second John and Beverly Martyn album, *Road To Ruin*, she was being made to feel lucky for getting a single solo credit and three co-credits. After that, John made it plain to her that *he* was the breadwinner:

> **Beverly Martyn**: Over the years there were songs that John and I wrote together that I never got credited for. They would come out of our late night jamming sessions. When our playing would begin to crystallise into something I would say, 'Please remember that I helped you to write this,' and he'd say, 'Yeah yeah. I'll do something about that,' but he never did. If I pushed the issue, he would get mad and call me a 'greedy Jewish bitch' and demand to know if I thought he didn't provide well enough for the family.

Her confidence shattered, Beverly Martyn withdrew into her shell. Her last attempt to write songs during her physically bruising marriage came when an equally withdrawn Nick Drake came to stay in 1971. Whether he had bought into the cult of authorship, or just some form of misplaced machismo, John Martyn decided he didn't want his wife's name on *his* records.*

Hank Williams, whose marriage to Audrey was equally prone to bouts of violence and binge drinking – in this case, from both parties – was equally disinclined to credit any contribution the first Mrs Williams made to his songs. As it happens, Audrey had none of Beverly's talent, or her husband's, while having a voice that could strip paint at a hundred yards. But never one to shy away from offering an opinion, every now and then she came up with a good idea for a song:

> **Audrey Williams**: Hank worked with ['A Mansion On The Hill'] . . . but he never could do too much good with it, and the reason he couldn't was because it wasn't his idea. One night I had just finished with the dinner dishes, and I started singing 'Tonight down here in the valley . . .' After I got through with it, I took it in to Hank and said, 'Hank, what do you think of this?' He really liked it, and [in the end] it was a mixture of my lyrics, Hank's lyrics, and Fred Rose's lyrics.

Generally, though, Hank liked to do it his way – the only input from his wildcat wife being to make him mad enough to pen a song like 'You're Gonna Change (Or I'm A-Gonna Leave)' or the defeatist 'You Win Again'. Even one of the greatest husband–wife songwriting partnerships of the twentieth century, that of Boudeleaux and Felice Bryant, seems to have been founded on the understanding that if in doubt about a song-credit, it would go to Boudeleaux Bryant – period.

Despite Boudeleaux fully admitting, 'Felice has more of a compulsion

---

* As proof, perhaps, that the universe of song has its own sense of karmic balance, Martyn's exquisite arrangement of the Highland folksong 'Eibhli Ghail Chiuin Ni Chearbhail' on *Inside Out* (1973) would constitute the melodic basis for 'Mull of Kintyre' six years later, giving Paul McCartney the UK's biggest selling single ever.

to write than I do – I can go for six months and not write anything more than a note,' very few of their published songs ever drew the solo credit Felice Bryant. On the other hand, 'Love Hurts', 'A Brand New Heartache', 'All I Have To Do Is Dream' and 'Bird Dog' all appeared with Boudeleaux receiving the sole credit.

If Felice missed out on the odd credit, she didn't seem to mind. Her husband and she were a team where the rewards were always shared. Communal property laws were not, however, applicable to most song-writing partnerships. Some partners didn't even ask for a credit, or care greatly whether they received one. Which is why Jimmie Rodgers was far more reliant on his sister-in-law Elsie McWilliams' lyrics than the song-credits at Southern Music ever suggested. (According to McWilliams's calculations, she 'alone composed or significantly contributed to some 39 of the 111 of her brother-in-law's issued recordings, though she is credited officially with only half that many'.)

Others just wanted a quiet life, letting the more egotistical partner have his way. In the case of Simon & Garfunkel, the pair had been work-ing as a duo, first as Tom and Jerry, since 1957 when they jointly composed their first minor hit, 'Hey Schoolgirl'. But by the time they reformed as a folk duo in 1963, only Simon was credited as songwriter, even though Art claimed he sometimes still lent a helping hand:

**Art Garfunkel**: There's so many times [I chipped in], who can remember? I wrote some of the lines [to 'The Boxer']. Never took a writer's credit because in spirit it was really a small two per cent factor. But there's some of my writing in there. In 'Punky's Dilemma', which was written for *The Graduate*, I wrote a verse in there ... I wrote a bunch of chords that make up 'Bridge Over Troubled Water'. The fact [is] that the verses end with a piano part that elaborates the ending and ... give it a turn-around that set[s] up the next verse. I wrote that stuff with Larry Knechtel on piano ... [But] Paul's the writer. Yeah, I wrote a little of that stuff, but that's just *technically* true.

Paul never wavered in his personal belief he was 'the writer'. When the pair went their separate ways in 1970, the single-minded Simon refused to accept their decade of success had ever been a partnership of equals, telling *Rolling Stone*, 'Musically, it was not a creative team, too much, because Artie is a singer and I'm a writer and player and a singer. We didn't work together on a creative level and prepare the songs. I did that.' Simon didn't want a helping hand; he didn't need a helping hand. He was a rock – not some songwriter for hire. Art left him to it.

# CHAPTER 18

# 1973–2015: Where Credit's Due

*Featuring*: 'Money'; 'Good Vibrations'; 'California Girls'; 'I Get Around';
'Graceland'; 'With God On Our Side'; 'Down Under'; 'Wimoweh'; 'Wild
Mountain Thyme'; 'Shakermaker'; 'Hello'; 'Whatever'; 'Bitter Sweet
Symphony'; 'American Tune'; 'Holding Back The Years'; 'Angels; 'Dazed
And Confused'; 'The Great Gig In The Sky'; 'The James Bond Theme'; 'Run
Through The Jungle'; 'Tupelo Honey'; 'Astral Weeks'; 'Hey Jude'

The [Bo Diddley] sound came from some African rhythm that was
passed along in the folk music tradition. It's [like] Robert Johnson,
who didn't invent a lot of *his* riffs. A lot of them were prior to him,
but you never hear about that. I feel sorry for Bo as he's always
saying he was cheated on his record royalties and that everybody
has been cheating him. It's not just Chess Records, he doesn't like
George Michael either! I saw him five years ago at the Rock And
Roll Hall Of Fame and I said, 'If you would let go of this and
forgive everyone, you'd become much more creative. Your energy
is being zapped in bitterness.' He patted me on the head like I was
still a little boy.

Marshall Chess

Marshall Chess, son of Leonard, hardly had a monopoly on patronizing
the performers his parents had fleeced. Wesley Rose at Acuff-Rose and
Stephen James at DJM both frequented the self-same tailor. All had learnt
their trade seeing how their dads handled the help.

And if Fred Rose was that blessed exception, a fair-minded publisher, his own son Wesley found he had a rare knack for feuding with
essential personnel, which meant he managed to alienate and ultimately
drive away from Acuff-Rose both the Everly Brothers and Felice and

Boudleaux Bryant. As for Marshall, when he inherited the Chess empire on his father's death in 1969, he was already on the defensive, telling Peter Guralnick, 'Oh sure, we done a little padding. Sometimes when royalty time come around, let's say that he had one group that was very big, my father might cut their royalty by $500 and add it to Wolf's statement. But he didn't ever put it in his own pocket.'

And if the sons' word would not suffice for the sins of such father-figures, when researchers came a-calling a steady supply of former friends and fellow workers leapt to the defence of credit stealers as morally compromised as Sam Phillips, Norman Petty, Alan Lomax and Moe Asch, citing their defining roles in the history of song as if it were some kinda mitigation. The law, though, was on their trail and catching up fast. From 1976 intellectual property became the new buzzword for those leaving law school with straight A's.

Bo Diddley had already seen the Chess brothers in their true colours, noting, 'When I left, they said I owed them 125 grand,' even though he had received less than half that in royalties in all the time he was there. The way Leonard (in tandem with his brother Phil) managed this was through 'a little known portion of copyright law called "Employee For Hire," which is generally used in a film, or if you're scoring something for a play. A music publisher hires a writer to write a specific score. The writer is paid a salary and then the publishing company, and not the writer, owns the rights to that song . . . Muddy and Willie, without comprehending, signed those kinds of agreements. Muddy signed his for two thousand dollars. It was retroactive back to the fifties. It meant that when he died his family would not have the right to any income derived from the copyrights.'

The ruse was uncovered by Muddy Waters' latterday legal eagle, Scott Cameron (whose words I've just quoted). Shortly after Leonard died, and Chess was sold, Cameron filed suits on behalf of Waters and Willie Dixon, alleging that Chess tricked these artists into signing contracts they did not understand, the devil being in a very specific detail designed to make them sign away rights they didn't even know they had. Chess stood almost no chance of winning this dispute in court precisely because these 'employee' contracts had been signed *retroactively.*\*

When Cameron instituted court action against Chess in 1976, on behalf of Waters and Dixon, the company's new owner, All Platinum, tried its very best to stall the legal process. But Cameron had the bit between his teeth, and was demanding not only a full accounting of previous royalties, but something unheard of in such suits: the return of copyright on the publishing, worldwide. Moreover, if Cameron could prove they had been defrauded, there would be punitive damages, potentially far higher than the actual amounts owed.

The new owners caved in shortly before the case was due to go to court, and returned the publishing to Dixon and Waters. (Only when Dixon was finally sure he owned his own publishing did he go after Led Zeppelin for the lion's share of 'Whole Lotta Love'.) Meanwhile, Cameron found himself enlisted to provide a similar service for other R&B innovators like John Lee Hooker, Lowell Fulson, Sonny Boy Williamson and Howlin' Wolf. Again, that 'employee-for-hire' contract reared its retroactive head. Again, Cameron offered to ride to the rescue.

As demonstrated by the estate of Robert Johnson after Stephen LeVere finally copyrighted Johnson's entire works in 1989 on behalf of 'the estate', actual evidence of authorship was no longer deemed necessary to claim a song's publishing. Hence, Morris Levy soon found Frankie Lymon's widow in his rear lights, even though all the evidence suggested Lymon had no more hand in the writing of 'Why Do Fools Fall In Love?' than he did (as finally proven in a separate court case).

It seemed if there was one moral to be had from the shenanigans at Sun, Roulette and Chess, it was that one is never too old to demand restitution

---

\* In any country other than the US, the issue would not have arisen in the first place because under the Berne Convention – of which the US remains a non-member after becoming a signatory in 1989 without Congress ever ratifying said treaty – one *cannot* assign such intellectual property, of which more later.

and reclaim one's own. But there were some old credit stealers who had yet to see the light – or the writ.

Berry Gordy at Motown had made a lucrative career out of bearing grudges and taking credit, memorably combining the two when he decided to remove Barrett Strong's name from 'Money (That's What I Want)' in 1962. A reconciliation of sorts saw Strong's (co-)credit restored in 1987, just as the copyright fell due for renewal under the twenty-eight year rule. But as soon as renewal was no longer an issue, Gordy, ever the opportunist, changed his mind again. Strong's name was crossed out the following year, though the songwriter was apparently unaware of this act of chicanery until 2010, when he took action to reclaim these lost royalties for a second time.

Unfortunately, yet again, an American artist fell foul of the country's unique determination to place a far lower time limit on reclaiming intellectual rights than it did assigning them – no matter how covertly they had been hijacked. Asked to comment on Strong's chances in a suit for an August 2013 *New York Times* feature, June M. Besek at the Columbia University School of Law opined, 'He's got an uphill battle. It's really a statute of limitations issue. He could be depicted as someone who did not conscientiously pursue his rights.' Or he could be depicted as someone who had been robbed blind by a fellow Afro-American.

To Gordy's mind, if it was on Motown, it was his. If it was made by someone once on Motown, it was his. If it even vaguely resembled the sound of Motown, it was his. After Holland-Dozier-Holland left the label, the song-credits to 'Please Mr Postman' – one of Brian Holland's early hits – acquired an extra song-credit, Gordy's, before being mysteriously removed again when another expensive suit threatened.

Gordy by this time had decided to live the fantasy, moving to Hollywood. And it was there he met fellow fantasist, Saul Zaentz, who had already reinvented himself as a film producer on the back of the money he made off John Fogerty's stellar songwriting.

Not only did Zaentz's Fantasy label own all six classic Creedence Clearwater Revival albums (and *Mardi Gras*), but Zaentz had gotten his grubby mitts on the publishing, too. For Zaentz had an even more peculiar idea of song 'ownership' than Gordy. Not content with feeding Fogerty scraps until the Creedence well ran dry – and smarting from the impudence of the artist switching to a label that actually accounted for its royalties – the brass-necked owner of Fantasy claimed that 'The Old Man Down The Road', the opening track of Fogerty's 1985 album, was a musical copy of the Creedence song 'Run Through the Jungle', which Fogerty had written fifteen years earlier.

It was Perry Bradford and 'Crazy Blues' all over again. Except 'The Old Man Down The Road' was not 'Run Through The Jungle', it was 'Run Through Long As I See Up Around The Bend Nos. 12 and 35'. A Californian jury decided it was derivative only in the sense that it came from the fertile brain of a songwriter whose only crime was not wanting to be part of Zaentz's Fantasy. Zaentz was left with with little option but to go back to his counting-house.

A suit like Zaentz's would have made many a long-serving rock artist nervous. What rocker hasn't reused and recycled their own work? Fortunately, by the time Dylan decided to reuse the 'Like A Rolling Stone' chord sequence on the likes of 'Handy Dandy' (1990) and 'Mississippi' (2001), he had already reclaimed his most famous song from Witmark Music (under a twenty-eight-year reversion clause casually included in his original 1962 contract). Likewise, when Van Morrison would occasionally segue between 1971's 'Tupelo Honey' and 1992's 'Why Must I Always Explain?' in concert, he knew he was safe suggesting they used the same chord changes, because he controlled the publishing on both.

But not everyone controlled all their publishing. And not everyone who did was able to prove it was all their own work. And the bigger the catalogue, the more likely it was that some former (or current) co-worker would step forward and say they'd had a hand in the one song that made the big bucks. Thus, the song-credit on the Police's 'Every Breath You Take' – thanks to a dispute over who 'composed' the guitar-break that was all anyone remembered – or sampled – had caused bad blood between Andy Summers and Sting for years. And if 'Another Girl, Another Planet' had been as big for The Only Ones as it should have been (and not just a favourite cover for the likes of REM and The Replacements), John Perry would have had just as sizeable a claim over his own inspired guitar intro.

At least one song's arranger managed to convince himself that, just because he later went on to great fame and fortune as a composer, he was the (co-)writer of a classic. As a result, in a spectacularly public spat, the most famous film composer of modern times was shown to be among the most brazen credit stealers of them all.

Fabled film composer John Barry had slowly convinced himself over a forty-year period that he *wrote* the 'James Bond Theme', and he was determined to convince the wider world. There was only one problem – he didn't write it. Which is why in 2001 he found himself, testifying in a libel suit brought by Monty Norman, the man who did, at a loss as to why the judiciary would not take him at his weasel word.

The *Sunday Times* had done so, not only publishing the libel in the original interview – in which his response to the question of whether Norman really wrote the theme was unequivocal, 'Absolutely not' – but defending the suit when Norman took understandable umbrage. Unfortunately for the *Times*, the articulacy Barry displayed during a friendly newspaper interview deserted him under cross-examination, as he sought to explain how *he* came to compose a theme that Norman had written five years earlier, for an abandoned musical, under the name 'Bad Sign, Good Sign'. Barry changed tack, insisting that, after growing to dislike Norman's contribution, he was left to work on the 'James Bond Theme' alone, but begrudgingly admitting using ideas from 'Bad Sign, Good Sign' in the riff and the start of the 'bebop' section. He now started to imply that while doing the job he was paid £250 to do – which was to *arrange* Norman's song – it alchemically became an act of (co-) composition.

Unfortunately for Barry, the prosecution had hired as their expert witness Dr Sadie, Professor of Music at Trinity College and a music critic for *The Times* for seventeen years. Sadie showed that the fundamental idea in the 'James Bond Theme', including the riff itself (the one play-ing in your head right now) was wholly derived from 'Bad Sign, Good Sign'; as, with modified intervals, was the main idea in the central section. The only part which wasn't so derived was the little vamp inserted by Barry; but, as Sadie went on to observe, such vamps have always tended to be common property. The defence's own chosen musicologist was far less impressive. Guy Protheroe, who had studied music at Cambridge and undertook post-graduate studies at Oxford, was as out of his depth as Barry and no match for Sadie.

Barry continued digging a grave for his own reputation by claiming under oath that he had never intended to claim royalties on the song, and had only been prompted to assert (co-) authorship because he had been repeatedly asked the same damned question year after year. The pros-ecution promptly produced two letters sent by Barry's solicitors at the start of proceedings, threatening to go after Norman for *all* royalties to the Bond theme unless Norman withdrew his libel action against the *Sunday Times*. At the time it was designed to scare Norman off; in the end it sealed Barry's fate. He lost the case, the *Times* faced a substan-tial bill for costs, and Norman was awarded £30,000. More importantly, Barry reminded the world what it had in fact forgotten, that no matter how many James Bond movies he ended up writing the score for, he did not write that trademark riff at the start of every one.

Having bought into the image of himself as the great film com-poser, Barry had been swiped by his own wet kipper. But he was hardly alone in seeing the need to preserve a carefully cultivated image of singular genius built up over decades, even when the evidence against him was enough to convince a court otherwise. There was the case of Brian Wilson, the unstable titular font of the Beach Boys' songwriting. Wilson's insistence on a sole song-credit on all those Beach Boys classics had never sat well with cousin Mike Love, who in the early nineties – as Capitol rolled out a CD reissue programme of the band's entire output – decided he would go after his own flesh and blood to claim his personal pound of flesh.

Founded by Murry Wilson, father to three of the band, the Beach Boys had as a rule consistently credited the Beach Boys' many hits to Wilson, starting with 'Surfin' USA', a tune he later had to give (back) to Chuck Berry. However, it was known inside the band that Mike 'Don't fuck with the formula' Love had contributed to a number of the early lyrics. Finally, Love decided it was high time someone set the record – and the accounts – straight. In a June 1994 interview he publicly voiced his sense of personal frustration that the matter had not been settled privately:

**Mike Love:** [My biggest] disappointment professionally . . . would be, honestly, my Uncle Murry not giving me credit for writing songs that I did write. Because I wrote all of the words to 'California Girls', but my name does not appear on the label. I've never been paid anything for that. The same with 'I Get Around'. I wrote most of the words . . . In fact, I came out with, 'I'm picking up good vibrations.' Brian has gotten, deservedly, a lot of credit, but I haven't been given the credit I deserve. Professionally speaking, that's the most personally impactful thing I can think of, when your own cousin and your own uncle cheat you . . . Brian has his excuses, I guess you['d] say, or excuses could be made . . . because he's had a series of mental problems . . . But, most of his adult life he's been under the control of other people . . . He's controlled right now by a couple of attorneys. They won't let him anywhere near me because of the ongoing litigation stemming from . . . the song rights.

The undisclosed settlement that was finally agreed reportedly ran to seven figures, but the damage had been done – in Wilson's case, years before. However, he wasn't the only Beach Boy who assumed the sole authorship of someone else's work. A more bizarre instance could be found on the *20/20* album, where the Boys recorded a song called 'Never Learn To Love', written by a then-friend of Dennis Wilson's, a certain Charles Manson. But when Manson was convicted of orchestrating ritual killings, the credit was changed to Dennis Wilson instead, presumably on the grounds that Manson could not collect on his composition from inside Corcoran Penitentiary.

Meanwhile, having discovered there was no such statute of limitations on this side of the pond, Jake Holmes finally decided to pursue Jimmy Page for a share of 'Dazed And Confused' in 2010. By now everyone knew Page had heard Holmes's version at the time he started performing the song. Yet, even after he privately settled the suit the following year, Page could not bring himself to admit 'Dazed And Confused' was not really his. He was the great creative force, the intuitive genius who crafted lead out of gold. And so, as a salve to his monumental ego and a solution of sorts to the suit, when a live version from Zeppelin's one-off reunion at the O2 Arena in 2007 was released in 2012 on the CD *Celebration Day*, the song was credited to 'Page, inspired by Jake Holmes' – a form of authorship not recognized by any copyright law. Inspired by a man one hasn't even heard? Now that's genius.

When it came to classic sixties and seventies rock albums, the prospect of an endless carousel of CD remasters seems to have prompted other folk to revisit the issue of credit (where due). Another of these was Clare Torry, whose contribution to the best-selling British rock album of all time, *Dark Side of the Moon*, had gone unacknowledged for too long. Torry had been paid a flat session fee for her spectacular vocal performance on 'The Great Gig In The Sky' – single-handedly transforming it from a meandering instrumental track into a song as wordlessly powerful as Blind Willie Johnson's 'Dark Was The Night':

> **Clare Torry**: They didn't say very much. Dave Gilmour was the only one who really communicated with me. That's my abiding memory. I went in and they just said, 'Well, we're making this album, and there's this track – and we don't really know what to do.' They told me what the album was about: birth and death, and everything in between. I thought it was rather pretentious, to be honest. And I said, 'Well, play me the track.' They did that,

and I said, 'What do you want?' They said, 'We don't *know*!' . . . [Finally] I thought, 'Maybe I should just pretend I'm an instrument.' So I said, 'Start the track again.' . . . I started getting this pattern of notes and they said, 'Well, that seems the right direction to go.' And I told them to put the tape on. At the end of the first take, Dave Gilmour said, 'Do another one – but even more emotional.' So I did a second take . . . and halfway through I realized that I was beginning to . . . sound contrived. I said, 'I think you've got enough.'

Finally, in the late nineties, she decided an overdue share of the publishing on 'Great Gig In The Sky' would be a nice way to supplement her pension. Any concerns she might have at being 'thought of as a troublemaker' were put aside when she realized how much was at stake. Surprisingly, the members of Floyd did not just hold up their hands; however, the case was eventually settled in Torry's favour, in time for an all-dancing, all-singing six-disc version of the album in 2011, where the song was now credited to 'Wright/Torry'. Cue tape loop of cash registers opening and closing.

It was perhaps inevitable there would be a flurry of would-be song claimants during the early nineties, as even the UK entered an age of 'no win, no fee' ambulance-chasers. As pop began to eat itself, what had once been a case of 'interesting people steal more interestingly' was not so much interesting any more as plain novel, perhaps because what qualified as post-modernism in modern art and respectful pastiche in cinema was still actionable in modern song. As to who was more inclined to take liberties, the Anglo-Saxons or the Eurovisionaries, it was a toss-up.

A Danish Eurodance singer of no great shakes who exploded on the pop charts in 1994 calling herself (just) Whigfield, was on the receiving end of a writ for her second single from a British songwriter who had taken a fair few liberties of his own in his past. Whigfield's first single, 'Saturday Night', which went to number one all around Europe, already suggested the lady had stockpiled snatches of her favourite late sixties and early seventies pop. 'Saturday Night' convinced both the Equals ('Rub A Dub Dub') and Lindisfarne ('Fog On The Tyne') she had referenced their earlier hits. But if so, she had done it skilfully enough to convince a court it was not plagiarism, just pop.

She was not so lucky with 'Another Day', which clearly conjured up 'In The Summertime', a 1970 number one for Mungo Jerry. The author of the latter song, Ray Dorset, had in past times taken a solo (*not* an arrangement) song-credit for Mungo Jerry's jugband arrangements of 'Ella Speed', 'Have A Whiff On Me', 'Milk Cow Blues' and 'Keep Your Hands Off Her', songs he knew belonged to the skiffle generation. Dorset admitted he had spotted the Whigfield 'nick' even before the song charted, but didn't 'want to complain too early as they may withdraw it. Better to wait until it sells and then make a claim.' He didn't, they hadn't, and he did.

But if Whigfield was again obliged to call lawyers for the defence, it was as nothing to the work Oasis demanded of theirs. Here was a Britpop outfit who appeared determined to reinforce their claim to be the next Beatles by proving they could be as light-fingered with others' songs as their Scouse brethren. The Gallaghers didn't need to make an appearance on *Magpie* to confirm they had canvassed the pop sounds of the seventies.

It was evident in their 'ironic' use of the New Seekers' 'I'd Like To Teach The World To Sing' – a song made world famous from its use in a Coca-Cola TV ad – on 1994's 'Shakermaker', for which they apparently ended up paying out half a million bucks. Sampling part of disgraced ex-pop star Gary Glitter's 'Hello, Hello I'm Back Again' for 'Hello', the opening track on their multi-million seller *What's The Story (Morning Glory)?*, would also cost Oasis dear. And when they attempted to palm off Stevie Wonder after lifting part of the chorus to 'Step Out' from Wonder's 'Uptight (Everything's Alright)', his publisher demanded (a not unreasonable) 10 per cent of the royalties. So the song was pulled from the album and put on the B-side of 'Don't Look Back In Anger', which promptly became Oasis's best-selling single ever.

Yet the song that perhaps best exemplified the Mancunian musos' laissez-faire attitude to the blatant cop was called, appropriately, 'Whatever', a non-album single from 1994 that bore an uncanny resemblance to ex-Bonzo Neil Innes's 'How Sweet To Be An Idiot'. The first Oasis Top Three single, it stayed on the English singles charts for an astonishing fifty-one weeks.

The Innes song had been title-track to his first solo album back in 1973, where it might have languished undiscovered had he not played it when sharing a stage with comedy touring troupe Monty Python's Flying Circus the night they filmed Python's 1976 Hollywood Bowl performance. It still took a phone call from Paul McCartney's brother, Mike, asking him if he had heard Oasis's new record, for Innes to take action. As Innes himself put it, 'Eventually they settle[d] out of court. They [now] give me a quarter of the song.'

In all these instances Noel Gallagher still hung on to a significant share of the publishing – unlike Verve vocalist Richard Ashcroft, who foolishly decided to sample the Andrew Loog Oldham Orchestra's instrumental arrangement of the first Jagger-Richards A-side, 'The Last Time', for Verve's instantly memorable 1997 single, 'Bitter Sweet Symphony'. According to Ashcroft, there had been a provisional agreement to split the publishing with ABKCO, but then Klein and co. claimed they had used 'too much' of the sample and demanded all the publishing *and* a credit that read Jagger-Richards-Ashcroft; all this for using a melody Richards had admitted was nicked from the Staple Singers in the first place. Klein's off-kilter moral compass had evidently not corrected itself in the quarter of a century since last he ransacked colonial coffers. Ashcroft acidly noted he'd given the Glimmer Twins their biggest UK hit since 'Brown Sugar'.

However, when it came to taking all the credit for half a song Gallagher and Ashcroft were mere bus-boy to that folk-rock maitre d', Paul Simon. The man who had stuck a forgettable instrumental ('Canticle') as a counterpoint to 'Scarborough Fair', claiming yet more of the publishing on this five-hundred-year-old song, was up to his old tricks again. The plaintive 'American Tune', from Paul Simon's strongest solo album, *There Goes Rhymin' Simon* (1973), was set to a tune he knew for sure was not American, but he liked his little joke. It had been written in 1529 by Martin Luther, when it housed the more sacral sentiment, 'A Mighty Fortress Is Our God'; thus making it public domain, but not anonymous. It seems he just couldn't help himself.

It was hardly Simon's last brush with controversy. The songwriter's unswerving self-belief appears to have been at the root of another controversial solo song-credit. After years in the commercial wilderness, Art's fairweather friend stormed back into the charts in 1986 with the platinum seller, *Graceland*, but this highly contentious album was dogged by accusations that Simon – a spiritual son of Seeger – had exploited Africa's musical heritage by taking snatches of quasi-traditional melodies from South African recordings and added them to a smorgasbord of world music.

And if the local African musicians were seemingly just happy to have the attention directed at them and their indigenous music, Simon did not confine his world tour of musical styles to the South African sub-continent. He also asked to work with Tex-Mex troubadours, Los Lobos; and according to the band, seemed to feel anything which resulted from two days of joint sessions was fair game for the Simon song-mill.

After a day and a half of doodling around the boys in the border-band broke out something they had been working on themselves:

**Steve Berlin**: There [had been] this uncomfortable silence and then Dave starts playing what would become 'The Myth of Fingerprints', because it was a song we were preparing for our next record. We'd been waiting around for two days for Paul to come up with something, but he had nothing. So to have something to do, we just started playing what we thought was our song, when Paul suddenly says, 'Hey, that's cool. What is that?' And we said, 'Oh, it's a song we've been working on.' He goes, 'Hey, can we do that?' and we just thought, 'Yeah – if it will get us out of this fucking studio!' So we started playing it and captured a take of it and finally escaped and thought, 'Thank God this is over with!' It was six months later the record comes out and we said, 'Oh, look at this: words and music by Paul Simon.' We thought, 'Well, obviously that's a mistake.' So we called up . . . the record company people that we had for Paul and asked them to fix the mistake. Silence, silence, silence. We're asking and asking, then finally six months later we hear from Paul and he says, 'Sue me. See what happens.' [2012]

In today's digital era one might have expected Los Lobos to issue a subpoena for the session tapes, which presumably might have shown how the song actually took shape. Instead, they contented themselves with bad-mouthing Simon at every turn, including for the twenty-fifth anniversary of the album, which prompted the above rant. By that time Simon clearly hoped the unwelcome accusation would have faded away, along with any sense of grievance. In this, as in so many other ways, he was mistaken.

Simon presumably felt Los Lobos had been well paid for their two days' worth of work, and what more did they expect? At least he was safe in the knowledge that he was not obliged to put their name on the tune: the USA, home of the brazen, was still not a signatory to the Berne Convention, which required the authorship of a work to be recognized irrespective of any financial agreement made between interested parties.

Whether that recognition came with a fair split of the proceeds was another matter. Thus, when Mick Hucknall formed Simply Red in 1983, he took with him the best song from his former band, The Frantic Elevators, 'Holding Back The Years', co-written (according to the 45 label of the Elevators' version) with co-founder Neil Moss. When the song became a worldwide hit, and Simply Red's only US number one, Mr Red seemed determined to claim the whole song for himself:

**Mick Hucknall:** I wrote 'Holding Back The Years' in its entirety. The reason I gave Neil a credit was because of the time we spent together, because of those years when we'd not had any success. In the beginning we did write some songs together, but after a while we started to have our own ideas and then have these meetings on a Friday night . . . and work them out together. We just came to an agreement that we'd call it Hucknall/Moss and that was it. [2010]

That 'agreement' did not wholly survive the transition to Simply Red intact. The song suddenly became 'words: Mick Hucknall, music: Mick Hucknall and Neil Moss', making Moss entitled to a quarter, not a half, of the song's very substantial revenue stream.

If Hucknall wasn't willing to split his good fortune entirely equally with his old buddy, he was Mr Generous compared to another singer who split from a band where he was the second-string songwriter to forge a solo career. Robbie Williams was desperate to prove he could step out from the shadow of Take That when he released his first solo album in 1997. But his first three solo singles failed to achieve that goal, leaving him staring failure in the face.. So when 'Angels' was released in December 1997, it was probably his last shot. At the time, his first solo album, *Life Thru A Lens*, had sold just 30,000 copies and was languishing at 104 in the album charts. 'Angels' would peak at number four, sending the album all the way to number one.

Whether it proved Williams was a songwriter in his own right, though, became a moot point. Because it soon emerged that the song's basic outline had been written by Ray Heffernan, an unknown Irish songwriter Williams had met around Christmas 1996 in a Dublin bar. According to Heffernan, he 'was in the pub with a friend of mine – we both had bleached blonde hair and white T-shirts on – Robbie came in alone and walked up to us. He asked us if we were in a boy band. We got on immediately . . . It was obvious he was having a lot of problems in his life. He said he was looking for a writing partner.'

After a few drinks, they reconvened in the wee small hours to

Heffernan's mother's house. There, according to the Irish songwriter, he played on an acoustic guitar 'Angels Instead', a song he had written about his own dead son. He only had the rudiments of the song at this stage: 'The verse and the verse melody was mine. The words at the start of the chorus were mine, but the big chorus melody . . . was down to Rob and Guy Chambers.' Nonetheless, Heffernan had the wit to record the song they 'made' that night on a Dictaphone. But when he tried to re-establish contact with Williams, visiting him at his Staffordshire home, Williams supposedly said, 'Look, man, why are you following me?'

After this incident, he was told all contact had to be made through Williams's management company, I.E. Music, who offered Heffernan a one-off payment of £10,000 for him to renounce all claim on the song. Heffernan wasn't greatly interested in the money, but believed that as part of a previous verbal agreement his name would be used on the single and album. It was not. Instead, on the sleeve of the single, the singer included the highly cryptic dedication, 'Even fallen angels laugh last, thanks to Ray Heffernan.' The Irishman was left embittered by the experience; and if not poorer for it, not noticeably richer, either:

> **Ray Heffernan:** The song has made millions, but the money side of it has never really bothered me. What is hurtful is that Robbie won't even acknowledge me. I was part of that song and I'm still angry about that. Robbie didn't steal it from me, but I just wish he had acknowledged my involvement in it. Even so, I am so happy that the song has touched so many people and that is more important than who wrote it.

In fact, it is doubtful any UK court would recognize the one-off payment made to Heffernan as having any legal validity, as Heffernan had not been advised to take legal representation and Williams had gone out of his way not to credit the song three ways. Whatever Williams would like to imagine, one *cannot* surrender one's moral rights under the Berne

Convention, meaning in this instance the right to be recognized as the (co-)creator of a song that has sold (and touched) millions.

Because that, surely, is what it's all about – striking a chord with listeners and staking a claim to a place in the pop pantheon. Not ending up just another sap chasing credit where credit's due. That Williams needed help became evident the minute he severed his songwriting partnership with Guy Chambers.

Because, like most of his kind, Williams the 'singer-songwriter' has needed all the help he could get to come up with such a catalogue of hits. He even went to live in LA for a while, hoping to get the creative juices flowing, as if proximity to the home of singer-songwriters – Laurel Canyon – might make him a mighty, mighty songsmith. It didn't. Others in this new breed have tried flying to LA on 'writing trips', though one suspects they couldn't find Laurel Canyon if they fitted satnav in their brand new Cadillac. But they know they need to write their own songs, at least in name, to fill their (and their managers') coffers; and yet the single name check is becoming as rare in modern pop as an original hook or a non-greeting-card sentiment.

The 'Record Of The Year', according to the 2015 Grammy committee, was a Sam Smith single called 'Stay With Me', which for all its trite catchiness required three names on the song-credits – and two more left unlisted but there in spirit. Because barely had Mr Smith been nominated than he was being asked to explain the astonishing similarity his song shared with a 1989 song by Tom Petty and Jeff Lynne, 'I Won't Back Down'. The problem was, he couldn't. It was, of course, a complete coincidence – but, if so, it was a costly one. The four-million seller was duly re-registered with ASCAP listing Smith, his cohort Jimmy Napes, Jeff Lynne and Tom Petty as the main songwriters. And behind closed doors, agreement was reached to pay Lynne and Petty 25 per cent of the publishing for this pure coincidence.

Petty announced himself satisfied, stating, 'All my years of songwriting have shown me these things can happen. Most times you catch it before it gets out the studio door but in this case it got by.' Quite how it got 'out the studio door' is not clear. A well-known New York guitarist, on hearing Smith's track for the first time on the radio, actually began singing 'I Won't Back Down' to it.

However, when Smith came to collect his award at the Grammy, in all humility and flanked by his 'two' co-authors, Jimmy Napes and William Edwards, Petty and Lynne were nowhere to be seen; and nor were they listed on the TV credits that scrolled across the bottom of the screen. Perhaps the idea that it took five 'songwriters' a quarter of a century to come up with a song that sounded like a computer-generated hit was one the Grammy Committee didn't want out there. Especially when announcing it as the Absolute Best Record of 2014. Maybe not.

# Outro: Who Knows Where The Money Goes?

The character of an era hangs upon what needs no defence. In this regard, few of us question the contemporary construction of copyright. It is taken as a law, both in the sense of a universally recognizable moral absolute, like the law against murder, and as naturally inherent in our world, like the law of gravity. In fact, it is neither. Rather, copyright is an ongoing social negotiation, tenuously forged, endlessly revised, and imperfect in its every incarnation. Thomas Jefferson, for one, considered copyright a necessary evil: He favoured providing just enough incentive to create, nothing more, and thereafter allowing ideas to flow freely, as nature intended.

Jonathan Lethem, 'The Ecstasy of Influence'

At a televised press conference held in San Francisco in December 1965, Dylan the folk-rock king was interrogated by a battery of Mr and Miss Joneses. Planted amid such prosaic philistines was beat-poet friend Allen Ginsberg, who had a pre-approved question he wanted to ask: 'Can you ever envisage a time when you'll be hung as a thief?' Dylan, who doubtless had a pre-prepared witty retort, just cracks up.

It was a private joke. Ginsberg knew Dylan had already been accused of being 'a thief of thoughts' and so was really asking, do you think your work will ever be treated as Art? The thief Dylan aspired to be was that Rimbaudian thief of fire, the true artist, who in the fullness of time would be hung in a gallery, his work embalmed by posterity (a case of infinity itself on trial).

Both Dylan and Ginsberg had become revolutionaries in their respective fields only after learning to plunder far and wide. For the elder Ginsberg, the poets who inspired him were long out of copyright, while there was no poets' union to which one need be affiliated to receive one's due. Indeed, when Lawrence Ferlinghetti published Ginsberg's *Howl*, it was on a handshake deal that was still being honoured forty years later when Allen made an appointment with Jahweh. Whereas Dylan had learnt – the hard way – to tread with a greater degree of care, weaving his take on tradition with strands of poetry and 'wild mercury music' that were all his own, trying to stay out of the joint.

Yet even back in 1914, when Handy broke the code, the line between song snatching and song writing was already hopelessly blurred. Twenty years later, when Leadbelly got out of jail, the line was still little more than footprints in the sand. After another twenty, with Elvis hot-wiring Crudup's recreation of the spirit of Blind Lemon, still the outline could be traced, but only by the clear-sighted. And fifty years after Handy, when Dylan introduced 'Mr Tambourine Man' to a captive audience at the Newport Folk Festival, the tidal outpouring of creativity on both sides of the pond seemed to be the direct result of decades of trawling tradition. Sixty years on, Robert Johnson, who died unknown in an unmarked grave having sold a few hundred records, was English R&B's cipher for the whole of Delta blues.

But then the lawyers moved in, and the mavericks moved out. The US Copyright Act of 1976 probably signalled the death knell of any kind of popular song which could be built from a tree with roots. It was replaced with the idea that a popular songwriter was de facto an Artist; and it came at the exact point when popular music stopped innovating. (And if evidence were needed to prove this point, just count how many times the unerringly inarticulate Lady Gaga uses the A-word in any given interview, applied in all seriousness to her own magpie muse.)

Perhaps this is because we have put a fence around the creative process; built a place where the songwriter can work to his (or her) heart's content without distraction or disturbance, removed from the continuum of song. It may look like a mansion on the hill, but it is really a prison. Plush and with all the luxuries, it still has bars on the windows and a high fence. On the other side lies a land where the likes of Leadbelly and Jimmie Rodgers, A.P. Carter and Chuck Berry are wont to roam. It is a place where you might meet a man like Captain Beefheart, who once said, 'I don't want to sell my music. I'd like to give it away, because where I got it, you didn't have to pay for it.'

So I hereby reveal that what you have been reading – hopefully from the beginning, not through Google's piratical prism – is one long love letter to creative thievery, which I have valiantly tried to distinguish the deeds of larcenous leeches, from the song borrowers. Removing the bloodsuckers from the pop form has proven a long, laborious process. The end result, ironically, suggests even leeches provide life-affirming properties, for without their kind – indeed, left to their own devices – the modern pop songwriter has become three parts businessman, one part artist.

What has been lost somewhere back in the swamps is the sense that in order to produce something which endures one needs to tap into what has already endured. To invoke David Evans' analysis of early blues performers again, 'Creation and recreation, then, are essential to some degree in folk music, yet they serve in part to produce material that will go on to become traditional . . . for they come from people who participate in the folk music tradition . . . Composers of popular music . . . sometimes do draw material from folk music. But when they do so, they present this material to their audience as a novelty or else recreate it in order to suit it for mass appeal.' In other words, pop songwriters who disguise tradition with the mantle of novelty still want to remain attached to the continuum.

It is these 'composers of popular music . . . draw[ing] material from folk music' who across sixty years of constant novelty (even innovation) tried to keep it rooted and real. Whenever these kinda creators stop selling, pop quickly becomes product. Actually, we may already have arrived

at our preordained destination. 'Creation and recreation' are now pre-
scribed by law, and a man in a powdered wig gets to decide which parts
of a song feed the cult of authorship, and which parts deny it. It is as
Dave Bartholomew, the original rapper, said, in his fifties N'Orleans classic, 'The Monkey Speaks His Mind': 'Another thing you will never see/A
monkey build a fence around a coconut tree . . . Why, if I put a fence
around this tree/Starvation would force you to steal from me.'

Modern pop music has forcibly cut itself off from a century of inspiration by building its own fence and then sitting on it. The notion that a
popular song is something other than a 'mere' bagatelle of musical and
lyrical ideas handed down to performers who cannot read music (or, in
some cases, lyrics) has been the task of twentieth-century lawmakers (and
credit stealers); and yet the *art* of the musically (and sometimes function-
ally) illiterate has frequently climbed into the sonic stratosphere on the
shoulder of similarly challenged giants.

Which is not to say that 'awopbopaloobop' is the level of articulacy
to which all popular music perforce aspires, or that musical articu-
lates are somehow exempt from song-snatching proclivities. The Velvet
Underground, co-founded by pupils of Aaron Copland and Delmore
Schwartz respectively, began their life covering Jimmy Reed and Rolling
Stones songs whilst trying to ride into the charts with 'The Ostrich', the
dumbest dance craze since 'Diddy Wah Diddy'. Yet even when the Velvets
in a matter of months made the most radical musical statement imagi-
nable – I am thinking of 'Venus In Furs' – the lyrics suggested Lou was
as light-fingered as his British cousins. On one level, 'Venus In Furs' is
'merely' a synopsis of a nineteenth-century fictionalized memoir of the
first masochist, von Sacher-Masoch, with some lines lifted verbatim from
our whip-happy wimp.

So in what way does his highfalutin' source set Reed apart from all
these other song snatchers who made recreation a creative act – and even
a career? The only difference between Reed and a 'thief of thoughts' like
Dylan may be that the former liked to lift lines (and in one of his last
works, the whole text) from nineteenth-century literati, whereas the latter

*integrated* lines from nineteenth-century literati as easily as he did those of illiterate twentieth-century bluesmen.\*

If all first-class songwriters had been obliged to pay their entire dues, a fair few would be spending their gilt-edged retirement in the debtors' prison. But for the first three-quarters of the twentieth century, there was some kinda unspoken rule that stopped short of lumping song borrowers and credit stealers together, even if these songwriters to a man moaned about how 'imitators steal me blind' (a line from Dylan's original 'Idiot Wind').†

Most rock bands meanwhile *evolved* into originality, passing through an intermediate process by which they made highly derivative but ostensibly original material for the masses – often their best work – on their way to full-blown originality (and, often as not, obscurity); a case of coming from nowhere and going straight back there, while hopefully leaving behind a worthy contribution to the continuum. Some never made it past the 'highly derivative but ostensibly original' stage. From Bo Diddley to Status Quo, there have been plenty reluctant to break the mould yet who still made their statement.

How we arrived at a lowest-common-denominator brand of pop music is really a subject for another day, another tome, some other iconoclast; but a key factor is undoubtedly the reluctance of new bands to 'pay their dues', playing and developing cover material that delineates points of reference for otherwise bemused audiences. They have bought into the cult of authorship to such an extent that they seem wholly unaware just how unlikely it is that their first songs will be worth hearing outside a rehearsal room. If talent is God-given, great songwriting is a process, painful, slow and hard-won.

Jeff Buckley was one songwriter who seemed to be on his way there

---

\* In 1993 Dylan described 'the people who originated this music' as 'all Shakespeares', and he did not mean because Bill the bard was a shameless plagiarist. He knew only too well unconscious geniuses once stalked the land, providing him with his cue.

† Dylan, for one, has recently acknowledged the role that Ralph Peer played, describing him as 'an overwhelming character in the music field, a true visionary, who realized the potential power of common music long before anyone else.'

but who never got the chance to complete that personal journey. He began writing songs, discovered his father's contemporaries, scrapped most of what he had already written and set out to invent himself anew. His A&R man at Sony, Steve Berkowitz, was convinced he would succeed, and gave him a whacking great publishing contract along with a (cross-collateralized) record deal.

Sadly, we'll never know if Jeff could have become even half the songwriter his father was. Berkowitz himself would end up explaining to a madly grieving mother how come there was no money in the bank, and just how royalties on an album as successful as *Grace* could be eaten up by Buckley's publishing advance. The endless permutations of Jeff's sliver-thin oeuvre have been released to recoup the ground Buckley lost the day he signed that cross-collateralized deal.

But that has been the deal with the devil required of most modern pop artists – even the most ungifted of songwriters. The voice of an angel is no longer enough. One must be seen to write, or at least, publish some producer's half-baked cast-offs; and perish the thought it should sound like a Louis Jordan song or a Carter Family classic. For the beneficiaries of pop's unique breed of pariahs now have attorneys willing to feed them scraps of carrion on the off-chance they can turn a writ into a retirement fund.

For this, we can thank a sorority of beneficiaries to the legacy of popular song. These beneficiaries of the protracted legal battles in the sixties, seventies and eighties, and copyright law changes in the nineties, have been almost entirely those whose sense of entitlement is their only connection to the creative process. In some instances, they are exactly the person a creative individual who crafted their canon from the debris of tradition least wanted living in the lap of relative luxury.

F'rinstance, the estate of English singer-songwriter Sandy Denny – though hardly in the same universe as those of Jimi Hendrix or John Lennon (the former controlled by a stepsister who never even knew the guitar-man) – is valuable enough to be administered by the second wife of her late husband, Trevor Lucas; the woman Denny believed in the last weeks of her all-too-short life was trying to take her husband away from her.

Yet when Sandy died intestate in 1978, her entire estate passed to that erring husband; who, when he also died intestate in 1989, bequeathed not only his own (largely worthless) estate but also that of his first wife to second wife Elizabeth Hurtt-Lucas – despite Sandy having a direct heir, in her daughter Georgia, who was only a year old when her mother died.

Now Universal Music, having gulped down Island Records, once the most progressive independent label in Christendom, have decided only a sixteen-CD boxed set will suffice for the collected, and some never-shoulda-been-collected, works of Sandy Denny – all to feed the twin behemoths of copyright holder/s and shareholders. The artist would have died of shame had she lived to see every inferior alternate take peddled to the punters, helping to fund the lifestyle of a lady Denny considered a stranger to herself.

The needs of the few who can stake a claim to some age-old copyright have been allowed to outweigh the needs of the many for whom popular song worked best when it was one great big melting pot, with a surfeit of cooks arguing over its ever-changing recipe. Such is the way of the world of estates where copyright confers rights on *generations* of oft-unrelated beneficiaries. It is Elizabeth Hurtt-Lucas's children who stand to inherit as much of Denny's estate as her actual daughter.

Whether it is the songs of Sandy Denny or the equally troubled Hank Williams, both have become in due time just another corporate revenue stream. Even the 'lost notebooks' of both artists, full of songs they never even finished, have recently been plundered – and copyrighted – for other artists' 'tribute' CDs. Meanwhile, Hank's old label, MGM Records, and Sandy's beloved Island Records have both been swallowed whole by Universal Music – which like Sony makes most of its profits from the publishing division, albeit fed by a stream of product. The recent all-consuming archival releases of Denny and Williams invariably required the okay of the estates, which in Williams's case was only possible after his beneficiaries fought themselves to a standstill.

His publishing initially proved such a productive battleground for lawyers and litigants precisely because two hard-as-nails women claimed to be the 'real' Mrs Williams (even to the point that both toured as Williams's widow). And both realized that Hank's posthumous publishing would dwarf his lifetime earnings.

Audrey, his first wife, had perhaps the better claim, simply because she had made Hank's life enough of a misery to inspire him to record songs as tortured as 'Take These Chains From My Heart' and 'Your Cheatin' Heart'. Shortly before he died in the backseat of a borrowed car he divorced the devil in a blue dress, and married the equally untalented Billie Jean. However, such was their hurry to get married that the contract was technically illegitimate. Billie Jean's divorce from her previous husband had yet to be finalized.

Suspecting she was standing on legal quicksand, Billie Jean agreed to relinquish her rights to a share of Hank's publishing for a one-off payment of $30,000, and Audrey finally had the beer money she needed to pursue her true vocation, drinking herself to death. But Billie Jean wasn't done; there was a final twist on Audrey's way to the cemetery. As biographer Colin Escott records: 'When Hank Williams's copyrights came up for renewal 28 years after they were first logged, [Billie Jean] sued for half of the publishing, contending that she hadn't signed away her right to the renewals because she couldn't sign away what she didn't have. She won, and Audrey got the news that she had lost just days before she died.'

Such tussles for control of song snatchers' estates have been a constant backdrop to the pop industry in the last quarter-century. With some disputes, it has been easy for the interested observer to take sides – Buddy Holly's widow versus Norman Petty was always a no-brainer for anyone save a series of US judges.

Equally, ABKCO's continuing control of The Rolling Stones' sixties oeuvre has continued to mean shoddy product and self-serving statements. As for The Beatles' continuing failure to regain control of Northern

Songs, there is at least the comforting thought that every owner of that catalogue has since gone to meet their Maker. Presumably, Dick James, Lew Grade and Michael Jackson were all surprised to find the devil at their door one morning, saying, 'I believe it's time to go.'

As for the man who wrote that line – and a handful of other blues commonplaces – Robert Johnson lived his life his way; and so it is perhaps fitting that the riches and rewards of it should pass to an illegitimate son, the product of a one-night stand with a woman who happily allowed her best friend to watch the single act of coitus that made our Detroit trucker into a steady rollin' man. When Claude was discovered by a BBC film crew in 1990, he was unaware Johnson had ever made records, let alone influenced Elmore James, one of his favourite bluesmen.

But soon the not-so-little bastard wanted to get his hands on copyrights that should have long ago lapsed. And only because Johnson's songs had not been registered in the first place, but had been belatedly copyrighted (by Steve LaVere) under a Copyright Act which didn't even become law until forty years after Johnson's death, songs that if copyrighted at the time would have fallen out of copyright instead *came into* copyright, leaving Claude to retrospectively reclaim what he had no moral right to in the first place.

Nor are Johnson's reworkings remaining in copyright a hundred years after his death the most absurd example thrown up by the byzantine maze that is modern copyright law.

Mildred Hill, the undisputed author of the tune to 'Good Morning To All' – and therefore to that of 'Happy Birthday To You' – published in 1893, had died in 1916. She went to her grave oblivious of the fact that somebody had started singing a new set of words to her tune – words that would not be copyrighted until 1925, and which would therefore be protected for a minimum of ninety-five years, not the twenty-eight that protected the original song pre-1909.

That copyright became in the fullness of time the most valuable single song publishing in the world:. According to court papers filed in 2013, challenging said copyright, the song still generates a staggering

$1.2 million per annum in royalties. And yet, as Robert Brauneis, a pro-
fessor at George Washington University Law School, informed the *New
York Times*, he has searched in vain for evidence of a copyright for a combination of the melody for 'Good Morning To All' with the lyrics for
'Happy Birthday To You'.

And still the byzantine absurdities of modern copyright law spiral
ever outward, and the absurdities of intellectual property law mount ever
higher, with the record for the longest – and most morally dubious – extension of copyright term surely residing with the family of Solomon Linda,
the man who recorded 'Mbube'. The family of the Zulu singer had done
nothing about (re-)securing rights to the song until South African journalist Rian Malan appeared on his metaphorical milk-white steed nearly
forty years after Linda's death, crying rip off and unleashing the dogs of
copyright law. But before they could go after the American copyright-
holders, they needed to get back the rights Linda signed away in 1939.

Fortunately for them, the deal Eric Gallo had struck with TRO back
in 1952 had been so badly constructed that he had made very little money
from a song that had earned tens of millions in the interim – and was
fair set to earn tens of millions more when it became a central pivot for
the stage show of the Disney film, *The Lion King*. As a result, the Gallo
family agreed to return all rights to the Linda family, on what terms we
know not. This meant that the Linda family could now contest the 10 per
cent cut they were receiving from 'The Lion Sleeps Tonight', by asserting
that Weiss's song was little more than a reworking of 'Mbube', which it
self-evidently was not.

If Weiss had been a more mean-spirited man, he could have returned
the entire copyright to the Linda family, knowing that he was probably
not long for this world. After all, when the case went to court in 2004, he
was already eighty-three years old, and had no need of the money himself. But ever the family man, he had his children to think about; and an
agreement was struck which allowed him and the Lindas to share jointly
this steady stream of revenue, primarily from *The Lion King*. What their
agreement actually meant was that, although Solomon Linda died in 1962,

a seventy-year copyright extension would only start when Weiss himself died, which he duly did in 2010; meaning that a traditional Zulu song that may or may not have been adapted by Linda in 1939 will still be in copyright in 2080!

For the crusading Rian Malan, the whole saga served as a vindication of a stance predicated on the idea that the Man dun stole 'our' songs. Tellingly, in his 2000 *Rolling Stone* article on 'Mbube', he cites three other examples of black singers whose songs have been ripped off, every one of which has been covered at length in this book: 'Robert Johnson's contribution to the blues went largely unrewarded. Lead Belly lost half of his publishing to his white "patrons." DJ Alan Freed refused to play Chuck Berry's "Maybellene."' In every single case I think I have demonstrated Malan's exemplars did *not* write the songs they said they did, at least not unaided; and in the latter two cases, it was a case of a black man 'stealing' from white tradition.

In fact, Malan's whole article – and subsequent TV documentary – reeks of a startlingly simplistic (and rather racist) analysis of so-called song stealing; one in which he whitewashes Pete Seeger, the original song-stealer in the whole 'Wimoweh' affair, while simultaneously blackening the name of Weiss, who seems to have acted with honour throughout the whole saga, and without whom 'Wimoweh' would be accruing as much as all the other Weavers classics we all still sit around and hum (i.e. nowt). It was the wise man Weiss who took a folk chant and made a pop song, thus providing in microcosm the story of twentieth-century song snatching.

Which returns us, a tad circuitously, to Jonathan Lethem's 'Ecstasy of Influence', which reminds us, 'The first Congress to grant copyright gave authors an initial term of fourteen years, which could be renewed for another fourteen if the author still lived. [Whereas] the current term is the life of the author plus seventy years.'

The kicker here is that 'plus'. We have already come across a merry band of widows who have proven adept at exploiting legacies and legal loopholes, with a view to looking after themselves. As far as they're concerned, any centuries-old sisterhood of song can go hang itself. Nor are they the only birds of prey picking at the carrion of some semi-original composition that struck a chord down through the ages.

In Nick Hornby's third novel, *About A Boy*, he creates a lead character who is an indolent wastrel living (comfortably) off a single song his father wrote. As he tells the nosey 'boy' of the title, 'It's a famous song, and I live off the royalties.' The kid replies, 'If you can live off it, we must have heard of it.' But that is not necessarily the case. Any list of the most lucrative melodies in twentieth-century song would certainly include 'Good Morning To All', 'Comme D'Habitude', 'Bad Sign, Good Sign' and 'I Believe I'll Make A Change' – but only because they are the originals of 'Happy Birthday', 'My Way', 'James Bond Theme' and 'Dust My Broom'.

A hundred years on from Handy's 'St Louis Blues', it is clear that if the 1976 Copyright Act had been substituted for the 1909 Copyright Act, there would have been no W.C. Handy, no Leadbelly, no Robert Johnson, no Muddy Waters, no Chuck Berry, no Bob Dylan, and certainly no Led Zeppelin. For in a world where some lucky blighter is living off 'Good Morning To All' a hundred and twenty years after it was written, or off 'Sweet Home Chicago' eighty-five years after its supposed author's death, or off 'St Louis Blues' a full hundred years on, there is precious little room left for creative recreation; for 'interesting people' to 'steal songs interestingly'.

'Steal a little and they throw you in jail/Steal a lot and they make you a king.' Bob Dylan said that, albeit sixteen hundred years after St Augustine of Hippo first told the story (from oral tradition) about the time Alexander the Great confronted a pirate who pointed out there was little distinction between what he did and the Emperor did. It was just a question of which side one was on.

So it is high time we collectively agreed that some rather well-known songs have paid their dues. It is also about time we let songs become whatever their DNA allows. Because ol' Tom Jefferson was onto something when he said he 'considered copyright a necessary evil [and] favoured providing just enough incentive to create'. The cult of authorship has created a century of inspired songwriting, but has it sustained the conditions for a deep creative well from which all-comers can drink? Methinks not. This is in a large part because, as Richard Hillesley states in his challenging essay, 'The Revolution Will Be Plagiarized':

> Intellectual property law may have been conceived to protect the rights of the little man, the individual creator, against the appropriation of ideas and inventions by corporate interests, but in the real world this is no longer the case. Intellectual property is big business and the little man seldom gets a look in . . . The truth about the [so-called] content industries is that control of copyright is owned not by the individual artist or performer, but by the corporate entity.

It is these corporate entities who 'administer' the songs of everyone from Bob Dylan to Paul McCartney, while disregarding the 'moral rights' of anyone in their path. It was just such an entity who pursued Neil Innes for his Rutles parodies of Lennon and McCartney against the express wishes of the authors themselves. They are hardly likely to consider the melodic and lyrical commonplaces of popular song to be fair game if they have stamped a big © across a given individual example, whether or not it is conjured from the recycling plant that is pop music. They eschew the very idea that such recycling will always be a necessary act of re-creation when put in the hands of those musicians aware enough to know the universe began not with a big bang, but with a single note, pure and easy.

The big bang itself came later, when song snatching became an art form. It came when W.C. Handy jammed together a bunch of chords with some blue notes and a whole set of couplets he'd heard down South. Even then it took Bessie Smith to light the blue touchpaper, and Blind Lemon to ensure it kept burning. And still it required Leadbelly to send it off into the night-time sky, Hank Williams to take it back to the country, Elvis to inject a beat and The Beatles to harmonize the results. Everyone of 'em would now be hung as a thief.

# Bibliography

Though I have refrained from notating every single article or book I scanned, skimmed or devoured while writing this rather wide-ranging tome, below are the various sources – printed and web-based – that I have actually drawn on in the text, and indeed quoted from. If there is a chapter bracketed after a reference, it is because I have quoted directly from that source or relied on it for information in the relevant chapter. The conclusions I have reached nonetheless remain mine alone.

### Reference sources

Bond, Johnny and Norm Cohen, *The Recordings of Jimmie Rodgers: An Annotated Discography* (pp, 1978). [ch4]

Dixon, R.M.W. and John Goodrich, *Blues And Gospel Records 1902–1943* (Storyville, 1982).

Harris, Sheldon, *Blues Who's Who: A Biographical Dictionary of Blues Singers* (Da Capo, 1994).

Humphries, John (ed.), *Music Master Tracks Catalogue* (John Humphries, 1989).

Meade, G.T., D. Spottswood and D.S. Meade, *Country Music Sources: A Biblio-Discography of Commercially Recorded Traditional Music* (University of North Carolina Press, 2002).

Russell, Tony, *Country Music Records: A Discography 1921–1942* (OUP, 2004).

Shemel, Sidney and M. William Krasilovsky, *This Business of Music* (9th ed., Billboard Books, 2003).

Wenner, Jann (ed.), *Rolling Stone Cover To Cover 1967–May 2007* (Bondi DVD-ROMx4, 2008).

**Useful general books**

Barker, Hugh and Yuval Taylor, *Faking It: The Quest For Authenticity In Popular Music* (Faber, 2007). [ch4]

Bufwack, Mary and Robert Oermann, *Finding Her Voice: The Saga of Women In Country Music* (Crown, 1993). [ch2]

Clarke, Donald, *The Rise and Fall of Popular Music* (St Martin's Press, 1995). [ch6, ch11]

Dannen, Frederic, *Hit Men: Power Brokers and Fast Money Inside the Record Business* (Vintage, 1991). [ch17]

Goodman, Fred, *Mansion On The Hill* (Times Books, 1997). [ch14]

Kittredge, George Lyman, *The English and Scottish Popular Ballads* (Houghton-Mifflin, 1904).

Leigh, Spencer, *Brother, Can You Spare A Rhyme: A Hundred Years of Hit Songwriting* (Southport: S Leigh, 2000). [ch7, 8, 9, 14, 17, 18]

Malone, Bill, *Country Music USA* (University of Texas Press, 1969).

Sanjek, Russell and David, *Pennies From Heaven: The American Popular Music Business In The 20th Century* (Da Capo, 1996). [ch2, ch4]

Whitburn, Joel, *Pop Memories 1890–1954: The History of American Popular Music* (Hal Leonard, 1989)

Zollo, Paul, *Songwriters On Songwriting* (Da Capo, 2003). [intro, ch9, ch17]


**Other books referenced**

Abbott, Kingsley, *Back To The Beach: A Brian Wilson and The Beach Boys Reader* (Helter-Skelter, 1998). [ch18]

Aeppli, Felix, *The Rolling Stones: The Ultimate Guide 1962–1995* (Record Information Service, 1996). [ch11, ch13]

Albertson, Chris, *Bessie* (Yale University Press, 2005). [ch1, ch2]

Amburn, Ellis, *Buddy Holly: A Biography* (St Martin's Press, 1995). [ch8]

Anthony, Ted, *Chasing The Rising Sun: The Journey of an American Song* (Simon and Schuster, 2007).

Azerrad, Michael, *Come As You Are: The Story of Nirvana* (Three Rivers Press, 1993). [ch16]

Baez, Joan, *The Joan Baez Songbook* (Hal Leonard, 1994). [ch12]

Belden, H.M. and Hudson, A.P. (ed.), *Frank C. Brown Collection of North Carolina Folklore vol. 2: Folk Ballads* (Duke University Press, 1952). [ch9]

Beer, Molly and David King Dunaway, *Singing Out: An Oral History of America's Folk Music Revivals* (OUP, 2010). [ch9]

Blake, Mark, *Is This The Real Life? The Untold Story of Queen* (Aurum, 2011). [ch15]

Blake, Mark, *Comfortably Numb: The Inside Story of Pink Floyd* (Da Capo, 2008). [ch15]

Bright, Spencer, *Peter Gabriel: An Authorized Biography* (Headline, 1989). [ch15]

Brown, Peter and Steven Gaines, *The Love You Make: An Insider's Story of the Beatles* (McGraw-Hill, 1983). [ch11, 13]

Burdon, Eric, *I Used To Be An Animal, But I'm All Right Now* (Faber, 1986). [ch9]

Burns, Robert and James Johnson, *Scots Musical Museum vols 1–6*, [single volume edition] (Folklore Associates, 1962) [ch17]

Cantwell, Robert, *When We Were Good: The Folk Revival* (Harvard University Press, 1996). [ch9]

Carr, Roy, *The Rolling Stones: An Illustrated Record* (Crown Publishing, 1976). [ch13]

Chappell, William, *Popular Music Of The Olden Time (2 volumes)* (Chappell and Co., 1858).

Charlesworth, Chris, *Deep Purple: An Illustrated Biography* (Omnibus, 1998). [ch15]

Cohen, Rich, *Machers and Rockers: Chess Records and the Business of Rock and Roll* (Norton, 2004). [ch18]

Cohen, Norm, *Long Steel Rail: The Railroad in American Folksong* (University of Illinois Press, 1981). [ch3, ch4, ch9]

Coltman, Bob, *Paul Clayton and The Folksong Revival* (Scarecrow, 2008). [ch9]

Coon, Caroline, *1988* (Omnibus Press, 1982). [ch16]

Cornyn, Stan and Paul Scanlon, *Exploding* (Harper Entertainment, 2002).

Cross, Charles, *Heavier Than Heaven* (Hodder and Stoughton, 2001). [ch16]

Curtis, Deborah, *Touching From A Distance* (Faber, 2005). [ch16]

Davies, Ray, *X-Ray: The Unauthorized Autobiography* (Penguin, 1995). [ch11]

Davis, Francis, *History of the Blues: The Roots, the Music, the People* (Hyperion, 1995). [ch1, ch2, ch5]

Dawson, Jim and Steve Propes, *What Was The First Rock'n'Roll Record?* (Faber, 1992). [ch7, ch8]

De Lange, Kees and Ben Valkhoff, *Plug Your Ears: Jimi Hendrix* (Up From The Skies, 1993). [ch10]

Dixon, R.W.W. and J. Godrich, *Recording The Blues* (Stein and Day, 1970). [ch3]

Dixon, Willie and Don Snowden, *I Am The Blues* (Da Capo, 1990). [ch12]

Doggett, Peter, *You Never Give Me Your Money* (Harper, 2010). [ch13]

Doggett, Peter, *The Man Who Sold The World: David Bowie and The 1970s* (Harper, 2012). [ch17]

Dunn, Tim, *The Bob Dylan Copyright Files 1962-2007* (AuthorHouse, 2008). [ch9]

Dylan, Bob, *Chronicles* (Simon and Schuster, 2005). [ch9]

Eliot, Marc, *Rockonomics: The Money Behind The Music* (Franklin Watts, 1989). [ch14]

Eliot, Marc and Mike Appel, *Down Thunder Road: The Making of Bruce Springsteen* (Simon and Schuster, 1992). [ch14]

Escott, Colin, *Hank Williams: The Biography* (Little Brown, 1994). [ch6, ch17]

Escott, Colin, *Sun Records: The Brief History of the Legendary Recording Label* (Quick Fox, 1980). [ch7]

Evans, David, *Big Road Blues: Tradition and Creativity In The Folk Blues* (Da Capo, 1987). [ch1, ch3, ch5]

Filene, Benjamin, *Romancing The Folk: Public Memory and American Roots Music* (University of N. Carolina Press, 2000). [ch3, ch5, ch10]

Flanagan, Bill, *Written In My Soul: Rock's Great Songwriters* (Contemporary, 1986). [ch7]

Fox, Jon Hartley, *King of The Queen City: The Story of King Records* (University of Illinois Press, 2009). [ch8]

Gallo, Armando, *Genesis: The Evolution of a Rock Band* (Sidgwick and Jackson, 1978). [ch15]

Glebeek, Ceaesar and Harry Shapiro, *Jimi Hendrix: Electric Gypsy* (William Heinemann, 1990). [ch10]

Goldrosen, John and John Beecher, *Remembering Buddy Holly* (Da Capo, 2001). [ch8]

Goodman, Pete, *The Rolling Stones: Our Own Story* (Bantam, 1970). [ch10, ch11]

Gordon, Robert, *Can't Be Satisfied: The Life and Times of Muddy Waters* (Pimlico, 2003). [ch10]

Gordon, Robert Winslow, *Folk-Songs of North America* (National Service Bureau, 1938). [ch3]

Gray, Michael, *Hand Me My Travelin' Shoes: In Search of Blind Willie McTell* (Chicago Review Press, 2007). [ch12]

Greenfield, Robert, *Exile On Main Street: A Season In Hell With The Rolling Stones* (Da Capo, 2006). [ch15]

Guralnick, Peter, *Sweet Soul Music: Rhythm and Blues and the Southern Dream of Freedom* (Harper-Collins, 1986). [ch7]

Guralnick, Peter, *Searching For Robert Johnson* (Penguin, 1989). [ch12]

Guralnick, Peter, *Feel Like Going Home: Portraits in Blues and Rock'n'Roll* (Penguin, 1992). [ch10, ch18]

Guralnick, Peter, *The Last Train To Memphis: The Rise of Elvis Presley* (Little Brown, 1994). [ch6, ch7]

Guralnick, Peter, *Careless Love: The Unmaking of Elvis Presley* (Little Brown, 1999). [ch8]

Hamilton, Marybeth, *In Search of The Blues: Black Voices, White Visions* (Vintage, 2008). [ch1, ch5]

Handy, W.C., *Father of The Blues: An Autobiography* (Da Capo, 1991). [ch1]

Handy, W.C. and Abbe Niles, *The Blues: An Anthology* (Da Capo, 1990). [ch1]

Harper, Colin, *Dazzling Stranger: Bert Jansch and the Folk and Blues Revival* (Bloomsbury, 2000). [ch12, 17]

Harris, John, *Dark Side of the Moon: The Making of the Pink Floyd Masterpiece* (Da Capo, 2005). [ch15, ch18]

Harrison, Daphne Duval, *Black Pearls: Blues Queens of the 1920s* (Rutgers University Press, 1990). [ch2]

Harvey, Todd, *The Formative Dylan: Transmission and Stylistic Influences 1961–63* (Scarecrow Press, 2001). [ch9]

Hayward, Keith, *Tin Pan Alley: The Rise of Elton John* (Soundcheck Books, 2013). [ch14]

Hell, Richard, *Artifact: Notebooks from Hell* (Hanuman Books, 1991). [ch16]

Hell, Richard, *I Dreamed I Was A Very Clean Tramp* (Ecco Press, 2013). [ch16]

Henry, Mellinger Edward, *Folk Songs From The Southern Highlands* (J.J. Augustin, 1938). [ch3]

Heylin, Clinton, *From The Velvets To The Voidoids* (Penguin, 1992). [ch16]

Heylin, Clinton, *Sad Refrains* (Helter-Skelter, 2000). [outro]

Heylin, Clinton, *Can You Feel The Silence?* (Viking, 2002). [ch11, ch14]

Heylin, Clinton, *Babylon's Burning: From Punk To Grunge* (Penguin, 2006). [ch16]

Heylin, Clinton, *The Act You've Known For All These Years* (Canongate, 2007). [ch13]

Heylin, Clinton, *Revolution In The Air: The Songs of Bob Dylan 1957–73* (Constable, 2009). [ch9]

Heylin, Clinton, *Dylan Behind The Shades* (Faber, 2011). [ch9]

Heylin, Clinton, *All The Madmen* (Constable, 2012). [ch15]

Heylin, Clinton, *E Street Shuffle* (Constable, 2012). [ch14]

Hilburn, Robert, *Johnny Cash: The Life* (Little Brown, 2013). [ch7]

Hill, Mildred J., *Song Stories For Kindergarten* (1892). [ch2]

Hinman, Doug, *All Day and All Of The Night: The Kinks Day By Day* (Backbeat Books, 2004) [ch11]

Hornby, Nick, *About A Boy* (Riverhead, 1998). [outro]

Hortsman, Dorothy, *Sing Your Heart Out, Country Boy* (Country Music Foundation, 1986). [ch3, ch4]

Hoskyns, Barney, *Trampled Underfoot: The Power and Excess of Led Zeppelin* (Faber, 2012). [ch12]

Humphries, Patrick, *The Boy In The Bubble: A Biography of Paul Simon* (Sidgwick and Jackson, 1988). [ch9]

Ives, Edward D., *Bonnie Earl of Murray* (Tuckwell Press, 1996).

Jackson, John A., *Big Beat Heat: Alan Freed and The Early Years of Rock'n'Roll* (Schirmer, 1991). [ch7, ch8]

James, Tommy and Martin Fitzpatrick, *Me, The Mob, And The Music* (Scribner, 2011). [ch8]

Jansen, David and Gene Jones, *Spreadin' Rhythms Around: Black Popular Songwriters 1880–1930* (Music Sales, 1998). [ch2]

Jones, Loyal, *Minstrel of the Appalachians: The Story of Bascom Lamar Lunsford* (The University Press of Kentucky, 2002).

Jones, Roben, *Memphis Boys: The Story of American Studios* (University Press of Mississippi, 2010). [ch8]

Jorgensen, Ernst, *Elvis Presley: A Life In Music* (St Martin's Press, 1998). [ch7, ch8]

Kirkeby, Ed, *Ain't Misbehavin': The Story of Fats Waller* (Da Capo, 1975). [ch2, ch3]

Klein, Joe, *Woody Guthrie: A Life* (Knopf, 1980). [ch5]

Ledbetter, Huddie, *Negro Folk Songs As Sung By Lead Belly* (MacMillan, 1936). [ch5]

Lee, George, *Beale Street, Where The Blues Began* (Ballou, 1934). [ch1]

Legman, Gershon, *The Horn Book: Studies In Erotic Folklore* (University Books, 1964). [ch9]

Legman, Gershon and Vance Randolph, *Roll Me In Your Arms: Unprintable Ozark Folksongs Vol. 1* (University of Arkansas Press, 1992). [ch9]

Leigh, Spencer, *Everyday: Getting Closer to Buddy Holly* (SAF Publishing, 2009). [intro, ch8]

Leigh, Spencer and Michael Heatley, *Behind The Song* (Cassell Illustrated, 1998). [ch9]

Lennon, John, Yoko Ono and David Sheff, *The Playboy Interviews* (NEL, 1982). [ch11, ch13]

Lewis, Dave, *Led Zeppelin: A Celebration* (Omnibus Press, 2003). [ch12]

Lewisohn, Mark, *The Beatles Live!* (Pavilion, 1986) [ch11]

Lomax, Alan, *Folk Songs of North America* (Doubleday, 1960). [ch9]

Lomax, Alan, *Penguin Book of American Folk Songs* (Penguin, 1964). [ch9]

Lomax, Alan, *The Land Where The Blues Began* (Random House, 1993). [ch10]

Lomax, Alan, Woody Guthrie and Peter Seeger, *Hard Hitting Songs for Hard Hit People* (University of Nebraska Press, 2012). [ch9]

Lomax, John, *American Ballads and Songs* (MacMillan, 1934). [ch2]

Lomax, John, *Adventures of a Ballad Hunter* (MacMillan, 1947). [ch5]

Lomax, John, *Cowboy Songs and Other Frontier Ballads* (Collier, 1986). [ch5]

Lomax, John and Alan, *Our Singing Country* (MacMillan, 1941).

Lomax, John and Alan, *Folksong USA* (Signet, 1966). [ch9]

Long, Eleanor, *The Maid and The Hangman: Myth and Tradition in a Popular Ballad* (University of California Press, 1971) [ch12]

MacKenzie, W. Roy, *Ballads and Sea Songs From Nova Scotia* (Folklore Associates, 1963) [ch3]

Marcus, Greil, *Mystery Train: Images of America In Rock'N'Roll Music* (E.P. Dutton, 1975) [ch6]

Martyn, Beverly, *Sweet Honesty* (Grosvenor House, 2011). [ch17]

Mason, Nick, *Inside Out: A Personal History of Pink Floyd* (Weiderfeld & Nicolson, 2004). [ch15]

Matlock, Glen and Pete Silverton, *I Was A Teenage Sex Pistol* (Omnibus Press, 1991). [ch16]

Mazor, Barry, Meeting Jimmie Rodgers (OUP, 2009). [ch4, ch17]

McDevitt, Chas, *Skiffle: The Roots of UK Rock* (Robson Books, 1998). [ch9]

McDonald, Ian, *Revolution In The Head: The Beatles' Records and The Sixties* (4th Estate, 1997). [ch13]

McGee, David and Carl Perkins, *Go, Cat, Go: The Life and Times of Carl Perkins* (Hyperion, 1997). [ch7]

Miles, Barry and Paul McCartney, *Many Years From Now* (Secker and Warburg, 1997). [intro, ch13]

Muir, Peter C., *Long Lost Blues: Popular Blues In America 1850–1920* (University of Illinois Press, 2010). [ch1]

Neill, Andy, *Have Me A Real Good Time: The Faces Before During and After* (Omnibus, 2011). [ch12]

Neill, Andy and Matthew Kent, *Anyway, Anyhow, Anywhere: The Complete Chronicle of The Who 1958–78* (Virgin, 2002). [ch11]

Odum, Howard, *Folk-Song and Folk Poetry As Found In The Secular Songs Of The Southern Negroes* (Journal of American Folklore vol. 24, 1911). [ch2, ch3]

Odum, Howard and Guy Johnson, *Negro Workaday Songs* (University of North Carolina Press, 1926). [ch3]

Oldham, Andrew Loog, *Stoned* (Secker and Warburg, 2000). [ch11]

Oliver, Paul, *Barrelhouse Blues: Location Recording and The Early Traditions of the Blues* (Basic Civitas, 2009). [ch3]

Olson, Ted and Tony Russell, *The Bristol Sessions: The Big Bang of Country Music* (Bear Family 5-CD boxed-set + book, 2011). [ch3]

Oster, Harry, *Living Country Blues* (Minerva Press, 1975). [ch3]

Palmer, Robert, *Deep Blues* (Viking Press, 1982). [ch12]

Pearson, Barry Lee and Bill McCulloch, *Robert Johnson: Lost and Found* (University of Illinois Press, 2008). [ch12]

Percy, Bishop, *Reliques of Ancient English Poetry* (3rd ed., 1775). [ch17]

Perry, John, *Meaty, Beaty, Big and Bouncy* (Schirmer, 1996). [intro, ch11]

Peterson, Richard, *Creating Country Music: Fabricating Authenticity* (University of Chicago Press, 1997). [ch3]

Platt, John, Chris Dreja and Jim McCarty, *The Yardbirds* (Sidgwick and Jackson, 1983). [ch12]

Porterfield, Nolan, *Jimmie Rodgers: The Life and Times of America's Blue Yodeler* (University of Illinois Press, 1979). [ch3, ch4]

Randolph, Vance, *Ozark Folksongs, IV: Religious Songs and Other Items* (University of Missouri Press, 1980) [ch6]

Reich, Howard and William Gaines, *Jelly's Blues: The Life, Music and Redemption of Jelly Roll Morton* (Da Capo, 2003). [ch1]

Richards, Keith, *Life* (WandN, 2010). [ch13]

Ritchie, Jean, *Folk Songs of the Southern Appalachians* (University Press of Kentucky, 1997). [ch9]

Ritz, David, *Hound Dog: The Leiber and Stoller Autobiography* (Omnibus, 2010) [ch8]

Robertson, David, *W.C. Handy: The Life and Times of the Man Who Made The Blues* (Knopf, 2009). [ch1]

Rodgers, Carrie, *My Husband Jimmie Rodgers* (Vanderbilt University Press, 1995). [ch4]

Rogan, Johnny, *The Kinks* (Elm Tree Books, 1984). [ch11]

Rogan, Johnny, *Starmakers and Svengalis: The History of British Pop Management* (Trans-Atlantic, 1988). [ch11]

Rolling Stones, The, *According To The Rolling Stones* (Weidenfeld & Nicolson, 2003). [ch11, ch13]

Sandburg, Carl, *The American Songbag* (Harcourt-Brace, 1927). [ch3]

Scaduto, Anthony, *Bob Dylan* (Grosset and Dunlap, 1971). [ch9]

Scarborough, Dorothy, *On The Trail of Negro Folk-Songs* (Harvard Uni. Press, 1925). [ch1, ch3]

Seitel, Peter, *The Anthology of American Folk Music: A Booklet of Essays, Appreciations and Annotations* (Smithsonian boxed-set, 1997).

Selvin, Joel, *Here Comes The Night: The Dark Soul of Bert Berns and The Dirty Business of Rhythm N Blues* (Counterpoint, 2014). [ch11, ch14]

Sharp, Cecil, *Folk Songs from the Southern Appalachians* (OUP, 1932). [ch9]

Simpson, Claude M., *The British Broadside Ballad And Its Music* (Rutgers University Press, 1966) [ch17]

Smith, Joe, *Off The Record: An Oral History of Popular Music* (Warner Books, 1990). [ch14]

Southall, Brian, *Northern Songs: The True Story of The Beatles' Publishing Empire* (Omnibus, 2006). [ch11, 13, 14]

Southall, Brian, *Pop Goes To Court: Rock'N'Pop's Greatest Court Battles* (Omnibus, 2008). [ch13]

Southall, Brian, *Simply Red: The Official Story* (Carlton Books, 2010). [ch18]

Spencer, Scott B. (ed.), *The Ballad Collectors of North America* (Scarecrow Press, 2011). [ch3]

Stenhouse, William, *Illustrations of The Lyric Poetry and Music of Scotland* (Blackwood and Sons, 1853) [ch17]

Stewart, Rod and Giles Smith, *Rod: The Autobiography* (Century, 2012) [ch9]

Stewart-Baxter, Derrick, *Ma Rainey and The Classic Blues Singers* (Stein and Day, 1970). [ch2]

Szwed, John, *The Man Who Recorded The World: A Biography of Alan Lomax* (William Heinemann, 2010). [ch9]

Tolinski, Brad, *Light and Shade: Conversations with Jimmy Page* (Virgin Books, 2012). [ch12]

Tooze, Sandra B., *Muddy Waters: The Mojo Man* (ECW Press, 1997). [ch10]

Tosches, Nick, *Country* (Secker and Warburg, 1989). [ch3, ch7]

Townshend, Pete, *A Decade of The Who* (Fabulous Music/Music Sales, 1977). [ch11]

Townshend, Pete, *Who I Am* (Harper-Collins, 2012) [ch11]

True, Everett, *Nirvana: The True Story* (Omnibus, 2006). [ch16]

Trynka, Paul, *Portrait of The Blues* (Hamlyn, 1996). [ch10]

Turner, Steve, *Van Morrison: Too Late To Stop Now* (Bloomsbury, 1993). [ch11]

Van Ronk, Dave and Elijah Wald, *The Mayor of MacDougal Street: A Memoir* (Da Capo, 2005). [ch9]

Wald, Elijah, *Escaping The Delta: Robert Johnson and The Invention of the Blues* (Amistad, 2005). [ch10]

Ward, Ed, *Mike Bloomfield: The Rise and Fall of an American Guitar Hero* (Cherry Lane, 1983). [ch10]

Wardlow, Gayle Dean and Jim Green, *Chasin' That Devil Music: Searching For The Blues* (Backbeat Books, 2011). [ch12]

Wedderburn, James and John, *A Compendious Book of Godly and Spiritual Sangs*, ed. David Laing, (W. Paterson, 1868).

Welch, Chris, *The Who: Teenage Wasteland* (Sanctuary, 1995). [ch11]

Wexler, Jerry and David Ritz, *Rhythm and the Blues: A Life In American Music* (Knopf, 1993). [ch11]

Wilgus, D.K., *Anglo-American Folk Scholarship Since 1898* (Greenwood Press, 1982). [ch5]

Williams, Alfred, *Folk Songs of The Upper Thames* (Duckworth and Co., 1923). [ch2]

Williams, Richard, *Phil Spector: Out of His Head* (Omnibus, 2003). [ch11]

Wilson, Lee, *All You Have To Do Is Dream: The Boudleaux and Felice Bryant Story* (House of Bryant Publications, 2011).

Wolfe, Charles K., *The Carter Family: In The Shadow of Clinch Mountain* (Bear Family 12-CD boxed-set + book, 2010). [ch3, ch4]

Wolfe, Charles K. and Kip Lornell, *The Life and Legend of Leadbelly* (Harper Business, 1993). [ch5]

Wyman, Bill and Ray Coleman, *Stone Alone* (Viking, 1990). [ch10, ch13]

Zwonitzer, Mark and Charles Hirshberg, *Will You Miss Me When I'm Gone: The Carter Family and Their Legacy In American Music* (Simon and Schuster, 2002). [ch3, ch4]


**Articles**

Behan, Dominic and co., *Letters to the* Guardian *January to February 1986*, as reproduced in the *Telegraph* #23. [ch17]

Brown, Cecil, 'We Did Them Wrong: The Ballad of Frankie and Albert in The Rose and The Briar', ed. G. Marcus and S. Wilentz, *The Rose and The Briar: Death, Love and Liberty In The American Ballad* (Norton, 2005).

Clerk, Carol [and Pink Floyd] – 'Lost In Space', in *Uncut* #73 (June 2003). [ch15]

Diacomo, Frank, 'Searching For Robert Johnson', (*Vanity Fair* 1/11/08).

Gabriel, Peter, 'Out, Angels, Out', (*NME* September 1975).

Gardner, Peter, 'Happy Lawsuit to You!' (*Daily Mail* 15/6/2013).

Gordon, Robert, 'Devil Work: The Plundering of Robert Johnson', (*LA Weekly* 5-11/7/91). [ch12, ch17]

Greenway, John, 'Jimmie Rodgers: A Folksong Catalyst', 'Journal of American Folklore' #277 (July-Sept. 1957).

Handy, W.C., 'I Would Not Play Jazz If I Could . . .', *Downbeat*, (August, 1938).

Heath, Chris, 'The Nirvana Wars', *Rolling Stone* (June 6, 2002).

Hillesley, Richard, 'The Revolution Will Be Plagiarized' [accessed from Tux Deluxe website, tuxdeluxe.org].

Howse, Pat and Phillips, Jimmy, 'Godfather of Delta Blues: H.C. Speir', *Monitor* #13 (1994).

Jones, Hugh and Bill Bratton, 'Zeppelin Sources: What They Covered, Borrowed and Stole', *Proximity* Vol 4, No. 11 (October, 1993).

Lethem, Jonathan, 'The Ecstasy of Influence', in *The Ecstasy of Influence* (Vintage, 2013). [outro]

Lyon, Peter, 'The Ballad of Pete Seeger', *Holiday* magazine, (July, 1965). [ch9]

Malan, Rian, 'A Story About Music: Mbube', *Rolling Stone* (May 25, 2000).

Michaels, Sean, 'Led Zeppelin Sued For Alleged Plagiarism . . . ', the *Guardian*, (June 30, 2010).

Morton, Jelly Roll, 'I Created Jazz in 1902, Not W.C. Handy', *Downbeat*, (1938).

Rohter, Larry, 'For A Classic Motown Song About Money, Credit Is What He Wants', *New York Times* (August 31, 2013).

Self, Joseph C., 'The My Sweet Lord/He's So Fine Plagiarism Suit', in *910* magazine, (1993).

Simmons, Sylvie [and Pink Floyd], 'The Making of The Wall', *Mojo* #73 (December 1999). [ch15]

Simpson, Dave, 'How We Made Blue Monday', the *Guardian* (February 11, 2013). [ch16]

Spivey, Victoria, 'Blind Lemon And I Had A Ball' *Record Research* 76, (May, 1966.) [ch2]

Sutcliffe, Phil, 'Whose Song Is It Anyway?', in *Q* magazine, 1999 [referenced from Rock's Back Pages website]. [ch17]

Scott, Paul, 'Heaven-sent hit that gave solo Robbie wings', the *Scotsman* (June 26, 2003). [ch18]

Svedburg, Andrea, *Newsweek* (October 26, 1963). [ch9]

Tonsor, Johann, 'Negro Music', in *Music* #3 (1892-3). [ch2]

Turner, Gil, 'Sing Out' (10-11/62). [ch9]

Wyatt, Lorre, 'New Times', (1974) [reproduced in Endless Road #4]. [ch9]

## Interviews

*Bob Dylan and related*

Slocum, Mick, the *Telegraph*. [ch9]

Dylan to Cameron Crowe, Biograph notes (CBS, 1985) [ch10]

Dylan and Robert Hilburn, *Acoustic Guitar*, (2004). [intro, ch9]

Pennebaker, D.A., in the *Telegraph*. [ch9]

Carthy, Martin, *Isis* #83. [ch9]

*Deep Purple and members thereof*
Blackmore, Ritchie, *Sounds* (8/2/75). [ch15]
Blackmore, Ritchie, *Sounds* (5/4/75). [ch15]
Blackmore, Ritchie, *Sounds* (2/8/75). [ch15]
Lord, Jon, *MM* (15/2/75). [ch15]
Lord, Jon, *Sounds* (19/7/75). [ch15]

*Genesis and members thereof*
Banks,Tony, *MM* (7/6/75). [ch15]
Collins, Phil, *MM* (7/6/75). [ch15]
Collins, Phil, *MM* (23/8/75). [ch15]
Collins, Phil, *NME* (15/3/75). [ch15]
Collins, Phil, *NME* (13/9/75). [ch15]
Gabriel, Peter, *MM* (6/12/75). [ch15]
Gabriel, Peter, *NME* (15/3/75). [ch15]
Gabriel, Peter, *NME* (27/12/75). [ch15]
Gabriel, Peter and P.J. Philbin, *MM* (20/7/74). [ch15]
Genesis, *Sounds* (13/9/75). [ch15]
Rutherford, Mike, *Musician*, (May, 1976). [ch15]

Rolling Stone *interviews*
Berry, Chuck, (November 23, 1972). [ch7]
Dylan, Bob, (September 27, 2012). [ch14]
Gilmour, Dave, (November 19, 1987). [ch15]
John, Elton, (August 16, 1973). [intro]
McCartney, Paul, (July 12, 1979). [ch14, 15]
Simon, Paul, (July 20, 1972). [ch1]
Spector, Phil, (November 1, 1969). [ch11]

*Miscellaneous*
John, Elton, *NME*, (22/2/75 – 8/3/75). [ch14]
McCartney, Paul, *Guitar Player*, (1990).
Peer, Ralph, *The Meridian (Miss.) Star*, (May 26, 1953). [ch3, ch4]
Plant, Robert, *Q*, (1990). [ch12]
Talmy, Shel, *NME*, (3/4/76). [ch11]
Taylor, Mick, *NME* (12/10/74). [ch15]

**Sleeve-notes**

Anderson, Clive, *Chuck Berry: Poet of Rock'n'Roll* (Charley, 1994). [ch7]

Calt, Stephen, *Henry Thomas' Texas Worried Blues* (Yazoo, 1989).

Costello, Elvis, *Reissues of My Aim Is True, This Year's Model, Armed Forces, Get Happy, Trust.* (Rhino, 2001-2003). [ch16]

Escott, Colin, *When The Evening Sun Goes Down (9 vols.)* (BMG/RCA Victor, 2002). [ch5, ch10]

Fairchild, Michael J., *Jimi Hendrix: Blues* (MCA, 1994). [ch10]

Fulchino, Anne, *Elvis Golden Records* (RCA, 1958) [ch8]

Gordon, Robert, *Elvis At Stax* (Sony, 2013). [ch8]

McCall, Michael, *The Lost Notebooks of Hank Williams* (Sony, 2011).

Patrick, Mick and Rob Hughes, *The Bert Berns Story Vol. 1: Twist and Shout* (Ace, 2007).

Russell, Tony, *Rarities From The Vaults* (Sony, 2011). [ch3]

Smith, Russell, *Dave Davies Hidden Treasures* (Universal, 2011). [ch13]

Taupin, Bernie, *Elton John Rare Masters* (Polydor, 1992). [ch14]


**Miscellaneous material**

Calt, Stephen, 'Hellhound On My Trail', unpublished mss. of Robert Johnson biography. [ch12, ch17]

Dylan, Bob, 'Blowin' In The Wind' 4-verse ms., (May, 1962). [ch9]

'Mills Music Inc. v. Cromwell Music, Inc.', US District Court, LEXSEE printout of opinion by Leibell, (July 29, 1954). [ch17]

Mazor, Barry, *Ralph Peer and The Making of Popular Roots Music*, proof copy (Chicago Review Press, 2014). [ch3, ch4]


**DVDs**

The Sex Pistols, *The Filth and The Fury*. [ch16]

*Genesis: The Lamb Lies Down On Broadway*, 2007 edition. [ch15]

*The Rutles, All You Need Is Cash*. [ch14]


**Websites**

Berlin, Steve, Interview w/ . . . , Rock Cellar Magazine website, www.rockcellar magazine.com, July 17, 2012.

Illustrated Howlin' Wolf discography: *www.wirz.de/music/howlwolf.htm.*

'Monty Norman v. The Sunday Times', eye-witness report on 2001 libel case: www.jollinger.com/barry/lawsuit.htm.

Petty, Norman, biography on International Songwriters [sic] Association website, www.songwriters-guild.co.uk

Shade, Will, 'Dazed and Confused: The Incredibly Strange Saga of Jake Holmes', Perfect Sound Forever website, www.furious.com/perfect, September 2001.

Springsteen, Bruce, key-note speech at South By South West, March 2012, on www.rollingstone.com.

Wight, Phil and Rothwell, Fred, The Complete Muddy Waters Discography: bluesandrhythm.co.uk/documents/200.pdf

Wikipedia entries for 'Hound Dog', 'Susie Q' and 'Whiter Shade of Pale'.

# Acknowledgements

Writing a book like *It's One For The Money* invariably requires a little more conversation and a lot more background reading than my usual fare. This is a book that has come about as a result of trawling the Central Reference Library in Manchester, the New York Public Library, the Lincoln Center's Library of Performing Arts and raiding friends' libraries, when even those esteemed institutions came up short.

But it is equally the product of swapping stories from a hundred years of pop, and forty years of music listening, with my fellow scribes and 'musos'. So to the following I extend my heartfelt gratitude: Peter Doggett, Steve Shepherd, Spencer Leigh, Mick Middles, Barney Hoskyns, Richard Hell, Andy Hasson, Roy Wittaker, Lee Ranaldo, Jeff Rosen, Mick Gold, Laura Cantrell, Jeremy Tepper, Nicholas Hill and Mike Decapite, for helping me (re) form my ideas, and throwing some tall-tales of their own into the mix. Yuval Taylor and Kevin Doughten also gave valuable feedback in the early stages of the endeavour, even as they were being called to editorial duties elsewhere.

A book like this has also allowed me to go back to some of my favourite music historians and writers and rediscover their work afresh. So the spirits of writers such as Peter Guralnick and Colin Escott stalk these pages, and I extend my thanks to them in absentia. In the instances of Elijah Wald and Robert Gordon, two equally fine writers from across the pond, not only did I plunder their work, but I somehow managed to convince them to look kindly on my efforts, and even read early drafts of some chapters, sparing my blushes into the bargain. Barry Mazur was another like-minded historian who shared information, on both Jimmie Rodgers and the late great Ralph Peer, while he was busy working on his own definitive biography of the latter, now published by Chicago Review Press.

Robert Hilburn shared a pint and a pie in London, and talked shop, regaling me with his own version of the 'Folsom Prison Blues' farrago; and though it has been a while since I rode shotgun with Joel Selvin, he is someone I must thank for the unpublished Janet Planet interview he shared with me, for his ongoing interest in the 'real' Bert Berns, and for wide-ranging half-remembered conversations about song snatches and snatchers.

A good friend, who as a copyright lawyer in the lion's den of corporate publishing is not about to waive his right to anonymity, nevertheless betrayed confidences and dished the compost when he could, for which many thanks. He knows who he is! And for seeing the project through, and trying to make the whole thing blend, I thank my editor, Andreas Campomar and all at Little, Brown (UK). Here's to the next dose of musical anarchy....

Clinton Heylin, March 2015.

# Index